China's Social Development and Policy

In China, social development has fallen far behind economic development. *China's Social Development and Policy* looks at why this is the case, and poses the question of whether the conditions, structures and institutions that have locked China into unbalanced development are changing to pave the way for the next stage of development. Based on an empirical examination of ideological, structural and institutional transformations that have shaped China's development experiences, the book analyses China's reform and development in the social domain, including pension, healthcare, public housing, ethnic policy, and public expenditure on social programs. The book moves beyond descriptive analyses to understand the role of broader changes in shaping and redefining the pattern of development in China.

Litao Zhao is Senior Research Fellow at the East Asian Institute, National University of Singapore.

China Policy Series

Series Editor
Zheng Yongnian
East Asian Institute, National University of Singapore

1. China and the New International Order
Edited by Wang Gungwu and Zheng Yongnian

2. China's Opening Society
The non-state sector and governance
Edited by Zheng Yongnian and Joseph Fewsmith

3. Zhao Ziyang and China's Political Future
Edited by Guoguang Wu and Helen Lansdowne

4. Hainan
State, society, and business in a Chinese province
Kjeld Erik Brodsgaard

5. Non-Governmental Organizations in China
The rise of dependent autonomy
Yiyi Lu

6. Power and Sustainability of the Chinese State
Edited by Keun Lee, Joon-Han Kim and Wing Thye Woo

7. China's Information and Communications Technology Revolution
Social changes and state responses
Edited by Xiaoling Zhang and Yongnian Zheng

8. Socialist China, Capitalist China
Social tension and political adaptation under economic globalisation
Edited by Guoguang Wu and Helen Lansdowne

9. Environmental Activism in China
Lei Xei

10. China's Rise in the World ICT Industry
Industrial strategies and the catch-up development model
Lutao Ning

11. China's Local Administration
Traditions and changes in the sub-national hierarchy
Edited by Jae-Ho Chung and Tao-chiu Lam

12. The Chinese Communist Party as Organizational Emperor
Culture, reproduction and transformation
Zheng Yongian

13. China's Trade Unions
How autonomous are they?
Masaharu Hishida, Kazuko Kojima, Tomoaki Ishii and Jian Qiao

14. Legitimating the Chinese Communist Party since Tiananmen
A critical analysis of the stability discourse
Peter Sandby-Thomas

15. China and International Relations
The Chinese view and the contribution of Wang Gungwu
Zheng Yongnian

16. The Challenge of Labour in China
Strikes and the changing labour regime in global factories
Chris King-chi Chan

17. The Impact of China's 1989 Tiananmen Massacre
Edited by Jean-Philippe Béja

18. The Institutional Dynamics of China's Great Transformation
Edited by Xiaoming Huang

19. Higher Education in Contemporary China
Beyond expansion
Edited by W. John Morgan and Bin Wu

20. China's Crisis Management
Edited by Jae Ho Chung

21. China Engages Global Governance
A New World Order in the making?
Gerald Chan, Pak K. Lee and Lai-Ha Chan

22. Political Culture and Participation in Rural China
Yang Zhong

23. China's Soft Power and International Relations
Hongyi Lai and Yiyi Lu

24. China's Climate Policy
Chen Gang

25. Chinese Society
Change and transformation
Edited by Li Peilin

26. China's Challenges to Human Security
Foreign relations and global implications
Edited by Guoguang Wu

27. China's Internal and International Migration
Edited by Li Peilin and Laurence Roulleau-Berger

28. The Rise of Think Tanks in China
Xufeng Zhu

29. Governing Health in Contemporary China
Yanzhong Huang

30. New Dynamics in Cross-Taiwan Straits Relations
How far can the rapprochement go?
Edited by Weixing Hu

31. China and the European Union
Edited by Lisheng Dong, Zhengxu Wang and Henk Dekker

32. China and the International System
Becoming a world power
Edited by Xiaoming Huang and Robert G. Patman

33. China's Social Development and Policy
Into the next stage?
Edited by Litao Zhao

China's Social Development and Policy

Into the next stage?

**Edited by
Litao Zhao**

R Routledge
Taylor & Francis Group

LONDON AND NEW YORK

First published 2013
by Routledge
2 Park Square, Milton Park, Abingdon, Oxfordshire, OX14 4RN

Simultaneously published in the USA and Canada
by Routledge
711 Third Avenue, New York, NY 10017

Routledge is an imprint of the Taylor and Francis Group, an informa business

First issued in paperback 2015

British Library Cataloguing in Publication Data
A catalogue record for this book is available from the British Library

Library of Congress Cataloging in Publication Data
China's social development and policy : into the next stage? / edited by Litao Zhao.
    p. cm. – (China policy series ; 33)
    Includes bibliographical references and index.
    1. China–Social policy. 2. China–Socil conditions–2000- I. Zhao, Litao, 1972- editor of compilation.
    HN733.5.C4418 2013
    303.3'720951–dc23
                2012047754

ISBN 978-0-415-64283-5 (hbk)
ISBN 978-1-138-18299-8 (pbk)
ISBN 978-0-203-49679-4 (ebk)

Typeset in Times New Roman
by Taylor & Francis Books

Contents

List of illustrations   ix
List of contributors   xii
Acknowledgements   xv
List of abbreviations   xvi

Introduction   1
LITAO ZHAO

PART I
China into the next stage of development   17

1   Society must be defended: reform, openness and social policy
    in China   19
    YONGNIAN ZHENG

2   China's new stage of development   40
    PEILIN LI

PART II
Social policy reform moving to the fore   49

3   Issues and options for social security reform in
    China   51
    SHI LI

4   China's fiscal expenditure on social security since
    1978   83
    YANZHONG WANG AND YUQI LONG

5   Healthcare reform: where is China heading?   99
    KAI HONG PHUA AND ALEX HE JINGWEI

 6 How successful are China's public housing schemes?   115
    BINGQIN LI

 7 China's rapid demographic transition and its challenges to
    the social security system   141
    DING LU

 8 Political dynamics of social policy reform in China   161
    YONGNIAN ZHENG AND YANJIE HUANG

 9 Developmentalism, secularism, nationalism and essentialism:
    current situation and challenges of the ethnic issue in China   186
    YONGJIA LIANG

PART III
China's social development in a comparative perspective   **205**

10 The evolving East Asian welfare regimes: the case of China   207
    CHACK KIE WONG

11 Singapore's social development experience: a relevant lesson
    for China?   230
    LITAO ZHAO AND JOHN WONG

    Index   253

Illustrations

Figures

1.1	Intergovernmental decentralization	25
1.2	Professional composition of CCP membership, 2006	31
3.1	Changes in income inequality in urban and rural China, 1978–2007	52
3.2	China's urban–rural income gap between 1978 and 2007	54
3.3	Poverty incidence of rural population based on official lines	54
3.4	Rural official poverty line as a percentage of household income per capita, 1985–2007	55
3.5	Number of urban unemployed people in China, 1978–2008	56
3.6	Urban registered unemployment rate in China, 1978–2008	56
3.7	The number of rural–urban migrant workers in China	57
3.8	Changes in consumption as a percentage of GDP in China	58
3.9	Saving rate of households in urban, rural areas and China as a whole	59
4.1	Fiscal allowance for social insurance	90
4.2	Net fiscal appropriation to national social security fund	92
4.3	Incidence of rural absolute poverty in China	92
5.1	Composition of China's health expenditure, 1978–2007	100
5.2	Coverage of risk-pooling schemes, 2003	102
5.3	Total health expenditure and government health expenditure, 1990–2007	102
5.4	Sources of income for Chinese public hospitals (General), 1998–2008	103
5.5	Coverage of risk-pooling schemes, 2008	106
6.1	Population growth in China	118
6.2	Total number of permanent residents and number of registered residents with *Hukou* in Beijing, Shanghai, Tianjin and Shenzhen, 1978–2008	119
6.3	Household size changes over time, 1982–2008	120
6.4	Household size changes of the whole country and of the four major cities, 2001–08	120

x   *Illustrations*

6.5   Share of households by household size   121
6.6   Newly built residential buildings in urban China   123
6.7   Number of employed persons at year-end in urban and rural
      areas, 1978–2008   130
6.8   Average wage of staff and workers, 1978–2008   130
6.9   Number of flats of residential buildings completed by enterprises
      for real estate development   133
6.10 Total investment in residential buildings   133
7.1   China's dependency ratios, 1950–2050   142
7.2   Birth rate, death rate, and natural growth rate of population,
      1949–2007   143
7.3   Fertility rates: China vs. India, 1950–2050   146
7.4   Total population and labor force: China vs. India, 1950–2050   147
7.5   Dependency ratios: China vs. India, 1950–2050   148
7.6   Median age: China vs. India, 1950–2050   149
7.7   Population age structures: China vs. India, 1995, 2010 and 2030   150
7.8   Estimated sources of per capita GDP growth   152
8.1   Coverage rates of five social insurance schemes   166
8.2   Urban and rural residents under the MSLS   166
8.3   Average share of welfare items in urban household
      total expenditure   167
8.4   Government expenditure on education, healthcare and
      public housing   179

Tables

1.1   Social groups that benefited the most and least since the reform
      and opening-up policy   26
3.1   Urban and rural population supported by the MLSG in
      China, 2000–08   62
4.1   Chinese government social security expenditure   86
4.2   Number of participants in China's social insurance programmes   88
4.3   Revenues, expenditures and balance of China's workers social
      insurance fund   88
4.4   Composition of fiscal expenditure on social security   89
4.5   Cumulative savings of the national social insurance fund,
      1989–2008   91
4.6   Minimum subsistence security and fiscal expenditure   93
4.7   Social security expenditure of some OECD countries, 1960–2001   94
4.8   Average monthly pension for different types of pensioner   94
4.9   Share of central and local government in fiscal expenditure and
      revenue in 2008   95
7.1   Estimated sources of per capita GDP growth (1981–2008)   152
8.1   Political dynamics of exit and voice in different social policy
      domains   181

10.1 Social expenditure as percentage of gross domestic product
(GDP) in China (selected years)   215
10.2 Employment of state-owned enterprises (SOEs) as percentage
of total urban employment   216
10.3 China's healthcare expenses and national wealth, selected years
(at current price)   220
10.4 Division of expenditure and revenue of central and local
governments in China   223
11.1 Singapore's major social indicators, 1970–2008   233
11.2 Socio-economic development in selected East Asian economies 234
11.3 Singapore's government expenditures, 1998–2009   235
11.4 The evolution of the CPF system   238
11.5 CPF contribution rates (for workers aged 50 and below)
since 1955   240
11.6 Selected indicators of Singapore's Central Provident Fund
(CPF)   241
11.7 Resident households by type of dwelling in Singapore   243
11.8 Singapore government expenditure on education   245

Contributors

Alex He Jingwei teaches in the Department of Asian and Policy Studies, at the Hong Kong Institute of Education. He received his PhD degree from the Lee Kuan Yew School of Public Policy, National University of Singapore, in 2011. Dr He specializes in health policy and public policy analysis with particular reference to the Greater China region. His work has appeared in leading international journals including *Public Administration Review*, the *China Quarterly*, *Public Administration and Development*, *China: An International Journal*.

Yanjie Huang is a Research Assistant at the East Asian Institute, National University of Singapore. While focusing on the economic aspect of China's development, he is also interested in other aspects of the ongoing modernization programme, such as political development, international relations, social changes, value shifts and institutional changes. He has written papers on China's contemporary centrally-managed state-owned enterprises and the institutional changes in the monetary systems in the 1940s and 1950s. Recently, he has conducted research into the evolution of China's political economy from its historical forms to current post-reform configuration.

Bingqin Li is an Associate Professor at the Crawford School of Public Policy, ANU College of Asia & the Pacific, Australia. Her research interests include social exclusion faced by rural to urban migrants, lon-term unemployed people and informally employed people. She has published numerous papers in these areas. Her research has covered coastal and inland cities in China. She has given guest talks in universities in Britain, China, Japan and Singapore. She has worked as a consultant for a number of international organizations such as UNDP, UNESCO, IIED and DFID.

Peilin Li is Professor and Director of the Institute of Sociology, the Chinese Academy of Social Sciences. He received his PhD in Sociology from University of Paris I. His research interests include enterprise organization, social stratification, and institutional transformation and development. He has published widely in Chinese and English on China's social transformation and social policy.

Shi Li is Professor of Economics at Beijing Normal University. His current studies focus on income distribution, poverty and rural migration in China. He has published in several journals such as the *Journal of Population Economics*, the *Review of Income and Wealth*, the *Oxford Bulletin of Economics and Statistics*, *Economic Development and Cultural Change*, the *Journal of Comparative Economics*, *Oxford Development Studies*, the *Journal of Development Economics*, *Asian Economic Journal*, *Development and Society.*

Yongjia Liang is Professor of Anthropology at China Agricultural University, after working for four years in the Asia Research Institute, National University of Singapore, as a Senior Research Fellow. He has combined interests in the ethnographic and historical studies of popular religion and ethnicity in PR China. His papers have been published in journals such as *The Asia Pacific Journal of Anthropology*, the *Asian Journal of Social Science*, and the *Chinese Sociology and Anthropology*. He is writing a monograph on the religious and ethnic revival in south-west China to be published by Routledge.

Yuqi Long received his PhD in Management from Remin University of China. He is now teaching at the School of Management, Capital Normal University, China. His research interests include social security and social policy. He has published 30 academic papers, one monograph on the civil servants' pension system from a comparative perspective, and has edited four books.

Ding Lu, a PhD from Northwestern University, is a Professor of Economics at the University of the Fraser Valley, Canada. His research interests include international trade and investment, comparative economic systems, and regional economic development. He has published several books and dozens of papers in peer-reviewed journals and book chapters. Most of his publications involve development issues of Asian economies. He is the author and editor of *Entrepreneurship in Suppressed Markets: China's Private Sector Experience* (New York: Garland, 1994), *State Intervention and Business in China: The Role of Preferential Policies* (Cheltenham: Edward Elgar, 1997), *China's Telecommunications Market: Entering a New Competitive Age* (Cheltenham: Edward Elgar, 2003), and *The Great Urbanization of China* (Singapore: World Scientific, 2011).

Kai Hong Phua is a tenured Professor at the Lee Kuan Yew School of Public Policy, National University of Singapore. He is frequently consulted by governments in the region and international organizations, including the Red Cross, UNESCAP, WHO, and the World Bank. He has lectured and published widely on policy issues of population aging, healthcare management and comparative health systems in the emerging economies of Asia. He is the current Chair of the Asia-Pacific Health Economics Network (APHEN), founder member of the Asian Health Systems Reform Network (DRAGONET), Editorial Advisory Board member of *Research in Healthcare Financial Management*, Associate Editor of the *Singapore Economic Review*, and was a past Associate Editor of the *Asia-Pacific Journal of Public Health*, and Vice-Chairman of the Singapore Red Cross.

Yanzhong Wang is Professor and Director of the Research Centre for Labour and Social Security at the Chinese Academy of Social Sciences. He received his PhD in sociology from Peking University. His main research areas are labour economics and industrial relations, pension systems, small and medium-sized enterprises, industrial organization and social policy studies.

Chack Kie Wong is Professor at the Department of Social Work, and Associate Director of Hong Kong Institute of Asia-Pacific Studies, Chinese University of Hong Kong. He received his PhD from the University of Sheffield. His research interests include welfare attitudes, comparative social policy, social security and welfare reform in Chinese societies. He has published in *Asian Social Work and Policy Review, Asian Survey, Development and Society*, the *International Journal of Social Welfare, Issues and Studies*, the *Journal of Contemporary China*, the *Journal of Social Policy, Social Indicators Research, Social Policy and Administration*.

John Wong is currently Professorial Fellow and Academic Advisor to the East Asian Institute (EAI) of the National University of Singapore. He obtained his PhD from the University of London in 1966. He has written/ edited 33 books, and published over 400 articles and papers on China and other East Asian economies, including ASEAN. He has done consultancy work for the Singapore government and many international organizations, including UN ESCAP, ADB, UNIDO, APO and ADI.

Litao Zhao is Senior Research Fellow at the East Asian Institute, National University of Singapore. He obtained his PhD degree in sociology from Stanford University. His research interests include social stratification and mobility, sociology of education, organizational analysis, and China's social policy. His research has appeared in *China Quarterly, Research in Social Stratification and Mobility*, the *International Journal of Educational Development, Social Sciences in China, Built Environment, China: An International Journal, East Asian Policy* and *Frontiers of Education in China*. He has authored or edited *Paths to Private Entrepreneurship: Markets and Mobility in Rural China, China's Reforms at 30: Challenges and Prospects, China's New Social Policy: Initiatives for a Harmonious Society*, and *Singapore's Experience in Social Development* (in Chinese).

Yongnian Zheng is Professor and Director of the East Asian Institute, National University of Singapore. He received his PhD in Political Science from Princeton University. He has studied both China's transformation and its external relations. His papers have appeared in journals such as *Comparative Political Studies, Political Science Quarterly, Third World Quarterly* and *China Quarterly*. He is the author of 13 books, including *Technological Empowerment, De Facto Federalism in China, Discovering Chinese Nationalism in China* and *Globalization and State Transformation in China*, and is co-editor of 11 books on China's politics and society.

Acknowledgements

Most of the chapters in this volume were presented at the International Conference on China's Social Policy Reform: Challenges and Direction, jointly organized by the East Asian Institute, the National University of Singapore and Research Department of Social Development, Development Research Center of the State Council, China, 30–31 July, 2010, in Singapore. I thank Professor Zheng Yongnian and Professor Ge Yanfeng for their strong support. I also thank Taylor & Francis and the Editor of *Journal of Contemporary China* for permission to re-publish Chapter 1. Finally, thanks go to Peter Sowden, Jillian Morrison, Hannah Mack, Dominic Corti and Susan Dunsmore for their assistance during the preparation of this volume.

Abbreviations

ACFTU	All-China Federation of Trade Unions
BHI	Basic Health Insurance Scheme
CCP	Chinese Communist Party
CDCs	Community Development Councils
CDRF	China Development Research Foundation
CMS	Cooperative Medical System
CPF	Central Provident Fund
CPFIS	CPF Investment Scheme
DRG	diagnosis-related groups
EH	Economic Housing
FDI	foreign direct investment
FFS	fee-for-service
GDP	gross domestic production
GIS	Government Insurance Scheme
GNI	Gross National Income
HDB	Housing and Development Board
HDI	Human Development Index
HPF	Housing Provident Fund
JSF	*Jingji shiyong fang* (price-subsidized housing)
KMT	Chinese Nationalist Party
LHR	Low Rent Housing
LIS	Labor Insurance Scheme
LZF	*lianzu fang* (rent-subsidized public housing)
MCA	Ministry of Civil Affairs
MLSG	Minimum Living Standard Guarantee
MSA	Medical Savings Account
NCMS	New Cooperative Medical System
NCSSF	National Council for the Social Security Fund
NGO	non-governmental organization
NIEs	Newly Industrialized Economies
NPC	National People's Congress
NRCMI	New Rural Cooperative Medical Insurance
NRCMS	New Rural Cooperative Medical System

NROIS	New Rural Old-age Insurance System
PAP	People's Action Party
PAYG	pay-as-you-go
PLA	People's Liberation Army
PNEO	private non-enterprise organization
PPP	Purchasing Power Parity
RMB	*renminbi* (Chinese currency)
SEZ	Special Economic Zone
SOE	state-owned enterprise
TVEs	township and village enterprises
UNDP	United Nations Development Programme
URBHI	Urban Resident Basic Health Insurance
URBMI	Urban Residents Basic Medical Insurance
WBMI	Worker Basic Medical Insurance
ZXB	*Zhuang xianjin butie* (housing cash-subsidy)

Introduction

Litao Zhao

Economic development and social development are often expected and argued to go hand in hand. To some extent, this has been the case in China. Various indicators clearly show China's progress in social development, as reflected in the fall in poverty rates, the rise in living standards, the expansion of education, and so on. As recently as 2000, ownership of automobile was rare for urban households, with every 200 urban households owning a car; in 2009, nationwide every 10 urban households owned a car. By the mid-1990s, about 5 percent of the college-age cohorts had access to higher education, as low as some of the least developed countries; in 2009, the gross enrollment ratio had increased to 24 percent (*China Statistical Yearbook* 2001, 2010).

The progress in social development, however, is not the main story. In fact, the overwhelming majority of discussions tend to highlight the contrast of economic development and social development in China. The contrast takes one of the two forms in most discussions. Some research focuses on a plethora of social problems, including the widening gap between the rich and the poor, the growing rural–urban divide, the rising regional disparities, the deteriorating environment, and the declining social trust and morality (Zhao and Lim, 2010). What makes China a puzzling case is the high social costs of economic growth. Society is not becoming happier and more stable. The most telling evidence for this are the surging social protests, known in China as the "mass incidents," despite China's spectacular economic growth for over three decades.

Some other studies look more closely at the relationship between China's economic development and social development. The World Bank has carried out a number of studies to suggest that the relationship is looser than it could be. For instance, economic growth in the 1980s removed millions of Chinese from living in poverty. Over time, however, this growth has become increasingly less effective in poverty reduction (World Bank, 2009). China's gain in life expectancy is also much less than would be expected from its high economic growth in the past 20 years. The United Nations Development Programmes (UNDP) reaches a similar conclusion in its Human Development Report. China is the second largest achiever in terms of the Human Development Index improvement since 1970s. Unlike other largest achievers, however, China's improvement is mainly due to income rather than health and educational achievements (UNDP, 2010). Survey data collected in China also suggest that the relationship between economic development and well-being is not as close as expected (Zhang *et al.*, 2010).

Given the high social costs of China's economic growth, there have been calls for more policy attention to social development. From a normative perspective, China should move from the current stage of development to the next stage. At the next stage, the relationship between economic development and social development should be remarkably different. China's social development should at least keep pace with its economic development, if not be given more priority. The key question is the driving force. For China to move into the next stage of development, certain changes are needed so that the conditions, structures and institutions that are locking China into unbalanced development will be transformed in favor of more balanced development. This volume sets out to examine China's transition to the next stage of development, less from a normative perspective, but based more on an analysis of the presence (or the lack) of the driving forces needed for the transition.

The first stage of development: why social development suffered

It is difficult and perhaps futile to define development by stages, and to determine the turning point that sets the first stage apart from the next. Nonetheless, in more general terms, China is still in a stage of unbalanced development. Most would agree that China's social development is lagging behind its economic development, the benefits of high growth have not been widely shared, and the role of social policy is weak in providing security and reducing inequality.

China is often viewed as one of the East Asian developmental states. To the extent that the successive generations of leadership since Deng are firmly committed to economic growth and that the state plays a pivotal role in steering the economy and society, China is undoubtedly in the same league as Japan and the four little "tigers" of South Korea, Taiwan, Hong Kong and Singapore. Yet China's development experience is complicated not just by its vast size and large regional variations, but also by its intertwined double transitions. In the late 1970s, China not only faced the challenge of developing from an agrarian economy to an industrial one, but also the challenge of what to do with the system that had been built on redistribution and central planning (Li, 2005). The second challenge was never faced by the other East Asian economies.

China had favorable conditions for the first transition. China had a huge surplus of young labor, known as the "first generation of migrant workers," who had basic skills for factory jobs and more importantly, were willing to work for long hours under harsh conditions for low wages. With the shift to the "open-door" policy, China also had access to foreign investment, technology, and markets. Moreover, China had a huge domestic market for all kinds of consumer goods after decades of severe shortages. In terms of capital, labor, skills, and markets, China was in a good position to take off economically in the late 1970s.

The bigger challenge is the transition from the planned economy to the market economy. This transition involves profound changes in almost every aspect of economic and social life. In terms of social value, money and wealth had to be reaffirmed as desirable and legitimate. Some people had to be permitted to become rich first. At the institutional level, prices of goods and services were to fluctuate in relation to supply and demand, private ownership of productive assets would be allowed, workers were to enjoy greater freedom to move between jobs and to different locations, and employers in turn would be less constrained in hiring and firing. The relationship between individuals and their "work unit" would change from the one of organized dependence to a looser one, and the state as a result had to think of new mechanisms of social control.

It is the transition from plan to market that sets China apart from other East Asian societies. China's challenge in balancing economic and social development has a great deal to do with this second transition, which occurred simultaneously with the first transition of industrialization and urbanization. The problem is not so much the older institutions holding back the transition to the market economy. Although there were powerful conservative forces blocking economic reforms, at the societal level the support for lifting the ban on private ownership and market exchanges was much wider and stronger. The reformists were in a much better position to mobilize support for their economic agenda. In fact, the shift to a monied lifestyle was so rapid and thorough that it was quickly seen as social problem to be termed "materialism" or the "moral vacuum" (Rosen, 2004).

The problem, from the long-term perspective of social development, was the reform strategies of decentralization, commercialization and marketization. There were political and practical reasons why China chose to embrace these reform strategies. The reformists allied with sub-national governments by making concessions, in exchange for their support for the reform agenda, in the face of resistance from conservatives in the central leadership and the ministries. Financial constraints at all levels of government also led to the decentralization of public services, to the point that rural education received very limited government support and was forced to rely on surcharges on farming households (Zhao, 2009). Local governments were given greater autonomy; meanwhile they were also made responsible for public service provision within their jurisdiction. The same practical concern also led the government to delegate greater autonomy as well as responsibility to every organization in the public sector, including government agencies, schools, hospitals, and so on.

Decentralization changed the central–local relationship. It also profoundly affected the incentives and behavior of individuals and organizations in the public domain. Wherever possible, they set up their own businesses or created new programs/opportunities to charge user fees for the services they provided. Marketization became the dominant strategy for public institutions to generate extra-budget and off-budget incomes for their own survival and also benefits. The ability to "marketize" their services of course varied widely across sectors, with public hospitals among those that were best able to take advantage of the newfound autonomy and responsibility. Nonetheless, China's public service providers quickly adapted to the new reality. For their part, governments, particularly those at the higher levels, were able to reduce their financial burden.

China's shift towards decentralization and marketization was therefore done out of practical concerns. Of equal importance is the fact that it was facilitated by the neo-liberalism of decentralization, marketization and privatization (Wong, 1998). Coincidently, China's reform and "opening-up" began at a time when neo-liberalism was gaining worldwide dominance. There was a natural affinity between the two. What was afflicting China—the low efficiency of the public sector, the lack of incentives for economic growth, etc.—was also what neo-liberalism was trying to combat. Meanwhile neo-liberalism provided justifications for the coherent agenda it proposed. Although privatization as a reform strategy was accepted relatively late in China, not until the mid-1990s, the neo-liberal ideology of decentralization and marketization became popular, to the extent that it became the dominant discourse in China (Mok, 1996).

The neo-liberal ideology, coupled with the financial incentives given to lower levels of government, enterprises, public institutions, and individuals, paved the way for rather radical changes in China. At one level, it encouraged "entrepreneurial" and profiteering behavior, transforming society from one lacking growth incentives to one with extremely strong growth incentives. However, at another level, the boundary between economic policy and social policy was blurred. The strategies of decentralization and marketization were used not only to guide the reform of the state-owned enterprises, but also to guide the reform in the social domain. In the area of education, primary education in rural China was heavily dependent on surcharges on farming households and fees from student families. In the area of healthcare, hospitals generated the overwhelming majority of revenues—up to 90 percent—from charging patients. Meanwhile, the social safety net built during the Mao era had largely disappeared with the dismantling of the rural communes in the early 1980s, and the large-scale restructuring of state-owned enterprises since the late 1990s. Not surprisingly, the welfare mix changed in such a way that households now found themselves heavily burdened to pay for education, healthcare and their other security needs. The 1994 tax reform, which changed the revenue structure in favor of the central government, while leaving the expenditure structure largely intact, worsened the situation for local governments and households, particularly for those in the poor areas. The wide rural–urban gap and the large regional disparity in access to education, healthcare, and assistance, and the soaring costs of education, healthcare and housing—China's three "new mountains" as opposed to the three "old mountains" of imperialism, feudalism, and bureaucratic capitalism—became a salient source of social grievances and protests.

The intrusion of the neo-liberal ideology of decentralization and market-ization into the social domain was the root cause of the divergent trend of economic development and social development in China. Applying the reform strategy for the economic domain to the social domain is also the key reason why China is so different from other East Asian developmental states in terms of social development. In other East Asian developmental states, although economic development was the priority, the strategies and policies for economic development were not assumed to work in the social domain as well. Even in explicitly anti-welfarism countries such as Singapore, economic development was able to benefit social development, through full employ-ment, steady wage increases, and its unique public housing program that benefited over 80 percent of its citizens. By contrast, in China, the boundary between the economic domain and the social domain was blurred during the reform process. In fact, the strategy for economic reform became a guideline for reforming the social domain. Public service providers engaged in income-generating activities just like private enterprises. Unaffordability, not surpris-ingly, became a problem. As a result, the relationship between economic development and social development was not as close and balanced as expected.

Is the next stage coming?

As of today, China has been grappling with problems stemming from its ear-lier unbalanced development. The Gini coefficient keeps rising to a high level of income inequality; the numbers of social protests have yet to show signs of slowing down; a sense of insecurity and anxiety is widespread in the Chinese society. Isn't it too early to talk about the next stage of development?

If we look closely at China, certain aspects remain unchanged or have experienced little change. Civil society remains weak vis-à-vis the state; social protests are largely contained without developing into a national movement with a clear and coherent progressive agenda; the emerging elites seem to be drifting away from the ordinary people without showing their social respon-sibility; and the central government has yet to play a larger role to ensure equal access to basic public services nationwide. Yet, some other aspects have been changing, which can have profound implications for the relationship of economic development and social development.

At the ideological level, neo-liberalism is no longer a dominant discourse, although it still has its strong advocates. There has been increasingly strong skepticism and criticism of neo-liberalism as a guide to social policy reform. The official discourse of "scientific development" and "building a harmonious society" endorsed by the Hu Jintao–Wen Jiabao administration was in sharp contrast to the growth-centered discourses under Deng Xiaoping and Jiang

Zemin. Hu Jintao's scientific outlook on development, written into the Party Constitution in 2007, is a guideline calling for less income inequality, less regional disparity, more social justice, better protection of the disadvantaged, higher energy efficiency and less pollution. The elite are more divided, however, with neo-liberals claiming that China's current problems are caused by too much government intervention and distortion, and the critics arguing that too much marketization, or the combination of power and capital in the form of cronyism, is the root problem. Consensus is lacking on what is the best way forward for China. Nonetheless, the criticism of neo-liberalism is gaining ground. There are calls for a clearer distinction between the economic domain and the social domain, and between the market principles and the role of government.

The shifting ideology is reflected in two important reforms in recent years. In 2009, China announced its blueprint for a new round of healthcare reform up to 2020. Prior to this, the Chinese government had commissioned several independent, parallel studies for reform proposals. Some were in favor of more marketization in healthcare delivery while others were in favor of a dominant role for government. The announced blueprint has elements of both approaches, but the pro-government approach is clearly the winner (Zhao and Huang, 2010).

Another case is China's public housing program. China's earlier housing reforms have created a country with over 80 percent of home-ownership. However, there are still many people who have been left out of this state of affairs. Low-income families who had not secured a flat from their work unit fall into this category. Also included in this category are many young people. Even college graduates with well-paying jobs have problems finding affordable housing in large cities. The problem of unaffordable housing is believed to be caused by too much marketization. The lack of differentiation between commercial housing and public housing, for whatever the reason, has led to an over-reliance on the housing market to meet diversified housing needs. Following this line of thinking, the 12th Five-Year Programme (2011–15) drastically expanded the public housing program. In terms of construction targets, in late 2008, China estimated that a total of 7.5 million urban low-income families needed help. It thus made a security housing development plan to provide housing for these 7.5 million families and another 2.4 million living in run-down urban areas within three years from 2009 to 2011. The 12th Five-Year Programme made an even bolder commitment of building 36 million housing units for 20 percent of the urban population. In 2011 alone, the plan was to start constructing 10 million housing units, an increase of 72 percent from 2010.

At the institutional and policy level, there are also changes in favor of social development. Under Deng Xiaoping and Jiang Zemin, social policy reform was either marginalized or carried out to support the market-oriented economic reform. With market institutions more or less in place by the early 2000s, policy attention began to shift to the social domain. The attempt to advocate, propose and perform social policy reform is being institutionalized, with government-affiliated think tanks and university-based research institutes competing in identifying social problems and proposing solutions. There are also cases where the central leadership group was formed involving over a dozen ministries for a social policy reform, such as the healthcare reform (Thompson, 2009). The trend of institutionalizing social policy reform has led to the proliferation of social programs since 2003. For instance, the social security programs have been greatly expanded, to provide basic healthcare and pensions to the entire population, including rural residents, migrant workers, and the urban non-working population who were not covered by the previous programs. Public assistance programs have also been extended to more rural and urban poor. However, there still remain many problems arising from segregated programs, fragmented administration and the immobility of social security accounts. Nonetheless, China is moving in the right direction towards universal coverage in the health insurance and pension programs arenas.

External and internal conditions are also changing in ways that reinforce the need for more balanced development. For the past three decades, China's economic growth relied heavily on investment and export, less on domestic consumption. At that time, social development was not that important for economic development. But after the 2008 global financial crisis, China faced the risk of declining demand from the US and the European markets. Although China's savings rate remains high, too much government spending can create problems of overcapacity and inflation, as China experienced in the aftermath of the 4 trillion yuan stimulus package. China felt the need to shift to domestic consumption as a major source of economic growth. This shift is likely to change the relationship between economic development and social development. Under the new circumstances, social development is important, not only for social stability, but also for economic growth.

China's level of urbanization is believed to lag behind the level of industrialization. This feature is seen as a result of unbalanced development that prioritized economic growth over social development. City governments did not want urbanization to happen too quickly, because a larger urban population would mean higher government spending on public services. As a result, farmers were allowed to migrate and become workers, but were denied the opportunity to become urban residents. The situation is likely to change in the coming decade. Instead of seeing urbanization as a burden for city governments, a new way of thinking is emerging, which views urbanization as a new engine of growth. When people move to the cities, they need their own housing, their life style and consumption behavior will change, which in turn can boost domestic consumption. Moreover, when the farming population declines, more rural land can be freed up for urban development.

Another argument emphasizes the importance of social development to economic development from a different perspective. China's future growth is conditioned and constrained by its current social structure. Growing income inequality means a polarizing social structure. This would affect the formation of a middle-class society focusing on mass consumption. The low-income groups lack the ability to consume, while the top income groups change their consumption behavior towards foreign brands, luxuries and overseas trips, not necessarily benefiting domestic consumption. As Peilin Li argues in Chapter 2 in this volume, boosting domestic consumption is more of a social issue than an economic one.

Similarly, the government can find new grounds to justify the expanded social programs. Increased spending on education, healthcare, public housing, and social security is not only pro-poor and therefore morally justifiable, or instrumental in maintaining social stability, but also economically justifiable because such spending can directly and indirectly promote GDP growth. Public housing programs are now being seen as a new engine for local economic growth. Therefore, even without fundamental political and ideological changes to empower society and link social policy to citizenship rights, China's economic and social conditions have changed to the extent that social development has become a prerequisite of or a facilitator for economic growth. This is good news for social development even if the local officials are still preoccupied with GDP growth.

Overview of the book

This book analyzes changes in the conditions, structures and institutions that are shaping China's social policies and its transition to the next stage of development. China has yet to find an ideological core for its social policies. It is still debating the meaning of "making equal basic public services nationwide" as well as mechanisms to achieve this goal. The debate is made difficult by the absence of a common understanding of citizenship rights. Nonetheless, as the chapters in this book show, China's social policy used to be an appendage to its economic policy. It now has its own momentum, likely to have a greater influence on China's future social development and economic development.

Chapter 1, by Yongnian Zheng, raises the question of central concern to this volume: whether China is entering a new stage of development in which social development is the key feature. Clearly high economic growth has been the hallmark of China's development in the first three decades of its reform and opening-up to the world. A great deal of its dynamics comes from greater openness, both externally and internally. By opening up the economy to new actors and forces, such as foreign direct investment, international trade, growth-minded local officials, and private entrepreneurs, the Chinese state has created favorable conditions for economic growth, overcoming the problem of social rigidities as discussed by Mancur Olson (1982). The degree of state-led openness, however, varies across sectors, regions and social groups. Those who can participate in and benefit from greater economic openness are also being co-opted by the state into the structures of political representation and participation; those who cannot do so will be the losers, economically, socially and politically. The marginalized groups in turn are responding by the growing number of social protests, spontaneous yet disruptive. What accounts for China's great economic success therefore also accounts for its mounting social challenges. What is occurring in China was observed by Karl Polanyi in industrializing England: the emergence of the modern market economy tends to destroy what holds society together, giving rise to the counter-movement of social protectionism (Polanyi, 1944). According to Zheng, if China is to follow the development sequences described by Karl Polanyi, the state should and would move onto the next stage of development. The Chinese state has created a market economy; now it has to deal with the market malaise through better protection of the economically and socially disadvantaged to avoid political and social upheavals.

Normative arguments have been strong in academic and public discussions on why China should enter a new stage of development. A more difficult issue is whether China can transform and develop into the next stage. Chapter 2, by Peilin Li, provides a more or less affirmative answer to this question. This chapter reflects new lines of thinking within China's policy circles. The Chinese government has endorsed the concept of "changing the mode of development" as a guideline for future development. The concept, similar to but broader than "sustainable development," highlights the transformative aspect of development, shifting from investment- and export-driven to domestic consumption-driven, moving up the value-added chain, and gearing towards more balanced and environment-friendly development. With this new concept, China is preparing for the next stage of development. The 2008 global financial crisis is undoubtedly a major factor pushing for the transformation. While many scholars are talking about the difficulties and challenges of the transformation, in Chapter 2, Peilin Li is more positive and bolder, arguing that the new stage of development is coming. Mass consumption of large consumer goods and expanded services is coming of age in China. China's economic structure (measured by the share of primary, secondary and tertiary sectors), employment structure (measured by the share of employees in each of the three sectors), and rural–urban structure are all reaching the stage of accelerated transformation. China's population structure is also changing, resulting in the growing need for elderly care and the rise of labor costs. Conditions or pressures have emerged for China to establish a more comprehensive social security system and gear itself towards industrial upgrading. In other words, China's transition to the next stage of development is inevitable. One important insight from Peilin Li's chapter is that this transition is more of a social issue than an economic one. To shift from an investment- and exports-driven economy to a domestic consumption-driven economy, China has to develop sound social policies to expand the middle class, increase labor income, and transform the social structure from a pyramid shape to an oval one.

In the next developmental stage, social security is expected to be one of the priority policy areas, due to its importance for boosting economic growth, equalizing income distribution, alleviating poverty and maintaining social stability. In Chapter 3, Shi Li provides a comprehensive and thorough review of China's social security reform. Social security is understood in a broad sense, to include social insurance, public assistance, education, and housing security. If in the earlier stage of development, social security was considered a liability for economic growth, remarkably it is now viewed in a much more positive light in the next stage of development. Social security is now expected to play an important role in stimulating economic growth, apart from its widely recognized roles in poverty reduction, income redistribution, consumption smoothing, and social stability maintenance. The debate of the priority of economic development versus social development is thus rendered unnecessary because social security covers both social development and economic development. Against this backdrop, broad consensus has emerged regarding the importance and direction of China's social security reform. There should be universal coverage, regardless of their age, employment, and location; the individual social security account should be portable across regions and jobs; and the benefit levels, which are low by international standards, should be raised incrementally within government fiscal capability, commensurate with economic growth. Disagreements over the specifics of social security programs remain, as discussed in great detail in this chapter. Ideological preferences between government control and market mechanisms, and practical considerations of regional disparities and local realities have all shaped the divergent views. The debates, it should be pointed out, are more about policy options regarding the means of delivery, the level of benefits, and so on, rather than the more fundamental and strategic issues over the role of social security in the next stage of development.

One way to gauge the priority of social security in the overall development strategy is to analyze government spending on social security. This is what Yanzhong Wang and Yuqi Long do in Chapter 4. In the 1980s, social security remained a privilege for public sector employees; in the 1990s, China gradually established the framework of a modern social security system for employees in public and private sector employees, including five types of social insurance program. The focus of the Hu Jintao and Wen Jiabao administration since 2002 was to expand such programs to rural residents, urban non-working populations, urban employees in the informal sectors, and migrant workers. Along with these changes, government spending on social security has been increasing, either as a share of total fiscal expenditure or as a percentage of GDP. As Wang and Long show, social security accounted for 1.78 percent of total fiscal expenditure and 0.25 percent of GDP in 1992, but rapidly increased to 11.95 percent and 2.19 percent respectively in 2002 and stabilized thereafter. If expenditures on education and public health are included, the figures were 24.5 percent and 3.41 percent for 1992, and 38.41 percent and 7.98 percent for 2002. From a comparative perspective, China's public expenditures on social security remain low by international standards. Meanwhile, China's social security programs have yet to be more effective in equalizing income distribution and protecting the poor. There is plenty of room for China's social security room to improve in the next stage of development. As Wang and Long suggest, much can be done to raise the benefit levels, to increase the financial transfer from the central government to poor areas in central and western China, and to optimize the expenditure structure for the purpose of equity and efficiency. In this light, China's social security reform is an unfinished project. It will continue to move from the periphery to the center of China's development agenda.

Healthcare reform is of particular importance to China's next stage of development. The Chinese government has decided to build a basic healthcare system by 2020. The new system would cover both urban and rural residents, and is expected to address the problems of expensive accessibility (*kanbing nan*) and medical impoverishment (*kanbing gui*) that are plaguing the current system. In Chapter 5, Kai Hong Phua and Alex He Jingwei provide an overview of the causes of the deteriorating health system, and document successive rounds of healthcare reform designed to address the problem of accessibility and affordability. With varying degrees of success, the earlier healthcare reforms set the stage for the subsequent reform. Through different schemes for different categories of population, basic health insurance has become nearly universal across the country. More financial resources are being channeled to public healthcare providers, with those at the grassroots level receiving particular attention. The more difficult challenge, as Phua and He explain, is to fix the incentive structure to strike a balance between providing quality services and containing soaring costs. This will largely define the agenda for the healthcare reform in the 2010s and beyond. The problem is a perennial one, not unique to the hospital sector. Since the 1980s, public organizations have been given much greater financial autonomy to make up the shortfalls due to insufficient budgetary allocation. Public hospitals were among the most adaptive ones to shift towards profit-seeking. When the government finally has the resources and willingness to tackle the problem of cost inflation, it will find an entirely different public hospital sector that has become accustomed to strong organizational autonomy and weak government regulation. Increasing budgetary allocation to public hospitals, however necessary, cannot change their profit-seeking behavior. China's healthcare reform is an unfinished project. How to make the public hospitals accountable to public interests is a bigger challenge than expanding the health insurance coverage and increasing the budgetary allocation to the health system.

The housing issue provides a unique lens for examining how much China has been transformed. As Bingqin Li describes in Chapter 6, housing was a largely self-contained policy area in much of the 1980s and 1990s. In the aftermath of the 1997 Asian financial crisis when exports were badly hurt, housing began to be seen as an important source of economic growth, and land sales became a newfound source of revenue for local government. Taking on an important economic function made housing a much more complicated policy area than before. A diversified housing supply system has emerged, with private housing, government-subsidized housing and cheap rental housing catering to different housing demands and affordability. In practice, local governments were incentivized to prioritize private housing for revenue and GDP growth. Public housing schemes, including government-subsidized housing and cheap rental housing, were marginalized on the policy agenda for a number of years. This in turn led to the soaring price of commercial housing, well beyond the reach of low- and even middle-income households. Moreover, the relatively small-scale government-subsidized housing program was found to be abused and manipulated by the powerful and the well-off. Unaffordability and injustice caused widespread complaints, making housing one of the top public concerns in China in recent years. The central government has identified housing as one of the development priorities in China's 12th Five-Year Plan (2011–15). Yet, as Bingqin Li argues, there have been gaps and misalignments between policy-making and policy implementation, and between different stakeholders with divergent interests. After more than 30 years of reform, housing has developed from a self-contained policy area to a complicated policy area that is both economic and social. Looking to the future, housing stands as a unique challenge for China's next stage of development. One way forward is to draw a clearer boundary between housing as an economic policy and housing as a social policy, not letting the former overwhelm the latter. Another option, which has been discussed in China, is to make public housing a new engine for economic growth, thus taking on an important role for economic and social development at the same time. Either way, a new kind of relationship between housing and economic/social development has to be established, if the current problems of unaffordability and injustice are to be addressed.

Demographic transition—from high fertility and high death rates eventually to low fertility and low death rates—is one of the most powerful factors shaping the socio-economic development of the modern world. China is part of this general pattern, except that the decline of fertility rate is much steeper there than in other societies and that the decline occurs at a much lower level of economic development. In Chapter 7, Ding Lu describes the process of China's demographic transition, some unique features, and the challenges for economic growth and social security. Demographically speaking, China has entered a post-transition stage, which features rapid population aging and slow population growth. When the dependency ratio rises, it will adversely affect the labor force employment rate, capital accumulation, age-related productivity, and eventually economic growth. It also poses a serious challenge for China's pension system. China, as the first country to "get old before getting rich," is not well prepared for providing old-age care to its fast-aging population. Although much progress has been made in expanding the coverage, the pension system remains fragmented, in terms of schemes and administration. This raises the issue of unequal benefit levels and the immobility of social security accounts. An even larger challenge is financial sustainability. China had set up a pension system with three pillars, namely, a risk-pooling social account, a personal savings account, and voluntary savings. In practice, all the balance in the personal savings accounts has been used to pay the current retirees, thus making China's three-pillar system a *de facto* one-pillar pay-as-you-go system and "hollowing out" the personal savings accounts. With the old dependency ratio continuing to rise, it will become more difficult to maintain such a system. In short, China's next stage of development is conditioned by its demographic transition. The sources of economic growth have to change; the challenges for social development have to be addressed.

In the absence of a citizenship rights-based ideology for social policy-making, China's social policy reform benefitted the politically advantaged more. In Chapter 8, Yongnian Zheng and Yanjie Huang note that past 30 years have seen the Chinese welfare system transformed from a state-dominated system to a system dominated by market-based social insurance and welfare provision. For many disadvantaged groups, this transformation has resulted in a steep rise in the costs of basic welfare and the worsening of welfare conditions. Since the mid-1990s and especially in the Hu–Wen era, there has been a sustained effort to complement the market with government welfare subsidy for the needy. But these reforms have seen very different outcomes across different policy domains, such as social insurance, social protection, and welfare provisions, including housing, healthcare and education. The varying degrees of success have much to do with the different political dynamics and mechanisms between top policy-makers, the social forces urging reform and the vested interests that resist reform. There is a further break-down of social forces between groups with the most access (the state sector employees), groups with moderate political access (the middle class), and groups without any access (the lower class) to power and welfare privileges. Employing a Hirschman exit–voice model, Zheng and Huang set out to address the reform dynamics in each domain by identifying welfare arrangements and access to the political system for different social groups for each specific category and type of social policy reform. They argue that fiscal subsidy and reform progress are by and large positively related to the welfare position of social groups with more access to political power; the exclusion effect is most severe and comprehensive, if the politically powerful groups enjoy most substantive welfare privileges. As a key policy implication, stronger reform dynamics demands the replacement of the politically based welfare privileges with a program of citizenship-based welfare rights to both markets and government subsidies, if the government wants to build a more inclusive distribution in social welfare.

A shallow understanding of the causes of social issues and challenges can lead to policy failure. This is the case with China's ethnic policy, as Yongjia Liang forcefully argues in Chapter 9. China's ethnic policy has its ideological roots. Without critically examining such ideological roots, it is difficult to understand where and how China's ethnic policy fails to sustain the loyalty of some ethnic minorities in the making of a unified, multi-ethnic nation. Liang identifies three ideologies that have informed and shaped China's ethnic policy since the 1980s. The first is developmentalism, which sees the ethnic issue largely as an economic issue. When ethnic minorities and ethnic minority regions can participate in sustained economic growth, ethnic tension is believed to ease as a result. The Chinese government adopted this approach in the 1980s. It did not work well, however, resulting in a shift to the hard-liners' approach of "maintaining stability" by any means in the 1990s. The hard approach did not work well either, as evidenced by the violence in Lhasa and Urumqi in 2008 and 2009, respectively. The pendulum is now shifting back to the softer approach of economic development and social welfare, without realizing that the ethnic issue is more than an economic issue. The second ideology is secularism. The state operates as a secular power and governs the country in secular terms. The problem is that the ethnic issue, often intertwined with the religious issue, is more than a secular issue. The third ideology is nationalism, promoted in China since the 1990s. In reality, nationalism often takes the form of Han nationalism, thus serving to alienate ethnic minorities rather than unifying them. The more fundamental problem, according to Liang, is "ethnic essentialism," which underlies the three ideologies. Ironically, attaching great importance to "ethnicity" can create its own problems. "Essentializing" the ethnic issue, as what the three ideologies do, serves to make ethnic boundaries clearer and makes ethnic consciousness more salient. Policies informed by such policies are counter-productive. Liang's analysis of China's ethnic challenges can shed useful light on the other social challenges China is facing, such as the erosion of social trust and the rise of social anxiety, in spite of China's significant improvement in measurable economic and social indicators.

In Chapter 10, Chack Kie Wong places China in a comparative framework of welfare regimes. Wong points out that the Western welfare regime has its ideological roots in the concept of citizen rights and property rights. In the East Asian context, however, citizen rights and property rights were either absent or weak for an extended period of time. Instead of a single dimension of institutional analysis, a tripartite framework of institutional, ideological and developmental dimensions is more appropriate to study the welfare regime in East Asia. The East Asian developmental states feature a relatively autonomous developmental elite, a powerful and competent bureaucracy, and a weak civil society. At the later stage, these states began to diverge towards different models, with South Korea and Taiwan moving towards a model that more resembles the Western model after democratization, while Singapore retains much of the developmental features, despite being at a much higher level of economic development. Wong sees China as a typical developmental state, although the legacy of the Maoist past sets China apart from other East Asian societies. Social expenditure data clearly demonstrate the retreat of the state in social welfare in the 1980s and 1990s when economic development and restructuring dominated the policy agenda. Social policy to a large extent was subordinated to economic policy until an ideological shift under the Hu

Jintao–Wen Jiabao leadership towards more balanced development. Substantial increases in social expenditure have occurred in recent years. Overall, however, China's expenditure on social welfare is still small by international standards. China remains a developmental state without evolving towards a Western type of welfare regime. Its political, institutional and ideological set-up makes it favor the Singapore model more than other models.

In the reform era, China is keen to learn from the outside world about development experiences. Singapore, a small city–state, surprisingly attracts disproportionately large interest from the Chinese leadership, despite the tremendous differences between the two countries in the size of population and territory and the level of economic development. Singapore as a model of a vibrant economy, a garden city, and a harmonious society has been aspirational to Chinese leaders from Deng till now. In Chapter 11, Litao Zhao and John Wong look closely at Singapore's social development experience, in an attempt to shed light on the relevance of Singapore to China. Singapore clearly is a variant of the East Asian developmental states. The ruling People's Action Party (PAP) very early on rejected state welfarism as a model for Singapore. The PAP leadership adopted a broad concept of social policy and social welfare, and a holistic view of the relationship between economic and social development. The best way to promote general social well-being is through economic growth and job creation rather than redistributive policies for a minority of disadvantaged. In terms of social development, Singapore's developmental elite has for decades focused on "socially productive" areas such as education, healthcare and public housing. Economic policy and social policy have been integrated in such a way that they reinforced each other to transform Singapore from a Third World country to a First World one in a short span of three decades. As China is rethinking the relationship between economic development and social development, Singapore serves as an important reference for China. China's strong interest in Singapore's development experience is clearly reflected in the expansion of government-to-government cooperation from the economic to the social domain. After the China-Singapore Suzhou Industrial Park, the two countries are jointly working on the Tianjin Eco-City project, which adds social and environmental dimensions to the economic dimension. In specific policy areas, China has learned from Singapore to incorporate the idea and practice of the Central Provident Fund (CPF) into its social security and housing reform.

In sum, China still faces a lot of challenges. To tackle these challenges, there has to be a paradigm shift in social policy. Although important aspects remain largely intact, China's social policy is shifting towards a new ideological ground and becoming more autonomous and differentiated from the economic policy. The paradigm shift is driven by China's demographic and social changes, which have transformed the ideologies, institutions and structures to the point that social development is becoming more important not just for social stability, but also for economic growth. Given such changes, it is time to raise the issue whether China is entering a new stage of development.

References

China Statistical Yearbook (2001) Beijing: China Statistics Press.
——(2010) Beijing: China Statistics Press.
Li, P. (2005) *Another Invisible Hand: Transformation of the Social Structure* Beijing: Shehui kexue wenxian chubanshe (in Chinese).
Mok, K.H. (1996) "Marketization and decentralization: development of education and paradigm shift in social policy," *Hong Kong Public Administration*, 5: 35–56.
Olson, M. (1982) *The Rise and Decline of Nations: Economic Growth, Stagflation, and Social Rigidities*, New Haven, CT: Yale University Press.
Polanyi, K. (1944) *The Great Transformation: The Political and Economic Origins of Our Time*, Boston: Beacon Press.
Rosen, S. (2004) "The victory of materialism: aspirations to join China's urban moneyed classes and the commercialization of education," *China Journal*, 51: 27–51.
Thompson, D. (2009) "China's health care reform redux," in *China's Capacity to Manage Infectious Disease*, a conference report, Washington, DC: The Freeman Chair in China Studies at Center for Strategic and International Studies, pp. 57–78.
UNDP (2010) *Human Development Report 2010*, New York: Palgrave Macmillan.
Wong, L. (1998) *Marginalization and Social Welfare in China*, London: Routledge.
World Bank (2009) *China from Poor Areas to Poor People: China's Evolving Poverty Reduction Agenda*, Washington, DC: World Bank.
Zhang, X., Lum, T. and Xu, Y. (2010) "Economic development and household economic well-being in urban China," in K.H. Mok and Y.W. Ku (eds.) *Social Cohesion in Greater China: Challenges for Social Policy and Governance*, Singapore: World Scientific, pp. 319–37.
Zhao, L. (2009) "Between local community and central state: financing basic education in China," *International Journal of Educational Development*, 29: 366–73.
Zhao, L. and Huang, Y. (2010) "China's blueprint for health care reform," *East Asian Policy*, 2: 51–9.
Zhao, L. and Lim, T.S. (2010) "Introduction," in L. Zhao and T.S. Lim (eds.) *China's New Social Policy: Initiatives for a Harmonious Society*, Singapore: World Scientific, pp. 1–10.

Part I

China into the next stage of development

1 Society must be defended

Reform, openness and social policy in China

Yongnian Zheng

Development dynamics and social consequences

Of the many intellectual questions on contemporary China, two have stood out for many years. First, how could China's open-door policy, which began in the late 1970s, provide dynamism to the transformation of China in almost all aspects? Second, what does this transformation mean to Chinese society?

Shortly after he came to power in the aftermath of the Cultural Revolution, the late Deng Xiaoping, China's great statesman after Mao Zedong, began his ambitious reform and open-door policy program. The reform of China's old systems and the opening of China's door to the outside world were two related but separate policy processes. The former turned out to be easier than the latter.

In the 30 years under Maoist rule (1949–79), China's doors were closed to the outside world, especially the West. The Chinese Communist Party (CCP) cadres and government officials—most of them old revolutionaries—lacked sufficient knowledge and experience in dealing with the outside world. They greatly feared opening China's door to the outside world as they were haunted by bad memories of the regular humiliation of their country by Western powers after China entered its modern age. Nevertheless, most cadres and government officials understood and accepted domestic reforms. Even under Mao, there were several waves of reforms, though terms such as "adjustment" and "rectification" were frequently used instead of "reform."

Drawing on China's history and experience with the outside world, the leadership under Deng Xiaoping focused on three main arguments (or three hypotheses) in justifying its open-door policy: (1) China had been bullied in the past because of its backwardness; (2) China's backwardness was due mainly to its isolation from the outside world; and (3) the only way that China could become a strong state again was to open its door to the outside world. This mindset provided the justification for China's opening-up policy, a policy which continues today after three decades of reform and opening-up.

So, the question is: how could the open-door policy lead to China's transformation? Over the years, China has persisted in implementing its open-door policy. The Tiananmen Square event in 1989 did not interrupt the process; instead, it unexpectedly became a powerful motivation for the Chinese leadership to open the country's door even wider to the outside world. China now ranks second in the world in terms of total GDP, only after the United States. The rise of China has become an important topic in both academic and policy circles. China's openness has served the most powerful driving force behind its rapid transformation. At the domestic level, openness creates an institutional environment in which different existing factors reorganize themselves, thus providing new dynamics for change. At the international level, openness links China and the world, with the interaction between China and the world producing the external dynamics that lead to changes within the former.

Openness, however, also has its social consequences. So, another important question is: what does this transformation mean for Chinese society? Put simply, while China as a whole has benefited from its open-door policy, the benefits of openness have been unevenly distributed. Like other societies, some social groups have gained more than others, with some being winners and others being the losers. A society can be understood as being in a state of equilibrium, a relatively stable state in which different member elements accept each other. Openness implies that new elements are introduced into this state, which upsets the existing equilibrium. If a new equilibrium cannot be reached, this society will become unstable and sustainable development problematic. How can such a new equilibrium be achieved? Social policy plays an important role in this regard. Empirically speaking, society often is the weakest part of the processes of globalization and opening-up. Therefore, society must be defended by all means and in all major policy areas.

This chapter attempts to examine China's grand transformation from different perspectives, including economic, social and political. It discusses how these transformations are linked to the country's open-door policy, and draws implications for China's social policy reform.

The term "openness" normally and mainly refers to China's open-door policy. In this chapter, this term refers not only to China's opening-up to the outside world, which I call "external openness," but also "internal openness," meaning the opening of economic, social and political processes to different social actors. Empirically speaking, external openness takes place first before generating the necessary dynamics for internal openness. Needless to say, the two kinds of openness reinforce each other.

Mancur Olson and Karl Polanyi

In reflecting openness and its social consequences, one can draw on two great thinkers, Mancur Olson and Karl Polanyi. Through Olson, one can understand how China's transformation is linked to its openness, while from Polanyi one can learn how openness can affect a given society and why social policy must play an important role in protecting society.

In *The Rise and Decline of Nations: Economic Growth, Stagflation, and Social Rigidities*, Olson (1982) forcefully argues that the behavior of individuals and firms in stable societies leads to the formation of dense networks of collusive, cartelistic, and lobbying organizations that make economies less efficient and dynamic, and polities less governable. The longer a society goes without an upheaval, the more powerful such organizations become and the more they slow down economic expansion. Societies, in which these narrow interest groups have been destroyed, by war or revolution, for example, enjoy the greatest gain in growth. Olson was very innovative in arguing that over time a stable democracy will tend to accumulate more and more distributional coalitions whose political power will accumulate, thus gradually impeding the economic growth of the society. He focuses especially on the post-World War II performances of Germany and Japan as compared with that of the United Kingdom, arguing that the defeat of Germany and Japan in the war led to the overthrow of narrow special interest groups that impeded growth. In the UK, such groups, then at the peak of their power, had been responsible for the relatively weak performance of the British economy.

At the very beginning of the book, Olson states that "many have been puzzled by the mysterious decline or collapse of great empires or civilizations and by the remarkable rise to wealth, power or cultural achievements of previously peripheral or obscure peoples" (ibid.: 1). Olson focuses on the economic side of the rise and decline of nation-states. His theory is also applicable to other aspects. Although Olson's book was published in 1982, when China was at an early stage of its open-door policy, and thus did not pay much attention to the case of China, his theory is helpful in improving our understanding of the dynamics of China's transformation. China's experience in the past three decades also proves the practicality of Olson's logic.

While I agree with Olson's starting point about stable societies, I disagree with his conclusion. I believe that all policies that encourage openness can replace upheavals, wars, and other forms of social conflict to provide greater dynamics for sustainable transformation which will prevent vested interests from becoming deeply rooted or, as Olson terms it, a society becoming too stable and lacking the dynamics for sustainable development. In China, the process of openness was initiated and sustained by the Chinese Communist Party (CCP), the only organization that is able to withstand all social forces.

While Olson focuses on how a society becomes rigid, Karl Polanyi, a Hungarian political economist, shows us how a society could be devastated by the rapid rise of a market economy (Polanyi, 1944). In *The Great Transformation*, Polanyi explores the social and political upheavals that took place in England during the rise of the market economy. He contends that the modern market economy and the modern state should be understood not as discrete elements, but as a single human invention that he calls the Market Society. He reasoned that a powerful modern state was needed to push changes in the social structure that allowed for a competitive capitalist economy, and that a capitalist economy required a strong state to mitigate its harsher effects. For Polanyi, these changes implied the destruction of the basic social order that had existed throughout all earlier history. The market society is unsustainable because it is fatally destructive to the human and natural contexts it inhabits.

In assessing the role of the state in the unleashing of market forces, Polanyi highlights the historical novelty of the nineteenth-century market economy and its concomitant ideological distortions. He argues that *laissez-faire* was planned; that the movement toward a market society was a conscious and planned phenomenon in which state action was the driving force. There was no natural evolution toward this occurrence. The road to the free market was paved with continuous political manipulation.

On the other hand, as opposed to the careful and deliberate construction of a market society, the counter-movement or social protectionism was spontaneous, unplanned, and came from all sectors of society in response to the devastating impact of the market. Polanyi argues that the construction of a "self-regulating" market necessitates the separation of society into economic and political realms. While the self-regulating market has brought unheard-of material wealth, it also resulted in massive social dislocation and spontaneous moves by society to protect itself. The market, once it considers land, labor and money as "fictitious commodities," subordinates the substance of society itself to the laws of the market. When the free market attempts to break away from the fabric of society, social protectionism is society's natural response, a response Polanyi calls the "counter-movement."

According to Polanyi, this counter-movement of protectionism is a movement of general interest toward the goal of general welfare; it especially included workers, yet also incorporated capitalists. All sought some form of protection from the vagaries and perils of the self-regulating market. The protection gained by the counter-movement impeded the efficiency of the self-regulating market, which in turn created more severe economic conditions and another round of demands for protection. The market system was unstable and its instability generated fear and action. Polanyi demonstrates, historically and comparatively, that market encroachment and political repression immediately inspire resistance and rebellion.

Therefore, for Polanyi, social demands against economic uncertainty and market malaise placed heavy pressure on the state to react with political intervention. The ensuing state action would have to, at least nominally, provide some relief and protection. The market society must be replaced by a society with democratic control of both political and economic institutions. These institutions can no longer control society, but should instead be controlled by society.

Many contemporary scholars have explored a similar line of thought to Polanyi when they come to review how globalization affects a given society. For example, Dani Rodrik (1997) believes that globalization has created three sources of tension between the global market and domestic social stability. First, it has reduced the barriers to trade and investment and accentuated the asymmetry between groups that can cross international borders and those that cannot, thus fundamentally transforming the employment relationship. Second, globalization has engendered conflicts within and between nations over domestic norms and the social institutions that embody them. As the technology for manufactured goods becomes standardized and diffused internationally, nations with very different sets of values, norms, institutions, and collective preferences begin to compete head-on in markets for similar goods. Third, globalization has made it exceedingly difficult for governments to provide social insurance—one of their central functions and one that has helped maintain social cohesion and domestic political support for ongoing liberalization throughout the post-war period. All these tendencies might lead to a loss of authority for those who govern in the name of the nation-state. The state cannot protect its citizens in ways they have been used to expect, and the state can no longer count on the loyalty of its citizens.

The relevance of the arguments of both Olson and Polanyi to contemporary China is quite apparent. From Olson, one can see how China has overcome the rigidity of society and achieved rapid economic transformation, while, from Polanyi, one can see how such a transformation has affected society. China's transformation from the planned economy to a market one was a state project. Similarly, solving the problems resulting from a market economy must also be a state project. Without effective state intervention, market malaise will undermine the very fabric of society. Compared to market forces, society is too vulnerable and weak to protect itself; it must be defended by the state. The Chinese state, however, is not neutral. There is a natural tendency for capital (market forces) to seek state protection and for the state to align with capital since both capital and the state can benefit tremendously from their cooperation. While society is also struggling for state protection, such protection will remain weak without effective mechanisms (e.g., democracy) through which it can exercise influence over the state. This is the dilemma that the Chinese state faces today. The state must make a decision to create a situation where market forces and society can play a win–win game. Such a situation is not impossible. Market forces are greatly needed to sustain economic development, but without effective state regulation, market forces have the tendency to self-destruct. Furthermore, without society exercising effective constraints, both state and market forces will destroy themselves.

Openness and market development

There is a fast-growing body of literature on how China's open-door policy has contributed to its economic growth, in particular to foreign direct investment (FDI), technological spill-over, China's access to the world market, and so forth.[1] This chapter focuses on how openness was established as a state project to overcome what Olson called "narrow interests" and which promoted great changes and transformation. While Olson demonstrated how stable societies are often associated with economic stagflation, he did not pay enough attention to why societies become stable and how they could become "de-stabilized." In this regard, China offers a good example.

China's transformation was triggered by economic openness introduced in the late 1970s. How did economic openness take place? In the pre-reform era,

China was a typical "rigid" (in Olson's term) economy and society. I do not need to go into detail on how individuals and firms behave in a planned economy. The system was characterized by inefficiency, egalitarianism and poverty. Apart from what was called the "new class," which referred to the privileged ruling class of bureaucrats and Communist Party functionaries (ilas, [1957] 1983), people were all equally poor and without freedom in all fields. It was not an easy task to open such a society to the world since the existing ruling class was strongly resistant to new policy initiatives. To overcome resistance from the ruling class, China's leadership under Deng Xiaoping adopted a strategy of "external reform first, internal reform later," namely, of using external pressure to create dynamics for internal reforms. The rationale behind this strategy was that external reforms were easier to undertake than internal ones. To engage in internal reforms first, the leadership would have had to be able to overcome resistance from deeply entrenched vested interests which had consolidated their positions in the three decades of Maoist rule. The leadership did not take this route. Instead, it engaged in external reform first. The goal was to create new interests apart from those vested ones. Once new interests were created, they were expected to generate pressure for internal reform.

Engaging in external reform first did not mean that internal reform (internal openness) was rendered unnecessary. By contrast, if there were no internal reform, external reform would not have been possible. The question was, what kind of internal reform? In the early stages of China's reform, China did not experience any radical movements such as privatization and democratization, both of which had taken place in the former Soviet Union and other Eastern European countries. Both privatization and democratization can be understood as processes of state–society decentralization. While privatization meant the decentralization of economic power from the state to firms, democratization implied the shift of political power from the state to social forces. China did not follow this path of reform. One major reason was that the ruling class was afraid that state–society decentralization would give rise to social forces which could in turn challenge the state. Instead, China's reform was aimed at first introducing internal competition, in other words, competition within the ruling class. Internal competition was realized through inter-governmental decentralization (see Figure 1.1). Compared to state–society decentralization, internal governmental decentralization was more acceptable for the ruling class because the process was more controllable than state–society decentralization, as shown by several waves of intergovernmental decentralization under Mao during the Great Leap Forward and the Cultural Revolution.

With inter-governmental economic decentralization, economic decision-making shifted to the local governments. With expanded power, local governments were able to play an important role in implementing China's external reform. They started lobbying the central reformist leadership for open-door policies and other preferential treatments. In many ways, China's political system is characterized by *de facto* federalism in which local governments at different levels play a key role in governing the country (Zheng, 2007).

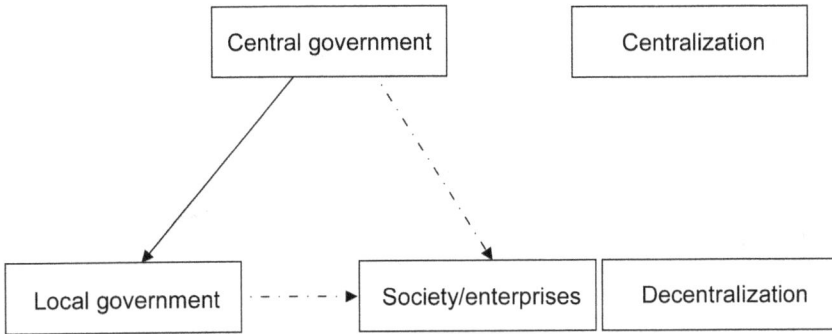

Figure 1.1 Intergovernmental decentralization

The ensuing economic openness can be regarded as a product of inter-governmental decentralization. As a state project, the opening of the country to the world had been carefully designed and implemented. It began with local trials. In the early 1980s, the reformist leadership approved the establishment of five Special Economic Zones (SEZs) in three coastal provinces— Guangdong, Fujian and Hainan. In these SEZs, local governments had considerable latitude to grant special privileges to exporting firms such as the right to import their intermediate inputs without duty.

Similar rights to encourage trade and foreign investment were subsequently granted to another 14 coastal cities in eight other provinces. These special economic zones and coastal open areas acquired considerable autonomy, enjoyed favorable tax treatments, and received preferential resource allocations. Thanks to these preferential policies, coastal provinces have been able to experience rapid growth as a result of the liberalization of international trade and investment flows.

It is important to note that inter-governmental decentralization from the very beginning was accompanied and indeed facilitated by China's regionalization and globalization. These two developments resulted in greater interdependence between the Chinese provinces and the outside world. The integration of China into international markets in turn created a conducive environment for China's entry into the World Trade Organization at a later stage. Of course, regionalization and globalization also had an impact on the relationships among Chinese provinces. There was a surprising decrease in inter-provincial interdependence. For example, according to a study by the World Bank in the early 1990s, internal trade as a percentage of GDP among the Chinese provinces was 22 percent, which was lower than the 28 percent in the former European Community and the 27 percent among the republics of the former Soviet Union.[2]

A high degree of openness had facilitated China's globalization process. China experienced a sustained period of high economic growth over the three decades, which could not have been possible without the country's opening-up policy. Through gearing (*jiegui*) itself up to integrate with the world economic system, China has, since the early 1990s, become one of the world's most favorite destinations for FDI. Over 80 percent of the Fortune-500 companies and the world's top 100 information technology firms have set up businesses in China. Driven by these investments, China has fast become the world's foremost manufacturing base. Its exports have increased at an average rate of 16 percent in the past two decades. The country has become one of the most successful "export-oriented" economies in East Asia, emulating the "economic miracles" of the "four little dragons," namely Hong Kong, Taiwan, South Korea and Singapore. It is now the world's largest exporter.

Unequal impact of openness

While openness has benefited China tremendously, it has also had a devastating impact on society. Openness produces distributive conflict among different social groups and regions. Some groups and regions have benefited more than others with some becoming winners and others losers. In other words, social groups and regions have benefited unevenly from the increasingly market-oriented economy and its openness (or globalization). While those who have been able to participate in the process of openness have profited, those who have not have become disadvantaged.

Who are the losers? Table 1.1 reflects perceptions among Chinese government officials and urban residents on the winners and losers in China's

Table 1.1 Social groups who benefited the most and least since the reform and opening-up policy

Social groups who benefited the most			Social groups who benefited the least		
Types of social groups	*Ranking*	*Choice as a %*	*Types of social groups*	*Ranking*	*Choice as a %*
Party and government cadres	1	59.2	Workers	1	88.2
Private enterprises bosses	2	55.4	Farmers	2	76.3
Acting personnel	3	43.0	Teachers	3	15.3
Urban and rural self-employed	4	33.0	Professionals	4	14.2
State-owned enterprises managers	5	29.3	State-owned enterprises managers	5	8.8
Professionals	6	24.3	Urban and rural sole proprietors	6	7.7
Teachers	7	14.9	Party and government cadres	7	5.1
Farmers	8	3.4	Private entrepreneurs	8	4.7
Workers	9	1.5	Acting Personnel	9	2.5
Others	10	0.5	Others	10	2.7

Source: Zhou (2003, pp. 159–60).

reforms in recent years. One can see from Table 1.1 that although government officials and urban residents generally disagreed with one another, they did agree that farmers and state-owned enterprise (SOE) workers were the biggest losers in this process.[3] The question then arises: why and how do they become losers?

Reforms dismantled the Maoist egalitarian policy and promoted China's economic growth which was accompanied by substantial gains in poverty reduction. Nevertheless, both the increase in welfare and reduction in poverty have been extremely uneven, such that reforms were not able to reduce income disparities among different social groups and regions. The World Bank estimated that, in 1981, China's Gini coefficient was 28.8, but by 1995, it was 38.8. It was still lower than in most Latin American, African and East Asian countries, and similar to that in the United States, but higher than in most of the transitional economies in Eastern Europe and many high-income countries in Western Europe (World Bank, 1997). Three main categories of income disparities can be identified.

Urban disparities

According to a study by the World Bank (1997), which is based on China's official data, the urban Gini coefficient increased from 17.6 in 1981 to 27.5 in 1995. In 1996, among the bottom 20 percent of households, nearly two-thirds found that their income had reduced. Among the next 20 percent of households, almost half the families found their income had declined. In contrast, the top 20 percent of urban households had enjoyed an increase in their income (State Statistical Bureau, 1998). In 1990, the average income of the top 20 percent of households was only 4.2 times higher than that of the bottom 20 percent. By 1998, the ratio had jumped to 9.6 times. The share of the richest 10 percent of households of total income increased from 23.6 percent in 1990 to 38.4 percent in 1998. On the other hand, the share of the bottom 20 percent of households of total income declined from 9 percent to 5.5 percent during the same period (Xu and Li, 1999). Urban residents used to be the safe "haves" who were cut off from the hundreds of millions of "have-nots" in the vast countryside. However, after more than two decades of economic reform, about 30 million urban residents were living in poverty, having incomes that were no more than one-third the national average (Wang, 2000). Today, urban poverty has become an increasing political challenge for the Chinese leadership.

Urban–rural disparities

There is also a widening of the urban–rural income gap. The urban–rural divide is not new; it can be traced back to the Mao era (Khan and Riskin, 2001). For example, when China began its economic reform, the per capita urban income was 2.6 times higher than its rural counterpart (Wang, 2000, p. 386). In the early years of the reform, urban–rural disparities were reduced after reform was first implemented in the rural areas. However, since the urban reform in 1984, the gap has widened continuously. According to the World Bank, China's rural–urban gap is large by international standards. In other countries, urban income is rarely more than twice the rural income. In most countries, rural income is 66 percent or more of urban income. In China, rural income was only 40 percent of urban income in 1995, down from a peak of 59 percent in 1983 (World Bank, 1997, p. 16). In 2003, per capita disposable income in rural areas was 2,622 *yuan* on average, compared with 8,742 *yuan* in urban areas (*China Statistical Yearbook 2004*). By 2006, the per capita income of the urban resident had reached 3.3 times that of the rural resident (Ru *et al.*, 2007).

Regional disparities

According to the World Bank, regional disparities were moderate compared to inequality within provincial borders. For example, in 1992, average income in coastal China was 50 percent higher than in interior provinces but in the same year, the rural–urban income gap was twice as large (World Bank, 1997, p. 22). In contrast, Shaoguang Wang and Angang Hu (Wang and Hu, 1999) have given us a more pessimistic picture. In a detailed study on regional disparities, they reached three conclusions. First, inter-provincial inequality has been widening; second, regional gaps were unusually large; and third, regional inequality was a multi-dimensional phenomenon. Income disparity in per capita GDP between China's coastal and interior provinces has been rising since 1983 and accelerated after 1990.

As in many other countries (Cramer, 2001), widening inequalities across social groups and regions as a result of an ever-deepening process of globalization are increasingly becoming a driving force for social conflict in China, especially when appropriate state policies are not in place. The Chinese government has made continual attempts to address the issues of income disparities. In 1998, the Zhu Rongji government launched the western development program (*xibu kaifa*) (Lu and Neilson, 2004). In 2002, the central government set up a program to revive the economy of the northeastern region (*zhenxing dongbei*). To bring the central Chinese regions under national regional programs, Wen Jiabao declared in 2004 that besides continuing to accelerate the growth of the eastern part of the country and support the development of the western and the north-eastern regions, the central government would speed up the development of central areas to achieve well-balanced regional development (Lai, 2007).

These regional development programs were launched primarily to ease the dissatisfaction of minority groups and narrow development disparities among ethnic groups. China is a diverse country in terms of ethnicity. About 86 percent of its ethnic minorities live in the western region with most of the rest in the northeastern and central areas. Minority groups are concentrated, in most cases, in the least developed areas. Compared to the coastal provinces, the economies in these areas are extremely weak (Mackerras, 1994). For example, as early as 1995, the industrial output of Jiangsu province accounted for 10.4 percent of the overall output of China, which was more than the sum of the other eight provinces and autonomous regions, including Gansu, Guangxi, Guizhou, Inner Mongolia, Ningxia, Qinghai, Tibet, and Yunnan. This excessive disparity is likely to cause conflicts between the majority and minority groups and could hinder the creation of a "harmonious society." All the development programs to a large extent have been implemented to support the development of the minority regions and improve the living standards of minority groups. The programs have also extended China's development to disadvantaged regions, and thus different social and ethnic groups.

In recent years, the government has proactively initiated social policy reforms to improve the state's capacity as a social service provider. Improving social security, healthcare and medical services, implementing mandatory education, and building an "eco-friendly society" have featured prominently in its policy package. Overall, the call is to build a "socialist harmonious society." The government has begun to establish effective means to implement these new policies. Economic indicators (e.g. GDP growth), while important, are no longer the overriding concerns when evaluating the performance of leading Party cadres and government officials. A more comprehensive appraisal system is in the making—one that includes (but is not limited to) social, environmental and human development indicators. This new appraisal system is being piloted by the Party's Organizational Department in selected provinces.[4]

One particularly important policy in this new policy package is to "build a socialist new countryside." Underpinning the 'socialist new countryside' initiative is an increase in the national budget allocation to address "*sannong*" issues (literally, 'the three farming issues'—rural areas, agriculture and peasants) through improvements in rural infrastructure, such as roads, water supplies, and hospitals. In addition, from 2006, all agricultural taxes and fees were abolished.

The mounting problems and dissatisfaction resulting from China's market-oriented development over the past three decades show that China's policy shifts are long overdue, but one should not read too much into the official rhetoric of a policy shift from growth to greater social service provision. On the one hand, China still depends on market-oriented development to deal with the socio-economic side-effects of growth. On the other hand, China's current governance system has a built-in bias toward market growth, particularly below the central state level. This market growth orientation discriminates against proposed goals, such as greater equality, improved quality of life, better environmental protection, and so on (Wong, 2006).

Political reform and interest representation

It was a state project that promoted the development of the market economy. It also takes a state project to cope with the consequences of the market economy. As Polanyi observed, the development of the market economy in China has resulted in many devastating consequences, including the rise of spontaneous social movements.

Dissatisfaction has provoked street protests and blockades, the storming of government buildings by protesters, filing of petitions, and an increase in court cases throughout rural China. In 2005, there were 87,000 "mass incidents," or incidents of public protest, up 6.6 percent from 2004.[5] Meanwhile, huge numbers of peasants have migrated to the cities for work, where they are not only often subjected to ill-treatment and poor working conditions, they also contribute to an increase in the crime rate. This has led to brooding tensions between the haves and have-nots, prompting social policy reforms on the part of the government.

The more important state project, however, is to open the political process up to the newly rising social classes created by the market economy. In this respect, the CCP is the key determinant. While the opening of the political process is so far the most important aspect of internal openness, it has also led to a situation whereby many social groups, especially weaker ones, continue to be marginalized. As I will discuss later, this implies that society must be defended.

Traditionally, the CCP was supposed to represent the interests of only five major groups, namely, workers, peasants, intellectuals, members of the People's Liberation Army (PLA), and government officials and cadres. As in other communist states, the CCP under Maoist rule was hostile to capitalism and capitalists. The CCP's Constitution stated that the goal of the Party was to eliminate capitalism. Despite the de-emphasis of the role of ideology in the post-Mao era, the issue of whether capitalists or private entrepreneurs should be allowed into the Party had been controversial for a long time. In the aftermath of the 1989 Tiananmen incident, the Central Committee of the CCP issued a regulation on 28 August 1989, entitled 'A Notice on Strengthening Party Building' (Document No. 9, 1989). The regulation stated, "Our Party is the vanguard of the working class. Since there is an exploitative relationship between private entrepreneurs and workers, private entrepreneurs cannot be recruited into the Party" (Office of the Documentary Research of the Central Committee of the CCP, 1991, p. 456). Jiang Zemin, then Party Secretary of the CCP, was one of the major political forces behind this regulation (ibid., p. 442).

But the CCP leadership has been pragmatic about the development of the non-state sector. In February 2000, the Party's leadership raised the new concept of *san ge dai biao* (literally meaning "three represents"). According to this concept, the CCP represents the "most advanced mode of the productive force, the most advanced culture, and the interests of the majority of the population" (Xinhua News Agency, 2000). The "three represents" theory is the CCP's affirmation of the non-state sector in the economy. More importantly, it also shows that the CCP has begun to consider how the interests of the newly rising classes and social groups can be represented.

During Mao Zedong's era, the CCP was a genuine revolutionary party made up overwhelmingly of workers and peasants. For example, in 1956, 83 percent of Party members came from these two groups. The figure remained high in 1981, at 64 percent. When Deng Xiaoping came to power, he initiated the so-called technocratic movement, replacing workers and peasants in the Party with technocrats. Overall, CCP members are now younger and better educated.

With the ideological justification of the market economy, the CCP has been undergoing a drastic transformation from being peasants- and workers-based to being a "catch-all" party. Party members now come from increasingly diverse social and economic backgrounds. In the past three decades, the percentage of workers, peasants, and soldiers in the CCP has dropped significantly. From 1978 to 2006, the proportion of workers declined from 18.7 percent to 11.1 percent. The proportion of peasants shrank from 46.9 percent to 31.7 percent while the share of soldiers declined from 6.9 percent to 2.2 percent. In the meantime, the proportions of Party members from other social backgrounds increased dramatically. White-collar Party members (including management personnel and engineers) made up 21.4 percent, and Party members with private business background accounted for 5.1 percent (see Figure 1.2).

The opening-up of the political process to the newly rising social classes is also reflected on the legal front. The Second Session of the Ninth NPC in 1999 passed a constitutional amendment which, for the first time since the establishment of the People's Republic, provides constitutional protection to the private economy (Zou and Zheng, 2000). In 2008, the Eleventh NPC passed the Property Law to guarantee private property rights. The Property Law marked an important step in China's transition to a capitalist economy.

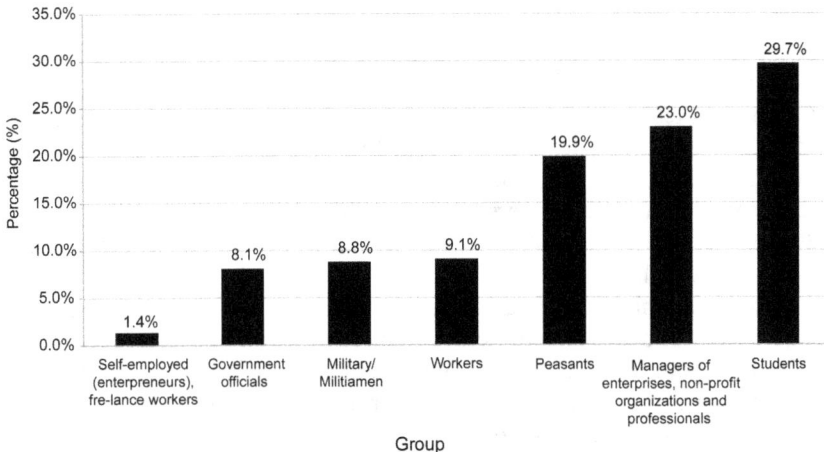

Figure 1.2 Professional composition of CCP membership, 2006

The travails involved in securing passage of the new law underscored the difficulties the leaders of China face as they attempt to put in place a coherent legal and financial system for the country. It had taken 13 years and eight readings (only three were technically—and in most cases, practically—required) for the property bill to come into force. This law was originally scheduled to pass in 2006, but was dropped after Party conservatives started a signature campaign against it, protesting that it would undermine the country's socialist system. The Property Law elaborated on the creation, transfer, and ownership of property in China.

The decision of the Party to recruit private entrepreneurs implies that the CCP is adjusting itself to suit China's changing political reality. Market-oriented economic development has rapidly changed China's social structure. The role of the traditional ruling classes, such as workers and peasants, is slowly being taken over by the entrepreneur class. Embracing the newly emerging social classes will certainly enable the Party to expand its social base. The accommodation of capitalism has also created dynamics for further changes. Being the only ruling party, the CCP has to represent as many social interests as possible. This also explains its policy shift in recent years under the leadership of Hu Jintao.

Since the 16th Party Congress in 2002, the Party's policy priority has gradually shifted to those less privileged social groups discussed earlier. The new leadership, however, has to continue to institutionalize the political influence of the newly rising social groups to sustain economic growth, demonstrated by the passing of the Property Rights Bill in March 2008 by the NPC, despite great controversy. The 17th National Congress of the CCP in 2007 also added representatives of new function groups, or what China termed as 'new economic organizations' and 'new social organizations', which included a lawyers' association (Xinhua News Agency, 2007). This means that the influence of the newly rising social classes is rapidly being institutionalized.

Social openness and uneven policy participation

In China, market-based economic development has given rise to a growing middle class, which has in turn encouraged political participation. When new social groups become proactive politically, reaction from traditional social groups is equally strong. Workers, peasants and other social groups, which the CCP represented in the past, feel that they are increasingly being marginalized in party politics, and their interests undermined. Meanwhile, the leadership has also made attempts to open China's political processes wider to include organizations that represent the interests of the less privileged social groups. For example, the NPC announced in 2008 that migrant workers would be regarded as a new function group to be represented in the NPC in future. Nevertheless, there is no doubt that the political door to the newly rising social classes has been opened wider than the political door to less privileged social groups.

Spontaneous social movements or protests have taken place, implying that such social groups still lack effective mechanisms for political participation. As Polanyi argued, while social movements are often spontaneous reactions to the rise of the market economy, such movements should lead to political changes through which society gains state protection. Historically, the development of the market economy had been associated with a series of social movements which in turn facilitated the transformation of the market economy. In China, although the state has effectively integrated the newly rising social classes, it has been appealing to all kinds of mechanisms to bring spontaneous social movements under control, and remains hesitant to accommodate the weaker social groups in the political process.

This is reflected in the development of non-governmental organizations (NGOs) in China, which has been quite drastic (Ma, 2006). This is especially true since the early 2000s after the leadership began to place an emphasis on social reforms. Reforms have led not only to a relaxation of state control over society, but also the active creation and sponsorship of NGOs by the state for the purpose of transferring certain functions to them which the state used to perform. Chinese NGOs have increased steadily in number over the years. Figures from the Ministry of Civil Affairs (MCA), which is in charge of NGO registration, shows that there were only about 100 national social organizations in China before 1978. By the end of 2003, this number had reached 1,736. Meanwhile the number of local-level social organizations grew from 6,000 to 142,121. The number of private non-enterprise organizations (PNEOs), which did not exist before the reforms, reached 124,491. By the end of 2005, there were 168,000 social organizations, 146,000 PNEOs, and 999 foundations. However, scholars found that many associations were unaccounted for. By adding different types of nonregistered NGOs, Shaoguang Wang believed that the total number of civil organizations had reached 8.8 million by 2003. Despite its rapid development, scholars have argued that NGOs in China are still underdeveloped. For example, the number of civil organizations per 10,000 people in China is 1.45, while that of France is 110.45, United States is 51.79, Brazil is 12.66, India is 10.21, and Egypt is 2.44.[6]

In the West, NGOs are autonomous and independent of the government. In China, however, the autonomy of NGOs depends on their relationship with, and thus their political 'distance' from, the government. Government regulations stipulate that a social organization must be approved and registered by the civil affairs departments at the county level or higher, while foundations (e.g. charity organizations) must be approved at the provincial or central government level. A civil organization which fails to register with the civil affairs department is considered illegal. Government regulations require every social organization to find a "professional management unit" (*yewu zhuguan danwei*) to act as its sponsoring agency. Only after obtaining the approval of its sponsor can an NGO apply for registration with the civil affairs department. The sponsor must be a state organ above the county level or an organization authorized by such an organ. It must also be "relevant" to the activities proposed by the NGO, i.e. it must have responsibilities in the same field as that of the NGO. Regulations also disallow NGOs with similar remits to coexist in the same geographical area.

As a result of such strict rules, many grassroots NGOs are unable to register, either because they fail to find government agencies willing to act as their professional management units, or because other NGOs with similar missions have already been registered in the geographical area where they intend to base their operations. In order to exist legally, some NGOs have registered with industry and commerce bureaus as businesses instead, even though they engage in public non-profit-making activities. There are also unregistered, hence illegal, organizations which operate openly but have been left alone by the government instead of being banned according to the regulations.

Nevertheless, the registration requirement does not apply to the eight big national social organizations which are often referred to more specifically as "people's organizations" (*renmin tuanti*) or "mass organizations" (*qunzhong tuanti*), such as the All-China Federation of Trade Unions, the All-China Women's Federation, and the Communist Youth League. These social organizations were created by the Party/state to perform administrative functions on its behalf. Indeed, they are independent organizations, and do not come under the supervision of the civil affairs department. Top appointments in these organizations are made by the CCP's top leadership. Exemptions from the registration requirement include "organizations formed within administrative agencies, social organizations, enterprises, or service units which are approved by these organizations and which only carry out activities internally" (State Council, 1998). Some grassroots organizations, such as property owners' committees (*yezhu weiyuanhui*) formed by owners of apartments in the same housing compound and urban community-based organizations, e.g. leisure activity groups formed by residents in the same neighborhood, are not required to register with the civil affairs department.

Moreover, the development of NGOs in different functions has been uneven. In the economic sphere, the government has attempted to reduce its direct management role by establishing intermediary organizations such as trade associations and chambers of commerce to perform sectoral coordinating and regulating functions. In the social welfare sphere, the government wants to foster the NGOs to take over some of its burden of service provision. In the social development sphere, the government wants the NGOs to mobilize societal resources to supplement its own spending (Howell, 1997; Wong, 1998). These NGOs will have to perform their role according to the party line—they will be "helping hands" rather than independent organizations.

The political influences of China's NGOs also vary widely across different areas as well as between different NGOs. In some areas such as poverty reduction, charity, and environmental issues, NGOs are encouraged to play a greater role, but in other areas such as religious issues, ethnicity, and human rights, the influence of NGOs is much weaker. Also, some NGOs are more powerful than others. Most commercial organizations are extremely powerful in influencing the government's policy-making process. It is not difficult to find business people sitting in the People's Congress and the Chinese People's Political Consultative Conference at different levels of the government. Workers and farmers, on the other hand, are not allowed to organize themselves, and thus do not have any effective mechanisms to articulate and aggregate their interests. In fact, the decline of workers and peasants in the total party membership implies their weak influence in China's political system.

When powerful social groups become organized, they become even more powerful. There is no effective means for weak social groups such as workers and farmers to promote their own causes. This is so partly because China is at an early stage of economic development and development continues to be given a higher priority than political participation. Workers and farmers might be able to play a more important role with further economic progress. We can take trade unions as an example. The government's attitude toward workers' rights is changing. Today, even the stodgy, government-dominated All-China Federation of Trade Unions (ACFTU) has recognized the need to take a more activist approach to workers' rights. China is now facing a rising tide of labor disputes, which could destabilize Chinese society and thus undermine the political legitimacy of the CCP. Therefore, there is a need for employers to better understand and honor their obligations under China's labor laws. In an apparent reflection of this new attitude, at the 2003 annual ACFTU congress, the federation made a direct appeal to multinational retail corporation Wal-Mart Stores, Inc. to allow its workers to establish trade unions. Following that event, more and more foreign firms have established trade unions. In some cases, they did it voluntarily; in others, they were asked to do so.

Why society must be defended

So, why must society be defended? This chapter has attempted to answer the question by examining how openness leads to the rapid development of the market economy and how the latter has had a devastating impact on weak elements of the society. Both economic and political transformations mean that 'money' and 'power' are now the two key players in China's development. Both players occupy strategic positions within the country's hierarchical system. That implies that while both play an important role in promoting development, they will continue to dominate the course of China's development. Meanwhile, these two players can exchange their resources, be it money for power or power for money, for their own benefit. While quite drastic changes have also occurred in the Chinese society, political participation by social groups remains very weak. This is especially true in the case of participation by weaker society groups such as workers, migrant workers and farmers. This partially explains why there has been a drastic increase in social protests in recent years. Social protests by weaker social groups can be interpreted as efforts to "voice" grievances on the part of these social groups. Without effective mechanisms for political participation by these social groups, social protests (similar to street democracy in the West) become inevitable.

As discussed in this chapter, the CCP leadership is fully aware of the "voice" of the weaker social groups. Social reforms have been on the top of the agenda and social policy has been given the highest priority. Nevertheless, when it boils down to policy enforcement, the problem arises. Policy performance in different social areas such as social welfare, healthcare, medical reform, and education continues to be less than ideal despite great efforts on the part of the central government. With the extremely slow development of political participation, weaker social groups continue to be excluded from the formation of key social policies, and they continue to be marginalized.

Needless to say, social policy is gaining weight in the maintenance of social stability and in turn, the sustainability of socio-economic development of China. Effective social policy, both in its making and implementation, depends on the political participation of relevant social groups. The exclusion of the weaker social groups from the political process will not lead to the improvement of their social well-being. Without an effective social policy, the openness of both the economic and political process will lead to a development pattern that only benefits certain elements of society. Society must thus be defended, especially the weaker elements of society. Apparently, defending society is not only an economic task, but more importantly, a political task.

In concluding, this chapter would like to quote Premier Wen Jiabao in length. Wen was interviewed by CNN journalist Fareed Zakaria on 23 September 2008. In answering Zakaria's question on market and socialism, Wen stated:

> The complete formulation of our economic policy is to give full play to the basic role of market forces in allocating resources under the macro-economic guidance and regulation of the government. We have one important piece of experience of the past 30 years: that is to ensure that both the visible hand and the invisible hand are given full play in regulating the market forces. If you are familiar with the classical works of Adam Smith, you will know that there are two famous works of his. One is *The Wealth of Nations*, the other is the book on morality and ethnics. *The Wealth of Nations* deals more with the invisible hand that are the market forces; the other book deals with social equity and justice. If most of the wealth is concentrated in the hands of the few in a country, then this country can hardly witness harmony and stability.

Wen Jiabao here touched on two actors, namely, the market and the government, or money and power. Society is not in this equation of money and power. In the same interview, Wen also mentioned that he was very much impressed by Stoic philosopher Marcus Aurelius Antonio's *The Meditations*, and drew the conclusion: where are those people that were great for a time? They are all gone, leaving only a story, or some even half a story. Only people are in the position to create history and write history (CNN, 2008).

Either regulate or die. This is the lesson one can draw from the current financial crisis in the United States. The issue is who regulates whom. While the government can regulate the market, the two sides can also share mutual benefits. If this is the case, then there will be no morality and social justice. No one can regulate money, and no one can regulate power. If one refers to Wen's conclusion on *The Meditations*, one can reach the conclusion that only society can regulate both money and power, and only by bringing society into the equation can social justice be served.

Notes

1 For a survey of China's reform process and economic development at different stages, see Barry Naughton's works, (Naughton, 1996), and (Naughton, 2007).
2 See World Bank (1994). For a summary of the World Bank report, see Anjali Kumar (1994).
3 This can also be illustrated by the increasing income inequality between rural residents and urban citizens and the rising disparity within the urban regions between the rich and the poor.
4 In the province of Zhejiang, for instance, environmental indicators have been integrated into the appraisal of officials in a trial conducted by the Party's Organizational Department. See *People's Daily*, "Organizational department uses Zhejiang as a testbed to include environmental protection into officials' appraisal," October 17, 2005.
5 See Reuters, "China to 'strike hard' against rising unrest," 26 January 2006.
6 Cited in He (2008).

References

China Statistical Yearbook (2004) Beijing: Zhongguo tongji chubanshe.
CNN (2008) "Transcript of interview with Chinese Premier Wen Jiabao," available at: www.cnn.com/2008/WORLD/asiapcf/09/29/chinese.premier.transcript/index.html & accessed 1 October, 2008).
Cramer, C. (2001) "Economic inequalities and civil conflict," Centre for Development Policy and Research Discussion Paper 1501, School of Oriental and African Studies, University of London.
Đilas, M. ([1957] 1983) *The New Class: An Analysis of the Communist System*, 2nd edn, San Diego: Harcourt Brace Jovanovich.
He, Z. (2008) "Institutional barriers to the development of civil society in China," in Y. Zheng and J. Fewsmith (eds.) *China's Opening Society: The Non-state Sector and Governance*, New York: Routledge.
Howell, J. (1997) "NGO–state relations in post-Mao China," in D. Hulme and M. Edwards (eds.) *NGOs, States and Donors: Too Close for Comfort?* London: Macmillan.
Iredale, R.R., Bilik, N. and Guo, F. (2003) *China's Minorities on the Move: Selected Case Studies*, New York: M.E. Sharpe.

Khan, A.R. and Riskin, C. (2001) *Inequality and Poverty in China in the Age of Globalization*, Oxford: Oxford University Press.

Kumar, A. (1994) "China's reform, internal trade and marketing," *The Pacific Review*, 7(3): 323–40.

Lai, H. (2007) "Developing Central China: a new regional programme," *China: An International Journal*, 5: 109–28.

Lu, D. and Neilson, W. (eds.) (2004) *China's West Region Development: Domestic Strategies and Global Implications*, Singapore: World Scientific Publishing.

Ma, Q. (2006) *Non-Governmental Organizations in Contemporary China: Paving the Way to Civil Society?*, London: Routledge.

Mackerras, C. (1994) *China's Minorities: Integration and Modernization in the Twentieth Century*, Hong Kong: Oxford University Press.

Naughton, B. (1996) *Growing Out of the Plan: Chinese Economic Reform 1978–1993*, New York: Cambridge University Press.

——(2007) *The Chinese Economy: Transitions and Growth*, Cambridge, MA: MIT Press.

Office of the Documentary Research of the Central Committee of the CCP (1991) *Xinshiqi dang de jianshe wenjian xuanbian* [Selected Documents of Party Building in the New Era], Beijing: Renmin chubanshe.

Olson, M. (1982) *The Rise and Decline of Nations: Economic Growth, Stagflation, and Social Rigidities*, New Haven, CT: Yale University Press.

Polanyi, K. (1944) *The Great Transformation: The Political and Economic Origins of Our Time*, Boston: Beacon Press.

Rodrik, D. (1997) *Has Globalization Gone Too Far?* Washington, DC: Institute for International Economics.

Ru, X., Lu, X. and Li, P. (eds.) (2007) *Shehui lanpishu 2007 nian: Zhongguo shehui xingshi fenxi yu yuce* [Blue Book of the Chinese Society in 2007: An Analysis and Forecast of the Chinese Social Situation], Beijing: Shehui kexue wenxian chubanshe.

State Council (1998) *Shehui tuanti dengji guanli tiaoli* [Regulations on the Registration and Management of Social Organization], Beijing: The State Council.

State Statistical Bureau (1998) *Annual Prices and Family Incomes and Expenditures in Chinese Cities*, Beijing: Zhongguo tongji chubanshe.

Wang, S. (2000) "The social and political implications of China's WTO membership," *Journal of Contemporary China*, 9: 373–405.

Wang, S. and Hu, A. (1999) *The Political Economy of Uneven Development: The Case of China*, Armonk, NY: M.E Sharpe.

Wong, J. (2006) "Explaining China's 2005 growth and its problems (II)," *EAI Background Brief No. 269*, East Asian Institute, National University of Singapore.

Wong, L. (1998) *Marginalization and Social Welfare in China*, London: Routledge.

World Bank (1994) *China: Internal Market Development and Regulations*, Washington, DC: World Bank.

——(1997) *China 2020: Sharing Rising Incomes: Disparities in China*, Washington, DC: World Bank.

Xinhua News Agency (2000) "Jiang Zemin tongzhi zai quanguo dangxiao gongzuo huiyi shan de jianghua" [Comrade Jiang Zemin's talk at the National Party School's Working Conference], *Renmin ribao*, July 17.

——(2007) "Zhongzubu jiu dang de shiqida daibiao xuanju gongzuo da xinhuashe jizhe wen" [The Department of Organization of the Chinese Communist Party's Press Conference with the Xinhua News Agency on the election of the representatives of the 17th Party Congress].

Xu, X. and Li, P. (1999) "1998–99 nian Zhongguo jiuye shouru he xinxi chanye de fenxi he yuce" [Employment, income, and IT industry: analysis and forecasts, 1998–99], in X. Ru, X. Lu and P. Li (eds.) *Shehui lanpishu 1999 nian: Zhongguo shehui xingshi fenxi yu yuce* [Blue Book of the Chinese Society in 1999: An Analysis and Forecast of the Chinese Social Situation], Beijing: Shehui kexue wenxian chubanshe.

Zheng, Y. (2007) *De Facto Federalism in China: Reforms and Dynamics of Central-Local Relations*, Singapore: World Scientific Publishing.

Zhou, J. (2003) "2002 nian Zhongguo chengshi redian wenti diaocha" [Investigation of the "hot" issues in Chinese cities in 2002], in X. Ru, X. Lu and P. Li (eds.) *Shehui lanpishu 2003 nian: Zhongguo shehui xingshi fenxi yu yuce* [Blue Book of the Chinese Society in 2003: An Analysis and Forecast of the Chinese Social Situation], Beijing: Shehui kexue wenxian chubanshe.

Zou, K. and Zheng, Y. (2000) "China's third constitutional amendment: a leap forward towards rule of law in China," in A. J. de Roo and R. W. Jagtenberg (eds.) *Yearbook of Law and Legal Practice in East Asia*, vol. 4, The Hague: Kluwer Law International.

2 China's new stage of development

Peilin Li

Since China began to implement its reform and opening-up policies in 1978, its development and reform have centered on two T-changes, namely the transition of economic institutions and the transformation of social structure. The Chinese experience is often analysed in economic terms, with special attention given to the extent to which it conforms with or deviates from the more general development experiences. Attempts have been made to understand China from the theoretical framework of transition from a planned economy to a market economy. China is also analysed as the newest example of the East Asian development experience, following Japan and the Four Little Dragons of South Korea, Taiwan, Hong Kong and Singapore. More recently, China is also considered one of the four emerging big economies, along with Brazil, Russia and India, in a framework widely known as "BRIC."

The Chinese experience is, however, more than just economic development, thus it is different from the "China Miracle" (Lin *et al.*, 1994). The Chinese experience, not in its final shape yet, is not diametrically distinct from the Western experience of modernization. This stance does not agree with the so-called "Beijing Consensus" (Ramo, 2004). The Chinese modernization experience is that of an oriental country with a large population. This fact makes it makes it somewhat incomparable with the experience of Western countries. Examining the Chinese experience can contribute to a better understanding of the trajectory of human history in the context of globalization. As China's modernization is an ongoing process, the Chinese experience will be defined, to a large extent, by how China responds when it enters a new stage of development.

New challenges in the post-global financial crisis

Over the past 30 years, China has undergone rapid economic growth and enormous social transformation. But all of this has come at a heavy cost, especially in terms of natural resources and ecological environment. In the aftermath of the global financial crisis, China put forward a new concept of "changing the mode of development." The theme is close to, but has a broader sense than, "sustainable development." Undertaking "changing the mode of development" conveys at least three important messages. First, economic growth should no longer rely excessively on investment and exports, but more on domestic consumption. Second, the mode of economic growth should be changed from low-cost quantitative expansion to qualitative technological improvement, and from "made in China" to "created in China" to promote industrial upgrading. Third, the mode of development at the expense of natural resources and environment should be changed to a resource-saving and environment-friendly mode. Development should no longer be driven largely by industry, but to a greater extent by a modern service industry; and a low-carbon economy should be energetically promoted (United Nations, 1987).

There are three main factors that drive a country's economic growth: investment, exports and domestic consumption. As for exports, the global financial crisis hit China's exports badly. They registered negative growth of over 20 percent in 2009 for several consecutive months and bottomed out in 2010.[1] Due to the global financial crisis, international trade protectionism prevails in many countries due to unemployment pressures, giving rise to many trade disputes between China, the United States and the European Union. Even when the crisis is completely over, China is not likely to resume its 60 percent high dependency ratio on foreign trade, which is the ratio of the total volume of imports and exports to GDP. Moreover, unlike the export-oriented small economies in East Asia and Southeast Asia, China has a large population, making it risky, unsustainable and unstable for China to rely excessively on foreign trade for economic growth. It is well known that in terms of value added, China has to export about 100 million pairs of jeans in exchange for a Boeing airplane. To preserve and increase the value of foreign exchange earned through exports of large quantities of cheap products, China continues to buy the relatively secure US treasury bonds. However, in order to stimulate its economy, the US increases its investment by printing money, leading to the depreciation of the US dollar and dilution of its debts.

Since the reform and opening-up programme was launched in 1978, China's development mode has always featured high savings and investment ratios. Until now, the investment ratio has maintained a high level of 30 percent to 45 percent, averaging around 37 percent. Especially after 1993, China's investment ratio showed a rapidly rising trend. In 2007, it reached an even higher level of 45 percent. But this kind of high-investment and high-growth development is not sustainable. Long-term high investment is bound to cause excessive production capacity, reduced investment gains, redundant construction and an increase in non-performing bank loans.

Therefore, to meet the requirements for sustainable development and to sustain the trade balance within the context of the international economic order, China has to increase its domestic demands and consumer spending and shift to a development mode in which China's future economic growth will rely largely on domestic consumption. Yet it is difficult to change gears. Some scholars within China believe that China's economic growth should still rely largely on investment, because in the short term, it is difficult to increase domestic consumption, no matter how necessary it is. Moreover, it is believed that high savings and investment ratios are a feature of China's national condition and have been China's primary means of economic growth for quite a long time, so the transformation of the development mode should still rely more on changing the investment structure and increasing the investment efficiency.

A new possibility in the future

While it makes some sense to say that, in the short term, it is difficult to stimulate economic growth by increasing domestic consumption, this statement does not hold up under closer scrutiny. First, the hypothesis is based on the development experience of the past. Hitherto, when economic growth rates declined, China stimulated the economy by expanding its finances and increasing investment. To stimulate the economy by increasing consumption is only wishful thinking that has never been realized. On the other hand, high investment, as an alternative, would always lead to redundant construction, excessive production capacity, increased inventory, reduced investment gains, or even inflation after the crisis. It seems that some of these old problems are coming back in the aftermath of the international financial crisis.

There is, however, a new possibility as China's economic and social development has reached a new stage of growth, with significant changes. In the next 30 years, if the right policies are adopted, it is likely that China will experience a different trajectory of development.

The first question to be asked is why people lack confidence in spending. In the short term, consumption is constrained by income. China is now ready to change the situation. The proportion of resident income to national income is constantly declining. For example, from 1992 to 2007, the proportion of disposable income of Chinese residents to national income declined from 69 percent to 53 percent. Meanwhile, the proportion of disposable income of enterprises to national income rose from 12 percent to 23 percent, and the proportion of disposable income of the government to national income increased from 19 percent to 24 percent.

Why is consumption so low in China now? The state has no lack of money: from 1994 to 2008, China's tax revenue increased from over RMB 500 billion to RMB 5.4 trillion, at an average annual growth of 18 percent, which was far higher than the GDP growth. The Chinese people do not lack money either: from 1994 to March 2009, the savings balance of urban and rural residents increased from over RMB 2 trillion to RMB 24.1 trillion, at an average annual growth rate of 18 percent. Given the growing wealth, it seems puzzling why people do not spend as much as they might. From 1985 to 2008, the consumption rate of Chinese residents, namely the proportion of consumer spending to GDP, actually declined from 52 percent to 35.4 percent, which represents a very low level in the world, far lower than America's 70 percent and Japan's 65 percent. The 300 million Americans consume more than US$10 trillion's worth of commodities every year, while 1.3 billion Chinese people annually consume only about US$1 trillion. The two consumer markets differ widely.

The fundamental reason for China's sluggish consumption lies in the structure of income distribution. In other words, the greatest challenge that China faces in terms of consumption is actually the problematic structure of income distribution. Over the past 30 years, China's greatest achievement has been its rapid economic growth, whereas its most challenging problem has been income distribution. The Gini coefficient, which measures the income gap, is surging, just like the GDP growth curve. In the history of modernization, no country's Gini coefficient has increased from 0.2 to around 0.5 in over 30 years.[2] This amount of change within such a short span of time is unprecedented. It is estimated that nearly 60 percent of China's overall income gap can be explained by the income gap between cities and rural areas (Li *et al.*, 2008). This is the primary problem with income inequality. In recent years, China has abolished agricultural taxes and increased its investment and fiscal transfer payment for rural areas. In 2008, cities and rural areas saw nearly the same rate of growth in resident income. This was the first time this had happened in more than a decade. In 2009, however, the international financial crisis badly affected the income of rural migrants who had moved to cities for employment or business. Reducing the number of farmers and transferring rural labor to the cities are important means for China to increase the income of farmers and improve overall consumption power, and increasing farmers' consumption power matters a great deal to the total increase in consumption capacity.

The consumption structure is closely related to the structure of social stratification. The advent of a mass consumption era depends largely on the expansion of the middle class, which means that the structure of social stratification must change from a pyramid shape into an oval shape. Admittedly, the "middle class" is an ambiguous concept: economists often define it by income and property, while sociologists place emphasis on the occupation index. In other words, it is only when the tertiary industry of a country accounts for the largest proportion of the whole industrial structure and when the white-collar class accounts for the majority of the labor force, that the country's middle class is in the majority. According to other research by this author and Yi Zhang, if the middle class is to be defined by the three indexes including income, occupation and education, by 2006, China's middle class would account for 12 percent of the country's total active population, and around 25 percent of the urban active population (Li and Zhang, 2008). Since China has the largest population in the world, every percentage point of growth by the middle class represents a huge consumer group, that is, an enormous consumer market.

It is well known that the household consumption rate, namely the proportion of household consumption to household income, decreases progressively along with the increase in household income. This pattern holds in China as well. According to the sample survey of nationwide social conditions in 2008 conducted by this author and Li, the household consumption rate showed an obvious declining trend along with an increase in income: the lower the household income, the higher its consumption rate; the higher the household income, the lower its consumption rate; and the consumption rates differ greatly (Li and Li, 2009). Thus, how the increased income of society is distributed has a major impact on consumption. To increase consumption, China needs to increase the proportion of residents' income to national income, and increase the low income groups' proportion of income to resident income. On one hand, China must prevent saturated consumption among the affluent. On the other, it must prevent a situation where those who need consumption have no money.

There are three main factors that affect the day-to-day consumption of an ordinary household in China: spending on education, healthcare and housing. Educational and medical expenditures, in particular, account for far higher proportions of the total consumption of low- and medium-income households than of high-income households. Only spending on housing is an exception: the higher the income of a household, the higher the proportion its spending is to total consumption. Many high-income households have switched their household spending from day-to-day spending to property investment. Though this kind of housing investment, which is detached from consumption and based on the expectation of rapid appreciation, is likely to turn into asset bubbles, the excessively high shares of spending on education and healthcare by low- and medium-income households have restricted their day-to-day consumption.

A survey of the various purposes of household savings shows that spending on education and healthcare are often ranked top. Chinese people's propensity to save is not only a cultural issue. It is based on reasonable considerations, and is intended to avoid the risk of future household consumption. While Americans apparently live in a culture of credit consumption, with the current generation spending the money of the next generation, the Chinese live in a culture of savings accumulation, with the current generation saving money for the next.

To change people's consumption behavior, China needs to establish and improve a series of relevant systems, which will involve a series of social policies and social reforms. First, China must establish a mechanism for normal growth of labor wages, namely a mechanism for the annual growth of wages linked to the growth of enterprises' profits. At the same time, China should establish a mechanism for the growth of civil servants' salaries that corresponds with economic growth and the growth of enterprises' wages. Second, the structure of income distribution must be adjusted by levers such as finance, taxation, social security and social benefits, so as to divert more income to low-income groups, and the medium-income groups must be allowed to expand as the backbone of mass consumption. Third, China should provide public goods and services more effectively and universally, establish and improve social security systems that cover both urban and rural residents, equalize basic public services in urban and rural areas, and stabilize the public's expectation of consumption on education, healthcare, housing, old age, etc.

Increasing consumer spending is more of a social issue than an economic one, and is closely related to many social institutions (Lu, 2010). From an economic perspective, a large income gap inhibits consumption by the low- and medium-income classes. From a social perspective, this has a negative impact on the general growth of consumption and makes economic growth rely excessively on investment and exports. The large widening income gap has become the underlying cause of many social problems, leading to public discontent. As early as 1993, Deng Xiaoping warned that "Distribution poses an enormous problem. We talk about preventing polarization. In fact, it takes place naturally. We need to solve these problems by various means, methods and solutions." Otherwise, "such a way of development would eventually lead to unpredictable problems" (Central Committee of Communist Party of China Party Documentary Research Office, 2004, p. 1364).

A new stage of mass consumption

Whereas the high-speed growth of China's economy over the past 30 plus years relied mainly on investment and exports, its growth in the next 30 years should rely more on the growth of domestic consumption. That is, make domestic consumption the primary driving force for economic growth (Li and Chen, 2009).

The first feature of this new stage of growth is the coming of a mass consumption era. Calculated in US dollars, China's per capita GDP increased from only about US$300 to over US$800 in 20 years from 1980 to 2000. However, per capita GDP made gains from 2003 when it exceeded US$1,000: in 2006, it surpassed US$2,000; in 2008, it reached over US$3,300; and by the end of 2010, it had reached US$4,400. This development is closely related to three factors: rapid economic growth; a diminished net increase of population; and an appreciation of the *renminbi* (RMB). The Engel coefficient for Chinese residents is continuously declining. The proportion of food consumption to total household consumption has actually fallen to nearly 30 percent. According to the experience of various countries, a coefficient at this level signifies the coming of a mass consumption era during which large consumer goods, such as houses, automobiles, etc., begin to gain popularity among average households, and spending on education, healthcare, tourism, communications, etc., becomes of key priority. Most Chinese scholars are not yet aware of the coming of the mass consumption era. They still lack confidence in mass consumption.

The second feature of the new stage of growth is that industrialization and urbanization come to an intermediate stage of acceleration. This stage is also closely related to consumption growth. In industrialized and urbanized countries, consumption has reached a saturation level, so it is difficult to stimulate consumption growth. But in China, the situation is different: China's structural transformation shows great elasticity and its consumption has great potential for growth. According to international experience, the defining features of a major transformation in the economic and social structures are a lower than 5 percent proportion of agricultural added value in GDP, a lower than 30 percent proportion of agricultural labor in the employment structure and a higher than 50 percent urbanization level. China's three major structures, including the production value structure, employment structure and urban–rural structure, have all reached a stage of transformation. Of China's GDP, the proportion of agricultural added value was expected to decline to below 10 percent in 2010, and to around 6 percent in 2015. Of the employment structure, the proportion of agricultural labor was to decline to below 38 percent in 2010 and to around 33 percent in 2015. Of the urban–rural structure, the urbanization level, as indicated by the resident urban population, exceeded 50 percent in 2011. These indicators show that China, in general, has reached an intermediate stage of acceleration in the process of industrialization and urbanization, and its economic and social structures will undergo a profound transformation. However, China faces the problems of urbanization lagging behind industrialization and the transformation of its social structure lagging behind the transformation of its economic structure. For example, hundreds of millions of migrant workers are doing non-agricultural jobs but are still maintaining their identity as peasants. They live in cities but their consumption is still mainly in the rural areas.

The third feature of the new stage of growth is that the population structure is undergoing significant changes, producing two results. The first is the aging of the population (Lu *et al.*, 2009). From 2015 or 2016, the dependency ratio will begin to increase as a result of the rapid increase in the elderly-dependency ratio. This tendency is forcing China to establish social security systems, particularly a pension system, which covers both urban and rural residents. The second result is the gradual decline of the low labor cost era. When the working-age population stops growing and starts to decline, labor prices will to go up, compelling China to transform its mode of development from "made in China" to "created in China" and its status from a major power of population to a world power of human resources. To maintain its comparative advantages China must devote more resources to labor training and education. To that end, it will inevitably choose to establish a mechanism for the normal growth of wages. Both results are related to the expansion of consumption. The former result is conducive to stabilizing consumption anticipation, while the latter is conducive to increasing consumption power.

Of all the outstanding issues concerning China's expansion of consumption in the next decade, acceleration of urbanization, particularly housing consumption, must be properly addressed. China can introduce a major policy to allow the listing of farmers' houses on the leasing and trading markets. By doing so, farmers can potentially obtain more income from their properties. Meanwhile, there is likely to be an enormous increase in the housing supply, thereby stabilizing the cost of housing and making it more affordable.

In addition, with respect to the expansion of consumption, income distribution remains an inevitable issue. Adjustments to the structure of income distribution entail not only properly adjusting the proportion of labor payment to capital gains in primary distribution, but also balancing the proportions of the incomes of the state, enterprises and residents to national income. The labor payment share in primary distribution should be increased, and the proportion of resident income in national income should also be increased. Furthermore, the role of such levers as finance, taxation, social security and social benefits should be brought into play in the redistribution.

Conclusion

To adapt to the "changing the development mode" and the needs of the new stage of growth, China needs to conduct a comprehensive social reform to provide momentum for future development. Over the past three decades of reform and opening-up, China's primary approach has been largely oriented towards the reform of the economic institutional system, although concurrent reforms have been introduced in other sectors. Thus far, China has basically established a socialist market economic system. However, the great changes in the economic and social structures require continued adaptation of the systems of all sectors. As the reform expands from the economic sector to the social sector, social reforms relating to employment, income distribution, social security, management of migration, social governance, operation of non-governmental organizations (NGOs) and the whole civil society are needed. Fully promoting and deepening social reforms will become the hallmark of the new stage of growth and a major task for China.

Notes

1 Unless otherwise specified, all figures in this article are measured according to the data published by the National Bureau of Statistics of China.
2 Measured according to data obtained from a comprehensive survey of China's social conditions conducted in 2006 by the Institute of Sociology at the Chinese Academy of Social Sciences. The Gini coefficient for China's per capita household income in 2005 was 0.496. See Li *et al.* (2007).

References

Central Committee of Communist Party of China Party Documentary Research Office (2004) *Chronicle of Deng Xiaoping's Life 1975–1977*, Vol. II, Beijing: Central Party Documentary Press.
Li, P. and Chen, G. (2009) "China steps into a new stage of growth," in X. Ru, X. Lu, and P. Li (eds.) *Shehui lanpishu 2010 nian: Zhongguo shehui xingshi fenxi yu yuce* [Blue Book of China's Society in 2010: An Analysis and Forecast of the Chinese Social Situation], Beijing: Shehui kexue wenxian chubanshe.
Li, P., Chen, G. and Li, W. (2007) "A report on the situation of social harmony and stability of China in 2006," in X. Ru, X. Lu and P. Li (eds.) *Shehui lanpishu 2007*

nian: Zhongguo shehui xingshi fenxi yu yuce [Blue Book of China's Society in 2007: An Analysis and Forecast of the Chinese Social Situation], Beijing: Shehui kexue wenxian chubanshe.

Li, P. and Li, W. (2009) "Investigative report on people's livelihood issues, 2008," in X. Ru, X. Lu, and P. Li (eds.) *Shehui lanpishu 2009 nian: Zhongguo shehui xingshi fenxi yu yuce* [Blue Book of China's Society in 2007: An Analysis and Forecast of the Chinese Social Situation], Beijing: Shehui kexue wenxian chubanshe.

Li, P. and Zhang, Y. (2008) "The scope, identity, and social attitude of middle class in China," *Society*, 2: 1–19.

Li, S., Sicular, T. and Gustafsson, B. (eds.) (2008) *Research on Income Distribution in China III*, Beijing: Beijing Normal University Publishing Group.

Lin, J., Cai, F. and Li, Z. (1994) *The China Miracle: Development Strategy and Economic Reform*, Shanghai: Sanlian Shudian.

Lu, X. (ed.) (2010) *Social Structure of Contemporary China*, Beijing: Shehui kexue wenxian chubanshe.

Lu, X., Song, G., Hu, J. and Li, X. (2009) 'The core task of social construction in the new stage: adjusting the social structure," in X. Ru, X. Lu, and P. Li (eds.) *Shehui lanpishu 2010 nian: Zhongguo shehui xingshi fenxi yu yuce* [Blue Book of China's Society in 2010: An Analysis and Forecast of the Chinese Social Situation], Beijing: Shehui kexue wenxian chubanshe.

Ramo, J.C. (2004) "China has discovered its own economic consensus," *Financial Times*, 7 May.

United Nations (1987) *Our Common Future*, Oxford: Oxford University Press.

Part II

Social policy reform moving to the fore

3   Issues and options for social security reform in China

Shi Li

It is widely realized that China is approaching a development stage where social security is playing a more important role than ever before in terms of stimulating economic growth, equalizing income distribution, alleviating poverty and maintaining social stability.[1] It is also recognized that the current social security system needs to be reformed in order to meet the challenges resulting from the transition of the system from one which protected the minority group of urban workers in the formal sector to one which protects all citizens (CDRF, 2009). There is, however, considerable debate as to what kind of social security system can be applied in China, given the large differences between urban and rural areas in terms of income level, employment structure, fiscal capability of local governments, and provision of social services (Zhao *et al.*, 2006). The issues become more complicated when one takes into consideration what type of social protection is suitable for millions of rural migrant workers who have low incomes, high job and location mobility and unstable employment (Zheng, 2008).

Like many other developing countries, China has been striving to make its economy grow as fast as possible. From 1978 to 2008, GDP grew at nearly 10 percent while household income in urban and rural areas grew at 8 percent. These are both incomparable. By the end of 2008, GDP per capita reached US$3,100, raising China to the status of a low- to middle-income country. While China has made remarkable progress in economic growth, its progress in social development, particularly the reconstruction of a social security and welfare system is still lagging. The transition of the social security system is still in progress and the present system contains many flaws. As the private sector and self-employment—which have become the largest employers of informal workers—have grown rapidly, the majority of the workers are not covered by the system. In addition, rural migrant workers, mostly employed in the informal sector in urban areas, are also left out of the system.

Although China has significantly reduced poverty, the country has not been as successful in narrowing income inequality which is now much wider than it was at the beginning of the economic reforms. The Gini coefficient for the whole country is currently estimated at around 0.47,[2] compared to 0.30 in the early 1980s (Adelmen and Sunding, 1987). The Gini coefficient in rural China rose from 0.26 in 1980 to 0.38 in 2007 (see Figure 3.1), while the poverty rate

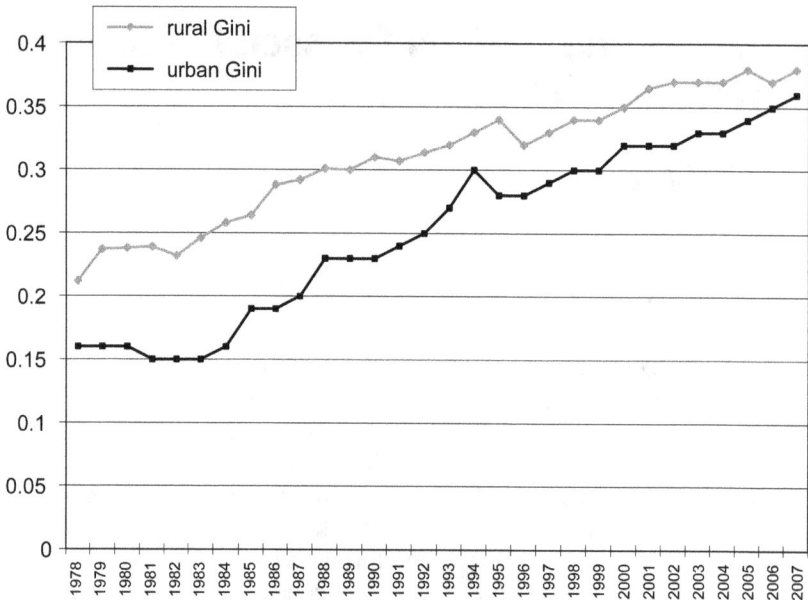

Figure 3.1 Changes in income inequality in urban and rural China, 1978–2007
Sources: Zhang et al. (2008).

declined from 30 percent to 3 percent. Since the mid-1990s, urban poverty has constituted a new phenomenon due to the increase in laid-off workers and consequently a widening income inequality as a result of the restructuring of state-owned enterprises (SOEs). The Gini coefficient in urban China surged from 0.16 in 1978 to 0.36 in 2007.

Though the poverty rate has declined over the past three decades, poverty still remains a serious social problem. It is well known that "official poverty" has been under-reported. The actual poverty incidence is certainly higher than the officially published figures (World Bank, 2009a). While official statistics indicate that the poor numbered less than 15 million in rural areas in 2007, the number of individuals receiving income allowance from the *Di Bao* programme (the minimum living standard guarantee scheme) approached 43 million. According to a World Bank estimate, the rural poverty rate would rise to over 10 percent if the 2-dollars-a-day poverty line was applied (ibid.).

In addition, the huge flow of rural migrant workers into cities exerts great pressure on employment for local urban workers. Unemployment is a huge challenge for the regional governments. The situation has been made worse by the global financial crisis, which impacted negatively on export growth and consequently, on employment.

Consumption as a proportion of GDP has decreased constantly since the mid-1990s, partly due to a decline in the share of labor income, and partly due to a fall in the average propensity to consume, resulting from uncertainties relating to expenditures on healthcare, education and housing. This is especially true for those in the population not covered by the social security system. To negate the impact of the global financial crisis, local governments have tried hard to stimulate domestic demand since the second half of 2008. The measures taken are focused on increasing investment rather than stimulating consumption. It is believed that expanding the coverage of social security and raising the protection level will help stimulate household consumption.

Social instability has become a major concern for the Chinese government since the number of social incidents and riots has escalated rapidly. According to the 2005 *Blue Book of China's Society*, the number of social conflicts increased from 10,000 in 1993 to 60,000 in 2003 (Ru *et al.*, 2005). It is also reported that social conflicts have intensified since 2008.

Building a comprehensive and fair social security system is one option, but not the only wise option for the government in the 12th Five-Year Programme. There is a general consensus among Chinese scholars on this, though debates are rife concerning the different approaches to a new system.

Social and economic challenges facing China

Widening income inequality

China was an egalitarian society 30 years ago and has experienced a sharp increase in income inequality since the beginning of the 1980s. As a developing country, China has implemented separate and urban-biased economic and social policies for urban and rural areas, resulting in large differences between urban and rural households in terms of income level, accessibility of public services and human development (Riskin *et al.*, 2001; Gustafsson *et al.*, 2008). As indicated in Figure 3.2, the income ratio of the urban household income per capita to the rural household income per capita rose from 1.8 times in 1996 to 3.3 times in 2007 in nominal terms.

Large-scale poverty

Whichever poverty measures are used, it is apparent that the number of poor has decreased by over 90 percent since the end of the 1970s (see Figure 3.3). However, when a different poverty line is adopted, a different figure is obtained. Poverty incidence is very sensitive to upward adjustment of the poverty line, especially if it involves a large proportion of low-income people with the income adjusted slightly higher than the official poverty line. In 2008, the government began to adjust the official line upwards by 43 percent for rural areas. As a result, the number of people defined as "poor" increased by over 200 percent.[3]

However, the new official poverty line is still believed to underestimate reality because it approximates to US$1 per person per day as suggested by

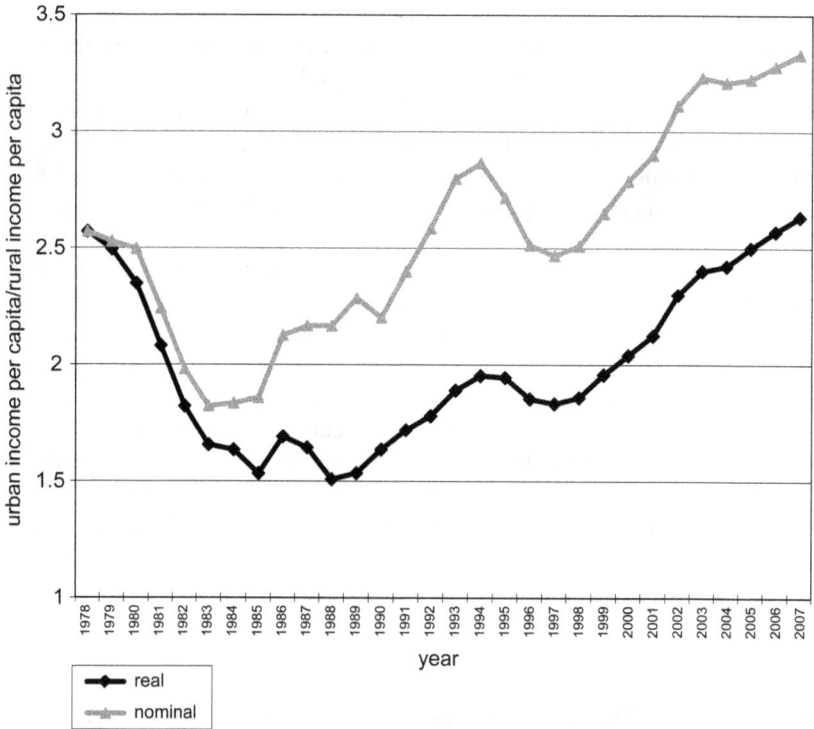

Figure 3.2 China's urban–rural income gap between 1978 and 2007
Source: China Statistics Abstract (2008), p.101.

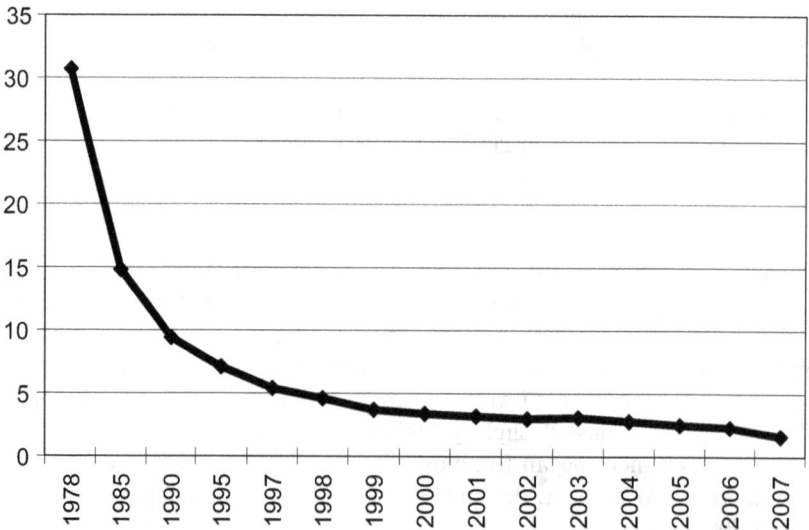

Figure 3.3 Poverty incidence of rural population based on official lines
Source: China Statistical Yearbook, various years.

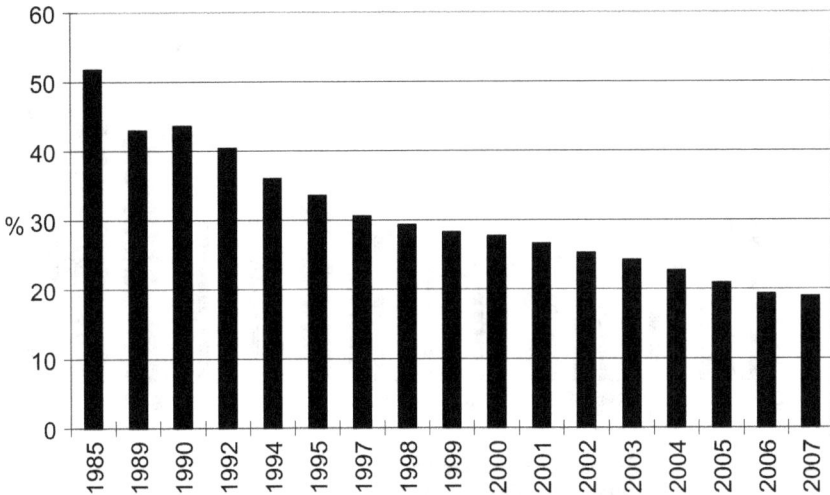

Figure 3.4 Rural official poverty line as a percentage of household income per capita, 1985–2007
Source: Author's calculation.

the World Bank. If the official line is raised to US$2 per person per day, the poverty rate doubles, meaning that in 2008, the rural poor population would have been around 100 million (Figure 3.4) (World Bank, 2009a).

High unemployment pressure

It is difficult to obtain an accurate estimate of the unemployment rate for a developing country like China which has millions of rural surplus laborers, rural–urban migrant workers and informal sector workers. Even in urban areas, the government has never published re-employment rates comparable to the international benchmark. The government simply publishes an annual registered unemployment rate for urban areas. By definition, the unemployed are people who are registered in labor offices, covered by unemployment insurance and seeking employment services from governments. This implies that most rural–urban migrant workers and those in the informal sector are unlikely to be registered. Therefore, the official registered unemployment rate has been considerably underestimated (Figures 3.5 and 3.6). Some studies state that the underestimation is around 2–5 percent, depending on the timing and whether or not rural migrant workers are included.

Increasing labor mobility

Like other developing countries, China is now still a labor-surplus economy with a large proportion of its labor force engaged in farming activities though

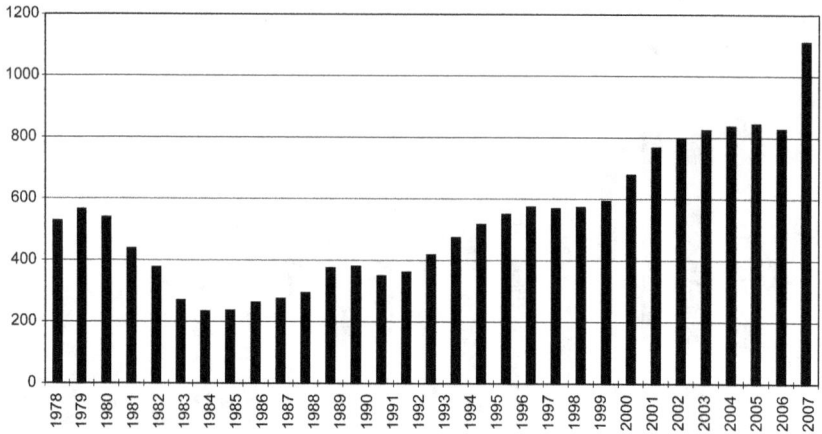

Figure 3.5 Number of urban unemployed people in China, 1978–2008 (millions)
Source: China Statistical Yearbook, various years.

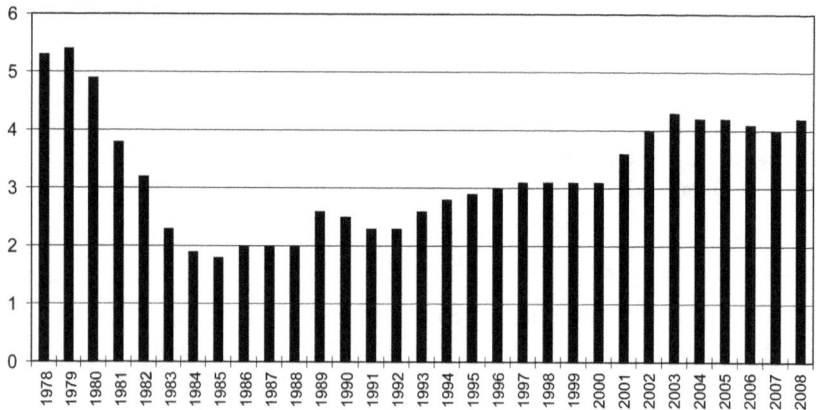

Figure 3.6 Urban registered unemployment rate in China, 1978–2008 (%)
Source: China Statistical Yearbook, various years.

the urbanization process has accelerated since the mid-1990s. The latest statistics indicate there were 480 million laborers in rural areas in 2007, accounting for 62 percent of the total number of laborers in China (*China Statistical Abstract 2008*, p. 43). Nearly half were mobile, employed either in rural industry or in urban areas. The number of rural–urban migrant workers has been increasing and reached more than 130 million in 2006, as shown in Figure 3.7. Based on experiences in developed countries, the process of rural–urban migration in China will likely continue for the next two decades.[4] The majority of these workers are less-educated, unskilled, highly mobile, low-income earners not covered by social security (Deng and Li, 2008; Li, 2008). As migrant workers are registered in rural areas, they are generally at a

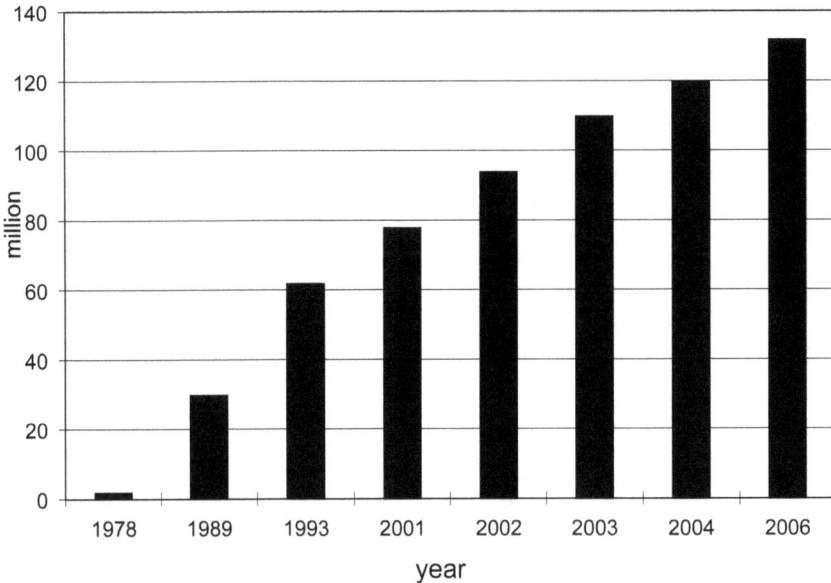

Figure 3.7 The number of rural–urban migrant workers in China (millions)
Source: Li, S. (2008).

disadvantage in the urban labor market in terms of employment opportunities, salary payment and accessibility to social security and public services.

Declining consumption propensity

Since the 1990s, China has experienced declining consumption as a percentage of GDP. As can be seen in Figure 3.8, total consumption as a percentage of GDP declined from 67 percent in 1981 to 49 percent in 2007. The decline was largely due to the fall in the share of household consumption. At the same time, the share of household consumption in GDP decreased by 17 percent while the share of government consumption stayed in the range of 13–16 percent.

Data from the annual household survey conducted by the National Bureau of Statistics also indicates that the household saving rates have been increasing since the early 1990s in both the urban and rural areas. Figure 3.9 shows that the household saving rate increased sharply from 10 percent in the mid-1980s to 27 percent in 2007 in urban China, while in rural China, a stunning rise occurred in the 1990s.

The decrease in the propensity to consume and the increase in household savings have had a negative impact on macroeconomic growth, which is increasingly dependent on export growth. Major reasons for the decline in consumption are the emerging economic uncertainties and transition of the social security system. Households feel the impact of rising unemployment, and higher payments for

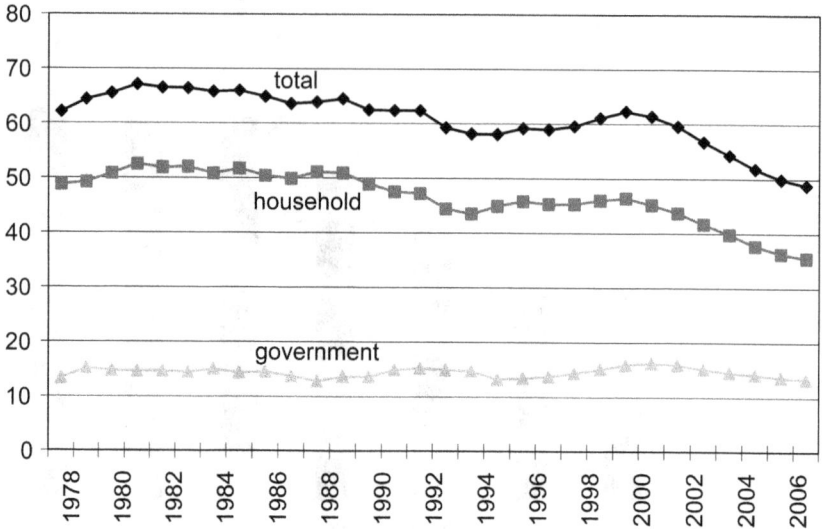

Figure 3.8 Changes in consumption as a percentage of GDP in China
Source: China Statistical Yearbook, various years.

social security and public services such as healthcare and education. To deal with these uncertainties, they have been increasing their savings.

Rising social conflict

Social unrest is recognized as a major problem that can trigger social instability in China. According to diverse sources, the numbers of incidences of social unrest have increased over the past decade. For example, citing Chinese Communist Party sources, Lum (2006) indicates that social unrest grew by nearly 50 percent from 2004 to 2005 and that there were 87,000 cases of "public order disturbances," including protests, demonstrations, picketing and group petitioning, in 2005 compared to 74,000 in 2004. Although there are no reliable official statistics on the latest situation, it is expected that social unrest may now be even worse in some regions (Peng, 2009).

Strategic objectives of social security

It is important for China—a developing country and a transition economy— to establish a desirable social security system to deal with its economic and social challenges. A well-functioning social security as well as a social welfare system is essential to achieve the overall objectives of providing insurance, poverty relief and income redistribution. Social security is expected to play an important role in stimulating domestic demand by reducing the saving rates of households, particularly for low- to middle-income groups, and maintaining social stability.

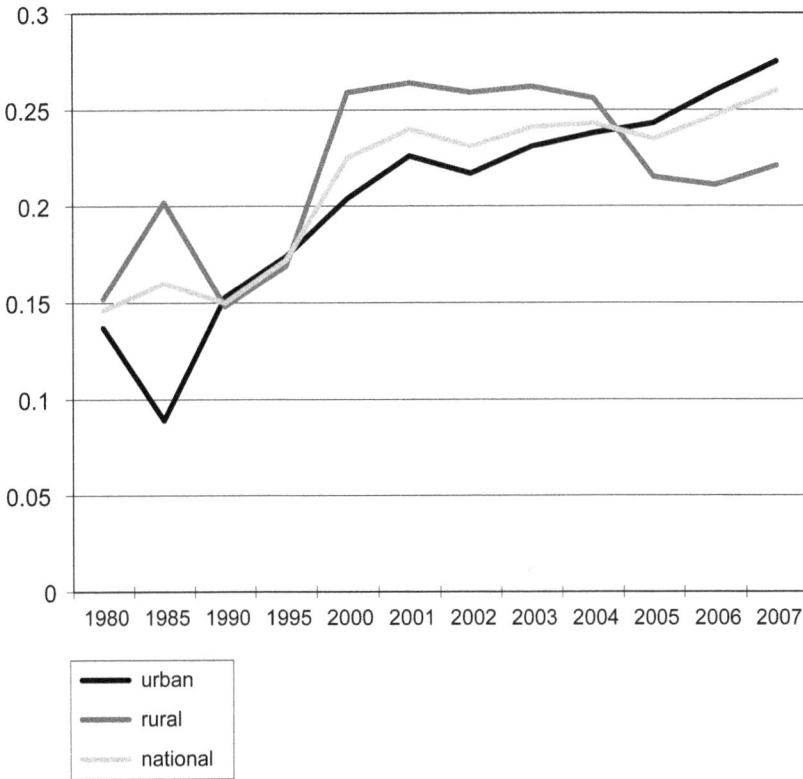

Figure 3.9 Saving rate of households in urban, rural areas and China as a whole
Notes: The saving rate was calculated by using household income and consumption expenditure data from the household survey conducted annually by NBS.

The six objectives of social security

The objectives of social security, widely recognized by economists and sociologists, with applications particularly focused on China, can be summarized as follows (Barr, 2001; Barr and Diamond, 2008):

1 *Insurance.* Social security has two major components—social insurance and social assistance—including social relief and financial support for specific population groups such as the aged and children. Social insurance is frequently referred to as social transfer programmes that deal with risks: the risk of unemployment, healthcare expenses and inadequate income support during retirement (Feldstein, 2005). For China, social security has a very important role in reducing risks, especially those resulting from uncertainties related to the transition process of an economy in terms of employment, income mobility, and healthcare. The unemployment insurance, minimum income guarantee programme and medical insurance

provide good examples of coverage in these aspects. Social insurance differs from private insurance in that it is mandatory and requires more intervention and obligation by governments, which may lead to disincentive effects on job-seeking and inefficient use of medical resources. It is crucial to design a desirable social security system to provide an optimal combination of insurance and incentives. While most countries, either developed or developing, are seeking solutions with their own specific conditions, China is no exception (Feldstein, 2005; Barr and Diamond, 2008).

2 *Poverty relief.* Without social security and social support, it is difficult for the poor to rise out of poverty. As modern poverty theory explains, poverty by nature easily generates poverty and even more poverty when low-income people fall into a poverty trap (Bowles *et al.*, 2006). In circumstances where public services are lacking, poverty and illiteracy and/or illness form a vicious circle. Knight *et al.* (2010) provide strong evidence showing that children from low-income households in rural China have higher drop-out rates in compulsory education than those from better-off households, and they have fewer opportunities to secure decent jobs and non-agricultural employment with higher compensation when they enter the labor market. The poverty structure has shown significant changes over the past decade. One is the increase in the proportion of rural population falling into poverty due to illness and disability, reflecting inadequate access to medical insurance and services in rural China. The Minimum Living Standard Guarantee (MLSG) scheme has been quite successful in alleviating poverty in urban China since its widespread implementation in 2000, but it plays a limited role in narrowing income inequality (Li and Yang, 2009). Drawing on experience from the MLSG scheme in urban areas, the government started to implement the same scheme in 2007 in rural areas, where the income level of households who qualified as recipients is much lower compared to that in urban areas. Believed to be a more effective measure of poverty reduction in China, the MLSG scheme is also a supplementary measure to the traditional measure—through supporting economic development in the poor regions—of alleviating poverty.[5]

3 *Income redistribution.* Social security's function is income redistribution, but it is still debatable whether income redistribution should be a priority objective in designing a social security system (Feldstein, 2005). Theoretically, social security has direct and indirect redistributive effects in society. The direct effects may not be so obvious and explicit, but the indirect effects cannot be ignored. A pension system such as pay-as-you-go (PAYG) has little effect on income redistribution in urban China since pensions are closely indexed to the previous wage of recipients, but there is no doubt that PAYG has an indirect effect on intergenerational distribution of income. The indirect effects become more significant in an aging population. Medical insurance and compulsory education have even greater indirect effects on income distribution in the long term. Equal opportunities in access to education are crucial in narrowing income inequality

within cohorts and generations. Over the past decade, rising returns to education have played an increasingly important role in widening wage inequality in urban China, but a significantly unequal educational attainment among urban employees also contributes to wage disparity (Li, 2008). Social security and welfare, such as an income allowance programme and free or subsidized education, have at the same time generally positive effects on income redistribution, from which the low-income population will benefit more.

4   *Consumption smoothing.* Social security in the form of a pension system has the obvious function of consumption smoothing—also called the piggy bank function—for individuals in the long term. Chinese households, particularly low-income households in rural areas, frequently experience income fluctuations due to unemployment, volatility of product prices, disease outbreaks and natural disasters. Income fluctuation is one of the major causes of rural population falling into transient poverty (Whalley and Yue, 2009). It is not surprising that income fluctuation inevitably leads to household consumption fluctuation. Therefore, social security, such as unemployment insurance, medical insurance and income support programmes like the MLSG, have a strong impact on household consumption smoothing, especially in low-income households.

5   *Consumption stimulation.* This objective is particularly important for countries like China with a continuing decline in the propensity to consume in the long term. The global financial crisis hit China's export sector seriously. Chinese economists and sociologists then appealed to the government to expand spending more on social security and public services in order to reduce consumers' risks and uncertainties and raise their propensity to consume (Cai and Du, 2009). Although there is no strong evidence showing that inadequate social security is a major cause of the decline in consumption in China, some attitudinal surveys indicate that saving for education, future medical needs and housing purchases are the primary reasons why people save.[6]

6   *Social stabilizer.* From China's perspective, this is integral to social security. Many studies indicate that crime and social conflict are strongly correlated with unemployment, income inequality and poverty (Fajnzylber *et al.*, 2002a, 2002b). The correlation increases in countries which have no or inadequate social programmes to protect the poor and unemployed. To reduce social conflicts and create a more stable society, it is important for China to expand and strengthen the current system of social security. This will help build a harmonious economic and social environment for the implementation of the 12th Five-Year Plan.

The role of the government in social security

How governments in developed countries, and especially in welfare states, should contribute to social security has been an ongoing debate for a long time. There seems to be no single uniform rule applied to all countries (Feldstein, 2005). In China's case, the government should play an increasingly important role in the provision of social security. This does not mean that the government should take full responsibility. There should be a clear division of labor between the government and the market in the provision of public services. Households and individuals are also major financial contributors to funding security programmes.

The strategic objectives of China's social security in the coming decades and their relationship with overall development objectives should be clarified. A desirable system should encapsulate the following three basic principles. First, there should be complete coverage for all groups—the young and old, rural and urban residents, workers in the formal and informal sectors, the employed and unemployed. Second, there should be portability of benefits, which means a personal contribution to social security programmes; and qualifications should be portable with job mobility and migration across regions. Third, sustainability of coverage, that is, the standard of social security should not be maintained at a level beyond government fiscal capability, but should be raised incrementally with economic growth. It is widely accepted that expenditures on social protection in China are much lower compared to other countries, and even most developing countries (CDRF, 2009).

Elements of the social secruity system in China: problems and reform

The Minimum Living Standard Guarantee (MLSG)

Current situation and problems

The MLSG scheme was introduced in the late 1990s, but its implementation has expanded rapidly in urban areas from 2001 and in rural areas since 2005.[7] The number of people supported by the MLSG since 2000 is shown in Table 3.1. In 2000, only 4 million of the urban population received support from the MLSG, but this figure increased to almost 12 million in 2001 and 21 million in 2002. Since 2003, the number of urban residents receiving income allowance has been maintained at around 22 to 24 million. The increase accelerated over the subsequent years, as indicated in Table 3.1.

Table 3.1 Urban and rural population supported by the MLSG in China, 2000–08 (millions)

	2000	2001	2002	2003	2004	2005	2006	2007	2008
Urban	4.0	11.7	20.6	22.5	22.1	22.3	22.4	22.7	23.3
Rural	3.0	3.0	4.1	3.7	4.9	8.3	15.9	35.7	43.1

Source: China Ministry of Civil Affairs (2008).

In 2008, of the urban residents receiving income allowance, 3.5 percent were formally employed, 16.3 percent were informally employed, 13.6 percent were aged people, 24.3 percent were registered unemployed, 17.2 percent were unregistered unemployed, 15.3 percent were students and 9.8 percent were other children. The average threshold level was 205 *yuan* and the average income received was 144 *yuan* per person per month in urban China in 2008, an increase of 13 percent and 40 percent, respectively, compared to that in 2007.

The programme currently covers all the population institutionally, but criteria for urban and rural residents are different and vary from one region to another. Although the number of rural residents supported by the MLSG exceeded the number of urban residents, the threshold level for rural residents to qualify as recipients and the average income received by rural residents are much lower than their urban counterparts. In 2008, the average threshold level for rural residents was 82 *yuan* and the average income each person received was 50 *yuan* per month.

Another problem is that the programme excludes certain population groups such as migrant households and college graduates. Since the programme is implemented by city or county governments, residents without local *hukou* (household registration) are not eligible for the programme.

Debates and policy options

Policy debates for the urban programme include whether rural–urban migrants should be covered and whether the differences in protection level across cities should be based on living costs rather than the financial ability of the government. Policy debates for the rural programme are concerned with the extremely low welfare standards and the wide differences in coverage and protection levels across regions. Some scholars believe that the programme should be more comprehensive, aimed at the most needy, and should be implemented with employment promotion measures that encourage the unemployed to return to the labor market quickly (Jiang, 2009; Xu and Zhang, 2009).

One of the notable problems of the MLSG in urban areas—which is not widely discussed and not deemed a problem by some scholars—is the exclusion of rural–urban migrant households from the scheme. The argument is that the programme is likely to generate a moral hazard for rural–urban migrants. Where the income of rural households is very much lower, the programme would induce rural people to move to urban areas if they qualify as MLSG recipients. It is, however, more critical to provide employment services, such as job training than to provide income allowance to rural migrants in urban areas (Lin, 2006).

The aim of the MLSG is to reduce poverty in urban and rural areas, but households which are considered marginally less poor are more likely to be ignored by the programme in less developed areas since the threshold level is set below the poverty line in these areas due to insufficient government revenue.

Also hotly debated is whether college students should be covered by the MLSG. Given that scholarships and education loan coverage are limited, the programme should target students from poor households who can barely maintain their basic living standards (Liu *et al.*, 2009).

How to maintain the credentials of the programme in the long term? It should be adjusted frequently with considerations for changes in consumer prices and economic growth. For example, the threshold level should be indexed to consumer prices and should rise with household income growth. It should also be adjusted with changes in the minimum wage and unemployment benefits (Song and Guo, 2008).

It is critical for China to narrow the regional differences in terms of threshold level and coverage of the programme. The differences arise mainly from the varying financial capacity of local governments. To raise the threshold level and coverage in less developed areas, it is crucial for the central government to take more financial responsibility by transferring more funds to less developed areas (Zhao, 2008).

Given the fact that the threshold level in some areas is underestimated, even below the poverty line, not all of the poor households are supported by the programme. To solve this problem, which happens in some cities and counties with financial difficulty, local governments should increase the threshold level in order to support and include households that previously did not qualify for the programme because their household income just scraped above the old threshold level. For instance, Anshan city in Liaoning Province started to provide special support to households with an income within 20 percent above the threshold from 2009. The special support includes subsidies for employment, education, training, healthcare, food, heating, etc.

Basic healthcare: financing and delivery

Current situation and problems

Since the mid-1990s, China has tried to work out a more efficient and economic healthcare system. In 1998, the State Council issued *The Resolution on Establishing the System of Basic Medical Insurance for Workers in Urban Areas*, drawing on the experience of earlier local pilot reforms, which indicated the need to introduce a national system of medical insurance. Currently, there are three types of medical insurance schemes. The first is the Worker Basic Medical Insurance (WBMI) scheme, which was transformed from public healthcare implemented under the old planned system, covering urban workers and retirees. The second is the Urban Residents Basic Medical Insurance (URBMI) scheme for urban residents who are not covered by the first insurance type, including children, students and aged seniors without employment history. The third is the New Rural Cooperative Medical Insurance (NRCMI) scheme, covering only rural people.

The key challenges facing the current healthcare system are incomplete coverage of medical insurance, low funding from the government, high fees required from patients for medical services and unbalanced regional allocation of medical resources (CDRF, 2009). By the end of 2008, nearly 150 million urban workers plus 50 million retired people had joined the WBMI scheme, and 118 million urban residents and 815 million rural residents have joined the URBMI and NRCMI schemes, respectively. However, the coverage for the WBMI, URBMI and NRCMI schemes was 99 percent, 60 percent and 85 percent, respectively.

A more serious problem with the NRCMI scheme is its low reimbursement ratio, which is below 50 percent in most rural areas. Given the rising medical costs in recent years, it is reported that most low-income rural families cannot afford medical services, even though they are covered by the NRCMI.

Debates and policy options

The debates center on the following two interrelated issues: Who should be the financial contributors: the government, enterprises or individuals? Should market mechanisms be introduced into medical service delivery? If the government finances healthcare through taxation, it will be inevitable that the service options will be provided mainly by public hospitals. There would be a very limited role for the market mechanisms (like the British model). Another argument prevails that medical insurance, either public or commercial, should be a priority option and public hospitals should be privatized (similar to the American model).

For rural migrant workers, the question is, what kind of medical insurance will be beneficial to them? Zheng (2008) and Du (2009) proposed a further classification for migrant workers: long-term migrant workers who settle in a city to be covered by the WBMI; short-term or seasonal migrant workers to be covered by the NRCMI; and highly mobile migrant workers to be covered by special arrangements, for which an ideal solution is difficult to find because the current system is not transferable across regions. You Chun suggested that coverage for high mobility migrant workers should be provided by commercial medical insurance that is subsidized by the government (You, 2009).

Encouraging migrant workers to join the WBMI scheme is a problem as the high contribution to be paid by the individual makes it unaffordable for low-income workers (Luo, 2008; Du, 2009). The WBMI requires that workers and their firms contribute 8 percent of the total wage to WBMI: 2 percent coming from the worker's contribution and 6 percent from the firm.

In Shenzhen, one of China's largest cities, the majority of the urban workers are rural migrants. To attract more migrant workers to participate in the medical insurance scheme, the city initiated new forms of medical insurance suitable for migrants. Meanwhile, the range of medical services covered and reimbursed by the insurance plan was expanded and the permitted reimbursement ratio was increased by more than 10 percent.[8] As a result, over 70 percent of the migrant workers participated in the medical insurance scheme by the end of 2008, a much higher figure than the national average.

A national integrated healthcare system

Most areas have adopted a healthcare system that encompasses the three medical insurance scheme types, namely, the WBMI, URBMI and NRCMI, but some cities have tried to create new systems. Yuhang in Zhejiang Province and Zhuhai in Guangdong Province, have merged the URBMI with NRCMI schemes into one system, whereas Dongguan in Guangdong Province merged the three types of medical insurance schemes into one system.

How medical services should be delivered to the population is still hotly debated in China. Now public hospitals are a dominant player in the medical service sector, accounting for over 90 percent of all healthcare institutions. Since the 1990s, the local governments have reduced subsidies to public hospitals, which must earn the major part of their revenues from patients and the WBMI scheme. Some hospitals receive subsidies from the governments, which are only 10 percent of their total revenue. To sustain business and operations, the hospitals raise medical fees and coerce patients into paying for expensive medication and unnecessary diagnostic tests. As a result, medical costs have reached an unaffordable level for ordinary households. On one hand, high medical costs mean high contributions to medical insurance from workers and firms. On the other, it deprives households of medical services, particularly rural households that are not covered by medical insurance. These problems have led to heated debates on how best to deliver medical services to individuals, and whether public hospitals should be subsidized by governments directly or compete with each other for patients.

Opinion is divided into two schools of thought. One camp is in favor of market mechanisms in the medical service industry. Hospitals, whether public or private, should create strong incentives to provide economic and efficient medical services to patients. The best way to achieve this is to tie and link the salaries of medical staff to their performance, and offer incentives to hospitals to operate more efficiently. This is just one side of the coin. The other side is to limit medical demand by cost-sharing whereby a portion of the medical cost would be borne by patients themselves. For this, the framework of medical services would be consistent with demand and supply.[9] For employees, payment contributions come from three parties: the government, firms, and individuals. For non-employees (such as children and the unemployed, etc.), payment contributions come from the government and individuals. Individuals buy medical insurance from insurance companies, which pay hospitals for the medical services rendered to individuals. As commercial agents, insurance companies have an incentive to propose that hospitals lower medical costs and overcome the problem of the abuse of medical services. Insurance companies can be state-owned, therefore the government is justified in regulating their business behavior.

The other camp is in favor of free provision of medical services by the government. The government instead of the market should play a more important role in financing and delivering medical services (Li, 2006). The more extreme argument is that the government should give full financial support to public hospitals, which are required to provide free medical services to patients. In this system, government funding comes from taxation and medical insurance is unnecessary since the government is a "large medical insurance company." There are two problems envisaged in this model. The first is how to make public hospitals operate more economically and efficiently. The second is to solve the "free rider" problem associated with patients.

The government has not made any final decision on the future direction of healthcare system reforms while pilot reforms are being conducted in several areas. However, all parties have reached a consensus that China needs a strong healthcare system at the community level, and that this should be the main responsibility of the local governments. Therefore, at the beginning of 2009, the State Council issued two documents concerning further medical insurance reforms: "Suggestions on Deepening Reform of the Medical System," and "Implementation Programmes of Deepening Reform of the Medical System in 2009–11." The three target goals for 2012 are: (1) basic medical insurance coverage for all residents in both urban and rural areas; (2) significant improvement in accessibility and quality of medical services; and (3) substantial reduction in the financial burden for citizens receiving medical services.[10] To achieve the goals, four proposed measures, to be implemented in the next three years are: (1) coverage of basic medical insurance for urban and rural residents is to be raised to over 90 percent; (2) the contribution to the NRBMI (from both individuals and governments) is to be increased to 120 *yuan* per person, a considerable rise compared to 30 *yuan* in 2005; (3) a medical system at the community level is to be established; and (4) public hospitals are to be reformed.

Basic education

Current situation and problems

Over the past ten years, China has implemented a nine-year compulsory education programme. By now, all children in rural and urban areas should be receiving at least nine years of school education without paying any tuition fees. However, an acute problem with compulsory education is the significantly large disparity in the quality of education between urban and rural areas, and between regions (CDRF, 2009). Unlike children in cities, children in rural areas have little chance of receiving a pre-school education due to the shortage of kindergartens.

Due to lower quality of teaching and the lack of teaching facilities, compulsory education in rural areas is not as good as that in urban areas. This contrast is even more strikingly stark between remote rural villages and mega-cities. The central government has recognized and mitigated the problem by increasing financial resources given to rural areas and the western region to improve the quality of education in these areas. It will, however, take time to overcome the problem.

Low-middle school graduates from rural areas, due to the low-quality education that they have received, have no competitive advantage in labor markets when they move into cities. They typically are employed as unskilled workers by small firms with low pay and are more mobile across cities and jobs. They are also more likely to remain in the low-income category throughout their lives.

Debates and policy options

Now that the nine-year compulsory education programme has been realized, China should turn its focus to basic education. Perhaps it should either initiate a more ambitious programme, that is, a 12-year compulsory education programme as most developed countries did some years ago, or concentrate on improving the quality of the present compulsory education programme, especially in rural areas.

Debates on policy for basic education revolve around issues about whether compulsory education should be extended to 12 years and whether more resources should be channelled to improve the quality of the current nine-year compulsory education. The bigger issue is how to improve the quality of compulsory education in rural areas, which is much lower than that in urban areas. The following policy options are proposed for the next five years. First, there is no doubt that rural primary and secondary education needs more financial support from the governments at all levels. In poor areas, financial support from the central government is crucial. Second, to improve the quality of rural education, it is crucial to attract more qualified teachers to teach in primary and secondary schools in poor and remote areas. Given the oversupply of college graduates resulting from the rapid expansion of higher education since 1999, the central government may consider initiating a special programme to encourage college graduates to teach in primary and secondary schools in rural areas.

Education of migrant children is another issue sparking policy debates. There are millions of rural-migrant children of school age living in cities, but most have difficulty gaining admission to public schools and have to go to private schools. The conditions in these schools are extremely unsatisfactory. Most teachers are unqualified, classrooms are unsafe and the quality of education is much lower than in urban public schools. Some of these schools are regarded as illegal by local governments, but they play an important role in providing education to migrant children. The current Chinese education system stipulates that local governments should take the main responsibility for financing the compulsory education of the local children in their communities, but for migrant children the local governments find no incentive to do so. As the central government has not implemented any nationwide policy concerning compulsory education for migrant children, local governments are concerned about more migrant children moving into their areas if the central government decides to implement a policy allowing migrant children to study in public schools. It is a huge dilemma for city governments. The central government also faces a dilemma since any change in the education system in favor of the migrant children in the cities would cause an influx of rural children into the cities.

The attitude that city governments adopt towards providing compulsory education for migrant children is understandable, but the consequences of their policy are unacceptable. Most migrant children will be disadvantaged and edged out in the urban labor market, thus generating inter-generational immobility among migrants in urban areas. To solve the problem, city governments must provide migrant children with a public education, the same education that local urban children are entitled to. To coordinate policy implementation across cities, the central government should create a uniform nationwide curriculum. Meanwhile, the central government and provincial governments should increase and transfer funding to cities which face difficulties in expanding their educational capacity to migrant children.

In most parts of China, children enter primary schools at age 6 or 7 years and the the enrollment rate is almost 100 percent in urban and rural areas. However, not all have the chance of a place in kindergarten. Some estimates indicate that about 30 percent of 5-year-old children in urban areas do not attend kindergarten and the percentage in rural areas is even higher. Therefore, the Chinese government should consider ensuring that all children receive at least one year of pre-school education. To encourage parents to send their children to kindergarten, local governments should give subsidies to either parents or to kindergartens. In more affluent areas, there is the option for governments to provide free pre-school education for all children.

Junior-middle school graduates face difficulty in finding employment and are disadvantaged in terms of salary. What they learn in schools is often not what employers require and does not enhance their employability. A way to solve the problem is to provide skill-training to these junior-middle school graduates which could last six months to a year, and should be free or highly subsidized. In 2008, about five million junior-middle school graduates left school and entered the labor market.

Higher education

Current situation and problems

Tertiary education in China has expanded rapidly in the past decade. College student enrollment has increased from 1.1 million in 1998 to 6.3 million in 2009, at an annual growth rate of 17.2 percent (*China Statistical Yearbook*

2008, p. 415). The gross enrollment rate in tertiary education reached 23 percent in 2009. The central and the local governments have at the same time increased their budgets for tertiary education. Spending by governments increased at 15.5 percent annually from 1998 to 2006 (ibid., p. 430).

However, with the rapid expansion of tertiary education, many problems have surfaced. The Chinese higher education system has maintained the typical features of the Soviet-style education system, mixed with the legacy of the Chinese economic planning system introduced in the 1950s. The problems in the higher education system have been widely criticized following Premier Wen Jiabao's question in 2006, "Why can't our education system foster great academic masters?"[11] The criticisms can be summarized as follows:

- Chinese universities lack creativity, motivation and mechanisms for innovation. Even though evidence shows that the publication of academic papers by Chinese scholars has increased considerably over the past decade with higher research funding, still very few papers appear in top journals. The fundamental reason is that innovation and innovation-related research are not given enough attention by Chinese universities and the governments (Wang, 2009).
- There is strong intervention from the government in the internal activities of universities. Due to the control and regulations in the teaching and administrative activities, there is very limited room for universities to exercise their autonomy in student enrollment, faculty and staff recruitment, as well as setting the academic curriculum and disciplines (Ruan and Hu, 2009).
- There is a lack of good governance structure within universities (Yang, 2009). The current administrative structure in Chinese universities is a system of the "president's responsibility under the Party Committee's leadership." A serious flaw in this system is that there is no clear division between the tasks of the university's president and the Party Secretary. In most cases, Party Secretaries are more powerful than presidents, though presidents are also in the Party Committee. Presidents are appointed by the Ministry of Education or local governments instead of being appointed via recommendation and election by professors within universities. This puts presidents in an awkward position as they must report to and be accountable to the higher-level governments, and less accountable to their university colleagues. Although the 1995 Education Law stipulated that Chinese universities should draft a university charter specifying their responsibilities and accountability, none have actually taken the initiative towards better governance (Yang, 2009; Zhu, 2009).
- Professors and teaching staff have little autonomy in administrative and academic matters within universities, even in choosing curriculum and textbooks. They have little role in decision-making processes. Some universities have a professor committee, which is supposed to be a decision-making organization within colleges and universities, but in reality the

roles of the committee are very limited (Zhu, 2009). As a result, professors have little incentive to work hard and perform well.

- There is no innovation-based evaluation system to gauge the performance of Chinese universities. The current evaluations are conducted by the Ministry of Education or local governments and they emphasize quantitative indicators such as the number of students, teaching staff, published papers, organized academic meetings, ongoing and completed research projects, etc. The assessment pays little attention to activities and outcomes associated with innovation. Thus allocation of financial and human resources are misleadingly channeled into activities and projects that have little or no breakthrough potential and innovativeness. In addition, the promotion benchmarks for teaching staff in most Chinese universities are based on seniority and publication quantity, whereas key criteria based on meritocracy such as creative research and new ideas are often ignored.
- There are many restrictions on the development of private universities. The majority of the higher education institutions are public universities. There is, therefore, no political and social environment for private universities to thrive. The governments impose too much red tape for private higher-education institutions to obtain any form of approval.
- The supply of university graduates cannot meet market demand due to the outdated curricula which are not oriented towards industry. As a result, the employment rate of college graduates within the first year of graduation has been declining (MACOS, 2009). The employment rate of the college graduates within the first year of graduation was slightly above 85 percent in 2008 due partly to the impact of the global financial crisis and partly due to the demand/supply mismatch of college graduates in the labor market (ibid., p. 7). Thus, over 750,000 or nearly 15 percent of the new college graduates were unemployed. Of the college graduates who were employed in their first year of graduation in 2008, nearly one-third found jobs that were unrelated to their field of study (Li and Wang, 2009).

Debates and policy options

The Chinese economy has reached a stage where growth is increasingly dependent on the improvement of product quality and efficiency of enterprises. Innovation will play a critical role at this stage. Chinese universities should thus take responsibility for the promotion of innovation. To meet this challenge, the following reforms are needed for Chinese tertiary education:

- Set up effective mechanisms to encourage innovation and creative research. Financial resources from the governments or from other sources should be allocated to innovative research, especially projects that emphasize originality and cutting-edge ideas. Researchers should be provided with sufficient funds for their innovative work and be sufficiently rewarded for their contribution to academic and technology innovation.

- Reduce intervention from governments in internal affairs of universities. It is crucial for universities to be independent academically and administratively if they are expected to establish themselves as institutions known for innovativeness. The governments must understand that too much intervention in universities leads to inefficiency and low productivity.
- Establish an appropriate governance structure within universities, including re-organizing leadership of the Party in higher education. Under the current political system, the leadership of the Party in universities and education is *de facto*, and calling for withdrawal of Party leadership is absolutely unacceptable. However, there is still some room for redefining the role of the Party leadership in higher education by reorganizing the Party committees in universities (Yang, 2009).
- Give more autonomy to professors by designing and reorganizing the professor committee in universities and colleges. The committee should be one of the major decision-makers in the allocation of human and financial resources within universities. Committee members should be elected by professors and teaching staff and take primary responsibility for their votes.
- Set up an authorized and innovation-guided evaluation system for the performance of universities. The system should be independent from government, political intervention and interest groups. The evaluation outcome should become one of the bases for governments to allocate research funds among universities.
- Provide special and preferential policies for the development of private higher education institutions, apart from the implementation of a comprehensive set of regulations that would not discriminate against private providers of higher education. The policies should include simple legal registration and approval procedures for private universities, tax reductions or tax exemptions for donations and charitable contributions to private higher education institutions, and removal of barriers to obtain credit.
- It is important to give greater autonomy to universities in terms of student enrollment. The current national college entrance exams can be considered one method—but not the only method—for universities to enroll new students. Universities should be given the freedom to determine the best admissions system and requirements, and to organize and determine the form of entrance examinations so that students with potential and creativity are identified and enrolled.
- Reform the academic curriculum in order to equip college graduates with professional knowledge and skills to better meet employer expectations (Ren, 2009). A World Bank project on skills development in Guangdong Province stresses that a good balance has to be achieved between hardware, which includes facilities and equipment for education, and software, which encompasses curriculum, instructional materials and trained qualified teachers (World Bank, 2009b). This emphasis can be applied to Chinese universities and colleges. Transforming the learning environment from

one that is teacher-centered to one that is learner-centered is necessary. The learner-centered approach trains and equips students with skills such as problem-solving, teamwork and communications that are much sought after by employers.

Housing security

Current situation and problems

Like all other countries in the world, China faces challenges in providing decent housing to low-income groups. Since the launch of housing reforms in the 1990s, most public housing has been privatized through apartment sales to tenants. Surveys have shown that the percentage of urban households living in public housing decreased from over 80 percent to less than 20 percent from 1988 to 2002. Along with housing privatization, the commercial property market has also developed rapidly. In 2008, total revenues from the housing and real estate industry accounted for over 5 percent of national GDP, becoming one of the major driving forces of the country's rapid economic growth. However, the growth of housing and real estate has resulted in unexpectedly high housing prices, especially in large cities. Local governments stopped giving housing subsidies to urban households since the late 1990s, as a stimulus for housing market development. As a result, the low-income households, together with millions of rural migrant households, cannot afford to buy their apartments. With skyrocketing housing prices, even middle-income households in cities face difficulties in affording larger and better apartments through the housing market. To some extent, the housing market has become a speculation playground for the rich and affluent.

The problem is very clear: high housing prices drive low-income households out of the housing market and rule out any possibility of them improving their housing situation. One solution is to reduce housing prices to an affordable level. Even though this solution is technically and economically feasible, it cannot be implemented politically: the local governments would strongly oppose this measure because their revenue from land sales would decline with falling housing prices. The second solution requires the governments to take responsibility for providing low-rent or low-price housing for low-income households, even for middle-income households.

Debates and policy options

There are three alternative solutions to the housing problem of low-income groups in urban China (CDRF, 2009):

1 Subsidized-price housing (*Jingji shiyong fang* or JSF) is restricted to low- and middle-income households. Housing is sold at prices lower than

market prices to households that qualify as the most needy and with an income below the threshold level set by local governments. The local governments' contribution is to provide free land to estate developers and to set housing prices. However, the subsidized housing prices in large cities such as Beijing, Shanghai and Shenzhen have been rising with market prices to a level that is beyond the affordability of the low-income group.

2 Rent-subsidized public housing (*Lianzu fang* or LZF) caters only to poor households, not migrant households. This programme has not attracted much attention from city governments because city governments need to spend more resources, both financially and in terms of land, to provide LZF rather than JSF, and the costs of managing and maintaining LZF are relatively higher.

3 Housing cash subsidy (*Zhufang xianjin butie* or ZXB) provides cash relief to households which have already bought housing or rented apartments in the market. This programme is not widely implemented and is in the pilot stage in developed areas.

Currently, most cities are implementing both JSF and LZF programmes at the same time, though the two are not "balanced." There are debates suggesting either JSF or LZF should become a priority housing policy for city governments. Some scholars, on the other hand, strongly argue for the abolishment of JSF based on the following rationale: first, the JSF programme is not justified on fairness. For example, one qualifying criterion for a JSF buyer is his/her current income instead of permanent income. This is a possible scenario whereby some buyers are not really categorized as low-income if their past income records are taken into account. To qualify for and own a JSF apartment means a lifetime benefit. Second, the programme would encourage corruption. Due to the large profit gain involved in huge price differences between commercial housing and JSF, rent-seeking activities are common in the allocation of JSF. This argument augurs well for the LZF programme—whose merits are morally acceptable—to be considered a priority in urban housing policy in the future.

There is still a strong voice in favor of the JSF programme because it is, first, more acceptable to city governments and can be quickly implemented, and second, the programme helps meet the housing needs of middle-income households.

Another housing policy debate is how to provide housing for migrant households in cities. Currently, most rural migrants live in factory dormitories, temporary dormitories on construction sites, or in the basements of high-rise buildings in city communities or in suburban areas. Several case studies indicate that the housing conditions of rural migrants are worse than their urban counterparts, and even worse than those of rural people left behind in their hometown (Li, 2008). Since rural migrants are low-income earners, they have no financial ability to buy apartments in the property market, and cannot even afford housing from the JSF. The only solution is permit them to be entitled to access to the LZF programme. Some cities recently initiated several pilot projects to provide LZF for rural migrant households.

The housing accumulation fund (*Zhufang Gongjijin*), a scheme which lacks fairness, should undergo reform. The current arrangement is that employees in the formal sector, such as civil servants and SOE workers, hold individual accounts for the housing accumulation fund. It is stipulated that both employee and employer should contribute 10 percent of his/her wage to the account, which has a very similar approach to the housing subsidy, but with a regressively distributional function factored in. That means higher-income earners obtain higher subsidies from this programme. There are two reform options for *Zhufang Gongjijin*. One is to completely abolish it, terminating payment of housing subsidies to these relatively higher wage earners. Second, if the programme name is to be maintained, it can be transformed into a scheme specifically for low- and middle-income employees who urgently need to improve their housing conditions.

Unemployment insurance and employment assistance

Current situation and problems

China is a developing country with large numbers of surplus labor in the rural areas. As its red-hot economy undergoes a transition, large numbers of workers are being laid off from state-owned enterprises. Therefore, China must deal with the challenges of unemployment in urban areas and under-employment in rural areas. Ironically, the official unemployment rates are not as high as expected and are believed to be overestimated. Nevertheless, the government is certainly aware of the unemployment pressures. One of the major motivations for the governments' desire to maintain high economic growth is to increase employment and alleviate unemployment pressures. After 10 years of rapid economic growth, the problems of unemployment and underemployment are not as serious now as they were in the late 1990s, when large numbers of workers were laid off from state-owned and urban collective enterprises. However, the recent global financial crisis no doubt intensified the problems as many export-oriented, labor-intensive enterprises closed down in the coastal areas.

Unemployment pressures cannot be significantly mitigated over the next five years. One reason is that about 25 million middle-school and college graduates are expected to enter the labor market each year from 2011 to 2015. This was due to a baby boom in the late 1990s. First, it is important to reform and improve the efficiency of the current unemployment insurance system and coverage. Second, it is even more imperative to encourage firms to create new employment opportunities and motivate graduates to actively search for new jobs. To deal with unemployment, it is widely recognized that state institutions, rather than private insurance, should play a more significant role. As Nicholas Barr points out, even in developed countries, what seems more important is how to design an unemployment insurance plan which provides genuine protection and serves as an incentive for the unemployed to look for jobs (Barr, 2003). In China, the issue of protection is currently more important than the issue of incentive.

A major problem with China's unemployment insurance system is that only workers in the urban formal sector are covered. In 2008, the number of urban workers accessing unemployment insurance reached 124 million, but that was only 41 percent of the total number of urban employees. At the same time, the number of rural migrant workers covered by unemployment insurance was 15.5 million, accounting for less than 12 percent of the total number of rural migrant workers in urban areas.[12] This implies that the majority of workers in informal sectors, such as rural migrant workers and workers in small private firms, are not covered by the current unemployment insurance system. Expanding the coverage of unemployment insurance should be a priority in the 12th Five-Year Programme.

Debates and policy options

Among the many policy debates generated in this issue include questions revolving around whether migrant workers and workers in the informal sector should be covered by unemployment insurance, and whether they should be covered by the current system or whether an alternative system that is more suitable for them. The Chinese governments at all levels have reached a consensus that migrant workers should not be ignored in the unemployment insurance system.[13] However, there has been no agreement as yet on how to provide a system for migrant workers. Since migrant workers typically move frequently between jobs, employers and cities, it is obvious that the current insurance system is unsuitable for them. One option proposed in the *2009 Annual Development Report* is that the unemployment insurance system for migrant workers be transferable between cities and provinces. The governments should be a major contributor to the system and the contribution from migrant workers should be as low as possible or at least affordable.

College graduates are now more and more likely to become unemployed. It has become a social and even a political problem. Debates arise over whether unemployed graduates should be covered by unemployment insurance, and who should be the main financial contributors to the insurance, etc.

Provision of various training programmes is part of the employment assistance, targeting different population groups. An example is the Sunshine Project for migrant workers. However, there are questions about the effectiveness of training projects and the role that the government can play in assisting the unemployed and job-seekers.

The current training programmes for rural migrant workers are generally short-term, spanning two to three weeks. One such programme is the so-called urban life guide training, which helps migrant workers accommodate to urban life, but may not be very useful in helping them find a job because what they need most are skills or professional training. Therefore, the governments should provide migrant workers more skills or professional training opportunities.

The Chinese governments may also consider setting up a national information network that provides and disseminates free and instant information for migrant workers on labor demand and supply, job opportunities, wage and social security and labor protection.

Conclusion

China has made great achievements in economic growth, but has been lagging behind in terms of social protection and the provision of public services over the past three decades. As a result, China is facing serious social and economic challenges such as widening income inequality, large-scale poverty, high unemployment pressures, increasing labor mobility, declining consumption propensity and increasing incidence of social conflict and unrest.

Studies and experiences from other countries indicate that an ideal social security system encompasses strategic objectives for both economic development and social stability.

The Chinese governments at all levels have recognized the importance and necessity of a new social security system that incorporates wider coverage, higher efficiency and greater sustainability (Zheng, 2008; CDRF, 2009). Moreover, China is now financially capable of providing a system benefitting the entire population instead of focusing exclusively on urban workers in the formal sector. One of the challenges China faces is quickly and impartially transforming the current system into a new system accepted by all parties.

It was a remarkable achievement for China to establish a nationwide poverty relief system, namely the minimum living standard guarantee scheme, which now supports nearly 70 million poor individuals in urban and rural areas, in less than 10 years. Now the system needs to be improved in terms of targeting accuracy, wider coverage and higher threshold levels (poverty lines), particularly in rural areas.

China is making a great effort to reform the current medical system, including financing mechanisms and delivery of medical services. A consensus has been reached for some issues, while others are tabled for debate. It has been agreed that the governments should assume greater responsibility for managing medical insurance systems and commit more financial contributions to them. The government's medical relief should be given to the poorest people, especially those living in rural areas.

Compulsory education is the responsibility of the government. The problems associated with compulsory education are low educational quality in rural areas, unequal allocation of financial resources in favor of urban schools and scant attention to preschool education. To deal with these problems, it is imperative for the central government to centralize allocation of financial resources by increasing fund transfer to rural education and education in less developed areas. Moreover, the governments should devise a plan to provide free preschool education to children in order to encourage early development of children's cognitive ability. In addition, it is proposed that governments look into setting up a free post-school professional training programme of six months to one year duration for middle-school graduates as they are presently having difficulties securing a job in the competitive labor market.

Higher education reform is imperative in China. The main problem with higher education is insufficient incentive for professional staff to develop innovative breakthroughs and ideas. One explanation is the extensive intervention from the governments in the internal affairs of universities (Lu and Zhang, 2007). Therefore, the first step towards higher education reform is to reduce this intervention and interference and accord full autonomy to universities.

Housing problems have been on the rise since the governments withdrew the provision of public housing to urban residents. Given the surging housing prices, a major problem is how to guarantee at least basic housing for low-income households, and even middle-income households in urban areas. The city governments can employ three alternative solutions, namely, JSF, LZF and ZXB, to deal with this problem. Over the long term, the JSF scheme should be gradually phased out and the LZF scheme should be expanded to solve the housing problems of poor urban households.

Unemployment insurance, with the coverage extended to workers in the informal sector and rural migrant workers, plays an integral role in maintaining social stability in China. The insurance offers income support to the unemployed, on one hand, and helps them to find employment or self-employment opportunities, on the other (Barr, 2003). To some extent, employment assistance plays a more important role in helping the jobless and protecting the employed from losing their jobs, especially in developing countries. The provision of a comprehensive information network offering employment information and a skills training programme would be very useful to the unemployed and migrant workers with high job mobility.

Acknowledgements

This research was supported by the Cairncross Economic Research Foundation in Beijing. The author is very grateful for the constructive suggestions from Dr Edwin Lim, Dr Ian Porter and Professor Zhao Renwei and comments from Professor Nicolas Barr, Professor Tony Atkinson, the participants in a project workshop held on 27 July 2009 in Beijing, as well as from the participants in the China Social Policy workshop held on 9 November 2009 in Beijing. The author would also like to acknowledge the research assistance provided by Ms Yang Sui and Ms Yang Xiuna.

Notes

1 It is important to note that social security has different coverage in different countries. For instance, the term is specifically related to the old age, survivors and disability programmes in the USA, while in the UK it is used to refer to all cash and tax transfers, both social insurance and social assistance. The Nordic countries, however, use the term in a broader sense, covering all measures to combat social insecurity. This chapter adopts the latter concept.
2 The China Household Income Inequality Project collected data in 2007 and made a preliminary estimation of the national income inequality. The Gini coefficient was found to be 0.47.
3 While the previous official line was 836 *yuan* for rural households in 2008, the new line was adjusted upwards to 1196 *yuan*, an increase of 43 percent. At the same time, the rural poor population increased from less than 13 million to 40 million, or 207 percent. The new line and the corresponding poor population figure can be found in the National Bureau of Statistics (NBS) of China (2009).
4 There were around 300 million rural workers engaged in agriculture in 2007, accounting for 39 percent of the number of total labourers in China as a whole. Assuming the number of rural workers declines by 1 percent each year, it will take 20 years for it to reach 10 percent of the total workers.
5 For a detailed discussion of the supplementary role of the MLSG scheme in reducing poverty in rural Jiangxi Province, see 'The rural MLSG and poverty alleviation: the same or supplemental role'. Available at: http://www.fupin.gansu.gov.cn/zwzx/1181004710d3661.html (accessed 10 June 2007).
6 See discussion summary of 'Why Chinese love saving'. Available at: http://news.xinhuanet.com/fortune/2006–04/10/content_4405567.html (accessed 10 April 2006).
7 A pilot program to guarantee minimum living standards started in Shanghai in 1993. The central government issued the State Council's notice on establishing the minimum living standard guarantee system for urban residents in the whole of China in 1997, and in 1999, decrees of urban minimum living standard guarantee, which then became a nationwide urban relief program.
8 See *Xinhua Agency* report, 19 March 2009. Available at: www.gov.cn/jrzg/2009–03/19/content 1263218.htm (accessed 19 March 2009).
9 A detailed discussion of the argument can be found in Gordon Liu's seminar, 'Deepening reform of Medicare system, development as hard justification' (Liu, 2009).
10 See a report in *China Labour and Social Security* (a Chinese newspaper) on 23 January 2006.
11 See the speech by Premier Wen Jiabao given at a meeting held on 20 November 2006 with six university presidents, *People's Daily*, 28 November 2006.
12 Ministry of Human Resources and Social Security and National Bureau of Statistics (2009).
13 It was reported that the Ministry of Human Resources and Social Security decided to modify the 'Unemployment Insurance Decree' by adding specific clauses regarding unemployment insurance for migrant workers. See *Economic Observer*, 19 June 2009.

References

Adelmen, I. and Sunding, D. (1987) "Economic policy and income distribution in China," *Journal of Comparative Economics*, 11: 444–61.
Barr, N. (2001) *The Welfare State as Piggy Bank: Information, Risk, Uncertainty, and the Role of the State*, Oxford: Oxford University Press.

——(2003) "Preface," in *The Economics of the Welfare State*, Beijing: Press of Labor and Social Security (in Chinese).

Barr, N. and Diamond, P. (2008) "Reforming pensions: principles, analytical errors, and policy directions," *International Social Security Review*, 62: 5–19.

Bowles, S., Durlauf, S.N. and Hoff, K. (eds.) (2006) *Poverty Traps*, Princeton, NJ: Princeton University Press.

Cai, F. and Du, Y. (2009) "To achieve economic recovery with employment growth". Available at: http://blog.voc.com.cn/blog.php?do=showone&uid=337&type=blog&itemid=539446 (accessed 7 February 2009).

CDRF (China Development Research Foundation) (2009) *Reconstructing Welfare System in China*, Beijing: Press of China Development.

China Ministry of Civil Affairs (2008) *Statistical Report of China's Social Development in 2008*, available at: http://cws.mca.gov.cn/article/tjbg/200906/20090600031762.shtml, (accessed 22 May 2009).

China Statistical Abstract (2008) Beijing: Zhongguo tongji chubanshe.

China Statistical Yearbook (2008) Beijing: Zhongguo tongji chubanshe.

Deng, Q. and Li, S. (2008) "Wage structures and inequality among local and migrant workers in urban China," paper presented at the Rural–Urban Migration in China and Indonesia (RUMiCI) Workshop, Australian National University, 10–12 December 2008.

Du, P. (2009) "Exploration of the deficiency of China's medical insurance for migrant workers," *Population and Economics*, Supplement: 145–6.

Fajnzylber, P., Lederman, D. and Loayza, N. (2002a) "What causes violent crime?," *European Economic Review*, 46: 1323–57.

——(2002b) "Inequality and violent crime," *Journal of Law and Economics*, 45(1): 1–39.

Feldstein, M. (2005) "Rethinking social insurance," Working Paper 11250, National Bureau of Economic Research (NBER), Washington, DC.

Gustafsson, B., Li, S. and Sicular, T. (2008) *Income Inequality and Public Policy in China*, Cambridge: Cambridge University Press.

Jiang, L. (2009) "On the secondary issue of minimum living standard guarantee system for urban residents in China," *Journal of Shandong Institute of Business and Technology*, 23: 19–25.

Keidel, A. (2005) "The economic basis for social unrest in China," paper presented at the Third European-American Dialogue on China, the George Washington University, 26–27 May.

Knight, J., Li, S. and Deng, Q. (2010) "Education and the poverty trap in rural China: closing the trap," *Oxford Development Studies*, 38: 1–24.

Li, C. and Wang, B. (2009) "Survey on current employment of Chinese college graduates," Discussion Paper, Institute of Sociology, Chinese Academy of Social Sciences.

Li, L. (2006) "Yiliao weisheng shiye fazhan ji yiliao tizhi gaige de shikao' [Thoughts on development and reform of the medicare and sanitation system]. Available at: www.southcn.com/nflr/zhongxinzu/fdbg/200612200398.htm (accessed 20 December 2006).

Li, S. (2008) "Rural migrant workers in China: scenario, challenges and public policy," Working Paper no. 89, International Labor Office (ILO), Policy Integration and Statistics Department, Geneva.

Li, S. and Yang, S. (2009) "Impact of *Di Bao* Programme on inequality and poverty in urban China," *Chinese Journal of Population Science*, 5: 19–27.

Lin, X. (2006) "Feasibility study on constructing the system of ensuring a minimum standard of living for rural labor migrants," *Population and Economics*, 1: 75–9.

Liu, G. (2009) "Deepening reform of Medicare system, development as hard justification," seminar paper delivered at the Unirule Institute of Economics, Beijing, 22 June 2009.

Liu, X., Liu, B. and Liao, X. (2009) "Ponder over the establishment of minimum livelihood guarantee system for college students," *Education Research Monthly*, 1: 88–9.

Lu, N. and Zhang, Y. (2007) "Changes in the role of government in higher education under globalization," *Peking University Education Review*, 5: 138–49.

Lum, T. (2006) *Social Unrest in China*, a report to Congress, 8 May 2006. Available at: www.fas.org/sgp/crs/row/RL33416.pdf (accessed 8 February 2009).

Luo, W. (2008) "Preliminary exploration on the employment flexibility in urban area," *Health Economics Research*, 3: 31–3.

MACOS (2009) *Report of Employment of College Graduates in China 2009*, Beijing: China Social Sciences Literature Press.

Ministry of Human Resources and Social Security and National Bureau of Statistics (2009) *Statistical Report of Human Resources and Social Security Development in China in 2008*. Available at: www.stats.gov.cn/tjgb/ndtjgb/qgndtjgb/t20090226_402540710.htm (accessed 26 February 2009).

Peng, J. (2009) "China may face social unrest as unemployment rises, report says," *Bloomberg*, 6 January 2009. Available at: www.bloomberg.com/apps/news?pid=20601080&sid=aG8JAH3FwkmY&refer=asia (accessed 6 January 2009).

Ren, Y. (2009) "Higher education reform in the 'educational revolution'," *Journal of Higher Education in Sciences and Technology*, 28: 71–3.

Riskin, C., Zhao, R. and Li, S. (2001) *China's Retreat from Equality: Income Distribution and Economic Transition*, New York: M.E. Sharpe.

Ru, X., Lu, X. and Li, P. (eds.) (2005) *Shehui lanpishu 2005 nian: Zhongguo shehui xingshi fenxi yu yuce* [Blue Book of China's Society in 2010: An Analysis and Forecast of the Chinese Social Situation], Beijing: Shehui kexue wenxian chubanshe.

Ruan, L. and Hu, Y. (2009) "Reconstructing the role of universities in higher education reform: defining relationship among government, market and university," *Heilongjiang Researches on Higher Education*, 183: 5–8.

Song, Q. and Guo, X. (2008) "Improve the minimum subsistence guarantee system for urban residents," *China State Finance*, 15: 36–7.

Wang, L. (2009) "Studies on some issues in reform of high education," *World Education Information*, 10: 48–50.

Whalley, J. and Yue, X. (2009) "Rural income volatility and inequality in China," *CESifo Economic Studies*, 55: 648–68.

World Bank (2009a) *From Poor Areas to Poor People: China's Evolving Poverty Reduction Agenda: An Assessment of Poverty and Inequality in China*, Washington, DC: World Bank.

——(2009b) *Skills Development in Guangdong Province: Reducing Inequality for Shared Growth in Guangdong Province*, Policy Note, no. 8, Washington, DC: World Bank.

Xu, Y. and Zhang, X. (2009) "Investigation on questions about social security system in rural and urban China," *Dong Yue Tribune*, 30: 32–7.

Yang, F. (2009) "How to establish a modern system for Chinese universities?," an interview report by Ma, G., *Economic Observation*, 22 May.

You, C. (2009), "The solution and problems on migrant workers' medical insurance," *Shanghai Insurance*, 1: 15–18.

Zhang, D., Liu, H. and Wang, X. (eds.) (2008) *Annual Report of Household Income Distribution in China*, Beijing: Economic Science Press.

Zhao, H. (2008) "The situation of rural lowest-level life security system and its problems," *Journal of Zhejiang Provincial Party School*, 5: 54–9.

Zhao, R., Lai, D. and Wei, Z. (eds.) (2006) *Economic Transition and Reform of Social Security in China*, Beijing: Beijing Normal University Press.

Zheng, G. (2008) *Zhongguo Shehui Baozhang 30 Nian* [Social Security in China in the Last Three Decades], Beijing: The People's Press.

Zhu, Q. (2009) "The essence of universities is to pursue excellence rather than power," an interview report by Ma, G., *Economic Observation*, 29 December.

4 China's fiscal expenditure on social security since 1978

Yanzhong Wang and Yuqi Long

Social security, a primary aspect and principal part of modern government fiscal and public expenditure, plays an important role in ameliorating poverty, improving social well-being and safeguarding social stability, equality and justice. Due to the fact that different countires are at varying stages or modes of development, the total amount, structure, scope, focus and working mechanism of social security expenditure differ across countries.

The concept of social security varies worldwide. In European welfare states, social security refers to social protection or social expenditure, while in the United States social security means all types of poverty alleviation pro-grammes and security expenditure directly covered by government finance. In China, social security is viewed as a broad concept covering social assistance, social insurance and social welfare. This chapter breaks down the scope of social security expenditures in China into three grades. The narrow grade (Grade 1) is used in the current government fiscal social security expenditures, including expenditures on pensions and social welfare, expenditures on relief, retiree expenditures of administration and public institutions and social security subsidy expenditures. Grade 2 is Grade 1 combined with social insurance fund expenditures. Grade 3 is Grade 2 combined with government fiscal expenditures on education and health.

China's social security system has undergone major changes since the late 1970s. In the 1980s, social security provided for employees in state-owned enterprises, and government organs and public institutions constituted the principal part of the social security system. Government finance offered only subsistence security to the absolute poor in the strict sense and provided limited social welfare to beneficiaries of preferential policy. In 1992, the expenditure on the social pension fund, welfare and assistance totaled 6.6 billion *yuan*, which was 1.78 percent of the entire fiscal expenditure and 0.25 percent of the GDP.[1]

From the 1990s to the beginning of the 2000s when the focus was on the establishment of the socialist market economy and pilot reform, China gra-dually set up the framework of a modern social security system, including the minimum subsistence security system and social insurance system comprising basic old-age insurance for urban workers, basic medical insurance, unem-ployment insurance, work injury insurance and maternity insurance. Despite the fact that the insurance payment mechanism and shared multiparty responsibility were introduced in the social insurance system, the amount and share of government fiscal expenditure on social security have been constantly expanding due to the continuous expansion in social security coverage and the rise of social security benefit levels. In 2002, the Chinese government's fiscal expenditure on social pensions, welfare and assistance reached 37.3 billion *yuan*. Together with the pensions for retirees of the administrative entities and public institutions and the expenditure on different types of social security allowance, the total fiscal expenditure on social security in China hit 263.6 billion *yuan*, which was 10.95 percent of the entire fiscal expenditure in the same year. Meanwhile, 347.2 billion *yuan* was financed by the growing social insurance fund (the revenue of the social insurance fund in 2002 totaled 404.87 billion *yuan*), which became the main source of the social security expenditure.

The 16th Communist Party of China (CPC) National Congress convened in 2002. The new leadership, Secretary-General Hu Jintao and Premier Wen Jiabao in particular, attached greater importance to improving people's livelihoods, introduced the *Scientific Outlook on Development* and proposed building a harmonious society. During the first half of 2003, the outbreak of SARS accentuated the problem of China's unbalanced development favoring economic over social, urban over rural, and coastal regions over inland regions. It can be regarded as a turning point in the construction of the Chinese social security system.

Starting from the second half of 2003, the new rural cooperative medical system was introduced on a trial basis across China and covered almost 90 percent of the rural residents by 2008. In 2007, the State Council put forward the system of basic medical insurance for urban residents, and after three years of development, over half of the residents in all the towns and cities were covered. A minimum livelihood protection system for rural residents was also set up in some regions and it covered the entire countryside by the end of 2007. The State Council also introduced the new rural social old-age insurance system in 2008 and launched pilot projects in over 300 counties across the country in 2009. At the same time, fiscal expenditure continued to expand correspondingly. By the end of 2008, China's fiscal expenditure on social pensions, welfare and assistance reached 680.4 billion *yuan*, which was 10.96 percent of the total fiscal expenditure in the same year. Even though the proportion is similar to that in 2002, the absolute amount is much larger, indicating that the revenue and expenditure of the social insurance fund have been growing at an even faster rate. In 2009, the expenditure of five social insurance funds reached 992.5 billion *yuan*.

While developing social insurance and expanding fiscal expenditure on social security, the government is also attaching greater emphasis to the development of education, public health, and so on. Funding for the nine-year compulsory education policy has been regularized as part of public finance. The "National Outline for Long and Medium-term Educational Reform and Development (Draft for Comment)" promulgated in 2010 proposed a larger apportionment for public finance for education. To address the deep-seated woes of "difficult and expensive access to healthcare," it was decided to initiate a new round of reform on medical and healthcare service systems in 2009, aimed at increasing government spending in this area by 850 billion *yuan* within three years.

Rapid urbanization, growing demand for better housing and soaring housing prices have caused the housing problem to loom large in China today. To arrest this problem, and as a means of offsetting the effects of the global financial crisis, the construction of low-rental housing and the reconstruction of dilapidated buildings in urban and rural areas have become a primary part of the programme supported by the government. In 2008, it was decided to invest 900 billion *yuan*, part of which came from public finance, in the construction of low-income housing. The central government provided a special subsidy of 55.1 billion *yuan* to build low-rental housing in 2009 and pledged to increase this to 63.2 billion *yuan* in 2010. Similar to education and public health, housing security has, in a broad sense, become a salient part of social security in China. In 2008, the central government spent 1.2 trillion *yuan* on education and public health.

With the gradual development of the social security system, investment in social security has been constantly expanding. The government has recognized its role in providing social security to its citizens. Supported by rapidly growing government revenues, the government—particularly the central government—is willing to increase spending on social security in both the narrow and broad senses. As a result, not only the total expenditure, but also the share of social security in total fiscal expenditure has been rising.

The rise of fiscal expenditure on social security

Since China's reform and opening-up in the late 1970s, the fiscal expenditure on social security has been growing rapidly. In terms of absolute quantities, expenditures on pension and social welfare, expenditures on relief, retiree expenditures for administrative and public institutions and social security subsidy expenditures (narrow social security expenditure) increased 401.3 times from 1.9 billion *yuan* in 1978 to 760.7 billion *yuan* in 2009 (Grade 1). Based on the narrow social security expenditure, combined with social insurance fund expenditures, the expenditure scale has also grown dramatically (Grade 2), increasing 7.2 times from 221.1 billion *yuan* in 1998 to 1.8 trillion *yuan* in 2009. If it is premised that equal access to public services is fundamental to building a socialist harmonious society, social security expenditure should include both financial security and basic public services, including education and health. For Grade 3, the total expenditure scale has been considerable, from 452.7 billion *yuan* in 1998 to 3.3 trillion *yuan* in 2009.[2]

The proportion of total fiscal expenditure as a share of total social security fiscal expenditure for Grade 1 increased from 1.65 percent in 1978 to 9.97 percent in 2009; for Grade 2 from 17.81 percent in 1998 to 20.88 percent in 2009; and for Grade 3 from 11.53 percent in 1978 to 37.51 percent in 2009

Table 4.1 Chinese government social security expenditure (billion) (%)

Year	Grade 1	Grade 2	Grade 3	Proportion of total fiscal expenditure			Proportion of GDP		
				Grade 1	Grade 2	Grade 3	Grade 1	Grade 2	Grade 3
1978	18.91	–	129.40	1.65	–	11.53	0.52	–	3.55
1986	35.58	–	432.53	1.61	–	19.62	0.35	–	4.21
1992	66.45	–	916.77	1.78	–	24.50	0.25	–	3.41
1994	95.14	–	1456.20	1.64	–	25.14	0.20	–	3.02
1996	128.03	–	2005.35	1.61	–	25.26	0.18	–	2.82
1998	595.63	2210.98	4527.34	5.52	17.81	36.47	0.71	2.62	5.36
2000	1517.57	3604.52	6493.56	9.55	20.05	36.13	1.53	3.63	6.54
2002	2636.22	5590.43	9604.93	11.95	22.36	38.41	2.19	4.65	7.98
2004	3116.08	7223.71	12368.39	10.94	22.16	37.95	1.95	4.52	7.74
2006	4361.78	9950.23.	16898.14	10.79	21.63	36.73	2.06	5.18	7.97
2008	6804.29	15098.51	26865.76	10.87	21.30	37.90	2.26	5.02	8.94
2009	7606.68	18132.95	32564.68	9.97	20.88	37.51	2.23	5.33	9.56

Note: See text for explanation of grades.
Sources: Calculated from *China Fiscal Statistics Yearbook*, *China Statistical Yearbook* and *Chinese Health Statistics Yearbook* (various years).

(see Table 4.1). The grades' expenditure increased the most in 1998, mainly due to increased social insurance funds expenditure focus on state-owned enterprise reform. The figures for proportion of GDP in social security expenditure are quite different: Grade 1 increased from 0.52 percent in 1978 to 2.23 percent in 2009; Grade 2 increased from 2.62 percent in 1998 to 5.33 percent in 2009; and Grade 3 increased from 3.55 percent to 9.56 percent.

Since the late 1970s China's social security expenditure has reflected, to some extent, the significant features of the various development stages. In the early stage, the absolute value of social security expenditure and the proportion of total fiscal expenditures were relatively low. With the deepening of the reforms and opening-up and acceleration of economic and social development, social security expenditures increased year by year. In the first decade of the twenty-first century, China has paid more attention to the development of people's livelihoods, the social security system framework has been established and been gradually improved and the scale of social security expenditure has been widened. As GDP growth and fiscal revenue growth are both very high, the share of social security expenditure is relatively stable, but the demand for social security, especially in education, health and housing continues to grow exponentially.

Expansion of the balance of the social insurance fund

The social insurance fund constitutes a major source of funding for social security. The social insurance fund is not considered in the analysis above because it has not been included as an item in fiscal budget management. In fact, with the deepening reform of state-owned enterprises and the development of the socialist market economy, the traditional security system in workplace units has been transformed into the social security system.

The current social insurance system in China is comprised of two categories. The first category includes old-age insurance, medical insurance, unemployment insurance, work injury insurance and maternity insurance for employees working in the formal sector in towns and cities. The second category includes the new rural cooperative medical system (NRCMS), the basic medical insurance system for urban residents and the new rural old-age insurance system (NROIS), which, being carried out as pilot projects, provides protection for urban and rural residents and employees in the informal sector. The basic old-age insurance system for urban residents is under consideration. Different from social assistance (supported by government fiscal revenues), healthcare and education, the social insurance system involves tripartite relations among the employer, employee and the government. However, the three parties play different roles in each programme. For employee old-age insurance, medical insurance and unemployment funds, the majority portion of the premium is paid by employers while employees pay roughly one-third of the premium, and the government gives a subsidy to make up the gap. For employee work injury insurance and maternity insurance, employers bear the primary responsibility of footing the premium, whereas employees and the government hardly contribute. Due to a lack of undertakings from employers for old-age insurance and medical insurance for urban and rural residents, the government provides the majority of financial support so that employees and families who participate in the insurance programmes need only pay a small amount of the premium.

From the establishment of the social insurance system in the 1990s to the current process of implementing basic old-age insurance for urban and rural residents and basic medical insurance, the coverage of social insurance in China has been gradually expanding (see Table 4.2). Meanwhile, the rapid development of the Chinese economy and rising wage and income levels have contributed to a growing balance of the social insurance fund (see Table 4.3).

According to Table 4.3, the balance of social insurance funds and the five social insurance funds for employees in particular, has been growing rapidly. The total revenue of the five insurance funds reached 100 billion *yuan* in 1995, exceeded 1 trillion *yuan* in 1997 and hit 1.6 trillion *yuan* in 2009.

The structure and characteristics of fiscal expenditure on social security in China

The fiscal expenditure pattern of social security has varied considerably over the past three decades. In the beginning of the reform and opening-up programme, fiscal expenditure on social security and its share in the overall fiscal expenditure were relatively low. With deepening reform and rapid economic growth, fiscal expenditure on social security has been growing. Particularly in the 2000s, under the guidelines of the Scientific Outlook on Development, the Chinese government attached great importance to the development of social welfare and maintaining a harmonious society. The framework for a social

Table 4.2 Number of participants in China's social insurance programmes (10,000)

Year	Basic old-age insurance	Basic worker medical insurance	Unemploy-ment insurance	Injury insurance	Maternity insurance	Cooperative medical insurance	Urban citizen medical insurance	Rural old-age insurance
1989	5710.3	–	–	–	–	–	–	–
1995	10979.0	745.9	8238.0	2614.8	1500.2	–	–	–
1998	11203.1	1878.7	7927.9	3781.3	2776.7	–	–	–
2000	13617.4	3786.9	10326.3	4350.3	3001.6	–	–	–
2001	14182.5	7285.9	10354.6	4345.3	3455.1	–	–	–
2002	14736.6	9401.2	10181.6	4405.6	3488.2	–	–	–
2003	15506.7	10901.7	10372.4	4574.8	3655.4	–	–	–
2004	16352.9	12403.6	10583.9	6845.2	4383.8	8000	–	–
2005	17487.9	13782.9	10647.7	8477.8	5408.5	17900	–	–
2006	18766.3	15731.8	11186.6	10268.5	6458.9	41000	–	–
2007	20136.9	18020.3	11644.6	12173.4	7775.3	72600	4291.1	5171
2008	20136.9	19995.6	12399.8	13787.2	9254.1	81500	11826.0	5595
2009	23550.0	21937.0	12715.0	14896.0	10876.0	83300	18210.0	8691

Source: The 1989–2008 data are from *China Labour Statistical Yearbook 2009*. The new rural cooperative medical data is collated from *China Health Statistics Yearbook 2009*. The new rural social pension insurance, labour and social security data is compiled from *Statistics Bulletin*, various years. The 2009 data is obtained from the related *Statistical Bulletin* of 2009.

Table 4.3 Revenues, expenditures and balance of China's workers social insurance fund (billion yuan)

Insurance	Elements	1989	1995	1998	2000	2002	2004	2006	2008	2009
Old-age insurance	Revenues	14.67	95.01	145.90	227.85	317.15	425.84	630.98	974.02	1149.10
	Expenditures	11.88	84.76	151.16	2115.5	284.29	350.21	489.67	738.96	889.40
	Cumulative savings	6.80	42.98	58.78	94.71	160.80	297.50	548.89	993.10	1252.60
Medical insurance	Revenues	–	0.97	6.06	17.00	60.78	114.05	174.71	288.55	367.20
	Expenditures	–	0.73	5.33	12.45	40.94	86.22	127.67	201.97	279.70
	Cumulative savings	–	0.31	2.00	10.98	45.07	95.79	175.24	330.36	427.60
Unemployment Insurance	Revenues	0.68	3.53	7.26	16.04	21.56	29.10	40.24	58.51	58.00
	Expenditures	0.20	1.89	5.61	12.34	18.66	21.10	19.80	25.35	36.70
	Cumulative savings	1.36	6.84	13.34	19.59	25.38	38.60	72.48	131.01	152.40
Injury insurance	Revenues	–	0.81	2.12	2.48	3.20	5.83	12.18	21.67	24.00
	Expenditures	–	0.18	0.90	1.38	1.99	3.33	6.85	12.69	15.60
	Cumulative savings	–	1.27	3.95	5.79	8.11	11.86	19.29	33.50	40.40
Maternity insurance	Revenues	–	0.29	0.98	1.12	2.18	3.21	6.21	11.37	13.20
	Expenditures	–	0.16	0.68	0.83	1.28	1.88	3.75	7.15	8.80
	Cumulative savings	–	0.27	1.03	1.68	2.97	5.59	9.69	16.82	21.20

Source: The 1989–2007 data are collated from *China Fiscal Statistics Yearbook 2008*. The 2008 data are from *China Labor Statistical Yearbook 2009*. The 2009 data are compiled from the *2009 Human Resources and Social Security Statistics Bulletin*.

security system has thus taken shape, and social security is one of the priority areas featuring higher fiscal expenditure growth.

The expenditure on social security rose faster than the increases in investment on education and public health

In terms of fiscal expenditure, the investment on social security in the narrow sense is relatively small compared to that on education and public health sectors, which have been the foci of government fiscal expenditure. In 1994, government spending on education and public health accounted for 23.5 percent of total fiscal expenditure. The government later continued to increase spending on education and public health, but its priority shifted to other sectors. As a result, the share of education and public education in total fiscal expenditure decreased, and stabilized at 18–19 percent since 2000. In fact, since 2000, the social security system in the narrow sense has been a priority growth area. Its share in total government spending has therefore been increasing (see Table 4.4). In 2006, social welfare expenses, the pension fund for retirees in administrative and public institutions and the fiscal allowance for social security accounted for 10.5 percent of the total fiscal expenditure. In particular, the fiscal allowance for social security reached as high as 5.3 percent. The allowance from public finance channeled to the social insurance fund increased 79.8 times from 2.2 billion *yuan* in 1998 to 177.7 billion *yuan* in 2009 (see Figure 4.1). The fiscal allowance for the social insurance fund between 1998 and 2009 totaled 851.3 billion *yuan*. This change took place as China was shifting from the traditional work unit-based security system to the social insurance system.

Table 4.4 Composition of fiscal expenditure on social security (billion yuan)

Year	Education		Health		Social welfare/ social assistance		Retirement expenditure of administrative unit		Social security subsidy	
	Amount	% of fiscal expenditure	Amount	% of fiscal expenditure	Amount	% of fiscal expenditure	Amount	% of fiscal expenditure	Amount	% of fiscal expenditure
1978	7.51	6.69	3.54	3.16	1.89	1.69	–	–	–	–
1982	13.76	11.19	6.90	5.61	2.14	1.74	–	–	–	–
1986	27.47	12.46	12.22	5.54	3.56	1.61	–	–	–	–
1990	46.24	15.00	18.73	6.07	5.50	1.78	–	–	–	–
1994	101.88	17.59	34.23	5.91	9.51	1.64	–	–	–	–
1998	172.63	15.99	59.01	5.46	17.13	1.59	27.44	2.54	15.00	1.39
2000	217.95	13.72	70.95	4.47	21.30	1.34	47.86	3.01	82.60	5.20
2002	310.60	14.08	90.85	4.12	37.30	1.69	78.88	3.58	147.44	6.69
2004	385.11	13.52	129.36	4.54	56.35	1.98	102.81	3.61	152..5	5.35
2006	516.91	12.79	177.89	4.40	90.78	2.25	133.02	3.29	212.39	5.25
2008	901.02	14.39	275.70	4.40	–	–	–	–	–	–

Note: Due to item adjustments of revenue and expenditure, expenditure on social security and employment expenditure for 2007/2008 includes special care and social welfare expenditures, retirement expenditures of administrative units and social security subsidies.

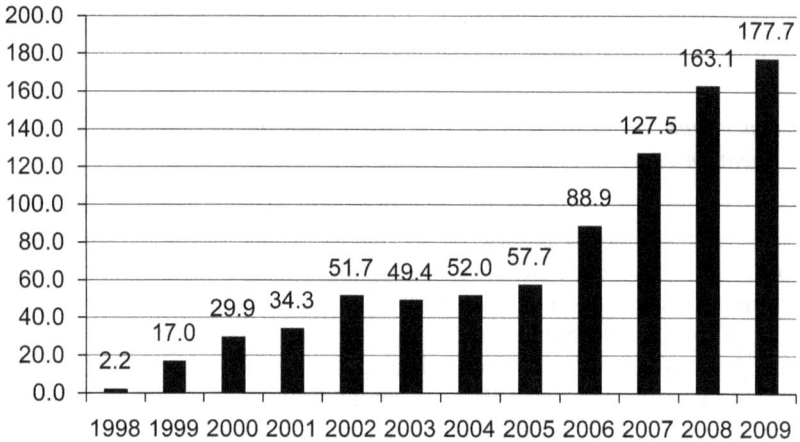

Figure 4.1 Fiscal allowance for social insurance (billion *yuan*)
Source: China Statistical Yearbook, various years.

The growth of fiscal expenditure on social security in China promotes the social insurance system's transition from a pay-as-you-go system to a partially accumulated system

At the beginning of the reform and opening-up programme, China's social security system featured pay-as-you-go. In the process of establishing a modern social security system, the government decided to shift to a system that features a combination of a social pooling account and an individual account. The social pooling account adopts the pay-as-you-go system, which, in essence, plays the role of mutual assistance and relief. The individual account is accumulated by personal contributions as well as government subsidies to social insurance to ensure the smooth implementation of the new system. By the end of 2008, the balance of the national social insurance fund amounted to 1.5 trillion *yuan* (Table 4.5). In addition, the individual account system (e.g., enterprise annuities, housing provident fund, etc.) and family account (e.g., new rural cooperative medical system, and new rural old-age insurance system) were also introduced to the social insurance system, making it a partially accumulated system.

The transition to the new system was unfavorable to "middle-aged people" (who entered the workforce before 1997 and are still working) and "old-aged people" (who had already retired before 1997). To deal with this problem and also meet the needs of the ageing population, the National Council for the Social Security Fund (NCSSF)—which is responsible for the management of the social security fund allocated by national finance and collected from other sources as well as some of the social insurance accumulated fund—was established in 2000. The NCSSF reported that from 2000 to 2009, the net allocated funds from public finance to the national social security fund totaled 380.3 billion *yuan* (Figure 4.2). Management of the social security

Table 4.5 Cumulative savings of the national social insurance fund, 1989–2008 (billion yuan)

Year	Five social insurance funds	National social security fund	Accumulated contributions on housing fund	Enterprise Annuity	New cooperative Fund	Rural old-age insurance fund
1989	8.16	–	–	–	–	–
1990	11.73	–	–	–	–	–
1995	51.68	–	–	–	–	–
1998	79.11	–	–	–	–	–
1999	100.98	–	–	–	–	–
2000	132.75	–	241.92	–	–	–
2001	162.28	80.51	332.62	–	–	–
2002	242.34	124.19	413.06	–	–	–
2003	331.38	132.50	556.27	–	–	–
2004	449.34	171.14	740.03	–	1.12	28.50
2005	607.37	211.79	975.94	–	1.36	31.00
2006	825.59	282.77	1268.74	91.00	5.78	35.40
2007	1123.66	439.69	1623.03	151.90	8.14	41.20
2008	1517.60	562.37	2069.98	191.10	12.23	49.90
2009	1572.10	776.62	2609.12	253.30	18.51	68.10

Source: The data on the five social insurance funds, including the urban basic old-age insurance, basic medical insurance, unemployment insurance, industrial injury insurance and maternity insurance were obtained from the State Council Development Research Center. The data on the National Social Security Fund were collated from the *National Social Security Fund Council Annual Report*, various years. The housing fund data were provided by the Ministry of Housing and Urban-Rural Development. The enterprise annuities and rural social old-age insurance data were obtained from the previous issues of the *Labour Statistics Bulletin*. The new rural cooperative medical data was obtained from the *2010 China's Social Security Green Paper*, with 2009 data ending in September.

fund and investment has become an important and challenging task in the development of the social security system.

The increasing fiscal spending on social security helps expand the coverage of the minimum livelihood protection system

China's rapid economic growth has substantially raised the income levels of both urban and rural residents. As an indicator of the improving living standards, the Engel's coefficient for urban and rural households decreased dramatically. In 2008, the Engel's coefficient of rural households was 43.7 percent, down from 67.7 percent in 1978. In 2000, the Engel's coefficient for urban households dropped to below 40 percent and that of rural households decreased to below 50 percent.[3] The absolute poverty headcount rate also dwindled, from 30.7 percent in 1978 to 4.2 percent in 2008 (see Figure 4.3).

However, a large number of people are still trapped in poverty. For decades, China has offered only minimal guarantees to extremely impoverished people

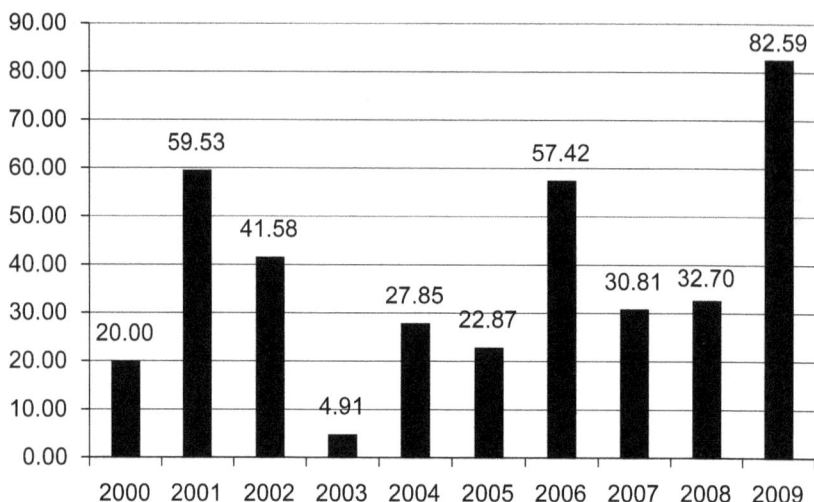

Figure 4.2 Net fiscal appropriation to national social security fund (billion yuan)
Source: National Social Security Fund Council. Available at: www.ssf.gov.cn/zjcj/dzqk/201005/t20100510_2685.html (accessed 28 June 2010).

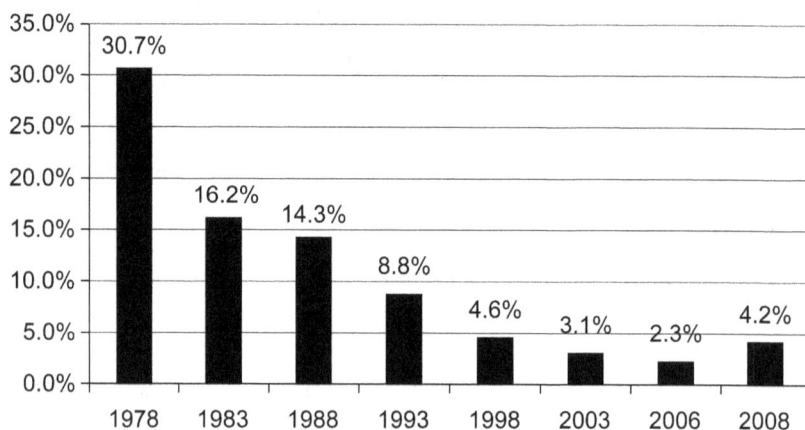

Figure 4.3 Incidence of rural absolute poverty in China (%)
Source: Database of the Development Research Center of the State Council.

(the "five guarantees" are: proper food, clothing, medical care, housing and funeral expenses). Following the reform of state-owned enterprises, a large number of laid-off workers, whose problems cannot be solved by the traditional social assistance system, became the new disadvantaged group. In the mid-1990s, the minimum livelihood protection system for this disadvantaged group was first set up in Shanghai. From the late 1990s, the government carried out the policy of "realizing universal coverage for eligible residents," expanding the system

Table 4.6 Minimum subsistence security and fiscal expenditure

Year	Urban minimum livelihood protection		Rural minimum livelihood protection	
	Number of beneficiaries (1,000)	Fiscal expenditure (billion yuan)	Number of beneficiaries (10,000)	Fiscal expenditure (billion yuan)
2000	4,026	2.72	3,002	–
2002	20,647	10.87	4,078	–
2004	22,050	17.27	4,880	–
2006	22,401	22.42	15,931	–
2008	23,348	39.34	43,055	22.87
2009	23,456	48.21	47,600	36.30

Source: *China Civil Affairs Development Statistical Bulletin* (2000–09).

nationwide to rural China by 2007. In 2009, 23.5 million urban residents and 47.6 million rural residents benefitted from the minimum livelihood protection programme (see Table 4.6). This programme has become the most important line of defense against absolute poverty in China. Another line of defense, which offers a higher level of benefits than the minimum livelihood protection programme, is unemployment insurance. The rapid increase in fiscal expenditure on social security facilitates the operation of the unemployment insurance system, allowing it to play the role of "stabilizer" and "safety network" during the critical period of state-owned enterprise reform, which accelerated since the mid-1990s.

Problems of fiscal expenditure on social security in China

Total fiscal spending on social security remains inadequate

Despite the fact that total fiscal expenditure has been increasing rapidly, it remains inadequate to meet the social security needs of urban and rural residents. As a percentage of GDP, China's expenditure on social security is extremely low by international standards. In 2002, the Chinese government spent about 2.2 percent of GDP on social security in the narrow sense, and 5.5 percent, if education and public health are included, far lower than the countries listed in Table 4.7.

The expected function of reducing income inequality has not been fully realized

The main purpose of the social security system is to promote social equity and justice. It is expected to play an equalizing role when it comes to income distribution. However, this function has not been fully realized in China, as evidenced by the widening income gap between the haves and have-nots, and the growing disparity between the coastal provinces and inland provinces and between urban and rural areas. From 1981 to 2009, the net income of rural residents increased 22.1 times, while that of urban residents increased 36.1 times. Instead of playing an equalizing role, some social security programmes

Table 4.7 Social security expenditure of some OECD countries, 1960–2001 (% of GDP)

Country	1960	1980	1985	1990	1995	1998	2001
Canada	–	14.3	17.4	18.6	19.6	18.4	17.8
France	13.4	21.1	26.6	26.6	29.2	29	28.5
Germany	20.5	23	23.6	22.8	27.5	27.4	27.4
Japan	5.8	10.2	11	11.2	13.5	14.5	16.9
Mexico	–	–	1.8	3.8	8.1	8.8	11.8
Sweden	12.8	28.8	30	30.8	33	30.4	28.9
Turkey	–	4.3	4.2	7.6	7.5	11.1	–
United Kingdom	13.9	17.9	21.1	19.5	23.0	21.5	21.8
United States	10.3	13.3	13.0	13.4	15.5	14.5	14.8

Source: Ministry of Finance of Social Security Research Group (2007: 36–4). Data for Japan are based on OECD data in 1970 instead of 1960. The per capita GDP of the United Kingdom, Sweden, the United States, France and Germany in 1960 was US $1,363, US$1,641, US$2,783, US$1,297, US$1,345, respectively. China's per capita GDP in 2004 was US$1,532.

have actually increased income disparity. The old-age insurance programme is a case in point. In 1990, the ratio of monthly pension per capita between urban enterprise retirees, public institution retirees and retired civil servants was 1:1.06:1.10. However, in 2005, it changed to 1:1.89:2.06 (see Table 4.8).

The structure of fiscal expenditure on social security needs to improve

Another problem is that, to some extent, the structure of fiscal expenditure is biased in favor of the privileged. It therefore needs readjustment and optimization. A large portion of fiscal expenditure goes to subsidizing the social insurance fund and the national social security fund. On one hand, due to the biased structure of the social insurance system structure, the high-income groups enjoy more benefits from the social insurance subsidy than low-income groups. This results in "robbing the poor to benefit the rich" and exacerbates the already large and still growing income disparity. On the other hand, the accumulated

Table 4.8 Average monthly pension for different types of pensioner (yuan)

Year	Urban enterprise retirees (A)	Public institution retirees (B)	Retired civil servants (C)	A:B:C
1990	134	148	143	1:1.06:1.10
1995	321	422	435	1:1.35:1.32
1997	402	549	548	1:1.37:1.37
1999	481	702	707	1:1.46:1.47
2001	531	921	964	1:1.73:1.82
2003	644	1,151	1,121	1:1.79:1.90
2005	714	1,346	1,469	1:1.89:2.06

Sources: The *Labour Statistical Yearbook*, 1990–2006; and Yang (2008: 9–12).

large amount of funds does not perform its due function and its management and investment have become big problems. Areas in dire need of government financial support are healthcare and public health. In recent years, the share of public health expenditure in total government budget expenditure has been declining year-on-year. In 2008, fiscal spending on healthcare and public health accounted for only 4.4 percent of the total fiscal expenditure. Education is another area that should receive greater government support. Its share in total fiscal expenditure was more stable than that of public health, but has also declined in some years. Low-rental housing, which is a kind of pro-poor invest- ment, is also inadequate in meeting the needs of low- and medium-income groups, despite the fact that government spending increased from 4 billion *yuan* in 2006 to 72.6 billion *yuan* in 2009. At the same time, the huge amount in the housing provident fund has yet to perform its function to safeguard housing security against the backdrop of soaring housing prices in the cities.

The responsibility of central and local governments in financing social security needs realignment and readjustment

The inconsistency between the revenue structure and the expenditure struc- ture has created many problems for financing social security in China. The revenue structure is skewed in favor of the central government since the 1994 tax reform, as the share of central government in total government revenue keeps rising. However, the expenditure structure features the opposite pattern, as local governments are primarily responsible for funding and providing various social services, including social security. For example, the central government accounted for 40.3 percent of fiscal expenditure on social security in 2008, 30 percent of expenditure on healthcare and public health and 17.8

Table 4.9 Share of central and local government in fiscal expenditure and revenue in 2008 (%)

Expenditure	Level of government	Share (%)
Social security and employment	Central	40.3
	Local	59.7
Health	Central	30.0
	Local	70.0
Education	Central	17.8
	Local	82.8
Total fiscal expenditure	Central	53.3
	Local	46.7
Total fiscal revenue	Central	21.3
	Local	78.7

Source: The authors' calculations are based on the 2008 fiscal revenue and expendi- ture accounts. The total fiscal revenue and expenditure data are obtained from the *ChinaNational Statistical Yearbook 2009.*

percent of expenditure on education. In contrast, the central government accounted for 53.3 percent of the total government revenue, while 46.7 percent went to local governments (see Table 4.9). Without the adequate financial transfer from the central government, local governments in poor areas have faced enormous difficulties in developing their social security systems, in terms of expanding the coverage rate and raising the benefit levels.

Recommendations for strengthening and improving fiscal expenditure on China's social security

To further increase fiscal spending on social security and improve the coverage rate and benefit levels of social security

In order to create a universal social security system covering urban and rural residents, the government should further increase spending on social security and establish a mechanism to keep the growth of social security expenditure in line with economic growth. In this process, the coverage rate and the benefit levels of social security should be further increased. Currently, China's social security system is biased, favoring urban residents in the formal sector either in terms of the coverage rate or benefit levels. Although China has pledged to establish a universal social security system, which is expected to be basically in shape by 2012, challenges abound to include rural residents, urban workers in the informal sector, the non-working urban population and especially rural migrant workers who are mobile and do not have urban household registration. The new social security system, which aims to reach "full coverage," is in need of investment funding estimated to be up to 2.6 trillion *yuan*. By 2020, with fiscal spending of 5.74 trillion *yuan*, "full coverage" is expected to be realized and fiscal expenditure on social security is expected to reach 9 percent of GDP (He *et al.*, 2009). To this end, the government must substantially readjust its expenditure structure to contribute towards social security.

To optimize the fiscal expenditure structure on social security and enhance the performance of fiscal expenditure on social security

The current social security expenditure consists mainly of pensions, healthcare, education, housing and minimum livelihood protection. There is a need to improve the expenditure structure. Apart from raising the benefit levels for citizens under the programme of minimum livelihood protection, China should aim to reduce the demand for minimum livelihood protection through sustained economic development and effective poverty reduction programmes. Increasing fiscal expenditure on medical care and public health should be of high priority. In the short term, government spending on healthcare and public health should be increased to 6 percent of total fiscal expenditure, and gradually to 8–10 percent by 2020. In education, government spending should be raised to 4 percent of the GDP by 2012, and above 5 percent of the GDP and 20 percent of the total fiscal expenditure by 2020. With regard to the housing security, given the huge demand for low-rental housing among low-income groups, larger fiscal inputs are urgently needed (Zhu, 2008). It is expected that government spending on housing security will reach 260 billion *yuan* by 2012 and 700 billion *yuan* by 2020. Taking the rapidly ageing population into account, fiscal expenditure on old-age security is expected to reach 800 billion *yuan* by 2012 and hit 1.4 trillion *yuan* by 2020 (He *et al.*, 2009). Priority should be given to the elderly who are not covered by any pension programmes. In the process of adjusting the fiscal expenditure structure on social security, China should devote greater effort to ensuring efficiency and fair distribution of fiscal expenditure. One way to achieve this is to establish a performance evaluation system to monitor and enhance the performance level of fiscal expenditure on social security (Lin, 2007).

To improve the shared responsibility mechanism among all levels of governments

China needs to clearly define the responsibility of different levels of government in financing social security. The current expenditure structure is misaligned. The central government finances about 30 percent of the expenditure on social security although it receives more than half of the total government revenue (Kou and Zhou, 2007). To realign the revenue and expenditure structure, the central government should play a larger role in financing social security. Financial transfers from the central government to poor areas can be a major mechanism for balancing the expenditure responsibility of different levels of government and reducing the regional disparities in social security expenditures.

To improve the adjustment mechanism of income distribution of fiscal expenditure on social security

The large and widening income inequality has become a social and political concern in China. So far China's social security system has not played an equalizing role in this regard. One important reason for this is that China's social security system is fragmented and biased in a way that favors the privileged—the urban employees in the formal sector, particularly those working for the government—who receive more benefits. Another reason is that historically, rural residents have been excluded from the urban-based social security system. Although attempts have been made to establish separate social security programmes for rural residents, the coverage remains an issue, particularly for rural migrant workers, and the benefit levels are substantially lower than those for the urban residents. To have a more equitable social security system, the government should play a larger role in equalizing the social pooling account to partially offset the bias built into the individual account. Greater efforts should be made to include rural residents and rural migrant workers in the social security system. Meanwhile more financial transfers from the central government should be channeled to local governments in poor areas, which can help reduce the regional disparity in government spending on education, healthcare and social security. A combination of such measures can strengthen the capacity building, increase the income level and provide better protection for low- and medium-income groups in China.

Notes

1 This calculation is based on the relevant statistics from the *China Fiscal Statistics Yearbook* (1993).
2 We based our calculations on available relevant statistics. We were not able to obtain housing security expenditures.
3 China National Bureau of Statistics, "Urban and rural peoples' lives step from poverty to all-round well-being." Available at: www.stats.gov.cn/tjfx/ztfx/qzxzgc160zn/t20090910402585849.htm (accessed 28 June 2010).

References

He, P., Li, S. and Wang, Y. (2009) "Research on public fiscal support to the development of China's social welfare system," *Fiscal Research*, 6: 2–11.

Kou, T. and Zhou, B. (2007) "International experience of responsibility differentiation on government expenditure and its reflection: a comparative analysis based on the government expenditure structures of developed and developing countries," *Fiscal Research*, 4: 77–81.

Lin, Y. (2007) "Government performance on social security and its evaluation index system," *Journal of South-Central University for Nationalities* (Humanities and Social Sciences), 1: 115–19.

Ministry of Finance of Social Security Research Group (2007) "International comparison of social security expenditure," *Fiscal Research*, 10: 36–42.

Yang, G. (2008) "Pension treatment gap between Chinese enterprises and administration and institutions," *Gansu Social Sciences*, 6: 9–12.

Zhu, Q. (2008) "Concern about people's well-being: direction and means of the restructuring and adjustment of fiscal expenditure," *Finance and Trade Economics*, 7: 24–30.

5 Healthcare reform

Where is China heading?

Kai Hong Phua and Alex He Jingwei

Introduction

The People's Republic of China has achieved spectacular improvements in healthcare since its founding in 1949. Its public health system developed from a very low base inherited from the old regime but underwent rapid development under the planned economy. During the period between 1950 and 1978, in spite of fluctuations as a result of political movements, mortality rates, however, were reduced significantly while the life expectancy of the Chinese population almost doubled. Major communicable diseases were curbed by mass mobilization through major public health campaigns. A three-tier public health network was established both in urban and rural areas with *Prevention First* held as the overall principle and widespread primary healthcare provided at low costs.

From the late 1970s, China's economic reform has brought about far-reaching implications to its health sector. Expensive accessibility (*kanbing nan*) and medical impoverishment (*kanbing gui*) have become the twin acute symptoms of the Chinese healthcare system that have drawn intense public discontent. A series of structural and institutional changes were made along the path of market transition in reforming the healthcare system. This chapter explains key reasons for the deterioration of the Chinese healthcare system and reviews the major waves of healthcare reforms in China as well as their implications for overall health system performance. Without doubt, the recent national healthcare reform programme will provide an unprecedented opportunity to strengthen the healthcare system with the massive budgetary allocations. In this chapter, we argue that greater emphasis in this new round of reforms should be put on improving the governance of administrative structures towards the implementation of policies and coordinating the organizational functions of provision, financing and regulation of healthcare with better realignment of incentives embedded in the system.

Deterioration of the health system and its causes

China's transition to a market economy has boosted a significant growth of healthcare facilities, but it has also produced a wide range of destabilizing social costs. The market-oriented healthcare system in China now is faced with "market failures," including problems such as limited access to health services for the poor and the shortcomings of market mechanisms for services characterized by positive externalities, such as public health programs. The practice of financial autonomy has given healthcare providers the incentives to maximize revenues instead of health outcomes. Past government interventions to contain costs and improve efficiency have shown that excessive reliance on the price mechanism is insufficient and should instead be tackled on a more systemic and holistic basis.

China's enormous economic success over the past decades is not mirrored in its healthcare sector. In spite of impressive advancements in medical science and technology, the current healthcare system stands in stark contrast with that in the Maoist era which impressed the world by achieving universal coverage at fairly low cost although economic development was affected by political movements. The old socialistic "welfare state" under the planned economy was quickly dismantled as the country attempted to switch to a market-oriented healthcare system from the 1980s. An immediate effect was the drastic decline in the proportion of the population with health insurance coverage. With the bulk of the health expenditures paid out-of-pocket (Figure 5.1),

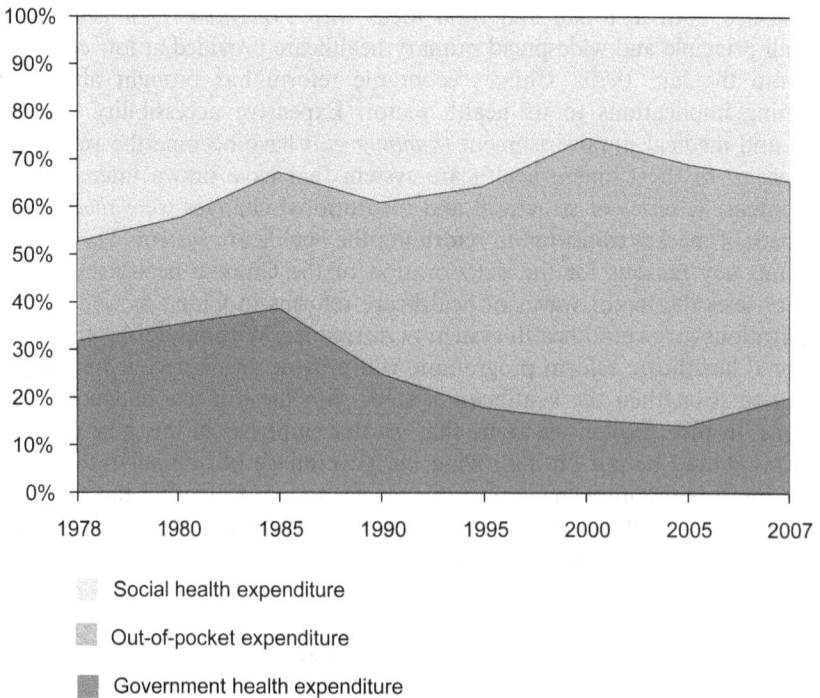

Social health expenditure

Out-of-pocket expenditure

Government health expenditure

Figure 5.1 Composition of China's health expenditure, 1978–2007

the Chinese healthcare system is considered one of the least equitable in the world (World Health Organization, 2000). This is compounded by the intractable cost escalation which tops the list of concerns for the general public. These have become a major cause for household impoverishment that is further aggravated by the low coverage of risk-pooling schemes and the reliance on fee-for-service as the dominant provider payment method (Blumenthal and Hsiao, 2005; Ge and Gong, 2007; Development Research Center, State Council, 2005). Soaring fees have plunged many people into poverty and have made medical services less affordable for ordinary citizens.

There is a rich body of literature explaining the reason why the Chinese healthcare system deteriorated at such a rapid pace from its previous internationally lauded model to a widely criticized system. By and large, the root causes can be attributed to the following aspects.

Collapse of health insurance schemes

The market transition has changed dramatically the way in which healthcare is financed in China. In the urban sector, economic reforms severely undermined the capacity of state-owned enterprises (SOE) to fund healthcare for their employees. As SOE restructuring took place, the economic basis for the previous Labor Insurance Scheme (LIS)—the backbone of the urban healthcare system—was severely eroded. The mass lay-off of SOE employees in the late 1990s left millions of urban workers outwith the state's financial protection (Grogan, 1995; Gao *et al.*, 2001; Hu *et al.*, 1999). A similar story is repeated in the rural sector. The dismantling of collective communes during the 1980s led to the demise of the Cooperative Medical System (CMS), leaving the vast majority of rural population without any form of healthcare coverage (Young, 1989; Feng *et al.*, 1995). Figure 5.2 is a snapshot of the coverage provided by major risk-pooling schemes in 2003. In the increasingly fragmented healthcare financing system, 70 percent of the population were without any form of financial protection while various available health insurance schemes covered merely 30 percent.

Insufficient budgetary allocation

Major changes also happened on the supply side. As a result of the severe loss of revenues from the SOE sector, the central government had to substantially limit funds available to the healthcare sector, which accounted for around 50–60 percent of hospital income under the planned economy (Yip and Hsiao, 2008). Despite the constant growth of government health expenditure, the increase in government subsidy to the healthcare sector could not keep pace with the rising costs of capital and other inputs due to the relaxation of various price controls (Figure 5.3) (Ramesh and Wu, 2009). This situation was exacerbated by major waves of fiscal reforms that made local

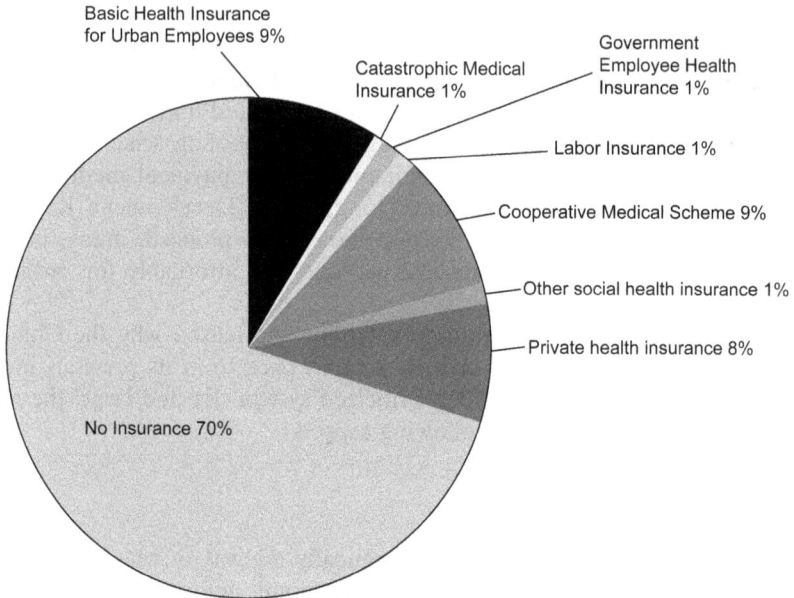

Figure 5.2 Coverage of risk-pooling schemes, 2003

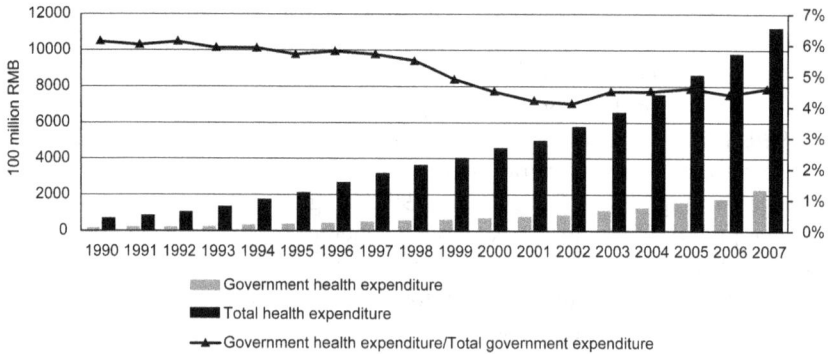

Figure 5.3 Total health expenditure and government health expenditure, 1990–2007

governments responsible for financing public health facilities under their jurisdictions. However, under the so-called policy of *local state corporatism* (Oi, 1992) and due to the fact that economic growth has been used as yard-stick to measure the performance of local cadres, local governments generally lack the incentives to invest in healthcare vis-à-vis developmental programs. With the financial autonomy given, hospitals were then allowed to generate most of their revenues from service charges and drug sales for their survival, which in turn, induced their revenue-maximizing behavior (Figure 5.4).

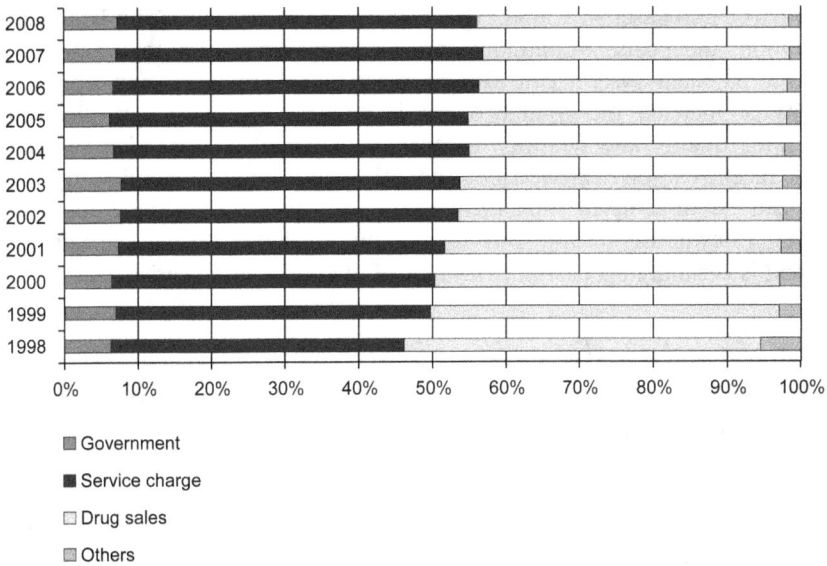

Figure 5.4 Sources of income for Chinese public hospitals (General), 1998–2008

Defective pricing system

Concerned about increasing access to care, the government set artificially low prices for primary care, basic pharmaceuticals and standard diagnostic tests and surgery, but allowed bigger profit margins for non-essential drugs and high-tech diagnostic tests. The original purpose was to guarantee the afford-ability of essential services to the public while letting the health facilities financially survive, but hospitals responded perversely to this fee schedule by increasing their supply of services that are not covered by controls, such as prescribing longer hospital stays and more expensive diagnostic procedures and pharmaceuticals—outcomes which went contrary to the policy-makers' intention. Over-prescription of drugs and unnecessary high-tech tests not only led to massive inefficiency but also fueled cost inflation. According to a study, 20 percent of all expenditure associated with appendicitis and pneumonia treatment was clinically unnecessary (Liu and Mills, 1999). Yip (2009) repor-ted that high numbers of 75 percent of patients suffering from common cold and 79 percent of hospital patients were prescribed antibiotics.

Reliance on the single payment method

Despite recent progress in some localities toward more rational payment methods, healthcare providers in China are still predominantly paid on a fee-for-service (FFS) basis, which is a weak method for controlling the provider's demand-inducing behavior, especially in the absence of a strong and prudent third-party purchaser in China. This contributes to the mounting healthcare utilization and costs. Admittedly, moving away from FFS to a fully pro-spective payment system can also be risky, since providers may skimp on quality or increase the volume of services unless the payer can effectively determine quality and quantity. Prospective payment systems also generally create incentives for risk selection, and risk-adjustment systems developed to date can be difficult to implement and often have considerable room for gaming (Newhouse, 1996). But relying on a single free-market payment method is certainly problematic, in light of international experiences.

Perverse internal incentives

In order to incentivize physicians to generate revenues for the hospital's financial survival, most Chinese public hospitals duplicated from the SOE sector the so-called *financial target responsibility system*, which virtually linked physicians' bonus to their performance in revenue generation. On average, the bonus could account for more than half of the income, and this system gave powerful incentives for physicians to induce demand (Liu and Mills, 2003). This was a result of letting medical institutions make their ends meet without minimal support from public financing.

Review of healthcare reforms in China

Recognizing the limitations of the old employer-based insurance schemes (GIS and LIS), China followed Singapore's lead in 1994 and began its own Medical Savings Account (MSA) scheme with a healthcare financing experi-ment conducted in two cities, Zhenjiang and Jiujiang. This so-called Basic Health Insurance Scheme (BHI) required all industry workers and govern-ment employees to have MSAs. Both employees and employers make com-pulsory contributions to the healthcare financing scheme. Employees are required to contribute 1 percent of their salaries into their individual accounts. Employers contribute 10 percent of the employee's salary, with 4 percent (or 6 percent if the employee is over 45) going into the employee's individual account and the remainder going into a risk-pooling social insur-ance account. When seeking medical care, individuals must initially finance care with their MSA. When the MSA funds are exhausted, individuals are required to pay a deductible which is equal to 5 percent of their annual salary. Once the deductible is reached, the social insurance account begins paying for part of the healthcare costs. However, the social insurance account does not pay for all costs; co-payments are required, although these decrease as costs rise. Supply-side controls exist through the Bureau of Labor and Social Security, which has a prospective budget for providers based on the previous year's expenditure.

Furthermore, fee schedules, drug formularies and other guidelines are employed. Five percent of the agreed budget is withheld for quality assurance.

Studies on the Zhenjiang experience have shown that MSAs have reduced cost inflation through reduction of hospital utilization rates, lengths of stay, and emergency visits via substitution with outpatient care. Zhenjiang's risk-pooling reform has been a successful story of health cost containment.

Overall, coverage under all insurance schemes together fell from 70 percent of the population in 1981 to 20 percent in 2003, according to figures released by the Development Research Center of the State Council in 2005. As a result, out-of-pocket payments rose significantly through the 1980s and 1990s. However, the rising out-of-pocket payments were accompanied by rising total health expenditures. Cost containment through higher co-payment has not restrained costs; it has merely increased the financial burden on the less well-off. The growing out-of-pocket payments coupled with escalating healthcare expenditure would therefore place a great burden on poor households.

In the past several years, the government has made attempts to revive rural health insurance schemes without much success. In 2002, it launched the New Cooperative Medical System (NCMS) on a pilot basis, funded from a government subsidy of approximately $2.50 a year and annual contributions of $1.25 per member. Differing from the old CMS, this new scheme operates on the national level and thus has a much larger risk pool. The plan only covers inpatient care and imposes high deductibles. The voluntary nature of this scheme and low level of financing make the viability of the scheme somewhat unpromising. Indeed, the contribution is less than a third of the existing per capita health expenditure in rural areas, suggesting that the scheme is seriously under-funded and, hence, financially vulnerable. Although the recent increase in government subsidy (from $2.5 to $6 a year) makes it more attractive to participate in the scheme as coverage rose to 86 percent in 2007, its effectiveness in containing medical expenditure and reducing poverty remains doubtful.

In the urban sector, although participation of the Basic Health Insurance Scheme was mandatory for all government agencies and state-owned enterprises, in practice, however, the compliance was still low for various reasons (Duckett 2001). More importantly, the scheme does not cover workers in the informal sector and migrant workers; nor does it cover dependents of enrolled workers. As a result, only 28 percent of all urban inhabitants were covered by the scheme in 2006. Based on the experience of BHI and NCMS, the government launched the Urban Resident Basic Health Insurance scheme (URBHI) in 2007 which started to bring the bulk of the previously uninsured under the risk-pooling umbrella. Like NCMS, URBHI is also funded by enrollee contributions and by increasingly generous subsidies from central and local governments. This scheme is voluntary but is limited at the household level so as to reduce adverse selection.

With these three major insurance schemes, the ratio of population covered by the basic medical insurance reached 87 percent in 2008 and is expected to surpass 90 percent by 2011 (Figure 5.5). Notably, major healthcare reforms from the mid-1990s to early 2006 were focused on financing issues while

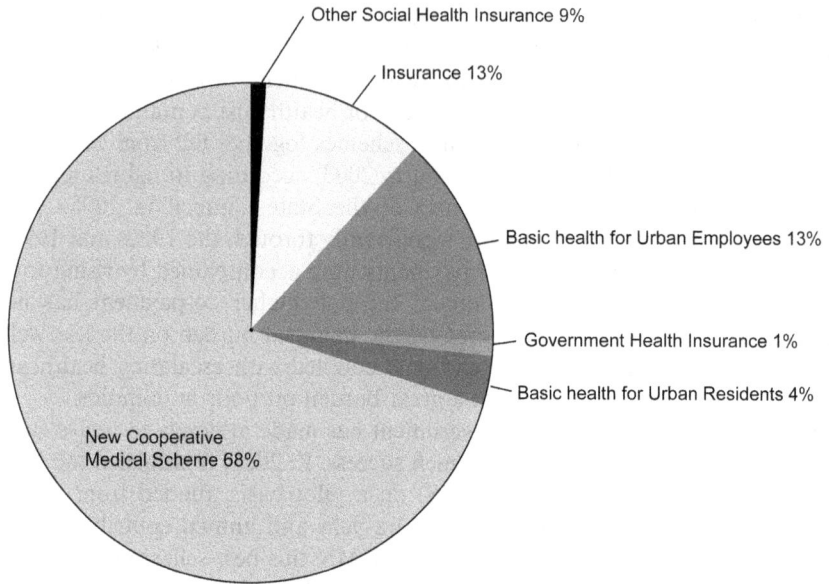

Figure 5.5 Coverage of risk-pooling schemes, 2008
Source: 2009 China Health Statistics Yearbook, Beijing: China Union Medical University Press.

provision reforms were largely confined to minor changes or local initiatives. It was not until 2006 that the Chinese government officially embarked on a systematic manner to reform the health sector.

Paradigm shift in public policy and the new healthcare reform

China's healthcare woes have not only caused individual hardships to its citizens but also posed political risks for the government. The rising inequality in access to healthcare is severely undermining the government's professed commitment to the ideal of the "harmonious society." The Chinese government has become increasingly aware of this dire situation and has been striving to grapple with the problems.

In fact, after the strategic goal to build a socialist harmonious society was set by the Chinese Communist Party (CCP), despite the persistent centrality of economic development, social welfare issues have been gaining higher profiles on the local governments' agenda. From this perspective, the overall policy environment in China has been undergoing a paradigm shift from "economic development-centered" to "harmonious development" (Liu and Rao, 2006; Wang, 2008). This trend became increasingly visible after the year 2003 when the SARS epidemic severely hit China and when the central government launched the New Cooperative Medical Scheme in its vast rural areas.

A high-ranking inter-ministerial task force was formed in 2006 to draft the new national healthcare reform agenda. In 2007, the government commissioned nine organizations—including the World Bank, the World Health Organization, Peking University and McKinsey—to recommend options for reforming the health system. In March 2008, Chinese Premier Wen Jiabao in his State of the Nation address announced a 25 percent increase in government health expenditure.

In April 2009, the central government of China promulgated the long-awaited healthcare reform plan after numerous revisions and extensive discussions and debates. For the first time, the blueprint in the paramount policy documents of the CPC acknowledged the nature of healthcare as public goods and highlighted the establishment of a basic healthcare system to cover all Chinese citizens—to be formed on the basis of systems of public health, medical services, medical insurance and pharmaceutical supply. The government will improve the public health network for disease prevention and control, health education, maternal and infant healthcare, mental health and emergency services (CCP Central Committee and State Council, 2009).

The Chinese government decided to spend 850 billion *yuan* (about US$123 billion) by 2011 to overhaul the country's entire medical system. The plan would bring 90 percent of China's 1.3 billion people under a primary medical insurance scheme that provides a better public healthcare system, basic pharmaceuticals, networks of improved local clinics and better services in public hospitals. The reform of public hospitals lies at the heart of the new plan, which had operated on profits from medical services and drug prescriptions due to the lack of past government financing. The reform is aimed at solving pressing problems that have caused strong complaints from the public, since there is growing criticism that medical services are difficult to access and increasingly unaffordable. More specifically, the reform is aimed at establishing a rational, effective and optimal healthcare system, fully motivating medical workers to provide the public with safe, effective, convenient and affordable medical services.

By 2011, according to the blueprint, a basic medical security system would have completely covered urban and rural residents, with an essential drugs supply system preliminarily established, urban and rural grassroots healthcare service systems further strengthened, basic public health services made available widely, pilot projects for reforming state-owned hospitals making breakthroughs, accessibility to the basic healthcare services markedly improved, and the burden of medical costs effectively reduced, and the problem of "difficult and costly access to healthcare services" would have been remarkably relieved.

By 2020, a basic healthcare system covering urban and rural residents will have been fundamentally established. The government aims to set up across the country, a fairly complete public health system and healthcare service system, a comparatively sound medical insurance system, a secure and relatively well-regulated pharmaceutical supply system, and a comparatively sound healthcare institutional management and operational system.

In order to realize such a comprehensive system, the government is striving to work out a multi-source health financing mechanism with the government playing the dominant role. It is clear that public health services will be mainly provided through government funding to urban and rural residents in an equitable manner. The expenses of the basic healthcare services will be rationally apportioned and borne between the government, society and individuals. But extra and discretionary healthcare will be paid for directly by individuals or borne by commercial health insurance.

In light of the principle of cost-sharing at all government levels, the blueprint called for efforts to rationally share the healthcare financing responsibilities between the central government and local governments at various levels. The local governments will take the principal responsibility, while the central government willl mainly subsidize national immunization programs, inter-regional prevention and control of major communicable diseases and other issues of public health, basic medical insurance of urban and rural residents as well as the development of relevant public-owned healthcare institutions. Special efforts should be made to increase special transfer payments by the central and provincial governments to financially constrained regions.

The government also pledged to invest more in urban and rural grassroots healthcare institutions. The government will take on the responsibility of providing funding for the basic construction, equipping and staffing of government-sponsored township health centers, urban community health centers, as well as the operational funds for public health services so that these institutions can function fully. Township health centers and urban community health service institutions sponsored by various non-public sources will be subsidized by the government. The construction of village clinics will be supported and reasonable subsidies will be granted to rural doctors who take the responsibility of fulfilling such tasks as public health services. The policy of granting government subsidies to public hospitals will be better implemented and increasing government investments will be mainly used for basic construction and procurement, and the development of key projects.

Public non-profit hospitals will continue to be the dominant providers of medical services, while more priority will be given to the development of grassroots-level hospitals and clinics in cities and rural areas, which are often ill-equipped and under-staffed. Patients will be encouraged to use more grassroots-level hospitals and clinics, which will be improved to provide more accessible and affordable services. Comprehensive hospitals in big cities will be asked to provide more support to small local hospitals in terms of personnel, expertise and equipment. Nevertheless, this would be rather difficult, given the absence of an effective referral system which should be responsible in part to reduce cost escalation. A so-called two-way referral system has been initiated in some localities acting as a gatekeeper to healthcare expenditure. In spite of moderate success, it is facing greater difficulties because the current health insurance schemes provide too little restraint on patients' behavior and choice of hospitals, and this is compounded by the hospitals' reluctance to refer downwards, as well as the inadequacy of grassroots health facilities.

Fixing the incentive structure: the way ahead

The healthcare market is, in essence, underpinned by a constellation of incentives. The role of government is essential to regulate and align the incentives appropriately so as to correct the natural market failures due to information asymmetry (Saltman, 2002). The Chinese healthcare market is one that has been severely distorted by the misaligned incentives for healthcare providers which is largely responsible for mounting health expenditure and issues of affordability (Liu and Mills, 2003; 2005; Gu and Zhang, 2006; Hsiao, 1995; Hu *et al.*, 2008). Many scholars have pointed out that the significant decline of budgetary allocation to the health sector had created perverse incentives. But substantial financial injections will not help unless the underlying misaligned incentive structure is corrected; otherwise more budgetary outlays would fuel an even further cost explosion (Ramesh and Wu, 2009; Yip *et al.*, 2010).

China's strategy of building a basic financing architecture before addressing the problems in the provision sector is generally in the right direction. More attention is now paid to the provider payment method in China's healthcare financing. With the newly-gained economic lever from health insurance reform, many local governments are now able to move away from fee-for-service (FFS) toward a system of prospective payment built on more rational incentives, and the effect in controlling cost inflation has been encouraging, as suggested from empirical studies (Yip and Eggleston, 2004; Yip and Eggleston, 2001; Eggleston *et al.*, 2008; Hu *et al.*, 2008). In the meantime, the shift from the dominant FFS to diagnosis-related groups (DRG) is featured in the reforms of some localities which aim to discourage physicians from inducing demand, while others have embarked on the so-called "price-ceiling schemes." Localities such as Shenzhen focus on disconnecting the physicians' bonus from revenue-collecting performance. In addition, the so-called "two-way referral system" was adopted on a pilot basis, aimed at acting as a gatekeeper and contributing to reduce inefficiencies prevalent in healthcare resource allocation. Physicians have been engaging in opportunistic behaviors so as not to be constrained, thus limiting the effectiveness of these reform initiatives and calling for more targeted institutional design.

Among other pilot schemes, breakthrough in this regard may come from the ongoing large-scale experiment of clinical pathway systems which will impose tighter but more scientific limits on physician behavior—if successfully implemented. This system prescribes standard pathways to diagnosis and treatment of major diseases that must be followed by physicians with exemptions that are very strictly controlled. The Ministry of Health is leading this experiment and has selected 110 public hospitals nationwide for pilot programs. The implementation of the clinical pathway is intended not just to standardize healthcare services, but also to pave the way for wider implementation of DRG.

While the realignment of economic incentives is without doubt crucial in the reform, the problem of political incentives are equally, if not more important. By and large, the relentless pursuit of economic growth still depicts the prevalent policy paradigm in China. It is believed that if China's economy were to continue to grow, health improvement for all would eventually follow. Under this overwhelming orientation, social policies, including health policies, have taken a back seat to other policy issues. Although there has been a visible shift of policy paradigm towards social welfare issues since Hu Jintao and Wen Jiabao came to power (Liu and Rao, 2006; Wang, 2008), local governments are still preoccupied by economic growth since it is still used as the yardstick for political appointment and promotion (Li and Zhou, 2005).

The Chinese political system since the 1990s has been characterized by the *de facto* federalism under which there is a growing discrepancy between what is seen as desirable in Beijing and what is implemented by local governments (Mertha, 2005; Zheng, 2006). Policies are often only half-implemented or in a very selective manner because local authorities may have other priorities (Meessen and Bloom, 2007; Huang, 2009). Largely driven by this, local cadres in China generally lack the motivation to engage voluntarily in healthcare reforms and the implementation of new healthcare policies that predominantly relies on a top-down approach. However, given the huge regional disparities in the country, more local initiatives are needed to tackle locality-specific problems. Nonetheless, this will be unlikely if the existing political incentive structure is not modified in favor of social welfare issues.

Furthermore, the inter-governmental fiscal system needs to be modified to the extent that responsibility is matched with corresponding financial capacity. Encouragement to embark on local initiatives ought to entail not only political incentives, but also fair fiscal distribution across the layers of governments. In fact, the primary obstacle to the on-going public hospital reform representing the core of the entire healthcare reforms is the local governments' inability to fully shoulder the major operational costs of their public hospitals.

Last but not least, success of the ongoing healthcare reform will also follow a strengthened and active role played by the Chinese health authorities. The failure of past rounds of healthcare reforms in China has often been attributed to the *policy gridlock* resulting from the buckpassing politics among related ministries (Huang, 2009). This is further compounded by the bureaucratic weakness of the Chinese health authorities who are often seen as incompetent in leading the reform. Yet, new evidence from some localities, especially Fujian, defies this notion and suggests that the Chinese health bureaucracy is not inherently incapable; with a supportive political environment and firm bureaucratic determination, it is able to initiate and engage in meaningful policy interventions with newly explored instruments accompanied by conventional command-and-control measures. These interventions should aim at restructuring provider incentives, particularly those of the managers, such that the incentive structure encourages hospital managers to seek benefits for their hospitals while discouraging them from taking advantage of market failures to undermine consumers' interests (OECD, 1992). While various reform initiatives are trying to establish scientific constraints on physician behavior, it is equally important to rebuild a sound accountability system governing the government–hospital relationship which collapsed during the marketization reform. Under the new accountability arrangement, hospital administrators should be motivated to serve the general public instead of responding to the bottom line, and be held fully accountable to the government.

Conclusion

The challenges confronting China's healthcare system have their roots in over-marketization and decentralization, beginning with the dismantling of the rural collectives and the state-owned enterprises as part of past reform and liberalization process. These reforms and the shift to a market-driven health system have led to an overall decline in the quality of care and a scramble for new sources of revenue that has undermined the provision of good quality services. The financial de-linking of government from local health units has resulted in the decline of the central government's oversight and effective enforcement of standards.

The present healthcare system in China is saddled with a multitude of problems. The most serious problem is a surge in healthcare costs. During the 10 years since 1995, the disposable income of urban dwellers increased 2.4-fold and the net income of rural residents doubled, while per capita healthcare cost for outpatients at general hospitals increased roughly three-fold. This situation is due to a number of factors. First, the government did not put enough money into the health sector; the ratio of government outlay to national healthcare expenditure stood at 36.2 percent in 1980. This figure declined gradually to a low of 15 percent to 17 percent in and after 2000. Personal payments, which accounted for 21.2 percent in 1980, increased to more than 50 percent in 2000. Second, healthcare resources are unevenly distributed. The number of general hospitals has increased steadily since 1980, but 80 percent of these hospitals are concentrated in urban areas. In contrast, the number of small public health clinics in rural areas has declined year by year. Third, government control and regulation have weakened considerably over the years. Since the 1980s, the government has promoted a self-supporting accounting system for medical institutions to reduce the financial burden on the state. This has resulted in the spread of rampant commercialism among medical institutions.

The common backdrop to these problems is the severe state of public finances. Since the 1980s, local governments have assumed responsibility for finance due to the introduction of a policy of partial decentralization of government financing. As a result, the capacity to run the healthcare and public health sector has declined in financially weak regions. Tax reform, which was effected in 1994, had strengthened the financial capacity of the central government, but a system to transfer power for finances to local governments has not been firmly established.

China has been giving priority to economic growth and largely ignoring social development, which has resulted in inadequate healthcare coverage. As a consequence, the cost burden on people for healthcare has sharply increased, caused by excessive commercialism on the part of medical institutions. Radical reform measures by the government are imperative. It is still possible for China to draw on the successful experiences of other countries to formulate its own healthcare policies and to reshape its future healthcare system.

The current orientation of healthcare reform in China seems clear. Priority will be given to public health measures directed at common, rather than serious illnesses, in order to spread healthcare more widely. In the long term, a universal health insurance covering every Chinese person will be established. Government leadership in healthcare will be further enhanced and supplementary roles will be assumed by the private sector. A better balance will have to be achieved by the reassertion of the state against the forces of the failed market in healthcare.

Last but not least, while a substantial amount of financial resources are allocated to the new national healthcare reform, it should be noted that a financial injection is not the end but the means, to make incremental reform possible. More efforts need to be made—through the new funds—to fix the long-distorted incentive structure in the healthcare system, especially in the hospital sector. The provider payment methods, physician bonus, drug dispensing and referral systems lie at the heart of any effective systemic overhaul. Greater emphasis in this new round of reforms should be put on improving the governance of administrative structures towards the implementation of policies and coordinating the organizational functions of provision, financing and regulation of healthcare with a better realignment of incentives embedded in the system.

References

Blumenthal, D. and Hsiao, W. (2005) "Privatization and its discontents: the evolving Chinese health care system," *New England Journal of Medicine*, 353(11): 1165–70.

CCP Central Committee and State Council (2009) "Zhonggong zhongyang guowuyuan guanyu shenhua yiyao weisheng tizhi gaige de yijian" [Opinions of the CPC Central Committee and the State Council on Deepening the Healthcare System Reform]. Beijing: Author.

China Health Statistics Yearbook, 2009 (2009) Beijing: China Union Medical University Press.

Development Research Center, State Council (2005) "Dui zhongguo yiliao weisheng tizhi gaige de pingjia yu jianyi" [Evaluation and recommendation of China's health policy reform], *China Development Review*, S1.

Duckett, J. (2001) "Political interests and the implementation of China's urban health insurance reform," *Social Policy and Administration*, 35: 290–306.

Eggleston, K., Li, L., Meng, Q., Lindelow, M. and Wagstaff, A. (2008) "Health service delivery in China: a literature review," *Health Economics*, 17: 149–65.

Feng, X., Tang, S., Bloom, G., Segall, M. and Gu, X. (1995) "Cooperative medical schemes in contemporary rural China," *Social Science and Medicine*, 41: 1111–18.

Gao, J., Tang, S., Tolhurst, R. and Rao, K. (2001) "Changing access to health services in urban China: implications for equity," *Health Policy and Planning*, 16: 302–12.

Ge, Y. and Gong, S. (2007) *Zhongguo yigai: wenti, genyuan, chulu* [Chinese Healthcare Reform: Problems, Origins, and Solutions], Beijing: China Development Press.

Grogan, C. (1995) "Urban economic reform and access to health care coverage in the People's Republic of China," *Social Science and Medicine*, 41: 1073–83.

Gu, E. and Zhang, J. (2006) "Health care regime change in urban China: unmanaged marketization and reluctant privatization," *Pacific Affairs*, 79: 49–71.

Hsiao, W. (1995) "The Chinese health care system: lessons for other nations," *Social Science and Medicine*, 8: 1047–55.

Hu, S., Tang, S., Liu, Y., Zhao, Y., Escobar, M. and de Ferranti, D. (2008) "Reform of how health care is paid for in China: challenges and opportunities," *Lancet*, 372: 1846–53.

Hu, T., Ong, M., Lin, Z. and Li, E. (1999) "The effects of economic reform on health insurance and the financial burden for urban workers in China," *Health Economics*, 8: 309–21.

Huang, Y. (2009) "An institutional analysis of China's failed healthcare reform," in G. Wu and H. Lansdowne (eds.), *Socialist China, Capitalist China: Social Tension and Political Adaptation under Economic Globalization*, New York: Routledge.

Li, H. and Zhou, L. (2005) "Political turnover and economic performance: the incentive role of personnel control in China," *Journal of Public Economics*, 89: 1743–62.

Liu, X. and Mills, A. (1999) "Evaluating payment mechanisms: how can we measure unnecessary care?," *Health Policy and Planning*, 14: 409–13.

——(2003) "The influence of bonus payments to doctors on hospital revenue: results of a quasi-experimental study," *Applied Health Economics and Health Policy*, 2: 91–8.

——(2005) "The effect of performance-related pay of hospital doctors on hospital behavior: a case study from Shandong," *Human Resource for Health*, 3: 11.

Liu, Y. and Rao, K. (2006) "Providing health insurance in rural China: from research to policy," *Journal of Health Politics, Policy and Law*, 31: 71–92.

Meessen, B. and Bloom, G. (2007) "Economic transition, institutional changes and the health system: some lessons from rural China," *Journal of Economic Policy Reform*, 10: 209–31.

Meng, Q., Cheng, G., Silver, L., Sun, X., Rehnberg, C. and Tomson, G. (2005) "The impact of China's retail drug price control policy on hospital expenditures: a case study of two Shandong hospitals," *Health Policy Plan*, 20: 185–96.

Mertha, A. (2005) "China's 'soft' centralization: shifting tiao/kuai authority relations," *The China Quarterly*, 184: 791–810.

Newhouse, J. (1996) "Reimbursing health plans and health providers: selection versus efficiency in production," *Journal of Economic Literature*, 34: 1236–63.

OECD (1992) "The reform of health care: a comparative analysis of seven OECD countries," OECD Health Policy Studies, No. 2, Paris.

Oi, J. (1992) "Fiscal reform and the economic foundations of local state corporatism in China," *World Politics*, 45: 99–126.

Ramesh, M and Wu, X. (2009) "Health policy reform in China: lessons from Asia," *Social Science and Medicine*, 68: 2256–62.

Saltman, R.B. (2002) "Regulating incentives: the past and present role of the state in health care system," *Social Science and Medicine*, 54: 1677–84.

Wang, Y. (2008) "The policy process and context of the rural new cooperative medical scheme and medical financial assistance in China," *Policy and Illness: Evidence for Policy*. Available at: http://www.povill.com/enjkw/cbwcont.aspx?id=46 (accessed 19 July 2010).

World Health Organization (2000) *The World Health Report 2000, Health Systems: Improving Performance*, Geneva: WHO.

Yip, W. (2009) "Disparities in health care and health status: the rural-urban gap and beyond," in W. Whyte (ed.) *One Country, Two Societies: Rural-Urban Inequality in Contemporary China*, Cambridge, MA: Harvard University Press.

Yip, W. and Eggleston, K. (2001) "Provider payment reform in China: the case of hospital reimbursement in Hainan Province," *Health Economics*, 10: 325–39.

——(2004) "Addressing government and market failures with payment incentives: hospital reimbursement reform in Hainan, China," *Social Science and Medicine*, 58: 267–77.

Yip, W. and Hsiao, W. (2008) "The Chinese health system at a crossroads," *Health Affairs*, 27: 460–8.

Yip, W., Hsiao, W., Meng, Q., Chen, W. and Sun, X. (2010) "Realignment of incentives for health-care providers in China," *Lancet*, 375: 1020–30.

Young, M. (1989) "Impact of the rural reform on financing rural health services in China," *Health Policy*, 11: 27–42.

Zheng, Y. (2006) *De Facto Federalism in China: Reforms and Dynamics of Central-Local Relations*, Singapore: World Scientific.

6 How successful are China's public housing schemes?

Bingqin Li

Introduction

Housing was probably one of the earliest areas of reform in the late 1970s. Over time, with the continued changes, the housing system and the housing outcomes in urban China are barely recognizable. Even if we only trace the process back to 1990, when major reform measures took place, there have been dramatic changes since then. In 1990, the average living space per person in Beijing was 7.2 square meters, in Shanghai it was 6.4 square meters and in Tianjin it was 6.5 square meters. The housing poverty line set by the central government in these large cities in the 1990s was 4 square meters per person. By the end of 2009, the average housing construction size[1] per person was 28.8 square meters in Beijing, 34 square meters in Shanghai and 29.9 square meters in Tianjin.[2] The actual size for household usage is much smaller though. Various sources suggested that it should be around 20 square meters per person at the national level. The size for large cities should be less than 20 square meters. By the end of 2009, about 87 percent of houses were privately owned. The improvement in the overall housing conditions seems to be obvious.

At the same time, the surveys by the mass media repeatedly suggest that housing is considered one of the biggest problems in daily life by the public. In 2010, it topped the list for the first time (Guo, 2010) and housing was the main subject area for discussion in the People's Congress in 2010 (Yu, 2010).

This chapter examines why the apparent improvements in housing have not led to a drop in public concerns. In the following sections, I first identify the sources of growing pressure for affordable housing. The second part tries to examine how successful China's public housing schemes are. I will first examine the housing outcomes and then look at whether the reforms have achieved the intended goals. The aim is to study how different interests have played out in the process of housing reform over the past 30+ years.

Criteria for evaluating the "success" of public housing schemes

To evaluate how successful public housing schemes are is an elusive task. In theory, a housing system should include different sectors of the housing market, such as owner occupation, shared ownership, private rental, either formal or informal. These sub-markets working together should be able to sort out the housing distribution through market pricing, i.e. everyone will have somewhere to live that matches their affordability. However, market solutions, such as shantytowns or even squatters areas, may not be pleasing to the eyes of urban middle class. The "miseries" associated with poor housing and the cry for better housing often drive the state, the representatives of the public (either democratically elected or not, and who want to maintain a relatively stable governing position), to do something in order to "improve" or appear to improve the housing conditions of the poor. This is where public housing policies kick in.

However, there are some complications regarding the public housing schemes when we try to evaluate whether they are successful. The outcomes of public housing schemes can be evaluated "objectively" and "subjectively." The objective ways are usually determined by "experts" based on their understanding of user needs. The first is housing adequacy. This is an area that has been studied by many researchers. Various indicators have been set by researchers in order to measure whether people are housed adequately in a society. This type of indicators is designed to measure hardship (Meyers and Garfinkel, 1999). However, these "objective" criteria are criticized for being manipulated by researchers, and may not reflect the actual experience and concerns of residents themselves (Newman, 1984). The second is about affordability. This angle of evaluation assumes that when the price to household income ratio is above a certain level, houses become unaffordable. When this happens, the state should try to offer assistance to improve the quality and affordability of housing. Therefore, evaluating public housing schemes should aim to look at whether the intervention has been successful in helping the targeted groups to obtain better and more affordable housing. Unfortunately, this type of evaluation is also open to criticism. It is because public houses, though more affordable, are often associated with poorer quality and high maintenance. Even if public housing is able to offer shelter to the poor, and even if it does not suffer from quality problems, it may also bring about social segregation (Turner *et al.*, 2009) and various social problems (Griffiths and Tita, 2009). The literature on public housing tend to suggest that many researchers consider public housing schemes are doomed to fail one way or another (Bloom, 2008). It is also very difficult for them to agree on the criteria for improved housing.

The subjective assessment looks at whether users are satisfied with their housing conditions. In this way, the objective criteria may be undermined, as the users could be very satisfied while others take an opposite view. This phenomenon can be observed in people's attitudes towards urban slums where slum dwellers have learnt to adapt to the life in slums and found slum life to be friendlier to the poor (Hasan, 2006), whereas outsiders, including the urban middle class and the government, often consider slums to be an eyesore, an inferior form of settlement that needs to be replaced by better houses

(Gilbert, 2007). However, champions for user satisfaction would unavoidably come across the difficult problem of voluntary under-consumption, especially by lower-income groups, i.e. some people may prefer to spend as little money as possible on housing (Li *et al.*, 2009).

Another type of evaluation tries to focus on the relationship between policies and outcomes. One perspective is to examine whether policy-makers have achieved their intended goals. However, these goals may not be about improving housing outcomes, but rather about achieving various social purposes, such as reducing crime (Beckett and Herbert 2008; Forrest and Murie, 2009), winning votes (McCarty, 2008), boosting economic performance (Harloe and Martens, 2009), or maintaining social stability (Lipman, 2008). Another view is to examine whether government interventions have made any difference, and whether these impacts have managed to achieve some socially desirable results. The problem with this approach is that if the interests of policy-makers are not in line with the needs of the lower-income group, a public housing policy that has successfully achieved its goals may actually harm the poor.

Given the restrictions, evaluating policy success becomes an elusive exercise. A realistic goal might be to strike a balance between objective and subjective views and at the same time look at the goals and outcomes. In this way, we may hope to build up a realistic picture to understand the possible causes of public discontent.

Pressure on the urban housing system

Several social trends may help to explain the increased pressure on urban housing system. They affect the demand and supply of housing in Chinese cities.

Changing population size and structure

The total population on China has grown over time, despite the One Child Policy, from 960 million in 1978 to 1.33 billion in 2008.[3] The growing urban population means that there need to be more houses to accommodate the increased number of people. Figure 6.1 also shows the pressure imposed by structural changes. The urban population has grown faster than the rural population. Therefore, unless an equivalent number of rural houses are also "urbanized," it means that there will need to be more housing supply in cities. What makes the scenario more serious is that the national level data only shows "rural" and "urban" populations according to the Household Registration. The reality is that there are also people moving from the rural areas, and working and living either long term or short term in cities, without being registered. They also need to be accommodated during their stay in cities.

Most information on migration is based on estimates. There are around 150 million migrant workers from rural to urban areas. Not all of them are

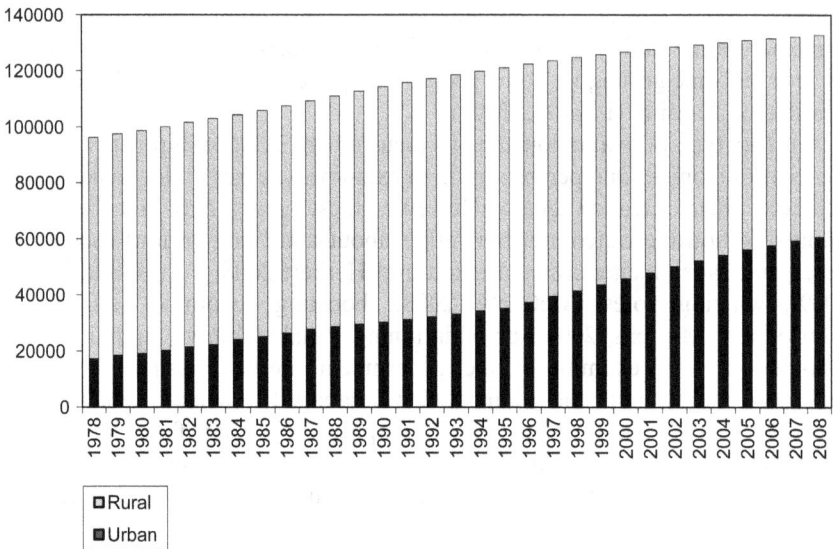

Figure 6.1 Population growth in China (10,000)
Source: China Statistics Yearbook, various issues since 1978.

permanent residents in cities. As shown in Figure 6.2, the registered population in Beijing (i.e. people holding Beijing *Hukou* (Household Registration)) had grown from about 8 million to more than 12 million. However, the total number of urban residents (who have stayed in the city for more than six months), including Beijing citizens and "people coming from outside the city" (*wailai renkou*), has been growing much faster than the registered population. By the end of 2008, the total number has reached 16.95 million. If we look at the left side of the figure on Beijing in Figure 6.2, the numbers between registered and total population are not very different in 1978. Moving toward the right side of the figure, by the end of 2008, there is a gap of more than 4.6 million people. According to the definition, these people are not registered as Beijing citizens and have lived in Beijing for more than six months. They are in essence the migrant population from other parts of the country. What is clear is that local rural population actually dropped from 1991 to 2008. The growth in the total population is mostly in the urban area of the city. In this sense, the pressure of population growth on housing mostly falls on the urban area. The official data in Shanghai do not report the same categories of population. However, even if we only examine the trend of total population and registered population, the similarity to Beijing cannot be missed.

There is a gap of five million between the afore-mentioned groups. Tianjin is an example of a second-tier city that is not as large as Beijing and Shanghai. There is also a gap of about two million people. Shenzhen is an example of the rapid growing industrial centers in southern provinces. The city grew from a fishing village to a multi-million people city in 30 years. As shown in

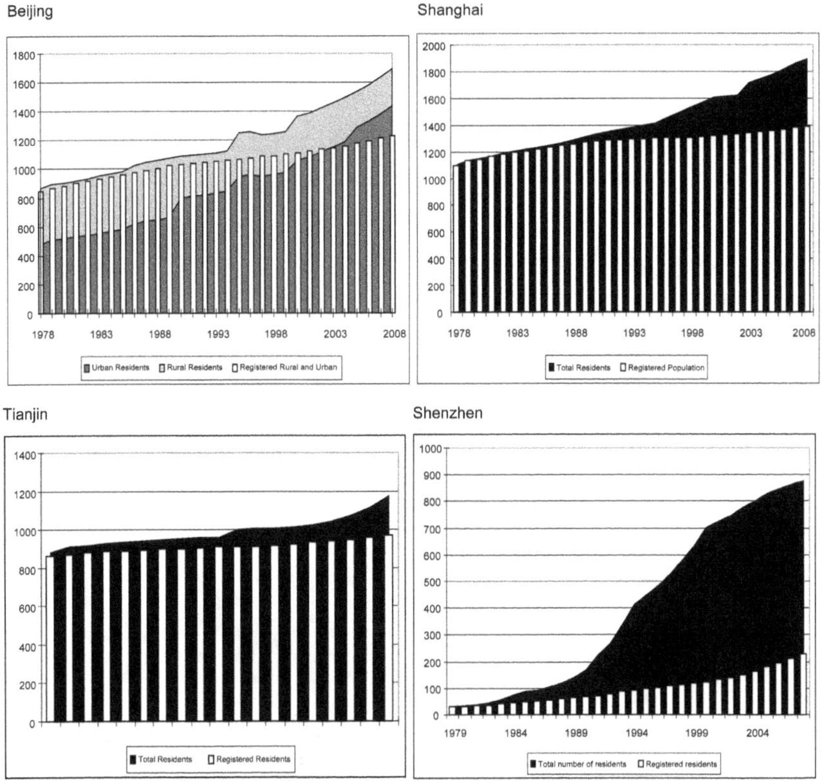

Beijing

Shanghai

Tianjin

Shenzhen

Figure 6.2 Total number of permanent residents and number of registered residents with *Hukou* in Beijing, Shanghai, Tianjin and Shenzhen, 1978–2008 (in 10,000s)
Source: Beijing Statistics Bureau, 2009, Beijing Statistics Yearbook, Table 3-4; Shanghai Statistics Bureau, 2009, Shanghai Statistics Yearbook, Table 3-4; Tianjin Statistics Bureau, 2009, Tianjin Statistics Yearbook, Table 3-1; Shenzhen Statistics Bureau, 2009, Shenzhen Statistics Yearbook, online version.

Figure 6.2, the growth in the registered population is much slower than the growth in the migrant population.

Shrinking household size

Starting from the early 1980s when the One Child Policy was enforced, the household size of Chinese families has declined over time. As shown in Figure 6.3, the number of household members dropped from 4.41 to 3.16 between 1982 and 2008. In large cities, household size is even smaller. Beijing has the smallest number of people per household, less than 2.6 at the end of 2008 (as shown in Figure 6.4). However, it was not only the One Child Policy that caused the shrinking household size. There is a growing trend for extended families to live separately from each other. This is clearly only made possible

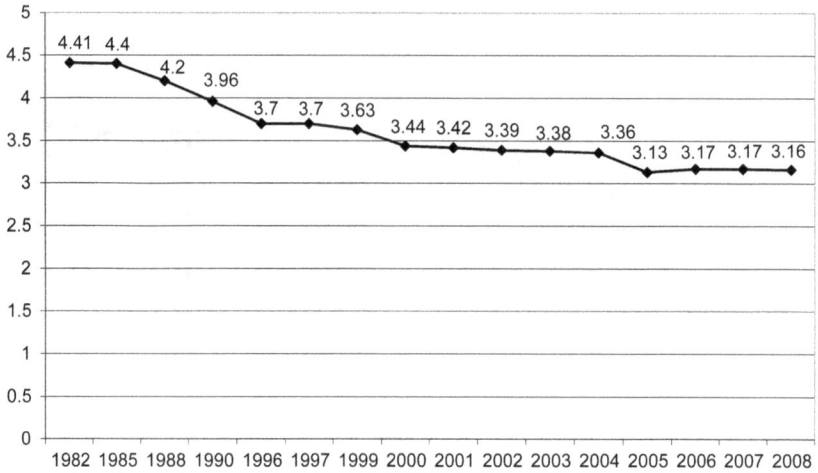

Figure 6.3 Household size changes over time, 1982–2008
Source: China Statistics Yearbook, various issues since 1978.

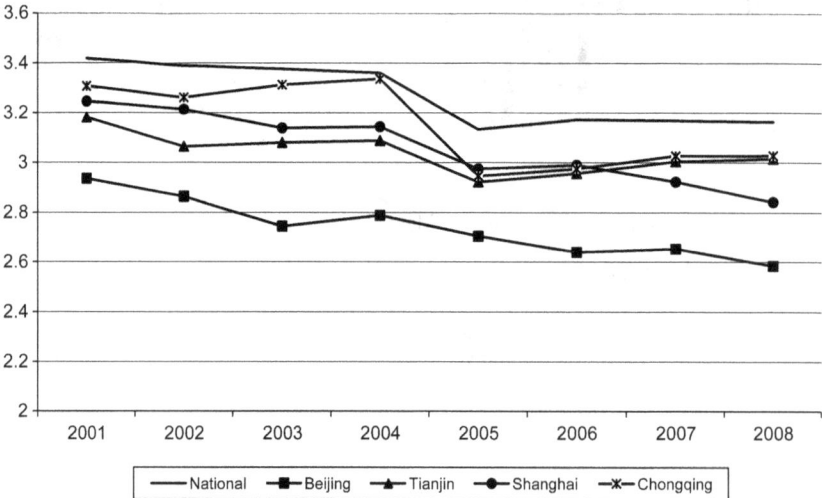

Figure 6.4 Household size changes of the whole country and of the four major cities, 2001–08
Source: China Statistics Yearbook, various issues since 2001.

by improved housing conditions. However, once it has developed into a norm, younger people would expect to leave home when they are married. Then this is automatically transformed into social pressure for greater housing supply. Another trend is the increased number of single person households. This is mainly older people who live independently on their own or young adults who delay their marriage either out of career or financial considerations. As shown

Beijing

Tianjin

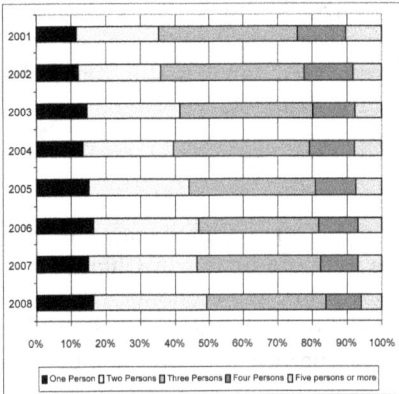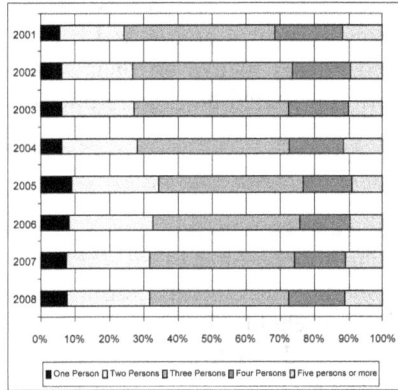

Shanghai

Chongqing

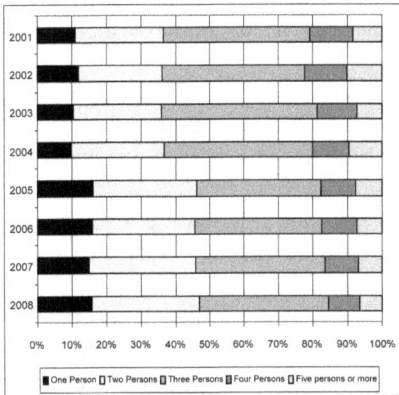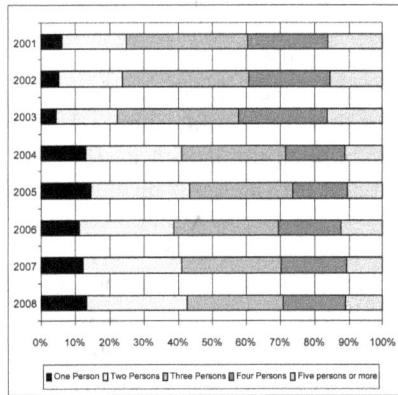

Figure 6.5 Share of households by household size
Source: China Statistics Yearbook, various issues since 2001.

in Figure 6.5, in large cities (except for Tianjin), one-person or two-person households have increased in importance.

Migration also affects household size. In theory, it has the potential to contribute to smaller household size. In the 1980s and 1990s, rural to urban migrant workers came to towns either on their own or at most with their partners. They rarely brought their school-aged children to towns. In 2003, when the restrictions on rural workers from working in cities were relaxed, migrant workers started to bring their children with them to the cities. Even so, the family size of the migrant workers was on average much smaller than that of local citizens (Guo *et al.*, 2006). However, this does not necessarily mean that migrant workers actually lived in smaller households. They might share houses or live in dormitories at very high density. As a result, the household size can be much larger than usual. Nevertheless, if we examine the life cycle of migration, it is not difficult to see that migrant workers also have a housing ladder to climb. As they stay longer in cities, they move out of employer-provided houses and become private renters; then they move out of shared houses to live on their own, or with their families (Li, 2006). This means that shared houses are only temporary solutions.

Pressure on urban housing

These demographic and social changes have a significant impact on urban housing supply. First of all, there need to be more houses in Chinese cities. Considering the difficult housing conditions before the economic reform, i.e. most households suffered from extremely poor housing conditions by today's standards (for example, most people needed to share facilities, and parents needed to share bedrooms with children), it was very difficult to further split up existing housing stock for newcomers. This means that for many years, even if the housing conditions of existing urban residents were to be improved slightly, there would still need to be massive increases in housing supply.

Second, as the total population grows and extended families split up, it means that the housing supply does not have to multiply the existing housing stock. Smaller families mean that smaller flats may be more manageable and affordable for the lower income groups.

Third, the increased numbers of temporary migrants require a much more developed private rental sector that can provide the flexibility for a large proportion of the highly mobile and low-income population.

Finally, it is also important to bear in mind that urbanization will reach its peak at some point. This means that eventually, natural growth in the urban population will be the main source of population growth. This will have two implications. On the one hand, the existing migrant population may move up the housing ladder and seek to live more like urban people. This in turn may impose greater pressure on "ordinary" urban housing supply.

Given these demographic and migration trends, the demand for housing can be roughly summarized as: (1) more houses are needed; (2) houses fit for smaller households are needed; and (3) houses are needed that can accommodate a large number of the migrant population who may or may not want to settle down in this city, and the household size may not be as stable as that of the local residents.

Are state interventions successful?

In the past 30 years or so, the state has enforced a whole range of policies trying to set up a housing system that will be able to maximize the use of the private market and at the same time relieve the social pressure on housing. This section examines the performance of state housing interventions against satisfying housing needs and the goals of the policy-makers.

Housing outcomes vs. housing needs

The macro-level statistics quoted at the beginning of the chapter are often challenged by the public, as it is unlikely that an average urban wage earner would be able to identify the massive improvement. A survey of Chinese Family Panel Studies carried out by the Institute of Social Science Survey at Beijing University offers some information on the living conditions of urban households. The household level data might be able to offer a better insight into the actual housing conditions in large Chinese cities. According to the summary statistics published in *Chinese Family Dynamics* (Institute of Social Science Survey 2010, pp. 27–31), in 2009, about 42 percent of urban households lived in owner-occupied houses; 43 percent were private renters. The rest shared houses with their parents. The average living space per person for owner-occupiers was 33 square meters. The size for renters was 23.5 square meters. About 25.2 percent of households had more than one house. At the same time, the proportion of people living in publicly provided houses (including government-provided and employer-provided free housing) was only 3 percent. In terms of housing difficulties, about 13 percent suffered from various difficulties.[4] These numbers, though not comprehensive, can give us a flavor of the issues related to housing poverty in Chinese cities.

Figure 6.6 shows that there have indeed been increases in the urban housing supply and the supply increased on a per capita basis. However, there are several problems with using the average housing supply figure.

The first problem is the increase in household income and income inequality. Urban household income has been growing in the past 30 years. The annual growth rate is above 10 percent on average. Such high growth in

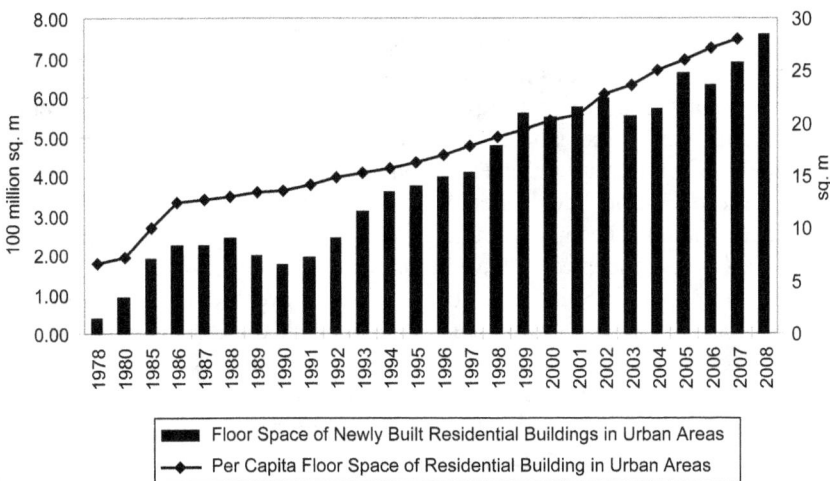

Figure 6.6 Newly built residential buildings in urban China
Source: China Statistics Yearbook, various issues since 2001.

disposable income means that households would be able to save more money than before. Apart from the financial market speculation, the housing market has been considered one major field for investment and speculation (Wang *et al.*, 2008). Sun and Zhang (2008) studied the data for 28 provinces and concluded that private savings in the banking sector helped to create real estate bubbles in all provinces, including the poorer provinces. These speculations made it very difficult for households that do not have much in the way of savings to be able to afford housing. Income and wealth also show a strong tendency of unequal distribution (Gustafsson *et al.*, 2008). According to the Chinese Family Panel Studies, the average income of the highest quintile was 15 times higher than that of the lowest quintile in 2009. This ratio varies across the country. For example, in Beijing, it is more than 20 times and in Shanghai, it is a bit higher than 10 times (Institute of Social Science Survey 2010, p. 10). Inequality in urban income within cities means there is a huge gap in housing affordability within a city. Not only can some families afford good quality housing, but they can also afford several houses. Also, speculators often bet on the booming market rather than buy-to-let, so as a result, large numbers of houses remain unoccupied and at the same time, many people struggle to get a place to live at all (Huque, 2005). It is estimated that around 30 percent of houses in Beijing are unoccupied. In some other cities, the ratio could be as high as 50 percent. According to a survey carried out by the National Electricity Network, there are at least 65 million empty apartments in 660 cities throughout China, which have not consumed any electricity for a period longer than six months. As estimated by Zhao (2010), these houses could potentially accommodate 200 million people. Although there are disputes over the accuracy of this number, it can still give us a rough idea of the potential scale of the problem.

The second problem is that there are only statistics on housing construction. However, very little is known about how many houses were demolished during the urban regeneration. The rate of housing demolition can mean two things: (1) the improvement in the housing statistics is accumulated construction size divided by population, not the net growth of housing supply. Therefore, the actual improvement can be less; and (2) swift demolition can cause uncertainty for households. Given that urban regeneration often targets poorer neighborhoods, they are the ones who have suffered most from such uncertainties. In recent years, demolition has become more aggressive in favor of business interests and the tensions over compensation have become more serious (Wu, 2004a).

Third, the population size used to calculate the average housing size is the number of urban residents who are registered with the local authorities, i.e. they are urban citizens. However, with the growing numbers of rural to urban migrants and the more relaxed household registration requirement, it is very difficult for the local authorities to capture all the people living in cities and there are numerous unregistered households.

Fourth, these statistics do not take into account the housing conditions of the rural to urban migrants. Apart from the small number of well-to-do migrants who are able to afford houses in the private market, the majority of migrant workers are stuck at the bottom end of the private housing market, in employer-provided dormitories and the informal sector. These houses are of very poor quality or offer unsuitable conditions for family living (Li and Duda, 2010; Li *et al.*, 2009). At the same time, migrant workers do not have the same access to urban housing benefits, even if they are also taxpayers. This has led to sustained disadvantage and difficulties for the migrant households (Wu, 2002; 2004b).

Finally, despite the fact that nearly more than 90 percent of houses are privately owned, they are not all owner-occupied houses. A much smaller proportion of people are private owners (Shen, 2008). This is, however, not the result of the existence of active private rental, but rather the higher rate of unoccupied houses. These can be houses that were bought by housing speculators or homebuyers or houses that were never sold. In contrast, the private rental market is seriously underdeveloped. The house price to (annual) rental ratio is well over 500 in cities like Beijing and Shanghai. In theory, when it is not worthwhile to buy, there should be more people trying to rent so that rent levels will increase. The high price to rental ratio shows the huge gap in housing affordability, i.e. some people can afford to keep their houses empty. It also shows the aspiration of urban residents to buy rather than rent. This is associated with the public discourse cultivated under the state home-ownership-oriented policies (Duda *et al.*, 2005).

Outcomes against goals

In this section, the chapter compares the goals and housing outcomes to see whether the reformers have achieved their intended results. There are many ways to mark the different stages of the housing reform in China. In this chapter, the reform periods are defined in order to highlight the changing goals and evolving housing market.

Changing attitudes (1970s–1992)

Housing reforms in China since the late 1970s can be perceived as a persistent attempt to "sell" the concept of private housing to urban households and break away from state-dominated housing provision. The public housing system to be discussed in this chapter can be summarized as a system in which the state provided funding and land for housing construction and allocated houses to urban residents through its agents at various levels. The allocation was based on a set of criteria set by the state. In this sense, even if there were a number of actors in this field, such as employers and local housing authorities, the central government imposed heavy-handed control, and local actors were merely policy enforcers.

The earliest reform began in the late 1970s when private ownership with heavy state subsidies was created. It was meant to be a pilot scheme to push for a radical shift to housing privatization. However, after the pilot schemes in several cities it was soon realized that such a radical change could not work, because even with heavy subsidies, the majority of urban residents would not be able to afford private houses. What is more, people were not willing to give up their welfare housing. In the mid-1980s, even though the state continued to allocate most of the funds for housing construction, the sources of funding began to diversify. For example, some employers encouraged workers to pay out of their own pockets a proportion of the construction costs and once the houses were built, the contributors could own the houses. However, this did not help to boost housing sales. The lack of enthusiasm for housing privatization was because of few incentives for public housing tenants to move into the private sector (Zhang, 2002) and the inability of the majority to afford private houses.

Later, a small number of cities started experimenting with rental reform. To avoid a dramatic increase in living costs, vouchers were introduced to assist households to pay the higher rents. The idea was to make people realize that welfare housing was in essence heavily subsidized houses. When subsidies were made explicit, they might also be withdrawn at any time. In this way, people might not feel secure in the public housing sector and would be motivated to purchase their own home. In 1988, the central government endorsed the experiments and decided to roll out the reform to the whole country. To help people to build up affordability, a Housing Fund was set up. It was meant to be a three-tier funding system jointly contributed by local governments, employers and individuals. In principle, individuals could use the money accumulated to exchange vouchers in order to pay rents and buy houses.

In sum, the reform in this period started from pushing for radical changes and ended up being a battle against the public tenants' struggle to stay put. On the surface, there were mounting complaints about the public housing allocation for its unfairness, inefficiency and the demoralizing effects at work. The employees wanted to be less dependent on the "mercy" of employers or officials in charge of housing allocation. There was also high hopes for the free market to be able to relieve the housing "burden" on the shoulders of the state and employers. However, when housing was indeed privatized, the level of resistance and the distance that people would withdraw from taking part in the newborn system were not expected by the reformers. The resistance came from several directions. First, people realized that not counting on employers or the government would mean spending more money out of their own pockets. Given that the average income level were very low, taking this major welfare item away meant that household disposable income would drop immediately. The Housing Fund was still in its early stage and the sums accumulated were not yet a significant amount for home buying (Li, 2001). Second, because of the limited funding for public housing in the past, there was a long waiting list to be cleared. People who had waited in the queue for a long time found it hard to accept if the allocation was stopped just when it was about time for them to be allocated a house. These were usually people at the bottom of the political and administration hierarchy. They were the ones who actively pleaded for continued (or at least another round of) housing allocation (ibid.). Finally, people were still uncertain about the future of the country. They would rather "wait and see" than venture into the uncertain part of the economy for fear of a reverse in the direction of reform.

Apart from the institutional rigidity, the reform in this period also had to face external constraints. First, wage control was not fully relaxed for a large part during this reform, so housing reform had to count on the very limited savings abilities. For most people, buying houses in this period meant the lion's share of their life-savings would be devoted to the house. Second, a formal housing finance system did not really exist. The informal fund-raising schemes were not encouraged by the state. People needed to pay off their housing debt at once. Third, when house prices increased, heavy subsidies meant even greater liabilities for the state and employers.

Therefore, after the initial enthusiasm for marketization, the reform to push for private ownership was put on hold. Radical reform measures were replaced by slower changes. A large amount of effort was devoted to using intermediate changes to send strong messages to the public that welfare housing would end, and if they did not move to the private sector as soon as possible, it would be even less worthwhile in the future.

By year-end 1990, 24 percent of residential houses were privatized, 7 percentage points growth from 1983. However, the higher private ownership rate was not really driven by the emerging housing market, but rather by the heavy subsidies.

At the same time, employers had to face the challenge of reduced public funds for housing allocation. The solution they came up with was to "look for" money to continue housing allocation, so that the existing waiting list could be cleared. At the same time, many employers started to sell the existing housing stock and the newly built houses to their employees at extremely low prices, in the hope that once everyone owned their house, there would be no more pressure on employer provision (ibid.). This meant that newly built houses were channeled into the pool of welfare housing. To make things worse, no rent would be paid in the future for these heavily subsidized new houses.

In this sense, the reform in this period was a failure. The aim was to reduce public spending on housing provision. However, pushing for private ownership led to even more spending.

There were some successes observed in terms of actual outcomes. After all, a private housing sector had been set up. In 1998, local governments were also allowed to sell the right to use land to private companies. These reforms paved the way for the private sector to play a bigger role in housing supply. Nevertheless, it could only function with a lot more reforms.

Separating the old and the new systems and improving affordability (1992–98)

Reform measures in this period were more cautious than in the previous period. To prevent newly built houses from being given away at too low prices, in October 1991, a new policy was issued requiring new houses to be treated differently from the old ones (*xinfang xinbanfa*; *laofang laobanfa*). At the same time, in the public housing sector, the rent levels of public housing were increased to cover the actual costs of maintenance, management and depreciation. The goal was that, by 2000, tenants of public houses would have to pay for maintenance and management, housing depreciation, interest for state investment and the property tax. Ideally, in the future, all houses would be commodities and public rentals would include more elements such as land usage fees, developers' insurance premium, and developers' mark-up. In other words, the gap between public and private rental houses would shrink or even disappear.

In practice, however, increasing the rent of public housing was not very easy, mainly because of the resistance from the tenants. In the public housing allocation period, people in higher positions were allocated larger houses. When the rent level was raised, they suffered the first as the income gaps between the senior and junior employees were not yet sufficient to cover the difference in house size. Under public pressure, the announced schedule for raising rents was delayed repeatedly.

Meanwhile, on the privatization front, selling existing public houses became heated. One only needed to pay the price that varied according to house size. Other factors, such as quality and location, were not taken into account. However, when they sold the houses on the private market, all the factors would count. This meant that public house owners with a good location and good quality houses, usually people in higher positions and with greater power, would receive a windfall gain because of privatization (Zhao and Sai, 2008). Therefore, they became very interested in buying the houses rather than waiting for the rent to increase and eroding their wealth and income. Soon, subsidized ownership became so popular that policy-makers started to worry that the heavy discounts would cause serious losses of state assets, and they banned subsidized sales in 1992 (Wang, 2003, p. 179).

This period marks the beginning of the first housing boom since the Communist Party came to power. From the second half of 1992 to early 1993, the housing boom reached many cities. The number of real estate developers increased dramatically. Land sales were active and prices were rocketing. In the southern provinces, land and housing speculation was rampant. This happened in the context of relaxed control over real estate development, the devolving power of approving construction projects to local governments, and the enthusiasm of banks to lend money to real estate developers. Facing the overheated market, the state decided to regulate the market more closely and tighten up the money supply (Chai, 2008). With the difficulties in raising public housing rent and the control of selling public housing, the housing reform was literally put on hold.

In July 1994, a new round of housing reform was initiated. The new policy set out to make houses jointly paid for by the state, employers and individuals. A social insurance scheme and housing finance were tested in some cities and rolled out to the whole country. Both employers and employees would contribute to a Housing Provident Fund (HPF). Individuals could take money out of HPF or borrow against it at favorable terms. This system was modeled against the Singaporean housing system. To encourage private ownership, all public housing, unless specified, was allowed to be sold to households. The idea was to make high-income households pay the market price (*shichang jia*), middle- and low-income households pay the "cost price" (*chengben jia*), and poorer households pay the lowest price, i.e. the "standard price" (*biaozhun jia*). At the same time, in the public rental sector, tenants of new houses would have to pay "new rents" which were much higher than the "old rents." The targeted rent level as announced by the central government was that by 2000, an average income household would have to spend 15 percent of the household income on rent. The intention behind the combination of these two sets of policies regarding home-ownership and higher rental level was clear: to make public rental less attractive and create a sense of urgency for people to shift to the private market. As a result, from 1994 to 1996, half of the newly built houses were sold to individuals.

In 1995, the "Housing Project for Low Income Households" (the Anju Project) was introduced in order to help low and mid-low income groups buy houses. It was considered part of the social security schemes. The targeted group was the people suffering from housing difficulties. By the end of 1997, about 6.5 million people had benefited from the Anju Project.

At the same time, the other major reforms initiated in this period also helped the progress in housing reform, the most important being wage and labor market reforms. With some preliminary changes in the 1980s, major wage and labor market reforms were launched in the 1990s. As a result, the private sector started to develop and moved on to become the most important employers in China, and the growth in average income accelerated in the second half of the 1990s (Yueh, 2004). The emerging private labor market meant that some workers might have to return the allocated houses to their employers before they could leave public sector jobs. However, they would soon find that they needed to acquire houses in the market. There were, for a while, workers flowing back to the public sector after realizing that their higher salaries in the private sector could not make up for the loss of giving up the housing benefit and other social welfare (Li and Gong, 2003) (Figure 6.7). These changes allowed urban skilled workers to bargain with private employers to increase their salaries. As we can see in Figure 6.8, the wage level in the private sector increased much faster than the wage level in the other sectors and was well above that in the public sector at the end of 1998. This trend was reversed when the 1998 housing reform stopped housing allocation to public sector employees.

Whether the reform in this period succeeded according to its original goals is not very clear. It had made some institutional changes that had left important marks on the housing system until then. First, the social insurance system, though regarded by many people as "insufficient" to play a big part in home purchasing when it started (Lee, 2000; Li, 2001), and people were not keen to borrow against this account, should be one of the most important institutional set-ups. There was disagreement on whether people should be

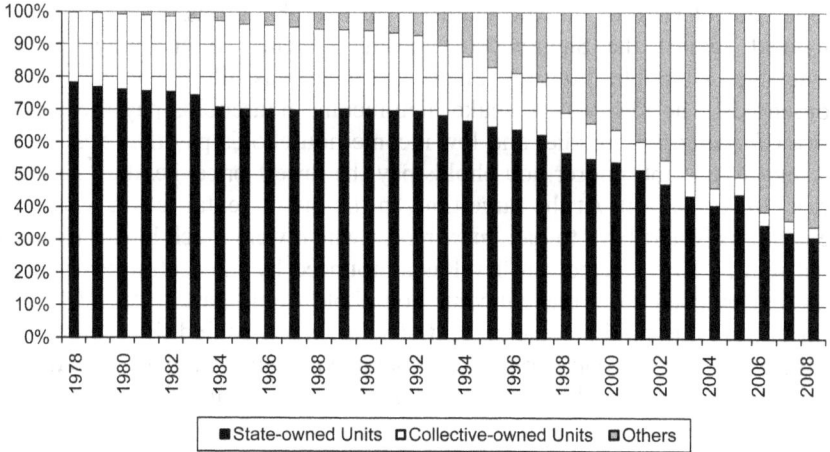

Figure 6.7 Number of employed persons at year-end in urban and rural areas, 1978–2008
Source: China Statistics Yearbook, various issues since 1978.

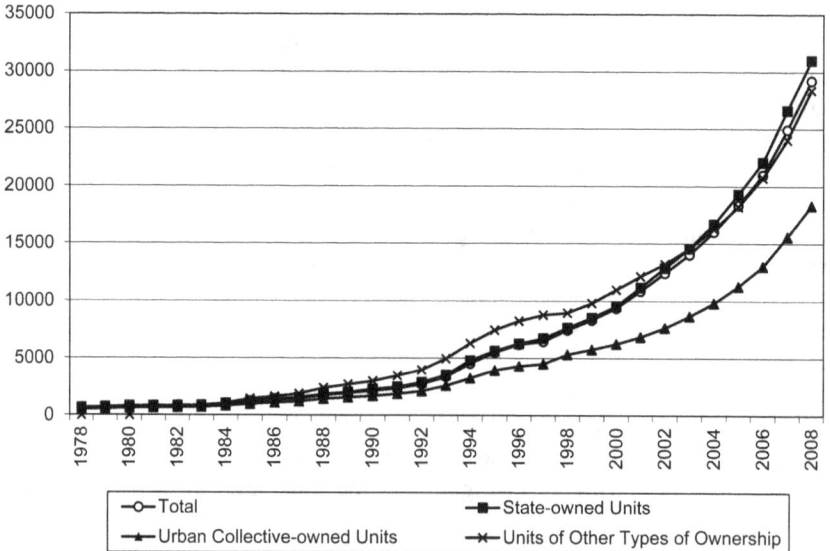

Figure 6.8 Average wage of staff and workers, 1978–2008
Source: China Statistics Yearbook, various issues since 1978.

"helped" by the state to save money for housing at all. However, we need to take into account the strong resistance to private housing at the beginning of the reform. Setting up the fund helped to develop a culture of saving money regularly for home buying. Up to the end of 2008, 7.7 million people had contributed to the HPF. The total amount paid into the fund in the year 2008 was 4.5 billion *yuan*. The total amount accumulated over time has reached 20.7 billion *yuan*. So far, about 41.5 percent has been used to assist people to buy houses (Ministry of Housing and Rural-Urban Construction, 2009). We cannot claim that it is a successful scheme in terms of participation and the level of usage. However, its potential to function as a supplement (when needed) cannot be ignored. Second, the housing project for low-income households (the Anju Project) was replaced by the Economical and Comfortable Housing Project (*Jingji Shiyong Fang*) in 1998. The latter enjoyed fewer subsidies. This policy suggested that the state wanted to stop people from depending on heavy state subsidies.

The outcomes were not as planned. The incremental reform in this period helped to build up the anticipation that the housing "doomsday" would indeed come soon. For individuals, it was rational to seize as much benefit from the state as possible before it was gone (Li and Gong, 2003). Employers, being the grassroots-level policy implementers, wanted to clear the existing waiting list before moving on to the next stage. As a result, they became the largest homebuyer in the private market (White, 1996). However, this turned out to be self-defeating. The housing boom led to soaring prices of construction materials, which increased the costs for construction. Further sales of houses at discount rates by employers meant greater loss of public resources.

During this period, housing reformers also had to cope with the consequences of reforms in other sectors, such as land, finance and real estate. The market transition in these sectors unleashed a series of "rational" responses from the private sector that could destabilize the economy. The state was forced to adjust its position and regulate the markets by tightening budgets and carrying out macro control. In this sense, housing was no longer an area that was restricted by other reforms. It also started to have an impact on the overall economic performance.

Pushing further towards marketization (1998–2005)

The year 1998 marked the end of employer housing allocation and the beginning of diversified housing supply and protection. It was a continuation of the earlier reforms but more "in-depth" and on a larger scale.

In 1998, "The State Council Notice No. 23" reiterated the government's determination to push forward urban housing reform. The key feature of this set of reforms was to replace "housing asset allocation" (*shiwu fenfang*) with "housing cash allocation" (*huobi fenfang*). According to the new regulation, employers should stop allocating houses directly to their employees. Employees should instead buy houses on the market. 'Houseless' households (*wufang hu*) or households living below the officially set minimum standard could receive one-off or monthly cash benefits to help with home-buying. The amount was subject to their status at work and current housing conditions. In addition, for the first time in the reform, the state put the Economical and Affordable Housing (*Jingji Shiyong Fang*)—i.e. houses built with state initiatives and sold to middle or lower-middle income households at prices below market level—on the agenda. The aim was to stop housing allocation directly and to set up a housing supply system, in which the state helped only the lowest income groups, and higher income groups were expected to buy on the market with/without subsidies. In this way, a multi-dimensional housing supply system was established on paper. It included three key sectors: cheap rental, subsidized ownership (*Jingji Shiyong Fang*), and private ownership. In practice, the system was steered towards making the private sector the dominant housing supplier.

Jingji Shiyong Fang, according to the original idea, should be able to cover a large proportion of urban residents. However, the supply was very limited. Between 1999 and 2008, about 4.5 million flats under the *Jingji Shiyong Fang* scheme (60–100 square meters each) were built.[5] This was equivalent to about 1.1 percent of the total number of urban households.

In 2003, a sense of uncertainty about housing reform emerged. Although the central government wanted to continue to provide public rental housing to the urban poor, local governments stopped it completely. People from the middle-income groups began to realize that the eligibility criteria and house size could be manipulated so that the middle-income groups would be priced out of the scheme. Higher-income groups and well-connected people, if could prove that they suffered from housing difficulties, would be able to apply for the subsidized housing (Yang and Shen, 2008). The public concerns over the potential of favoring well-to-do families and fraudulent practices never stopped. To make sure the direction of the reform would not be reversed, the state published a policy stressing that the majority of families should rely on the private market rather than the state subsidies to acquire their housing. The result was clear, as shown in Figure 6.9, from 2003 to 2005, subsidized houses played an even smaller role than before.

As discussed earlier, the housing outcomes for this period have several characteristics. Housing inequality became more serious. Income has become the differentiating factor for different neighborhoods. The well-to-dos moved into newly built, good quality and gated communities (Wu, 2005). Dilapidated, older or peri-urban neighborhoods often housed people who were not able to escape the poverty trap, or migrants (Wu, 2007; Wu and Huang, 2007). At the same time, households benefited from the previous system and were able to enjoy the advantage of using the older houses to finance the purchase the new ones (Chen *et al.*, 2011; Li and Li, 2006). What is more, starting from 2003, the urban labor market was opened to rural–urban migrant workers. They came to cities without much savings and often to work in low-income jobs. However, they were not entitled to the housing benefits that urban citizens could enjoy and usually lived in poor housing conditions (Li, 2006; Wu, 2004b).

However, these outcomes do not mean that the reformers had not achieved their goals in this period. In 1998, affected by the economic crises in Southeast Asia, the China's exports suffered. To maintain economic growth, the Chinese government used both monetary and fiscal policies to boost domestic demand. The banking system also faced looser credit control (Xiao, 2010). At

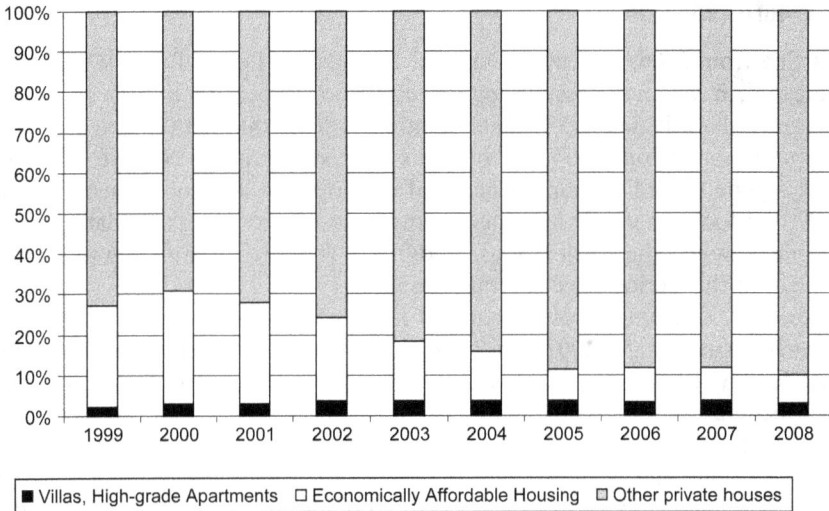

Figure 6.9 Number of flats of residential buildings completed by enterprises for real estate development

Source: China Statistics Yearbook 2010, Table 5-42.

the same time, the central government set growth targets and urged local governments to find new growth engines for the economy. Many local governments responded to this stimulus and treated housing, mostly private housing, as the key area for new sources of growth (Li and Piachaud, 2006). This was in line with the determination to push for further housing privatization stated in 2003. As shown in Figure 6.10, starting from 2003, private houses as a share of the total housing supply indeed grew faster than before.

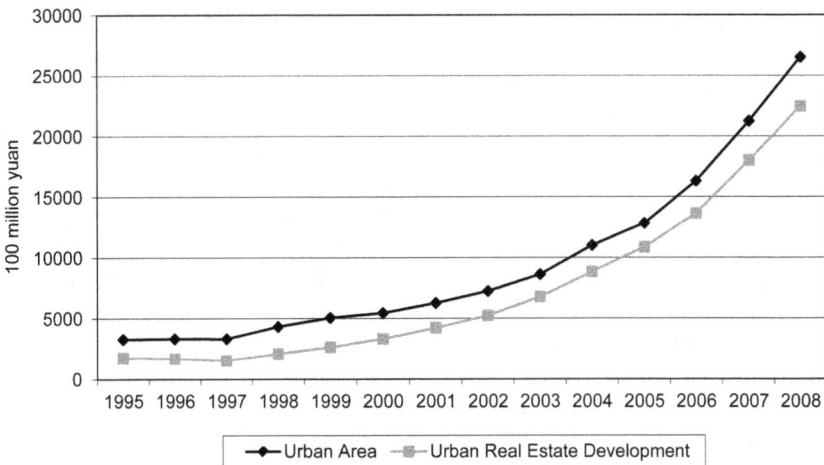

Figure 6.10 Total investment in residential buildings

Source: China Statistics Yearbook, various issues since 1995.

A U-turn (2006–)?

Starting from 2006, a greater consensus emerged that even if people's income increased, it was not possible for all urban households to be able to afford houses in the private market. The intention to force through full privatization was unrealistic (Wu, 2007). At the same time, in a broader context, the Hu–Wen regime started to emphasize social development and social harmony. In 2007, the focus of public housing schemes was on providing affordable housing for low-income urban households and rural to urban migrants. The policies in this period have several elements.

The first is resuming construction of houses for low-income families (State Council Issue No. 24, 2007). In 2009, the long-abolished term "housing projects for low income households" (the Anju Project) crept back into the official documents although the definition of the revived term is yet to be clearly defined. However, it is broadly understood that this type of flat should be relatively small and equipped with simple facilities. It should be different from the economical and comfortable houses (*Jingji Shiyong Fang*). When the Anju Project was replaced by *Jingji Shiyong Fang* in 1988, the idea was to remove the aim for people to depend on "social welfare" or "social security." However, the *Jingji Shiyong Fang* scheme has been plagued by corruption, fraudulence and abuse. Upper middle-income people try to get their hands on these subsidized houses and sell them at higher prices or rent them out. There are restrictions on the transactions of *Jingji Shiyong Fang*, for example, they cannot be sold within five years of purchase and the price should not be much higher than similar buildings in the same community. The purpose of these restrictions is to make the houses less attractive to speculators and reduce the opportunity for rent seeking. However, in practice, the restrictions did not prevent the owners from gaining handsome profits. The profit comes from several sources: (1) the houses are usually built much larger than the official size of 60 square meters[6] and are well equipped; each house if re-sold in the private market immediately can be worth hundreds of thousands *yuan* in profit; (2) the urban housing market has boomed in the past few years. Even if the owners wait for five years to sell, the profit is still handsome. Another problem with *Jingji Shiyong Fang* is that the eligibility to own this house is only checked before the transaction. There is no follow-up method to check on possible frauds or changes in economic status. There is no serious punishment for the rule-breakers. As a result, the penalties for fraud and rule-breaking are negligible. The reintroduction of the Anju Project aims to avoid the problems with *Jingji Shiyong Fang*. The idea is to impose tight control over the size of the houses and make them less attractive to higher-income groups and speculators.[7]

The second is increasing the supply of cheap rental houses. By 2008, less than 1 percent of the urban households lived in cheap rental houses (*Lianzufang*). The new enthusiasm for cheap rental houses led to an increase in the supply of the public rental houses. By the end of 2009, the share of urban households living in public rental houses increased to 2.8 percent. According to the government plan for 2009–11, another 7.47 million low-income households should be able to get out of housing poverty. The standard for cheap rental houses would be controlled at 13 square meters per person[8] and the house size should be less than 50 square meters. The houses would be equipped with only basic facilities. Central government would allocate part of the funds to local authorities. Local governments are expected to devote all the capital gains and at least 10 percent of the earnings from selling land-use rights to building cheap rental houses. The target is to increase the number of recipients of housing benefits to 6.6 percent of urban households in 2015, of which 62.7 percent will receive cheap rental houses directly (*Xinhua Newsnet*, 2009).

The backdrop for setting up these changes is related to the global economic recession. The Chinese economy used to rely heavily on exports to maintain growth and employment. It was claimed that to avoid high unemployment rates, GDP growth needed to be at least 7 percent (Sabin, 2009). To avoid recession, the state quickly turned to expansionary policies. Housing was one designated area for increasing public spending. Rhetorically, this also goes well with the intention to shift the focus of the state from pushing for economic growth to improving people's lives.

However, this strategy has to face up to several challenges. First, state investment in housing construction on a massive scale often has side effects. An increased housing supply may lead to lower housing prices. This may affect the income of private investors and cause a price crash in the housing market. If this really happens, the macro-economic goal of boosting economic performance can be undermined.

Second, organized speculation by institutional investors or informally formed investor groups had caused housing bubbles in many cities. To prevent speculation and cool down the over-heated economy, in 2010, a series of policies to tighten the control over money lending and home-buying eligibility was designed to make it difficult for hot money to flow. However, these measures came up against strong resistance. Local governments wanted investors to continue to borrow money so that they could continue to sell land to fund local services. Developers disliked the lower market price. Banks ended up with more bad debts because developers could not complete the projects. What is new to this period is that international investors have turned to China for investment opportunities since the economic recession. Slower growth caused by lending control means greater uncertainty and stress for these investors. Therefore, in the summer of 2010, we can see great efforts by the private sector and the local governments to persuade the central government to withdraw some of its earlier policies. So far, the state has held on to resist the pressure. However, the policies came at a time of recession after all. It is difficult to tell when the economic situation will improve, whether the state will or can continue to fulfill its promises on investing in cheaper housing for lower-income groups.

Another battlefront is urban regeneration and urban expansion. It has become a hotbed for social tension and protest. Violence breaks out over the disputes over the legitimacy of demolition procedures and compensation. Local urban governments, that are driven by the possibility to sell land to higher payers in order to earn money (Yang and Wang, 2008) are in favor of frequent urban regeneration and urban expansion driven by business interests (Shin, 2009; Tian, 2008; Wu, 2004a). On the other hand, developers constantly argue that better compensation to sitting residents will lead to even higher housing prices and the result will be to hurt the poor more. Entangled in these disputes, the more recent attempt to publish a regulation on urban regeneration and compensation has been put on hold.

Conclusion

The experience of China suggests that a "successful" state intervention is becoming more difficult to achieve. As the reform continues, housing has changed from a largely self-contained policy area into an important engine of the economy and is playing a bigger part in the national policy framework. The "context" of housing reform has expanded from targeting certain groups of people to facing the pressure from many stakeholders, some of whom are even abroad. As a result, it is difficult to push for housing policy changes without affecting the interests of some social groups or causing possible problems in other policy areas. Thus, the evaluation of the outcomes of a set of policies also becomes increasingly elusive, and a seemingly sensible policy could become counter-productive, either in the near future or in a broader context.

A narrower view is that housing has been playing a much larger part in the national economic and social development strategies. The public housing schemes, therefore, take on a role that is not directly related to the improvement of housing for the poor, but rather on boosting economic performances. Therefore, the satisfactory match between policy goals and outcomes might mean less desirable social outcomes.

These constraints also affect the state's ability to be consistent in solving the housing difficulties for the poor. Despite the central government's intention to change the situation, the poor are increasingly marginalized at the local level. Considering that the central government also has to deal with all the different interests, it is a fragile hypothesis to make that the central government will hold to its current stance unless there are major reforms regarding public finance and land policy.

Notes

1 Including shared public space that is inside the building but outside the private apartments. Private living space inside the walls of an apartment is much smaller. However, the data are not comparable for different cities. Therefore, we do not use the figures for private space.
2 Data quoted in this paragraph come from the Public Communiqué on Social Economic Statistics of each city as of each year.

3 Official statistics do not include Hong Kong and Macao. In addition, the data is often criticized for not including people who are not registered with the Public Security System.
4 The reported difficulties were mostly about over-crowding.
5 The most frequently quoted data are the total square meters completed in a certain period. However, these data cannot really reflect the actual housing supply as the house size can vary greatly. Therefore, we prefer to use the number of houses constructed. Given that one household is only entitled to one economical and comfortable flat, we can obtain a much better understanding of how many households actually benefited from this housing scheme.
6 Many local governments approved larger economical and comfortable houses of more than 100 square meters and the largest ones as reported in the media were 276 square meters in Yan'an, Shaanxi Province (*Xian Daily*, 2010, "276 square metres *jingji shiyong fang* appeared." Available at: www.chinanews.com.cn/estate/estate-qnht/news/2010 /05-29/2311693.shtml (accessed 22 July 2010).
7 There are other options. For example, Beijing and Shanghai, instead of reintroducing the Anju Project housing, simply put a cap on the size of *Jingji Shiyong Fang* and stopped offering subsidies to larger houses.
8 This is the construction size.

References

Beckett, K., and Herbert, S. (2008) "Dealing with disorder: social control in the post-industrial city," *Theoretical Criminology*, 12: 5–30.
Bloom, N.D. (2008) *Public Housing that Worked: New York in the Twentieth Century*, Philadelphia, PA: University of Pennsylvania Press.
Bottelier, P. (2010) "Beijing's new challenge: China's post-crisis housing bubble," *Policy Outlook*. Available at: http://carnegieendowment.org/publications/index.cfm?fa=view&id=41104 (accessed 21 July 2010).
Chai, Q. (2008) "Thirty years of real estate reform and market development," in D. Zou and R. Ouyang (eds.) *Report on China's Economic Development and Institutional Reform, No. 1*, Beijing: Social Science Literature Press. Available at: http://theory.people.com.cn/GB/49154/49155/8108609.html (accessed 22 July 2010).
Chen, J., Guo, F. and Wu, Y. (2011) "One decade of urban housing reform in China: urban housing price dynamics and the role of migration and urbanization, 1995–2005," *Habitat International*, 35: 1–8.
Duda, M., Zhang, X. and Dong, M. (2005) "China's homeownership-oriented housing policy: an examination of two programs using survey data from Beijing," *Harvard University Joint Center for Housing Studies*, Working Paper W 5.
Forrest, R. and Murie, A. (2009) "Residualization and council housing: aspects of the changing social relations of housing tenure," *Journal of Social Policy*, 12: 453–68.
Gilbert, A. (2007) "Inequality and why it matters," *Geography Compass*, 1: 422–47.
Griffiths, E. and Tita, G. (2009) "Homicide in and around public housing: is public housing a hotbed, a magnet, or a generator of violence for the surrounding community?' *Social Problems*, 56: 474–93.
Guo, Y., Ding, J. and Meng, Q. (2006) "Dachengshi liudong renkou juzhu xingtai yu juzhu kongjian biandong jili" [Metropolitan floating population's dwelling modes and its spatial changing mechanism: a case of Minhang, Shanghai], *Southern China Population*, 21: 40–5.
Guo, Z. (2010) *Tiwen 2010* [Questions about 2010 China], Beijing: Red Flag Press.

138   *Bingqin Li*

Gustafsson, B., Li, S., and Sicular, T. (2008) *Inequality and Public Policy in China*, Cambridge: Cambridge University Press.

Harloe, M. and Martens, M. (2009) "Comparative housing research," *Journal of Social Policy*, 13: 255–77.

Hasan, A. (2006) "Orangi Pilot Project; the expansion of work beyond Orangi and the mapping of informal settlements and infrastructure," *Environment & Urbanization*, 18: 451–80.

Huque, A. S. (2005) "Shifting emphasis in the role of the state: urban housing reform in China," *Asian Journal of Political Science*, 13: 53–74.

Institute of Social Science Survey (2010) *Chinese Family Dynamics*, Beijing: Beijing University Press.

Lee, J. (2000) "From welfare housing to home ownership: the dilemma of China's housing reform," *Housing Studies*, 15: 61–76.

Li, B. (2001) "China's housing reform and work incentive effects," PhD thesis, London School of Economics.

——(2005) "Urban housing privatisation: redefining the responsibilities of the state, employers and individuals," in S. Green and G. S. Liu (eds.) *Exit the Dragon?: Privatization and State Control in China*, London: Chatham House and Blackwell Publishing.

——(2006) "Floating population or urban citizens? Status, social provision and circumstances of rural-urban migrants in China," *Social Policy and Administration*, 40: 174–95.

Li, B. and Piachaud, D. (2006) "Urbanization and social policy in China," *Asia Pacific Development Journal*, 13: 1–26.

Li, B. and Duda, M. (2010) "Employers as landlords for rural-to-urban migrants in Chinese cities," *Environment and Urbanization*, 22: 13–31.

Li, B., Duda, M. and An, X. (2009) "Drivers of housing choice among rural-to-urban migrants: evidence from Taiyuan," *Journal of Asian Public Policy*, 2: 142–56.

Li, B. and Gong, S. (2003) "Social inequalities and wage, housing and pension reforms in urban China," *Asia Programme*, Working Paper 3, Chatham House, London.

Li, S.M. and Li, L. (2006) "Life course and housing tenure change in urban China: a study of Guangzhou," *Housing Studies*, 21: 653–70.

Lipman, P. (2008) "Mixed-income schools and housing: advancing the neoliberal urban agenda," *Journal of Education Policy*, 23: 119–34.

McCarty, D. (2008) "The impact of public housing policy on family social work theory and practice," *Journal of Family Social Work*, 11: 74–88.

Meyers, M.K. and Garfinkel, I. (1999) "Social indicators and the study of inequality," *Economic Policy Review*, 5: 148–63.

Ministry of Housing and Rural-Urban Construction (2009) "2008 nian quanguo zhufang gongjijin guanqi qingkuang tongbao" [Housing Provident Fund Administration Report, 2008]. Available at: www.cin.gov.cn/hydt/200903/t20090323_187675.htm (accessed 20 July 2010).

Newman, S. (1984) "Housing research: conceptual and measurement issues," *Surveying Subjective Phenomena*, 2: 143–55.

Sabin, L. (2009) "New bosses in the workers' state: the growth of non-state sector employment in China," *The China Quarterly*, 140: 944–70.

Shen, X. (2008) "Shengzhen jumin zhufang ziyoulv 83% de shuofa beizhi yangai pinfu chaju' [The 83 per cent of urban home ownership is accused of disguising inequality], *China Youth Daily*, 1 July 2008. Available at: www.360doc.com/content/08/0107/10/2760951891.shtml (accessed 22 July 2010).

Shin, H.B. (2009) "Residential redevelopment and the entrepreneurial local state: the implications of Beijing's shifting emphasis on urban redevelopment policies," *Urban Studies*, 46: 2815–39.

State Council PRC (2007) "Guowuyuan guanyu jiejue chengshi dishouru jiating zhufang kunnan de ruogan yijian" [State Council opinions on solving housing difficulties for urban low-income families]. Available at: www.google.co.uk/search? rlz=1C1CHMZenGB362GB335&sourceid=chrome&ie=UTF-8&q=国务院关于解决城市低收入家庭住房困难的若干意见 (accessed 20 July 2010).

Sun, L. and Zhang, S. (2008) "External dependent economy and structural real estate bubbles in China," *China and World Economy*, 16: 34–50.

Tian, L. (2008) "The chengzhongcun land market in China: boon or bane? A perspective on property rights," *International Journal of Urban and Regional Research*, 32: 282–304.

Turner, M.A., Popkin, S.J. and Rawlings, L. (2009) *Public Housing and the Legacy of Segregation*, Washington, DC: Urban Institute Press.

Wang, J., Wang, Z. and Chang, Z. (2008) "The research on controlling effect of taxation in the housing market of China," *Journal of Public Administration*, 6: 154–66.

Wang, Y.P. (2003) "Progress and problems of urban housing reform," in C.J. Finer (ed.) *Social Policy Reform in China: Views from Home and Abroad*, Ashford: Ashgate.

White, G. (1996) "Corruption and the transition from socialism in China," *Journal of Law and Society*, 23: 149–69.

Wu, F. (2004a) "Residential relocation under market-oriented redevelopment: the process and outcomes in urban China," *Geoforum*, 35: 453–70.

——(2004b) "Sources of migrant housing disadvantage in urban China," *Environment and Planning A*, 36: 1285–304.

——(2005) "Rediscovering the 'gate' under market transition: from work-unit compounds to commodity housing enclaves," *Housing Studies*, 20: 235–54.

——(2007) "The poverty of transition: from industrial district to poor neighbourhood in the city of Nanjing, China," *Urban Studies*, 44: 2673–94.

Wu, F. and Huang, N. (2007) "New urban poverty in China: economic restructuring and transformation of welfare provision," *Asia Pacific Viewpoint*, 48: 168–85.

Wu, W. (2002) "Migrant housing in urban China: choices and constraints," *Urban Affairs Review*, 38: 90–119.

Xiao, B. (2010) "A research on monetary policy's operational target from 1994 to 2007 in China," *Journal of Financial Development Research*, 1: 16–18.

Xinhua Newsnet (2009) "Cheap rental housing security plan, 2009–10," 2 June 2009. Available at: http://news.xinhuanet.com/fortune/2009–06/02/content_11476918.htm (accessed 21 July 2010).

Yang, D.Y.R. and Wang, H.K. (2008) "Dilemmas of local governance under the development zone fever in China: a case study of the Suzhou region," *Urban Studies*, 45: 1037–54.

Yang, Z. and Shen, Y. (2008) "The affordability of owner occupied housing in Beijing," *Journal of Housing and the Built Environment*, 23: 317–35.

Yu, F. (2010) "Zhufang wenti heyi ju lianghui guanzhu huati qianlie' [Why housing problem has become the biggest concern during the People's Congress]. Available at: www.china.com.cn/blog/zhuanti/2010rd/2010–12/26/content_19621626.htm (accessed 19 July 2010).

Yueh, L.Y. (2004) "Wage reforms in China during the 1990s," *Asian Economic Journal*, 18: 149–64.

Zhang, X.Q. (2002) "Governing housing in China: state, market and work units," *Journal of Housing and the Built Environment*, 17: 7–20.

Zhao, R. and Sai, D. (2008) "The distribution of wealth in China," in B. Gustafsson, S. Li, and T. Sicular (eds.) *Inequality and Public Policy in China*, Cambridge: Cambridge University Press.

Zhao, X. (2010) "When the sun of housing sets, it will not rise again," *Hexun Housing News*. Available at: http://house.hexun.com/2010-07-09/124204518.html (accessed 21 July 2010).

7 China's rapid demographic transition and its challenges to the social security system

Ding Lu

Introduction

China's hyper-economic growth in the past three decades has occurred in a period of rapid demographic transition that is highly favorable to savings, investment, and human capital improvement. Before the early 1970s, the high birth rates and falling death rates had contributed to over two decades of rapid population growth, which was only temporarily interrupted by the 1959–61 famine. After the government started family planning programs in the 1970s, fertility rates started falling quickly and the baby boomers from earlier decades joined the labor force in waves. The result is a three-decade decline of the overall dependency ratio and an expanding labor force that has grown faster than the population (Figure 7.1). This favorable demographic change co-occurred with the market-oriented reform that triggered the economy's takeoff.

Entering the 2010s, China's demographic transition is reaching a turning point: the dependency-ratio curve is at its bottom and will soon start on a steep rise while the population aging accelerates in coming years. In this chapter, we observe that, due to a series of historical events, China's population growth has developed some unique features. These features have contributed to a very rapid demographic transition, which is taking place at a speed much faster than elsewhere in the world. The quick evaporation of "demographic dividends" will have profound implications on China's economic prospect in the next two decades. A fast aging and shrinking labor force is likely to diminish the economy's growth vigor. The falling saving rates move to slow investment growth. A fast rising old-age support burden will pose serious challenges to the country's immature social security system. Whether the country is ready to grapple with these changes is a serious question.

China's past gains from demographic dividends

The pattern of demographic transition displayed in Figure 7.1 well illustrates the hypothesis of "demographic dividends." In the past three decades of hyper-economic growth, China has enjoyed tremendous gains from this transition.

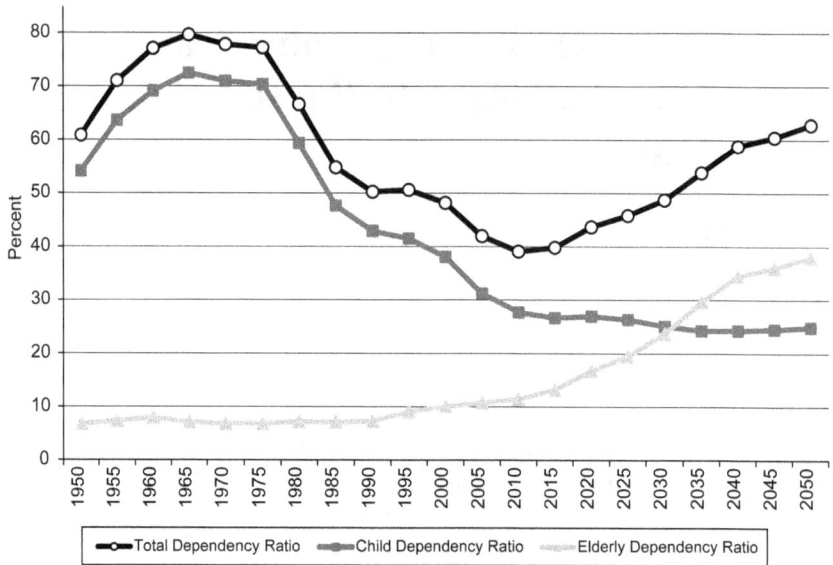

Figure 7.1 China s dependency ratios, 1950–2050
Notes: Child dependency ratio = population age 0–14 to population age 15–64; Elderly dependency ratio = population age 65 and above to population age 15–64; Total dependency ratio = (population age 0–14 and population age 65+) to population age 15–64. Source: United Nations (2009).

A typical demographic transition occurs as a society goes through economic modernization and thus experiences several stages of demographic changes. At the *initial stage*, both fertility rate and death rate are high and life expectancy is relatively short so the population growth is constrained and dependency ratio is high due to the large number of children an average working couple has to take care of. When economic modernization arrives with improved public healthcare, better diets, and rising income, the death rate (especially infant mortality rate) starts to plummet and people live longer. The growing divergence between the high birth rate and the falling death rate accelerates population growth and leads to an unprecedented expansion of the population size which features as the *second stage* of demographic transition. Sooner or later, with further modernization and rise in standard of living, the fertility rate starts to decline and the population growth slows and thus reaches the *third stage* of transition. Eventually, the falling birth rate converges with the lower death rate over time, resulting in a stable size of population. Among the world's richest countries, a post-transition era (or the *fourth stage*) is unfolding: As the fertility falls to and below the replacement level, population growth eventually comes to a halt and even starts to decline. With the low birth rate and lengthening life expectancy, the population age structure gets older and an aging society emerges.

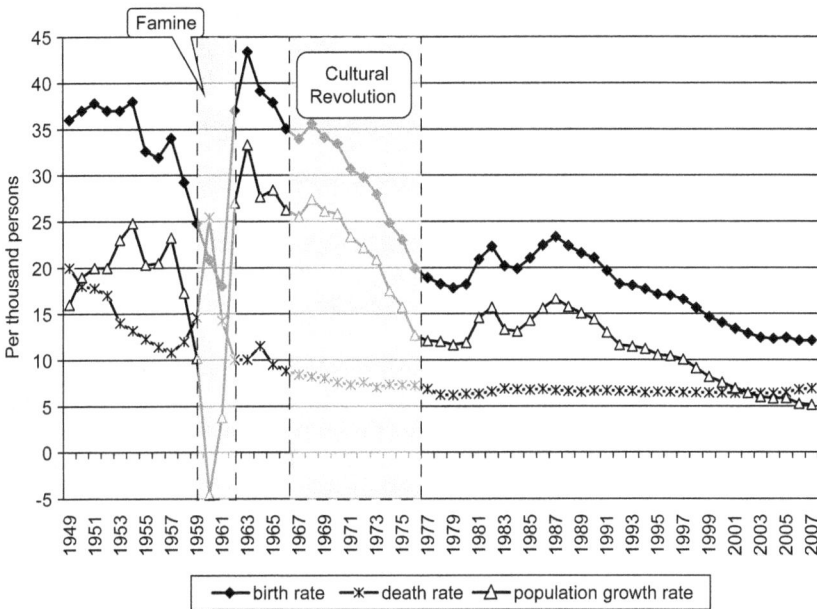

Figure 7.2 Birth rate, death rate, and natural growth rate of population, 1949–2007
Source: NBSC (various years), National Population and Family Planning Commission (2003).

A particular type of demographic change occurs when the demographic transition goes from the second stage to the third stage: As fertility falls and the earlier baby boomers enter the working age, there are fewer young mouths to feed and more youthful workers to produce (Lee and Mason, 2006), while the working-age population grows at a faster pace than the total population. If the working-age population is sufficiently employed, it will be a big boost to the growth for per capita income and thus offer a precious "window of development opportunity."

As seen in Figure 7.1, China's child dependency ratio (between the population aged 0–14 to the population aged 15–64) fell all the way from over 70 percent in 1970 to below 30 percent after the turn of the century, while the elderly dependency ratio (between the population aged 65+ to the population aged 15–64) remained relatively stable below 10 percent. The total dependency ratio (between the population aged 0–14 and 65+ to the population aged 15–64) thus fell from nearly 80 percent to below 40 percent. Such a drastic decline of dependency ratio has brought in a golden era of economic growth.

By international comparison, decline of China's dependency ratio during the demographic transition has occurred at a much faster pace than what happened in other parts of the world. A closer look at this transition reveals some unique features of the country's demographic trends, which can be attributed to a few historical incidents and state interventions in family size.

The first was the three-year famine (1959–61), which interrupted the population boom in the 1950s and caused a sharp and temporary fall in the population growth rate. According to official statistics, during the three-year famine, the death rate shot up to 25.4 per thousand people nationwide in 1960 and the birth rate fell for four years down to 18.0 per thousand people in 1961, resulting in a few years of unusually low and even negative population growth (see Figure 7.2).

The second event was the Cultural Revolution (1966–76), during which the state-administrated migration campaign sent over 17 million urban youth (mostly secondary and high school graduates) to live and work in the rural area during 1968–76. The consequence was not only quantitative but also qualitative: On the quantity side, many of these urban youth had to postpone their marriage till the Cultural Revolution period was over. On the quality side, the whole generation of youth lost the opportunity to receive a proper education while physically and psychologically enduring hard labor in farm fields and factories. The hardship and poor nutrition of the generation also have had long-term consequence on the cohorts' health conditions.

The third factor was the state-imposed birth control. It started with the family planning program of promoting "later marriage, longer birth intervals, and fewer births" in the early 1970s and evolved to the draconian one-child-per-couple policy that was implemented in the 1980s (Lu, 2009).

Last but not the least is the remarkable takeoff of the Chinese economy since the 1980s. In just one generation, China has successfully transformed itself from a secluded and poor centrally planned command economy to an open and prosperous market-based economy. By growing at about 10 percent per annum for three decades, the world's most populous nation has miraculously lifted itself from a low-income country to a middle-income one. Wealth creation of such a scale in such period of time is unprecedented in human history.

Due to these events, China's population growth has exhibited some unique features. As shown in Figure 7.2, from 1949 to the 1970, China was roughly in the second stage of demographic transition, with high birth rates and declining death rates. Except for the three-year famine period (1959–61), annual death rate declined continuously in most years, falling from 1.7 percent to 2.0 percent in 1949–52 to 0.76 percent in 1970. Meanwhile, the annual birth rate hovered between 2.9 percent and 4.3 percent for all years except for 1959–61. The famine-period setback to population growth broke up the baby booms in those years into two waves—the first wave came in the post-civil war period (1949–54) when the birth rate stayed above 3.6 percent for six years and the second wave arrived in the post-famine period (1962–65) when birth rate shot up above 3.7 percent for four years. The enlarged gap between birth rates and death rates led to an unprecedented expansion of the population at an annual rate above 1.6 percent through the period except for the three-year famine period.

During the Cultural Revolution, several factors caused the birth rates to fall fast and continuously in most years. In the context of political chaos and the state-coerced massive migration of urban youth, many had to delay their marriage and childbirth plans. Entering the 1970s, the family planning campaign was launched to promote late marriage and fewer births. Through the 1970s the female mean age at first marriage rose from 19.7 to 22.8 (Coale and Chen, 1987). Between 1970 and 1979, both the total fertility rate and annual birth rate fell sharply, with the former reduced from 5.81 births per woman to 2.75 births per woman and the latter from 3.34 percent to 1.78 percent. The decline of total fertility rate was further accelerated by the strong-handed state intervention in family reproduction after 1980 when the one-child-per-couple policy was initiated and practiced. With a combination of coercive and incentive-based interventions, the total fertility rate fell further in the 1980s and reached the replacement level of 2.1 per woman around 1990.

Despite the declining fertility rate, the crude birth rate bounced back in the 1980s, when 9 out of 10 years had birth rates above 2.0 percent (Figure 7.2). The bulging birth rates in these years were largely caused by the coincidental arrival of the marriage–childbirth tides with the two waves of baby boomers. In a normal situation, the first-wave baby boomers, who were born in the post-civil war period (1949–54), should on average have families and children at least 10 years earlier than the second-wave baby boomers, who were born in the post-famine period (1962–65). However, many first-wave baby boomers had to delay starting their families in the Cultural Revolution for various reasons, especially the state-administrated massive migration of urban youth to rural areas. When this policy was reversed in the early 1980s, most of the rusticated youth were able to return to their hometowns and many started their families at the age of late twenties to early thirties. The marriage–childbirth tide of the first-wave baby boomers thus coincided with that of the second-wave baby boomers in the 1980s to create the bulging birth rates.

By the end of the 1980s, the mini-baby boom of the decade soon gave way to a resumed falling trend of birthrates, which dropped all the way down to below 0.15 percent per annum by the turn of the century (Figure 7.2). China's fertility decline within a relatively short time period is drastic, rarely seen elsewhere in the world. Despite continuing debates over the extent of China's fertility decline, most researchers accepted that by the turn of the century the fertility rate had fallen to well below the replacement level of 2.1 births per woman. The United Nations estimated that the fertility rate in 2000–2005 was around 1.77 births per woman (United Nations, 2009).

A combination of several events caused a sharp fall in the birth rates: The rapidly rising standard of living thanks to the successful economic takeoff since the 1980s has reduced incentives for child-bearing, as in other parts of the world. The draconian one-child-per-couple policy further dampened the fertility rates. The peak age for marriage and childbirth among the second-wave baby boomers was phased out.

Thus follows another unique feature of China's demographic transition—its astonishing speed. The whole episode of transformation from the second-stage demographic transition to a post-transition aging society took place in merely a

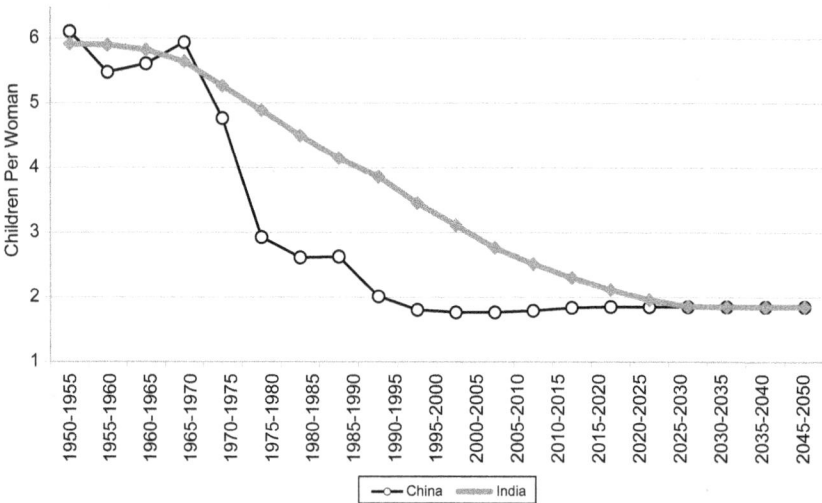

Figure 7.3 Fertility rates: China vs. India, 1950–2050
Source: United Nations (2009).

bit longer than one generation. Such a drastically rapid demographic transition has seldom occurred in other parts of the world. Figure 7.3 compares fertility rates between China and India. Between 1970 and 2000, the fall of fertility rates in China were astonishingly steeper than what happened in India.

Reversing the dividend

Now the curve of China's dependency ratio has hit its bottom and is set to rise in the coming years. That will inevitably reverse the demographic dividend. All indicators of demographic trends suggest that the population structure is becoming less favorable to economic growth (Cai and Wang, 2006). According to projections by Wang and Mason (2005), the drying up of the demographic dividend will reduce growth in per capita income by 0.45 percent annually between 2014 and 2050.

According to the World Bank, China's per capita GNI in 2007 was $2,360 (by Atlas adjusted exchange rate) and $5,370 (by Purchasing Power Parity, PPP), which position the country in the rank of middle-income economies (World Bank, 2009). This is a remarkable achievement made through fast economic growth over the past three decades. Despite the momentum of growth, however, the share of the poorest quintile of national income is only 4.3 percent, which implies that one-fifth of the Chinese population—264 million—are living on $1,150 per person (by PPP), even less than the mean per capita income of low-income countries. Entering an aging society at this level of development is worrying. Wu Cangping (2007), a leading Chinese demographer, coined the phrase "getting old before getting rich" to describe the predicament China faces.

China has already entered a post-transition era, in which the population is fast aging and the population growth has slowed significantly. This is rather unique among developing countries. By 2000, China's population age structure was that of a mature population with a median age of about 30 years old, where the largest shares are found in the working-age cohorts. By 2030, however, its median age will be 41 years old, ten years older than that of India (United Nations, 2009). That year will also likely to mark a turning point when the population size peaks before commencing its decline. By 2025, China would account for less than a fifth of the world's population but almost a quarter of the world's senior citizens (Eberstadt, 2006).

The rapidly aging population structure may severely undermine China's comparative advantage arising from its labor abundance, which has so far contributed to the economy's formidable competitiveness in labor-intensive exports. The United Nations projects that China's population aged 15–64 will peak around 2015 and then start to decline, eventually to be overtaken by that of India (Figure 7.4). This is consistent with the turning point of China's labor force size projected by the China Center for Population and Development and other scholars (Cai and Wang, 2006; Golley and Tyers, 2006). Cai and Wang (2006) warned that a possible gap between labor demand and supply may happen in the "very near future" (i.e. in the coming decade), causing "structural labor shortage in terms of region, sector and specific skills" from time to time.

Using the effective number of workers weighted by age-specific productivity varieties, Wang and Mason estimated that the growth rate of effective labor

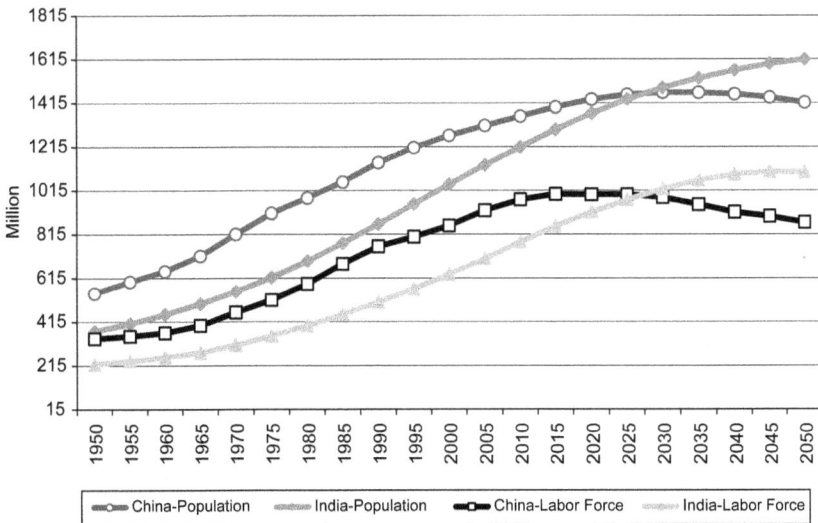

Figure 7.4 Total population and labor force: China vs. India, 1950–2050
Note: Labor force refers to population aged 15–64. Source: United Nations (2009).

force has been halved from its peak rate of 3 percent per annum in the late 1980s and early 1990s to the current rate of about 1.5 percent per annum. The steadily declining growth rate will continue and labor-force growth will cease altogether by 2020 and turn strongly negative thereafter (Wang and Mason, 2005). It is noteworthy that this timing of labor force decline compares China rather unfavorably with India and other emerging-market economies. As pointed out by Golley and Tyers (2006, p. 4):

> Even though India is also ageing, its most populous age groups are very young and, as these groups age, they raise the labor force participation rate and the crude birth rate. Thus, in a period during which China's labor force shows little net growth, that of India rises by half. The same pattern is observed in other populous developing countries in South Asia and Africa.

Yi Fuxian (2007), a fierce critic of China's birth control policy, disputes the validity of official demographic statistics by pointing out that the official figures of fertility rate (1.77 for 2000–2005) contradict the rate of 1.22 collected from the 2000 census data. He thus argues that actual aging rate should be much faster than the official projection.

This fast-forward play of demographic transition is bound to have two consequences. First, a V-shape movement of dependency ratios. As noted by Lee and Mason (2006), in industrialized countries, the type of demographic dividend period typically lasted five decades or more, which is also generally true for most other places in the world. In Figure 7.5, one can observe that

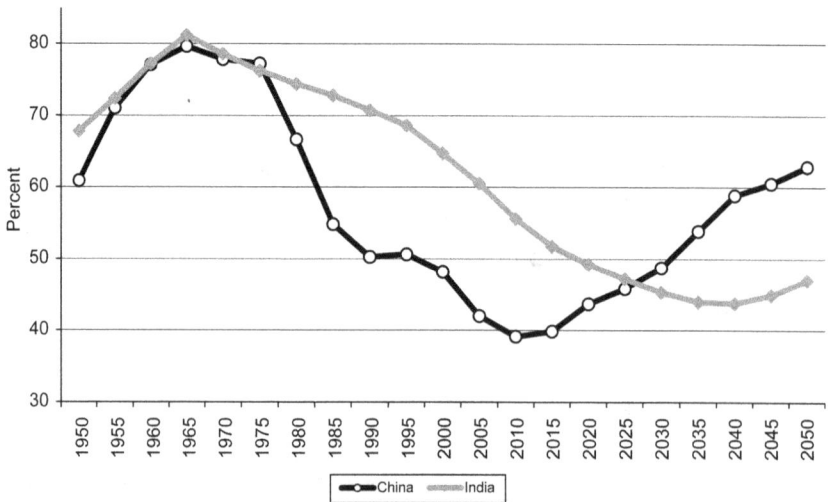

Figure 7.5 Dependency ratios: China vs. India, 1950–2050
Source: United Nations (2009).

India's dependency ratios started to fall in 1965–70, about the same time when China's did. It will take about seven decades for the ratio to reach its trough in around 2035–40. In China, it has only taken about four decades. The fall of dependency ratios in China is not only much steeper but also much deeper—the lowest dependency ratio is projected to be 39 percent in 2010, five percentage points lower than the lowest India is expected to reach in 2040.

The second consequence is an avalanche of a fast aging population. As shown in Figure 7.6, starting at about the same median age in 1970, China has advanced much faster than India towards an aged society. The difference between the two countries' aging progresses is shockingly evident when we compare their population age structures (or the population pyramids) in Figure 7.7. In the mid-1990s, China's population age structure still had a heavy base with every elderly person supported by more than 10 working-age people. This ratio has risen only slightly before 2010, when the population has a bulge of working-age adults. When China's median age rises from the current 30 years old to 41 years old in 2030, the country will have more elderly dependents than children. By that time, every elderly citizen will be supported by only four working-age persons. When the median age reaches 45 years old in 2050, it will have a 38 percent elderly dependency ratio, 13 percentage points higher than its child dependency ratio. Such a level of aged society will place China alongside those rich aging countries, including most Western European countries and Japan. In contrast, India's population age structure will continue to remain bottom heavy in the coming decades.

How will these two consequences affect the prospects of China's economic growth? We may consider the following ways in which these demographic changes may influence growth of GDP and standard of living.

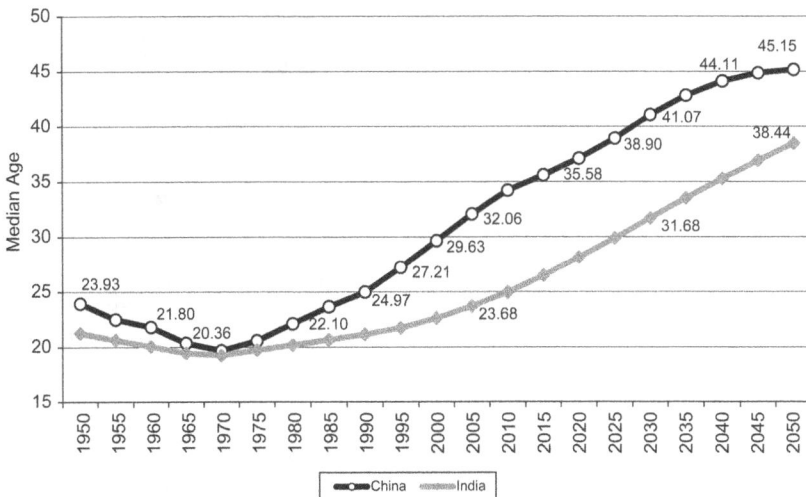

Figure 7.6 Median age: China vs. India, 1950–2050
Source: United Nations (2009).

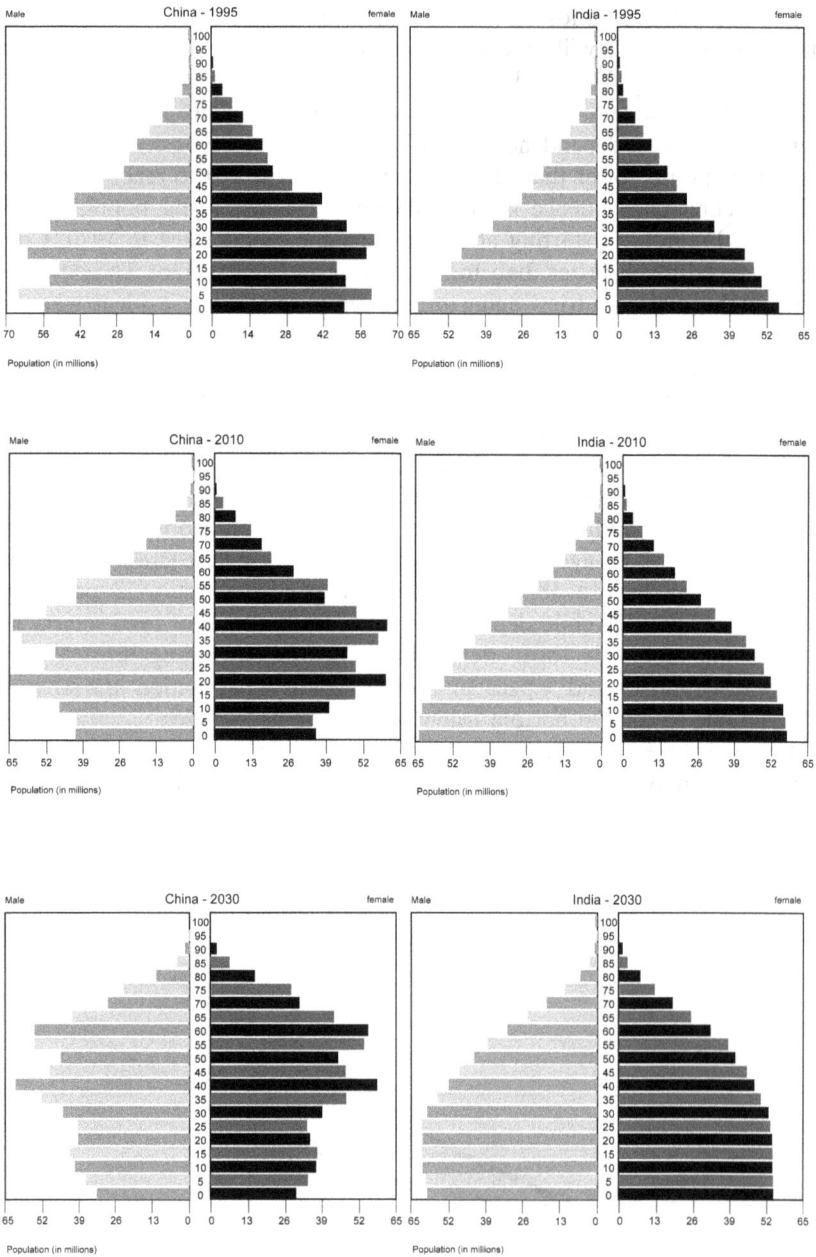

Figure 7.7 Population age structure: China vs. India, 1995, 2010 and 2030
Source: US Census Bureau, Population Division, www.census.gov.

First, when the dependency ratio falls, it allows the labor force to grow faster than the population. Other things being equal, if the larger proportion of population is sufficiently employed, per capita income will be higher. When the dependency ratio rises, the labor force will grow more slowly than the population and its influence on per capita income growth will turn negative.

The second channel is savings. When a greater proportion of people are of a working age, the society has the potential to generate higher savings. A falling dependency ratio thus enhances savings while a rising one dampens savings. A rising elderly dependency ratio tends to dampen savings even more: According to the life-cycle hypothesis, individuals save when they are working and use up their savings after retirement. When the society ages, the number of those who are not saving rises relative to the number of those who are saving, and thus reduces the aggregate saving. It is a well-known health economics norm that the medical expenses of the elderly increase exponentially with age. When China's elderly dependency ratio rises to overtake its child dependency ratio (which will occur around 2030, see Figure 7.1), the overall financial burden of dependency will certainly increase.

The third way is the link between age structure and productivity. In most careers, workers' productivity increases with training and experience in younger ages, gradually reaches a peak in mid-life, and then declines toward retirement age. Therefore, when the labor force grows older, the overall age-related productivity may rise at first and fall after reaching a peak.

To examine these implications quantitatively, we apply a neoclassical growth approach to analyze the relative contributions of capital accumulation, labor force employment rate (percentage of working-age population employed), working-age population rate (as percentage of total population), and productivity growth (growth unexplained by the other three sources). The methodology of this analysis is explained in the Appendix. The estimates of composition of per capita income growth are presented in Figure 7.1.

In Table 7.1 and Figure 7.8, we can observe that per capita income growth since 1982 has been mainly driven by capital accumulation (growth of per employee's capital stock) and total factor productivity growth as a result of technological progress and efficiency improvement. Of the average 9.08 percent annual growth in the 27-year period, growth in per capita capital stock has contributed 4.8 percentage points while total factor productivity accounted for another 3.7 percentage points of growth.

When China's population structure starts to age, saving rates will inevitably fall so that the resources for capital accumulation will become scarcer over time. In Figure 7.8, we use the linear regression of capital formation rate (fixed capital formation as percentage of GDP) on dependency ratios during 1981–2008 to project the downward trend of contributions of capital stock growth to per capita income growth, which is set to fall below 4 percentage points a year after 2020.

As for productivity growth, the trend of age structure is also not favorable. Currently, China's median age is about 30 years old (see Figure 7.6) and the

Table 7.1 Estimated sources of per capita GDP growth (1981–2008)

Period	Annual growth rate of per capita income	Contribution of				Dependency ratio
		Capital stock per employee	Labor force employment rate	Working-age population rate	Total factor productivity	
1982–1985	10.58	3.15	0.76	1.06	5.61	60.07
1986–1990	6.27	3.66	-0.07	1.01	1.66	52.87
1991–1995	10.96	5.45	-0.10	-0.05	5.66	50.07
1996–2000	7.62	4.49	-0.28	0.57	2.84	46.22
2001–2005	8.67	5.18	-0.29	0.70	3.07	40.67
2005–2008	10.40	6.97	-0.56	0.80	3.19	38.33
Average	9.08	4.82	-0.09	0.68	3.67	

Source: Calculated from data in NBSC (various issues).

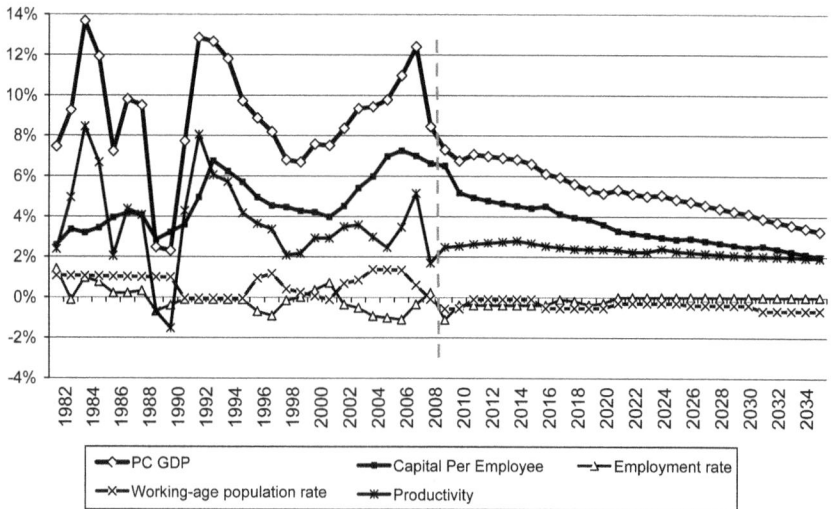

Figure 7.8 Estimated sources of per capita GDP growth
Note: see text for assumptions underlining projected data of 2011–2050.
Source: Calculated from data in NBSC (various issues), and United Nations (2009).

labor force median age (which is about 15 years older at around 45 years old) should have reached the peak of age-related productivity. When the labor force median age continues to rise, age-related productivity must fall. However, age-related productivity loss may be somewhat offset by the better human capital of the younger generations of workers and improved market-based institutions. A recent empirical study by Huh, Lee, and Lee (2007), based on data of 77 countries from 1993–2007, demonstrates the significant influence of the demographic burden of dependency ratios on economic growth. The same study also suggests that an increasing elderly dependency ratio has a greater negative impact on economic growth than an increasing child dependency ratio. Given such evidence, we hereby use the data of over-all dependency ratios and productivity growth since 1981 to project the future productivity growth trends and believe the projection is likely to be biased towards optimism.

In the early stages of the market-oriented reforms, job creation was buoy-ant so the labor force's employment rate rose until 1989, making a positive contribution to per capita income growth. Since then, employment growth has largely been a bit slower than labor force growth so its contribution to per capita income growth has been mostly negative, lowering per capita GDP growth more than half a percentage in 2005–08 (Table 7.1). Since the growth of the working-age population is slowing and will soon turn to negative after 2015, we expect the gap between job growth and labor force growth to close in the 2010s.

For most years since 1981, working-age population growth has roughly contributed a half to one percentage point to per capita income growth, reflecting the demographic dividends arising from a labor force growing faster than the population. These dividends are disappearing. Based on United Nations data, it can be projected that in the coming decades, labor force to population ratios are going to decline and will thus reduce annual per capita GDP growth by 0.3 to 0.7 percentage points from 2016–40 (Figure 7.8).

With the above analysis, we conclude that: (1) falling saving rates due to population aging will severely reduce the financial resources for capital accu-mulation, thus slowing down the most important engine of per capita income growth; (2) further aging of the labor force tends to retard productivity growth, another major engine of income growth; (3) in the past three decades, demographic dividends in terms of faster growth of productive population have been relatively small as compared to the contributions of capital accu-mulation and productivity growth. In the coming decades, when the share of the working-age population starts falling, its contributions to per capita income growth will turn from positive to negative; and (4) unless the employment rate of labor force can be raised, its contribution to per capita income growth will be minimal in the coming decades.

Challenges to China's social security system

Given the grim prospect of unfavorable demographic changes, reversing the draconian state-enforced birth control policy becomes increasingly urgent and inevitable for China's long-term well-being. Proposals to phase out the one-child-per-couple policy and even reverse the population policy from control-ling fertility to encouraging fertility have been debated by demographers and policy-makers.[1] Some reforms of birth control policies have been reported at the provincial level.[2]

By now even a drastic reversal of population policy towards fertility pro-motion will not be enough to deal with the avalanche of a fast aging popu-lation in the coming decades for several reasons. First, the fertility rate decline started in the 1970s before the era of the one-child-per-couple policy. The declining fertility and birth rates in the recent decades are a common phenomenon as has occurred in other parts of the world where economic development and rising standards of living increase the opportunity costs of raising children. The one-child-per-couple policy that started in 1980 just accelerated this declining trend. Second, even if a pro-fertility policy is adopted, it may not be effective in combating the falling trend of fertility rate, as testified by the experience of other low fertility countries like Japan and Singapore (Demeny, 2003). Despite various pro-birth public policies, the fertility rates in these more developed economies are still well below the replacement level. Finally, even if such policies do succeed in lifting the fertility rate above the replacement level by causing a "mini-baby boom" in a few years—which is unlikely—it will not change the fact that the dependency ratio will rise sharply in the coming two decades before the new wave of baby boomers reach their productive age at least twenty years later. As a matter of fact, if the fertility rate does rise at a time of fast aging of the elder generations, it will push the dependency ratio even higher in the next two decades.

To grapple with the avalanche effects of a fast aging society, China's social security system needs to be developed and consolidated. The current social security system was initiated in the late 1990s following the "three-pillar model" of old age security recommended by the World Bank (1994), i.e. a publicly managed system with mandatory participation and the limited goal of reducing poverty among the old; a privately managed mandatory savings system; and voluntary savings. In China, the first pillar of the system is called the "*shehui tongchou* (social pooling)" account, which actually functions as a pay-as-you-go (PAYG) system that makes transfer payments from the contributors to the beneficiaries. The second pillar is the personal endowment account, which is supposed to function like a fully funded personal-account based pension-cum-health insurance system, following the model of the Central Provident Fund system in Singapore.

Unlike the social security systems in OECD countries, China's is a fragmented one. Vertically, the system consists of three segments: (1) the basic old-age insurance for enterprise employees; (2) the pension system for government and public non-profit institutions; and (3) the rural old-age insurance.[3]

Of the three, the rural insurance is the most underdeveloped and before 2009 it was merely at the stage of experimental practice at the local (usually at county or even village) level. In September 2009, the State Council (2009) issued a guideline for developing a new nationwide rural old-age insurance system. All rural residents aged 16 or above can participate on a voluntary basis by paying an annual premium between 100 *yuan* and 500 *yuan*. The premium may be subsidized by the rural collectives and local governments. Every participant will have a personal account in a national social security system. When a participant reaches age 60, she/he can get an old-age benefit of no less than a minimum of 55 *yuan* per month and the total monthly payment will be one 139th (i.e.1/139) of the accumulated premium balance in the personal account.

The public-sector pension system is for government officials, civil service workers and employees in public non-profit institutions. Personal pension is proportional to the salary before retirement up to 90 percent, depending on the length of service. Generally, the public-sector pension system does not require personal contribution and is fully funded by various levels of governments. In recent years, there have been some local experiments of joint-premium contribution by the work units and individuals as well as personal endowment accounts. Overall, the public-sector pensions are much more attractive than those in other sectors.

The basic old-age insurance for enterprise employees is the most prevalent and well-developed segment of China's social security system. It covers almost all employees of for-profit entities in urban areas. By end of 2007, over 200 million urban employees had been covered and working-employees-to-retirees ratio was about 3:1.

The fund consists of a social pooling (pay-as-you-go) account and an accumulatively funded personal account. The employer contributes no more than 20 percent of the employee's wage and salary while the employee is required to contribute 8 percent of the wage and salary. Self-employed or part-time employed persons are required to pay 20 percent of annual wage earnings, of which 8 percent goes to the personal account. Old-age benefits consist of two parts. One is a basic pension benefit, which is calculated as follows: for every year of contribution made, the retiree will be paid 1 percent of a base amount, which is the average of the local average monthly wage and the retiree's average monthly (price-indexed) wage of the contribution years. The second part of benefit is equivalent to one 139th (1/139) of the balance in the retiree's personal account if the person retires at age 60, or one 170th (1/170) of the personal account balance if the person retires at age 55.

Apart from being vertically segmented into three major categories, China's social security system is also fragmented horizontally across regions. For the public-sector pension system, since there is no national pooling, some local governments or public non-profit institutions are short of funds to meet the pension payments to their retirees. The basic old-age insurance for enterprise employees is even more fragmented across regions. Since there is no nation-wide administrative system, personal endowment accounts cannot be transferred across provincial or even municipal or county boundaries. By end of 2007, of 32 provincial administrative regions, only 17 had a province-wide administrative system that allows social security funds to be coordinated and pooled. In other provincial regions, such coordinated use of funds was only at the county level. Progress has been made since then as is reported that by end of 2009 all provincial administrative regions in China had formulated systems of provincial-level coordination for social insurance endowment funds.[4]

After nearly three years of discussions and revisions since its first draft was submitted to the national legislature, China's Social Insurance Law was finally passed on October 28, 2010, by the National People's Congress. The Law sets the goal that the basic social insurance endowment funds will gradually realize national coordination and other social insurances will gradually realize provincial co-ordination. It, however, leaves the specific time and steps to be formulated by the State Council. By setting up a nationally uniform social security numbering system based on personal ID numbers, the Law has made a crucial move towards a nationwide social insurance regime. The Law, to take effect on 1 July 2011, also for the first time allows individuals to transfer their basic endowment and medical insurances freely across regions of different coordinating administrations.[5]

Compared to the problem of administrative segmentation, financial sustainability is an even more serious challenge. So far China's old-age insurance system is a *de facto* one-pillar PAYG program since almost all the money in the personal endowment accounts has been used to pay the current retirees like the money in the social pool accounts. This results in the so-called problem of "hollowed personal accounts." The overall ratio between the contributing employees and the retirees has declined quickly from 4.4 in 1993 to below 3 in recent years (China Economic Research Center of Peking University, 2007). With faster population aging in coming years, such a system will be equivalent to setting up a massive inter-generation wealth transfer scheme, which has to be supported by the younger generations of shrinking sizes. Without realizing the personal nature of the second pillar, participation incentives will never be strong and free riding will always be a serious problem for administration. If contribution to the system comes from tax-like levies on income, it may have a negative impact on work incentives. Meanwhile, the wealth-income transfer or redistribution will not create new wealth or faster income growth so it is a zero-sum game.

In the long run, a fully funded personal endowment account system has the advantages of ensuring a bottom-line level of personal savings for retirement and old-age medical needs while offering incentives for individuals to save and invest more in capital assets.[6] Based on the neo-classical growth model that assumes steady-state growth equilibrium, Wang and Mason (2005) calculate that, given the demographic conditions in China, if all old-age support is financed by capital accumulation, the incremental investment would raise capital-output ratio from of 2.6 in 1982 to 7.1 in 2050. An increase in the capital-output ratio of this magnitude would lead to a doubling of output per worker under some simple assumptions. This projection implies that public policies and institutional reforms should be geared to encourage savings and investment as a major vehicle for financing old-age support. A fully funded social security system will meet this demand while minimizing inter-generational transfers. It is therefore best suitable for an aging society.

However, the transition to a fully funded system is practically difficult since it would require a huge public fund injection to fulfill the hollowed personal accounts. Meanwhile, at the current stage, China still has one of the world's highest saving rates, which has been a reason for macroeconomic imbalance:

Since much of the high savings have not been fully converted into productive investment, China's excess savings have translated into a huge current account surplus. To develop a fully funded social security system may boost savings further in the intermediate future and thus aggravate this imbalance. It therefore is not only fiscally burdensome but also undesirable to do that.

For the above reasons, some scholars suggest that China should follow the "notional defined contribution" model, after Sweden's practice (Zheng, 2003). This model is essentially built on a pay-as-you-go system that transfers incomes from the younger generations of workers to support the elder retirees. However, retirees' benefits are calculated on the notional balance in their personal accounts, which can also be notionally subsidized by public funds. Since the scheme maintains a notional link between personal contributions and retirement benefits, it has the similar incentive advantage of a fully funded system. The benefit payment is also much more flexible than the old-age entitlements in a pay-as-you-go system, thus allowing adjustments to changes in demographic and fiscal conditions.

A research group at the China Economic Research Center of Peking University (2007) proposed a "transitional notional defined contribution" model, which formulates a social insurance system to begin with three pillars, a national pool of a basic fund (which aims at a 20 percent substitution rate of pre-retirement income), a notional defined contribution (that provides 40–80 percent substitution rate), and voluntary savings. As population aging continues, the notional part of the second pillar (i.e. personal endowment account) should be gradually replaced by fully funded contributions. It is proposed that one more percentage point of the contribution is replaced by fully funded contribution every other year starting from 2007. Based on a contribution rate of 24 percent of wage income, it is projected that by the year 2045 all incremental contributions to social insurance fund will be fully funded and by 2080 all personal accounts will be converted into fully funded ones. Accordingly, old-age social insurance deficit will first increase until reaching its peak about 1.5 percent of GDP around 2045 and will then start falling.

To prepare for a fast aging society, China not only has to reform and consolidate its social security system but also needs to adopt policies to prevent per capita income growth from stagnation. If savings will inevitably fall due to rising elderly dependency ratios, channeling savings to productive investment will become more important. Our analysis of sources of per capita income growth in Table 7.1 reveals that rising capital stock has been a major engine of economic growth. It is therefore crucial for China to maintain a rate of capital accumulation conducive to future economic growth. That requires further financial deepening to enhance investment efficiency.

Our analysis also highlights the importance of productivity growth to income growth. To counter the negative impact of an aging labor force on productivity, effective investment in education, better incentives for technological progress, policies to encourage entrepreneurship and innovation are all necessary to maintain the momentum of productivity growth.

Finally, the declining working-age population rate will be a drag on per capita income growth in coming decades. On the other hand, raising employment rates in the working-age population can nevertheless counter the loss. It is therefore important to implement policies that facilitate job creation and job search. One option to counter the negative impact of the declining working-age population rate is to raise the labor force participation rates among the aged population. This approach is feasible since China's labor force participation rates for old age groups are quite low as compared to some other Asian countries. These low participation rates were mainly due to two factors: (1) the statutory retirement ages of 60 for men and 55 for women, which were set at a time when life expectancy was only 50 years (compared with over 70 years now); and (2) economic reforms and transition in the late 1990s, especially the restructuring of state-owned enterprises, led to massive lay-offs, rising unemployment, and forced early retirements. Using a GTAP-Dynamic global economic model, Golley and Tyers (2006) simulated the effects of alternative policy approaches. Their results show that a transition to a two-child policy in China would boost its GDP growth, enlarging the projected 2030 Chinese economy by about a tenth. The approach, however, would slow the growth of real per capita income, reducing the level projected by the baseline scenario for 2030 by a tenth. Alternatively, almost the same GDP growth performance might be achieved with continued low fertility if China's aged labor participation rates can rise gradually through 2030 to approximate the rates currently observed in Japan. Starting from the current low level, the increased employment of the aged might be sufficiently life-enriching to offset the decline in leisure time. The simulated results suggest that the approach of raising aged labor participation offers superior per capita real income growth to what might be achieved via a policy-driven boost to fertility. To make this approach workable, a series of reforms are needed, including raising the statutory retirement ages (especially for women), introducing tax schemes and other policy incentives for old-age job creation and employment, and developing a pension system conducive to aged labor participation.

In conclusion, the upcoming demographic changes will be massive and profound. They will pose severe challenges to China's continuous prosperity in the coming decades. Whether China can answer these challenges successfully largely depends on its ability to build a sound and robust social security system.

Appendix: estimation of sources of per capita income growth

Suppose a Cobb-Douglas aggregate production function:

$$Y = A \, E^{\lambda} \, K^{\beta}$$

where Y = output, A = a coefficient that indicates overall productivity, E = employed labor, K = capital stock, and λ and β are elasticity-coefficients of output to labor and capital respectively. Assuming constant-returns-to-scale, $\lambda = 1 - \beta$.

To evaluate the impact of population structure, we introduce two more variables: population, N, and labor force, L, into this model to write per capita income as:

$$y = \frac{Y}{N} = \frac{AE^{1-\beta}K^{\beta}}{N} = \frac{AE^{1-\beta}K^{\beta}}{E} \cdot \frac{E}{N} = \frac{AE^{1-\beta}K^{\beta}}{E} \cdot \frac{E}{L} \cdot \frac{L}{N} = A \cdot \left(\frac{K}{E}\right)^{\beta} \cdot \frac{E}{L} \cdot \frac{L}{N}$$

The growth rate of per capita income is:

$$\dot{y} = \frac{\dot{A}}{A} + \beta \cdot \dot{k} + \dot{e} + \dot{l}$$

where $k = K/E$, $e = E/L$, and $l = L/N$.

We collected data on China's real per capita GDP (proxy for y), real value of fixed capital formation and capital depreciation rate (used for calculating K by the standard perpetual inventory approach), number of employees (proxy for E), working-age (15–64 years old, proxy for L) and total population (N) for the period 1982–2008. In real value, capital stock at time t is $K_t = K_{t-1} + I_t - \delta_t$, where I_t is investment (capital formation) and δ_t is depreciation. The value of δ is imputed from data of "compensation of employees" in GDP statistics. Data of "compensation of employees" and "capital depreciation" were published for years 1994, 1997–2003, 2005–7. For missing years, the values are estimated average of values in subsequent years or backward moving average.

Notes

1 "Family planning becomes a controversial topic," *Xinhuanet*, 30 December 2005.
2 Shanghai urges couples to have second child amid concerns over rapidly ageing population," available at: www.dailymail.co.uk/news, 23 July 2009.
3 Descriptions of China's old-age social insurance system in this section are based on the National People's Congress, "The Status Quos and Main Problems of Our Country's Basic Old-age Social Insurance System," National People's Congress website, available at: www.npc.gov.cn (accessed 22 December 2008).
4 "Endowment insurance to be implemented, coordinated as a whole in China," *China Daily*, 29 October 2010.
5 Social Insurance Law of the People's Republic of China, National People's Congress website, downloaded from www.npc.gov.cn (accessed 29 October 2010).
6 For more details, see Lu (2000, pp. 410–31).

References

Cai, F. and Wang, M. (2006) "Challenge facing China's economic growth in its aging but not affluent era," *China and World Economy*, 14: 20–31.
China Economic Research Center of Peking University (2007) *Transitional Notional Defined Contribution*, Peking: Author.

Coale, A.J. and Chen, S. (1987) *Basic Data on Fertility in the Provinces of China, 1942–1982*, Honolulu: East-West Population Institute Paper Series.

Demeny, P. (2003) "Population policy: a concise summary," Population Council, Policy Research Division, Working Paper No. 173.

Eberstadt, N. (2006) "Growing old the hard way: China, Russia, India—living longer but poorer," *Policy Review*, 136: 15–39.

Golley, J. and Tyers, R. (2006) "China's growth to 2030: demographic change and the labour supply constraint," Program on the Global Demography of Aging, PGDA Working Papers, No. 1106.

Huh, H., Lee, H. and Lee, Y. (2007) "Demographic transition and its impact on economic growth," paper presented at Korea and the World Economy VI Conference, University of Wollongong, Australia, 2–3 July.

Lee, R. and Mason, A. (2006) "Back to the basics: what is the demographic dividend?," *Finance and Development*, 43(3): 16–17.

Lu, D. (2000) "Choice of social security systems: Singapore's experience," in J. Yin, S. Lin, and D. F. Gates (eds.) *Social Security Reform: Options for China*, Singapore: World Scientific, pp. 410–31.

——(2009) "Diminishing demographic dividends: implications for China's growth sustainability," in D. Yang and L. Zhao (eds.) *China's Reforms at 30: Challenges and Prospects*, Singapore: World Scientific.

State Council (2009) "Guidelines for establishing the new rural old-age insurance," *State Council Gazette*, 2009, No. 32.

United Nations (2009) *World Population Prospects: The 2008 Revision*. Available at: http://data.un.org/ (accessed 18 June 2009).

Wang, F. and Mason, A. (2005) *Demographic Dividend and Prospects for Economic Development in China*, New York: United Nations.

World Bank (1994) *Averting the Old Age Crisis: Policies to Protect the Old and Promote Growth*, Oxford: Oxford University Press.

——(2009) *World Development Report 2009*, Washington, DC: World Bank.

Wu, C. (2007) *Wu Cangping Zixuanji* [A Collection of Self-Selected Papers], Beijing: Renmin University Press.

Yi, F. (2007) *Daguo Kongchao* [A Big Country in an Empty Nest: Wrong Direction of China's Birth Control Policy], Hong Kong: Da Feng Press.

Zheng, B. (2003) "Notional defined contribution: a feasible way to reduce transitional cost," *Management World*, 8: 33–45 (in Chinese).

8 Political dynamics of social policy reform in China

Yongnian Zheng and Yanjie Huang

Introduction

Effective social policy is the hallmark of modern states. In the developed world, social policy is an important dimension of state capacity and the institutional basis for social stability. In many Western countries, the development of social policy is underscored by a gradualist political process where state and society have undergone a mutual transformation and various social and economic institutions of modern states have gradually developed to maturity.[1] For developing countries, the state often lacks certain functions in providing social welfare. As a typical developing country, China's modern social policy is still halfway along a tortuous path, in the shadow of the prevailing paradigm of economic growth and social stability as the chief political agenda in the post-Mao era.

During the early periods of reform, social policy did not emerge as an independent policy concept. It was treated in concrete terms as welfare-related policy issues arising from economic reform. The politics of social policy likewise were only subsumed under the greater political agenda of economic reform and development. Most institutions of social protection were primarily designed to cope with the welfare consequences of the reforms of the state-owned enterprises (SOEs) and the township and village enterprises (TVEs). It was only when the economic development faced increasingly heavy social costs and encountered heightened social grievances that social policy gradually acquired its prominent presence because of the recognition of its importance to social stability and long-run sustainable economic growth. The Hu Jintao–Wen Jiabao administration in particular first made social policy an important area of reform under the grand project of the so-called "Harmonious Society" (Li, 2006). The term social policy itself was mentioned for the first time in the final report at the Sixth Plenary Session of the Sixteenth Party Congress in 2006.

Social policy-making in China has been the exclusive prerogative of the Party- state leadership and the political elites. Thus whenever social reform programs coincided with the political priority of economic growth, they were implemented promptly, such as the marketization of higher education, healthcare and housing. Otherwise, social policy was generally a delayed response to overwhelming social grievances and potential social instability. On the other hand, despite the fact that public participation in policy-making remains low and unofficial in China, the realm of social policy has become increasingly open to different voices and social forces, as the result of the great social transformation in China today and the emergence of the urban middle class, and the development of new media such as the Internet in particular. While the political elites still enjoy favored access to welfare privileges and political power, the middle class, the lower and the marginal classes are becoming increasingly vocal in asserting their own basic rights to state-subsidized welfare.

Varying sources of societal pressures have largely shaped the process of the Chinese social policy agenda. During the whole course of reform, the government has been more responsive to problems in certain policy domains than others, but not necessarily more successful in solving them. Some reform programs have been more systemically implemented throughout than others, such as the steadily increasing coverage of social insurance. Some policy reforms have been less satisfactory and sometimes riddled with rent-seeking. Some reform programs have been implemented more or less consistently since the very start, whereas other programs have been characterized by ad-hoc approaches, sometimes even contradictory ones. Still within different welfare domains, some programs have gradually developed a clear vision and blueprints, such as the new healthcare reform, while the domain of public housing lacks any comprehensive and feasible programs as such. The political processes underlying policy dynamics for specific policy realms have both similarities and certain particularities.

This chapter explores the political dynamics of social policy reform in contemporary China. We shall try to identify the progress of different social reform programs with different political mechanisms. The following discussion is divided into several parts. The first section provides an overview of the social policy reform in the reform era. In the next section an analytical framework will be developed based on Albert Hirschman's (1968) concepts of "exit" and "voice." The third section explains the dynamics, and the lack of dynamics, of the social policy reform in the areas of social insurance, social protection, welfare provision, education, healthcare, and housing. The next two sections will discuss how the lack of social policy reform is linked to social instability, and the related policy implications. In conclusion, we identify policy areas that will help China escape the social policy dilemma.

Social policy initiative in the reform era

China's great economic transformation in the past 30 years has brought about profound changes in the relations between the state and society. In the Maoist era, Chinese people lived in a highly centralized and closed system of a-society-within-the-state, where economic, social and political functions were all intermingled and integrated into the administrative framework of the socialist state. To compensate for low levels of wage income, the state provided a range of fringe social goods including housing, healthcare, child care and education through communes in the countryside and work units in urban areas. In particular, all the employees of urban work units and their households enjoyed a measure of communal healthcare, public-funded education and heavily subsidized public rented housing, among other price subsidies (Walder, 1986, pp. 59–67). In rural areas, a minimum measure of communal welfare was provided via the commune system, in particular, basic education and healthcare.

The Maoist system experienced a major crisis throughout the 1980s, first in the rural and then the urban areas. In the rural areas, the rise of the Household Responsibility System (HRS) marked the beginning of the end of the system of rural grassroots welfare provisions, since the decline and collapse of People's Communes deprived the rural welfare system of its formal institutional embeddedness. Some of the welfare function was transferred to the township and village enterprises (TVEs) and local governments. With the decline of the TVEs and fiscal demise of the local and grassroots authorities, the rural welfare system slipped further into disrepair.

In the cities, social reform encountered more complicated institutional and historical contexts. The initial reforms, which were intended to liberalize the state-owned enterprises (SOEs) and invigorate the urban market in fact enhanced rather than undermined the employment-based urban welfare provision (Naughton, 1995). However, since deeper reforms in the SOEs and financial sector in the mid-1990s, under the reformist Premier Zhu Rongji, social reform became an inevitable follow-up to economic reform, as the old system continued to lose much of its former institutional embodiment in the traditional SOE systems.

It came as no surprise that the first sets of social policy institutions were initiated in the immediate aftermath of the SOE reform. In order to cope with the consequence of the massive lay-offs from bankrupt or downsized SOEs, the central government implemented the first round of social reform in the area of pension and unemployment benefits. This part of social policy, which primarily dealt with the retrenched SOE workers, began to be institutionalized as complementary measures to economic reform and social stability. In 1993, the Minimum Standard of Living Scheme (MSLS, also known as the Minimum Living Standard Guarantee) was also introduced, initially targeted at laid-off elderly workers as a result of the SOEs' reform in Shanghai, China's major industrial center dominated by state enterprises (Tang, 2010).

In the Zhu Rongji era, social reform focused on setting up social insurance as an important mechanism to overhaul the old socialist welfare system. The gist of reform was to establish social insurance as the cornerstone in a new more socially based system to replace the old enterprise-based system. Various employment-related insurances were set up, first in employment, healthcare, old age pension, work injury and maternal leave. Beginning as programmatic responses to the SOE reform, the old-age insurance, a key social insurance scheme, was first instituted in 1991 and applied to all urban enterprises in 2005 as a concrete and standardized scheme (Chan *et al.*, 2008). As part of the rapidly progressing financial reform, this section of social policy reform gradually found its institutional embodiment in new state agencies, namely the Ministry of Labor and Social Security (later changed to the Ministry of Human Resource and Social Security) and the Social Security Management Fund.

As the socialist principles gradually gave way to the complementary paradigm of social instability, basic social policy concerns such as welfare provision and social protection also found their embodiments as institutional complements to the market-oriented social reform of the mid-1990s. In terms of policy design, marketization in the sphere of social welfare does not rule out the important policy goal of social protection. For example, in the housing sector, the central government has also set in place systems like Low Rent Housing (LRH) and Economic Housing (EH) for low- and middle-income families (ibid.).

Meanwhile, the market-oriented approach of social reform also met its limits, like the other economic reforms under Zhu. Politically powerful institutions tended to protect their members from potentially destructive policies, while fully embracing policies of social protection and insurance. Most significantly, marketization in the housing sector was firmly resisted by the politically powerful state sector. The downsized state sector agencies and large monopoly enterprises, thanks to their growing fiscal sinews, also provided the most generous subsidies and subscribed to the most comprehensive insurance programs.

The Hu–Wen social policy reform has inherited three distinctive institutional legacies. The first and most direct one is economic reform. At the dawn of the Hu–Wen era, China's welfare and social provision system is very similar to the libertarian model, with very limited scope of state involvement and market-based provision of welfare, with a very high level of societal self-reliance. Following the classic classification of a welfare regime by Gøsta Esping-Andersen, China's social policy reform involved a systemic shift from a statist model of citizenship-based minimum coverage to a predominantly liberal model, where means-tested welfare schemes and social insurances offer the bulk of social protection (Esping-Andersen, 1990; Gu, 2006).

The second and perhaps the most salient institutional legacy is a very unequal distribution of state-subsidized welfare provisions across different social groups defined chiefly by sectoral and regional identities rather than individual needs or merits. In the aftermath of the sweeping reform in the state sector in the late 1990s, the central government, the central monopoly SOEs and various government organizations emerged as powerful corporate entities retaining some key features of the old system of heavily subsidized welfare provision (Chan *et al.*, 2008). This left the institutionally downsized state sector as the bastion of corporate welfare programs compared with all other sectors, and the state employees among the most well-protected social groups. At the regional level, the Household Registration System (HRS) and the associated discriminatory policies against migrant workers are another set of major institutional hurdles that have constituted an inbuilt status-based welfare inequality between rural and urban, migrant workers and indigenous residents (Liu, 2005).

The last major legacy is the Maoist past. Although institutional vestiges remained of the Maoist paternalistic state, the ideology has inculcated in the Chinese psyche a widely shared value of basic social justice. Immediately after Hu Jintao assumed office, one of the first few things he did was to pay homage to the revolutionary sites and reaffirm his allegiance to selective ideas from Mao Zedong. Maoist paternalistic socialism also made an important imprint on Chinese political discourses especially for the politically vocal New Left. At the practical level, the memory of the Maoist socialist legacy also provided ideological support to many reformist forces, ranging from government think tanks and grassroots activists all the way to many disadvantaged social groups.

In late 2002, as Hu Jintao and Wen Jiabao succeeded Jiang Zemin and Zhu Rongji as CCP General Secretary and Premier respectively, China moved into the Hu–Wen era. Social policy reform as a coherent agenda began to appear as a reform priority. The Hu–Wen administration's approach to social policy is characterized by a mixed strategy of further market-oriented and more state engagement as the regulator of the market and the protectors of social stability. In the Scientific Development Outlook and Harmonious Society project, the new administration avowed its ideological commitment to protect society and achieve a basic measure of social equality and justice in the distribution of benefits and costs of the economic development (Hu, 2005).

The new social policy initiative of the Hu–Wen administration is twofold. First, it sought to strengthen and expand the basic institutions of social protection already put in place in the later days of the Jiang–Zhu era, such as the five employment insurances. Second, efforts were made to address the excesses of earlier market-oriented approaches to introduce a higher degree of equality and justice through direct state subsidy in the provision of education, healthcare and public housing. In economic terms, the Hu–Wen social policy reform is tasked with delivering social welfare with higher quality, lower prices and more equal access. Closely related to these two areas of social reforms was the recently proposed new reform initiative to curb the skewed income distribution in the interest of most urban workers.

The first major task of the social policy reform went relatively smoothly thanks to the fact that it did not involve the adjustment of interests of the parties involved and entailed only a limited increase in the government's fiscal commitment. In the Hu–Wen area, continued robust economic growth ensured a fairly stable rise in corporate and government revenue. The Hu–Wen era saw a significant rise in the coverage rate, total enrollment and accumulated funds in the various social insurance schemes, with the most substantial rise in the extent of coverage in healthcare and old-age (pension)

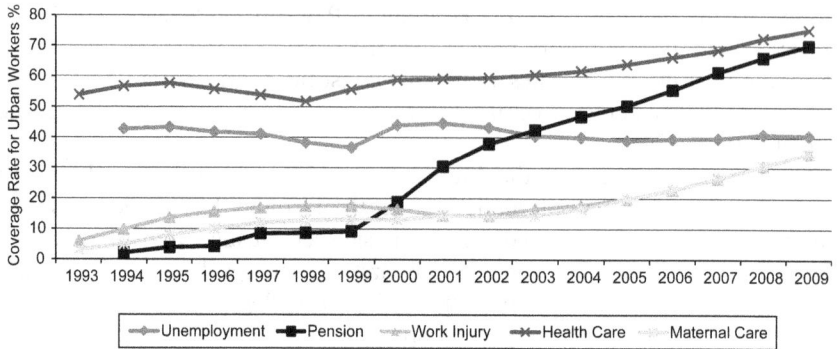

Figure 8.1 Coverage rates of five social insurance schemes (%)
Source: China Statistical Yearbooks, various issues.

insurance, two very important items in the whole social insurance scheme, from less than half to two-thirds coverage in the urban area. See Figure 8.1 for details.

The Hu–Wen administration has achieved significant progress in expanding the scale and raising the level of coverage of direct social protection. The MSLS, first put in place in 1993, only became an effective national institution in the new millennium. In particular, the Hu–Wen administration effectively extended MSLS to rural areas. From 2003 to 2009, rural MSLS grew from non-existence to cover 43.1 million rural poor. The new administration saw significant increases in coverage of all five major insurances and other policies (Figure 8.2).

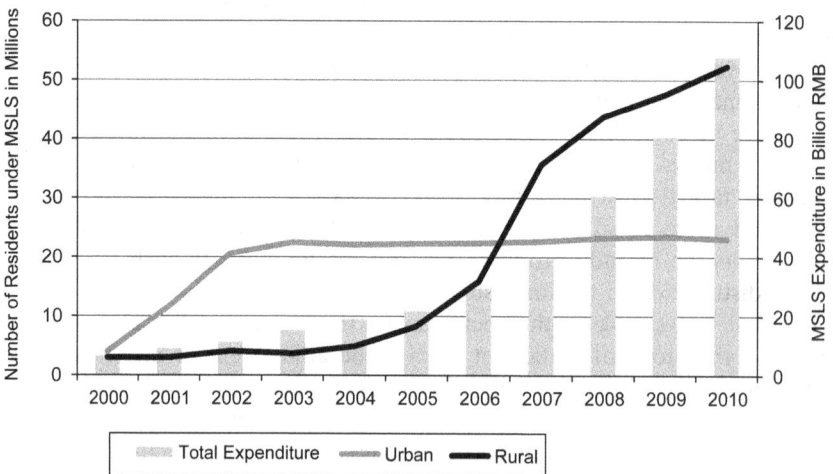

Figure 8.2 Urban and rural residents under the MSLS
Source: China Statistical Yearbook, various years.

The second area of social policy reform involves important changes in the market-oriented approach to social welfare provision. Most reform schemes hope to address the critical problems of high price, exclusion and inequality in the delivery of education, healthcare and housing via market channels. Little concrete success ihas been achieved on these accounts. Not only are healthcare, education and housing expensive for the ordinary citizen, but their provisions also involve significant inequality and exclusion.

The foremost government approach was to increase state expenditure in basic welfare provision to alleviate the effect of marketization while keeping household income on the rise. The level of exclusion is most severe in the healthcare sector. In 2003, 23–36 percent of patients in different areas declined hospital treatment, with levels as high as 75 percent in rural areas, citing high costs as the prime factor (Zhao, 2006). The new plan of healthcare reform was clearly spelt out in its mission to build state-subsidized and tightly regulated public hospitals and a network of grassroots medical centers to cover basic needs (Zhao and Huang, 2009). On the whole, the Hu–Wen administration has been able to align the financial burden of healthcare, education and housing with the average urban household income, with the share increasing from 15 to 32 percent in the last period of urban reform and this dropped slightly to 29 percent by 2008. See Figure 8.3 for details.

However, the present welfare programs were yet to find comprehensive solutions to inequity and exclusion, especially for those choosing to accept the market price. Despite achievements in checking excessive growth in welfare costs in general, the government is faced with many more significant problems as the new generation of the 1970s and 1980s come of age and the old generation of the 1950s and 1960s approach retirement age. The resulting surge in welfare demand poses a serious threat to the Chinese government still struggling to cope with unbearable rises in costs. The upsurge of social

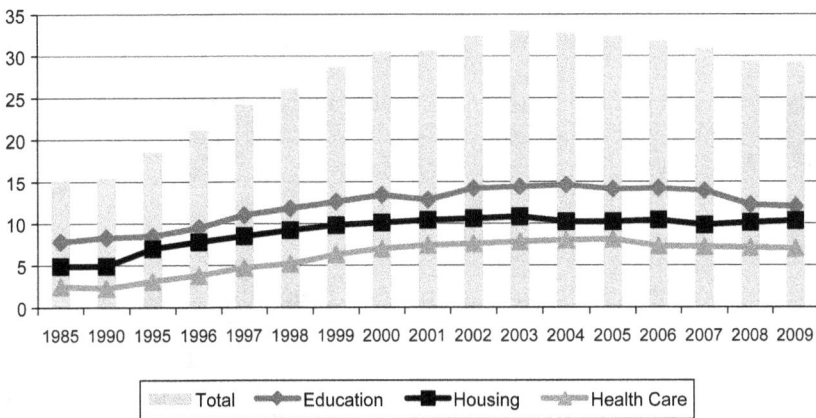

Figure 8.3 Average share of welfare items in urban household total expenditure (%)
Source: China Statistical Yearbook, various years.

grievances against fast rising housing price by the young generation is a clear sign of this change.

Another type of reform measure is the domestic response to crisis situations and the external pressures of globalization. The best example is the SARS crisis in 2003, which through a series of global engagements initiated a serious rethink about China's public health conditions and motivated the state to reform the public health and information sector (Chan *et al.*, 2010). The national project of "211" university-building and long-term technological development plan, which involves significant public funding to build research-based universities, is a clear systemic response to the challenge of globalization as well. In 2010, the reform of the income distribution system and the state monopoly gained momentum due to both intense domestic social grievances as well as the Sino-US debate on global economic structural imbalance.[2]

Despite the role of social policy reform in the Harmonious Society project, the ongoing reform is still primarily determined by the paramount agenda of economic development and market reform. Whenever global or regional economic downturns threaten domestic GDP growth, social sectors are opened up to stimulate domestic demands irrespective of the possible social consequences such as distributive justice and the affordability of basic welfare. The market-oriented reforms of higher education and healthcare in 1998 found their immediate application due to the Asian financial crisis of 1997. The post-crisis monetary policy in 2009 to achieve a GDP growth target of 8 percent likewise led to a build-up of bubbles in the housing price and caused many social problems down the road.

Most reform projects under the Hu–Wen social policy reform are still at an early stage. The Hu–Wen era has so far eschewed any abrupt and fundamental changes. Significant progress has been made in that employment-related social insurance coverage and labor protections have been extended to include most urban labor, including most migrant workers. But much less progress has been made towards achieving universal basic healthcare, fair access to education beyond the bare minimum, and providing affordable housing for all in need. Meanwhile, equality in welfare provision has in fact deteriorated, making China one of the least equitable nations in the world in the delivery of welfare services such as healthcare.

Exit, voice and social policy dynamics

At the heart of the politics of social policy is policy-making dynamics. Many Western scholars have made comprehensive historical studies of such dynamics of social policy in the developed world. In a classic study on American social policy, Skcopol (1992) indicated that successful social policy was critically dependent on nation-level civic engagement that organizes the interests of the disadvantaged and exercises a pressure on the political system. In the Chinese context, since voluntary autonomous political organizations are still unviable, it is more appropriate to assign the prime role to media and espe-cially the Internet as the platform of political input, where the social grie-vances are aggregated and politics of public policy are discussed publicly, overshadowing other official channels.[3] The only politically active organiza-tions are various government agencies within the formal framework of the Party-state.

Due to the exclusiveness of the policy-making process and the uniqueness of China's political systems, a detailed and documented analysis of the poli-tical process as in the example of Skcopol is not yet possible. Instead, we shall focus on the general pattern of policy dynamics and offer a conceptual fra-mework to address some key aspects of the policy-making process. The social policy process is defined as a strategic reaction by the Chinese political system to social grievances and social problems of different social groups under various institutional constraints.

Grievances and pressures can come from both inside the state apparatus and outside. For the convenience of analysis, only those directly working in various state agencies are regarded as insiders, such as Party and government organizations and to a lesser degree, government-sponsored institutions and the large SOEs, especially those managed by the central government. Thus, the Chinese social policy process runs on two levels, at one level, organized interests of the state agency, and especially central leadership, can directly influence policy; at the other level, organized social forces can input their grievances into the political system primarily through the media, in particular, the Internet.

Albert Hirschman (1968) advanced in his book *Exit, Voice and Loyalty* an interesting model to analyze organizational behavior from the vantage point of the members or parties to an organizational or transactional arrangement, such as customers of a firm or members of a political entity. When the quality of goods or services provided by the organization deteriorates, the individual transaction party can either terminate the contract to join another transaction arrangement, or alternatively, voice grievance or protest to urge the organiza-tionto change for the better if the exit option is costly or simply not available. The difference between exit and voice, as Hirschman pointed out, reflects the difference between economical and political acts of protest, the former dependent on the availability of alternative choices and the latter relevant to situations when exit options are unavailable or exit costs are too high.

In the Chinese context, the exit and voice model could be applied to both social welfare and public goods. Under the category of social welfare we subsume the provision of welfare such as public housing, healthcare and education. We further assume the state as the provider of social welfare and individual citizens is making the choice. The citizens may be further divided into the social elites, the middle class and the marginal social groups. The exit option can be interpreted as alternative options in welfare provision rather than the prevailing market for welfare supply. Exit options are few and available only to the elites. These would include exemptions from the market of welfare provision for the political elite, or access to the privately provided high-end welfare services for the economic elite. Lastly, there is the option of migrating to foreign countries for both the political and economic elite and to a lesser extent, the intellectual and technological elite as well (sometimes vaguely defined within the middle class), which offer a more open and merit-based society.

Voice naturally refers to political actions that citizens may take based on grievances against poor provision of social welfare. In the political as in any other systems, voice is dependent on political power. Four conditions for the magnitude of voice can be assumed. First, social groups with the closest and most direct relations to central state apparatus and official propaganda channels are considered to have the most powerful voice; second, voice is strongest among the most organized social groups; third, social groups with the highest social status, including the political, economic and intellectual elites, have the loudest voices; lastly, social groups which formerly had a significant stake and stand to lose most from reform should have the strongest incentive to protest and henceforth the most powerful voice. In short, social groups with direct access to the state powers either at the central or local levels have the most powerful voice in social policy-making and implementation.

The categorization of the middle class and the marginal class follows the social and economic positions of the relevant social groups in Chinese society. In general, the middle class has stronger voices and more opportunities for voluntary exit than the marginal groups. Here the middle class are broadly defined as social groups with secure jobs in the urban formal sector, most of the work-related social insurances and the financial means to access marketized welfare services. Most urban households under the HRS system with secure employment in the formal sector belong to this category. Marginal groups mainly refer to the urban unemployed population, the migrant workforce and most of the rural population. They usually lack the financial means or the basic social insurances, but more important, the full identity of residents in the city of their workplace under the HRS system. Both the middle class and marginal social groups exercise no voluntary exit option from the market of welfare provision. Whenever exit options are concerned, they can only be forced out of the market, with an absolute drop in social welfare, as in the case of "voluntary" withdrawal from treatment for serious illness, the act of abandoning further schooling beyond basic levels and the most recent crowding-out in urban housing market of most potential buyers.

Below-expectation performance of social policy induces a voice from the social groups adversely affected. As long as the social groups concerned could still afford the market price, their grievances are directed to price and quality and usually at controllable levels; however, if the social groups concerned are forced to exit the market, the grievances are mainly directed against the high price. In China, random voice ranges from causal grievances to anti-social violence at both the individual and collective levels. Voice can flow upwards through institutional channels like the media or petition-visits services of the state. Needless to say, a new pervasive form of dissenting voice is Internet protests. All voices from outside the institutional channels of the state in their accumulated forms lead to social instability. As commonly assumed, better positioned and organized social elites have much stronger voices since they can directly address the decision-making body of the state and its various levels of agency institutions from within when their key interests are at stake.

There are different channels of voices for people with different cultural, social and political capital. At the top level is the institutional embodiment of the state power, namely the government and party organizations themselves from central to local levels, where only the political elite have legal access. These high-level channels are considered as being within the political system. Closest to the state agencies at the formal institutional level are channels such as the National People's Congress (NPC) and the Chinese People's Political Consultative Conference (CPPCC). These are much weaker, but essentially and predominantly elite organizational actors. Less direct and but still influential channels are social agencies and intermediaries affiliated with the state, such as the media and NGOs. These channels can be considered outside the political system proper, but still within the boundary of stable political control. Lastly, for the social groups with no access to any of the above institutional channels, individual or collective acts of social protest are the least institutionalized and at best imperfectly controllable. This category will include random Internet protests to mass incidents in the streets. In extreme cases, voice can be expressed as violent crimes, suicide and self-immolations.

We assume the central government is motivated by two factors, namely the collective voice from society that is demanding reform, and the costs of reform, including resistance from institutional constraints and the direct costs of state subsidy or transfer. In each case the resultant voice from all the social groups affected, which is interpreted as political costs for delay or non-action in social reform, will be compared with the direct costs and the institutional resistance involved in possible social policy reform. The institutional resistance in most cases comes from the direct providers of social welfare, in most cases corporatized agency under the political control or auspices of the state. If the former outweighs the latter, we assume the government will be more likely to launch reform and make the necessary investment; otherwise the government will refrain from reform and make little investment. The resultant reform efforts will be measured in terms of the scale of state social spending, coverage of welfare policy, the clarity of the reform agenda and the level of institutionalization for each specific policy domain.

The following analysis will be based on different domains of social policy. As a matter of fact, the social structure and distribution of voice and exit opportunities vary widely across the specific domains of the social policy concerned. For convenience of comparison, social policies are categorized into three domains, namely, the corporate-based and state-managed social insurance schemes for the employed, the market-oriented welfare provisions under state supervision, and the social protection for the poor and needy in the form of minimum livelihood assistance. Exit and voice options in each category will be analyzed with regard to the social groups involved in order to estimate the possible reform pressure on the central government.

Social Insurance

Social insurance includes five work-related insurances associated with employment, namely old age pension, medical insurance, unemployment insurance, work injury insurance, maternal insurance and the Housing Provident Fund (HPF). The bulk of the urban workforce is involved in the five insurance themes and the HPF. Compared with other forms of welfare provision, social insurance has a number of features facilitating its implementation.

Addressed primarily to workers with secure jobs as opposed to the unemployed and part-time workers, social insurance has very wide political support among the urban working class. State enterprises and work units are naturally the first to benefit. Though necessarily vocal as political forces, regular employers of private enterprises, increasingly aware of their legal rights, tend to organize themselves for collective action. This tendency was further strengthened as labor-related social protests and massive incidents raised the urgency of labor protection.

Since everyone in the workforce is exposed to various types and levels of risks, the exit option is unavailable for any risk-averse employees for work-related social insurance, especially the state sector under the direct political control of the central and local governments. For instance, prior to the implementation of the New Labor Law, there was already wide social support for better protection of migrant workers by legislating basic insurance. Considering the instability and volatility of the lower end of the labor market in China, unemployment is certainly a most likely concern.

The risk pooling and sharing scheme in social insurance, except for the HPF, also serves to unite the strong and weak voices in the same direction of expanding coverage rate to achieve universal coverage. While risks may vary across different individuals, there is no clear variation and stratification of risks based on social status (except for work-related injury). This relative uniform distribution of risks aligns the interests of all urban employees from all social strata on the side of a nationwide insurance system.

The costs of setting up and expanding the work-related insurance system to cover all the urban employees are relatively low as long as China continues to enjoy its demographic dividends and rapid economic growth. Direct financial costs associated with the system are also not a serious problem for the state since it is funded by the corporate sector. Funds will be sufficient at least for the immediate future, if the government can maintain overall economic growth and a vibrant corporate sector. In overall assessment, as a socially based core part in the welfare system, social insurance is one of the relatively more successful social reform programs. As coverage grows steadily, exclusion is unlikely to become a major issue in this program.

However, the social insurance system today still lacks equality of access and sometimes suffers from many blind spots in its coverage. A major source of inequity is the dual-track pension scheme between the enterprises and the government sector. Since the SOE reform, the enterprises' pension scheme has been fully socialized and no longer administered by the state, however, the reform stops short of corporatizing civil servants and government-funded services, creating a dual-track pension system. The HPF contribution in particular displays very sharp corporate-based inequality due to the lack of specific regulations on its upper limits.[4] As the politically more vocal section of the workforce concurrently enjoys a measure of exit from the insurance-based system, there is a clear lack of political dynamics to increase the level of old-age insurance and a resistance to reform the dual-track system. The main constraints on social insurance come from the financial conditions of the individual enterprises. Many of China's small and medium-sized enterprises have always been living on a meager profit margin. Even as the New Labor Law made enterprises' contribution to insurance premiums a legal requirement, significant numbers of migrant workers are still under-covered by social insurance due to a lack of corporate funding and law enforcement capacity.

Social protection

Social protection is the direct transfer from the state as an institution of income redistribution. The classical example is the Minimum Standard of Living Scheme (MSLS) in China and to a lesser extent, the institution of the minimum wage. In China, following the liberal model of limited protection for the extreme needy, only means-tested marginalized social groups are eligible for minimum welfare support from the state.

The politics of social protection works by a simple mechanism. Since there is no exit for the absolute needy, the low-income group has very a strong incentive to push for the state transfer payment. However, lacking channels of expression and organizational capacity, the voice from below is likely to be very weak and must rely on social agency to express itself. Thus social protection for those in extreme need might be delayed for decades from being institutionalized, such as the rural MSLS. While poverty has long been an issue both in urban and rural China, it was not until 2005 that the Chinese government began to urge nationwide implementation of the rural MSLS to aid the desperate poor, long after the scheme was first introduced in urban industrial centers.[5]

The urban poor are relatively better protected in the social reform. This is not just because they are politically less marginalized. Thanks to the urban corporate reform, China's poverty relief started relatively early in the urban industrial regions. The MSLS was first institutionalized as a social policy to cope with the social consequences of the SOE reform, which resulted in massive urban unemployment in the industrial city of Shanghai in 1993. Later it spread with the pace of deepening SOE reforms to the inland provinces.

In a similar light, the Hu–Wen administration set up the minimum wage system in 2003 and made it a legal requirement in the New Labor Law in 2008, primarily to protect migrant workers in the coastal provinces. This institution of labor protection is envisaged as part of the administration's concerted efforts to introduce social inequality and in particular lessen the urban–rural income gap. In recent years, the minimum wage scheme has extended its coverage and been better enforced, but the level of minimum wage, as in the case of the MSLS, remained at a very low level and appeared sometimes inflexible to adjustment in some regions.[6]

The key issue of social protection is the level of protection. Politically, China's working and non-working poor are exactly the least vocal social groups politically. Weak and limited voice from the marginal social class often induces state inaction and constrains the extent and level of China's social protections. This is furthered delayed by the local authorities, often without political and fiscal incentives to aid the poor, especially the migrant workers. This policy lag can be very significant in that heavy state fiscal commitment only occurs long after the relevant institutions were first set up.[7]

Welfare provision in general

Welfare provision, covering the areas of housing, healthcare and education, is perhaps the most complicated and contentious domain of social policy in China today. The domain of welfare provision is first and foremost about the distribution of economic costs and benefits of the reform since the commodification and the marketization of housing, healthcare and education have transformed these social spheres into important sectors of the economy. The issue of welfare provision involves, among others, the key economic and social interests of China's emerging middle class as a politically strategic social group.

The market-oriented allocations of housing, education and healthcare are predominantly urban issues. In particular, the price and quality of these social goods are applicable in the most urbanized part of China where both the elite and the middle class are mainly concentrated. The highly differentiated distribution of voice and exit options between the elite and the middle class have so far created serious tensions in all the relevant policy domains, especially in the field of housing. For all three sectors concerned, the fault line between the elite and the middle class is the availability of the exit option and the level of voice.

In today's China, the elites have every means to circumvent and take advantage of the market mechanisms whereas the middle class, despite their growing political weight and growing voices in the media, often have no alternative but to accept the terms of the market. Market allocation is strictly based on the *dollar vote*, in that access priority to the limited supply of welfare goods is given to the highest bidders. As the market price for education, healthcare and housing continues to rise, some middle-class bidders are effectively crowded out and withdraw from the market. The crowded-out social groups have the most incentive to criticize the pricey welfare regime and resort to more violent means, whereas those who are not completely out of the game will have incentives to complain about the poor quality and high price of the welfare goods and services.

The game of welfare provision in China is thus typically played out among the central governments, the political and economic elites with an exit option, the middle class with no or some voice, the government agents with a stake in pricey welfare goods, and the often crowded-out marginal groups, in particular, those on the margin of haves and have nots. In terms of gain and loss, the elite enjoy absolute personal gain at little personal cost, the middle class enjoy relative social and personal gain at considerable personal costs and the marginal group face absolute social and personal loss. The agents are often rent-seekers and resistant to any reform. Forms of voice also vary across this social spectrum, from minor complaints to serious social grievances and violent retribution, while the channels of voice also shift from official government bodies to violent personal protest.

Education

For years, educational policy has attracted much media attention as one of the most problematic sectors across all social policy domains. However, it is in fact less problematic in terms of equality of access and exclusion than healthcare and housing. Unlike healthcare and housing, there are far fewer special privileges, such as state-subsidy and separate special arrangements in access to education for children from different social classes in a given region. This has made the political dynamics in education provision somewhat more efficient than other major social policy domains.

The exit option is less readily available for any social groups for public education. At the obligatory level, there is almost no exit for all social groups from the prevailing state-funded public school system, whereas at the higher education, the only significant exit lies in studying abroad, which is only available to the economically better-off. Despite the sharp rise in the opportunity of studying abroad, the exit is quantitatively less significant than the welfare privileges associated with housing and healthcare.[8] Political and economic elites, the middle class and the marginal class all have strong incentives to see the size of the education sector expand and the general quality improve.

At the level of basic education, China has made significant progress since the reform, both in terms of participatory rates and average years of schooling. Two important factors are at work. First, there is no exit for any social class in participating in the government-funded social policy domain of obligatory education, from the elites to the marginal groups. Second, the obligatory stage of education is not as commercialized as other domains of welfare policy and enjoys a unique legal protection. In the reform era the idea of basic education for all gained wide social consensus and unswerving political support from the central leadership. The legalization of the Nine Year Obligatory Education meant no exit for any social class from education at the stage of primary and junior high school.

The government has been overall successful in expanding basic education and improving the general quality of education. This progress notwithstanding, distributive inequity remains critical. Marginal social groups such as migrant workers are virtually excluded from the state-run urban basic education system, whereas financial and human resources vary widely among rural and urban, poor and rich regions. Since these weak social groups have only limited voices, there has been a lack of reform dynamics for years. As in the case of other domains of social services, the predominant choice for marginal groups is to choose an involuntary exit at some point beyond the mandatory level of education.

The marketization of higher education has spawned a phenomenal growth in the size of China's higher education sector. However, the newly available opportunities often cause a major deviation from the merit-based principles, since expanding enrollment and lower entrance quality controls induce a shift of access criteria from academic merits to family financial status. In other words, the economically better-off are provided with higher chance of a college education while those worse-off are levied with an additional cost. Decentralization and corporatization of higher-education also mean a larger playground for the political and social elites who have privileged access to the extra quotas. Since there is an obvious exit option for the poor household, namely opting out, it is not surprising to find an ever declining ratio of undergraduates from a rural background.[9]

Despite comparative under-financing, China's education system and especially the higher education sector, has enjoyed more profuse and generous state finance and other policy supports than other social welfare domains.[10] Thus the inequality in access to education is more of a market-based than an identity-based stratification or outright exclusion. The economic and political elites do have priority access to more quality education. The small voice of the socially disadvantaged in a country with few powerful autonomous organizations means a lack of social support for the weak, least of all from an organized body, to assert their interests and champion reform from outside the political system.

As a social policy domain, higher education reform faces a number of structural constraints specific to the powerful public education system. In China, education reform is tasked with a self-contained educational system composed of various levels of educational institutions, the local educational bureaucracy and the Ministry of Education. In the current framework of administrative control, the higher-education sector occupied prominent political positions as independent units from their local administration, whereas primary and high schools are locally based institutions. Of the independent institutions of higher education, universities with central ministerial filiations are even powerful vice-ministerial ranking administrative units. Such an organizational structure implies that the higher education system will continue to absorb more resources and pose more obstacles to reform than primary and high schools. The competitive expansion and the pursuit of scale rather than quality, which is in accordance with the vital corporate self-interests of the higher education system, are still hard to reform.

The future of China's education reform is as ambiguous as its achievements so far. While there are many media reports and discussions on various problems in China's higher education, there is no quick and effective means to overhaul it as long as China continues the process of marketization and globalization. The political significance of higher education is admittedly an important driving force for future reform, but reform in the near future, as the newly released medium- and long-term plan for education reform suggests, will focus on technical and governance issues rather than making fundamental changes to the course.

Healthcare

As another important domain of social policy, healthcare policy directly involves the well-being of every individual member of the society. In terms of the voice and exit, the interests involved are more complicated than education but not as complex as housing provision.

Access to healthcare in China is characterized by the existence of wide-ranging privileges of special social groups and virtually no legal protection for the marginal social groups. At the top of the pyramid sit the social groups who do not need to worry about medical bills. Incumbent and retired senior officials in the state sector of healthcare spending are fully or for the most part covered by state budget. The rich capitalists and entrepreneurial class can seek exit from the market system by seeking healthcare abroad. Exit options from the healthcare market are thus available for both top political and economic elites. At this level, there is no incentive for the privileged groups to voice any grievances as the actual beneficiaries.

At the next level are social groups whose socio-economic position and financial resources are sufficient to secure for themselves and their family members full or substantial levels of government- or corporate-funded medical insurance, such as civil servants and the upper middle class. These two classes enjoy at least a certain protection from the rising costs of healthcare services. Like the first class, they have limited incentive to voice protests against the current arrangement. But with at least partial self-contribution, they are still likely to complain about the quality of services.

Most of the middle class, with limited access to state subsidies and only minimum insurance coverage, are left with the sole choice of obtaining health service from the market partially financed by their savings. These social groups have strong incentives to challenge the present system since they have to pay heavy costs for most healthcare services. Collectively they have little direct influence over the actual agenda-setting, but their strong preference for state-funded public hospitals over continued marketization nevertheless will produce an accumulative effect.

At the lowest social echelon, some social groups are completely excluded from the healthcare market and basic insurance due to the prohibitive level of cost relative to their incomes and the incomplete social security system. As in many cases in the social policy domain, their collective voice is very weak, most choosing a voluntary exit from medical care. However, the scale of exclusion is larger and more consequential, as hundreds of millions of rural households are virtually cut off from any provision of healthcare.

Like education, inequity and exclusion are major problems in the present healthcare system. But both problems have been much more severe in the case of healthcare than education. The key factor at issue is the cost of medication, followed by the lack of coverage of basic medical insurance. Compared with education, the government has been more reluctant to increase direct healthcare expenditure instead of expanding medical insurance. Healthcare expenditure fell from 6 percent in 1994 to 2.6 percent in 2001. But more significantly for the middle class, rent-seeking and the resultant poor quality of service in hospitals are even more rampant and obnoxious than in education.

While linked to various levels of government as semi-autonomous institutions, public hospitals are mostly locally based, politically less significant corporate and administrative entities. In consequence, systemic reforms to deal with rent-seeking will encounter less resistance than education reform. Considering the social distribution of benefits and costs, healthcare reform is also unlikely to produce a serious conflict between the elite who are already enjoying full coverage and the excluded class desperately in need of basic coverage. The policy goal of building a mini-NHS, as clearly spelt out in the reform proposal in 2009, seems a plausible resolution. Indeed, the current new healthcare reform is already making headway in this direction. The whole process will take very long, especially in providing equal service, as long as the elite insiders feel no compelling incentives to pursue such directions on account of their own fully protected interests.

Housing

In many respects, housing is the most critical of all China's social policy domains as demonstrated by prohibitively high housing prices. Indeed, the interests involved are more complicated than any other spheres of social policy and the stakes much higher for most parties.

Housing policy is not as much a concern for China's older generation as for the younger generation, since the last two rounds of reform only monetized but not marketized housing, offering housing as part of the welfare provisions of work units rather than full private goods. Since the 1990s, the central government has implemented several welfare schemes to provide housing through state subsidy and to ensure the price is within the affordable range.

However, the pervasive tendency of rent-seeking at the local level soon led to an effective impasse in these state-subsidized housing programs.

Since the social provision of housing is highly marketized for most in the urban region, the most clear-cut division line in housing allocation is drawn between those who are exempt from the high-price market and those who must bid in the market. The former refer to employees in organizations that could provide cheap housing as a part of the welfare package, including civil servants, government-affiliated sectors and employees of some monopoly SOEs. The latter group is the rest of the buyers who have no such privileges.

Like any other sector, reform in the housing sector critically lacks the necessary political dynamics from inside. But the incentive mechanism in the housing sector is even more skewed, since houses can serve as a form of speculative investment. Political and economic elites with access to a limited supply of land and finance stand to profit hugely from manipulating supply and speculating on price, a process naturally bidding up the price for others. Thus, in the housing market, unlike in healthcare and education, the economically privileged propertied middle class have a strong incentive to ally with the powerful political forces in favor of price increase, against the other part of the emergent not-yet-propertied young middle class. Therefore, the expenditure on public housing has been both sluggish and inadequate for many years until the disastrous housing bubble in 2009–10, as shown in Figure 8.4.

Exclusion in housing provision is particularly politically destabilizing since much of the middle class are primary victims of crowd-out. The subsequent social grievances are not distributed linearly according to relative economic

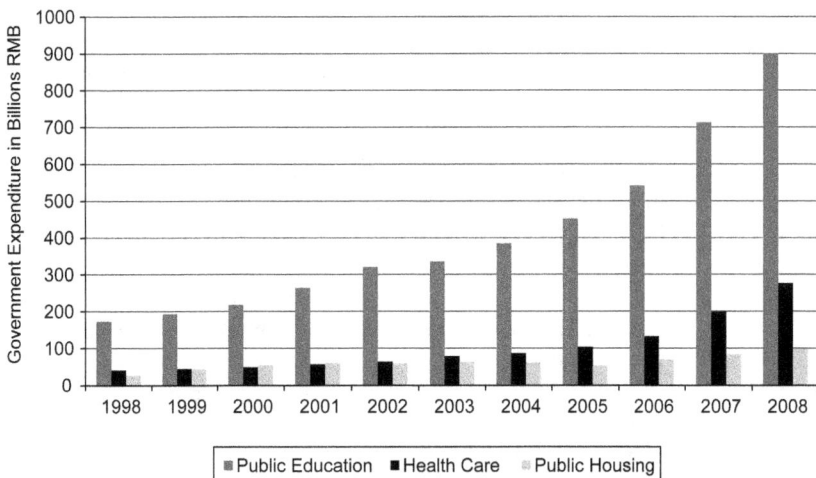

Figure 8.4 Government expenditure on education, healthcare and public housing
Source: China Statistical Yearbook, various years.

and social status, as in the cases of healthcare and education. Rather, grievances are concentrated in the aspirant middle class, mostly the young generation of university graduates as middle-class urban migrants in the non-state sector. Denied direct access to government bodies, they represent nevertheless the most vocal voices in the media, wielding significant power in shaping public opinion, particularly on the Internet. The indirect political pressure on the central government to tackle the current housing price hike and perhaps take on a completely new reform is strong and well represented at the political periphery.

Unlike the healthcare sector, contention centering on housing policy has yet to produce any unambiguous policy agenda. On balance, for the economic, financial and fiscal stakes of the powerful state agents, central government in general will not be motivated to force housing prices down, neither will there be very motivations for public housing, which offers the agents little profits. There is likely to be an increase in public housing expenditure, but the increase will most likely be inadequate to fundamentally restructure the housing market. Popular demands for affordable housing will prove to be difficult to achieve in practice at least for the near future. In this connection, the voice of the young middle class is likely to turn more political.

Across all the spheres of public policy in China today, social policy is uniquely and invariably characterized by varying degrees of elite exits. This not only makes social policy a hotbed of inequality and injustice, but also induces a lack of political dynamics for systemic reform. In all the domains of social policy discussed, there is almost complete absence of voice from outside the state apparatus when the policy was formulated. Rather, there is strong resistance to the pro-society policy orientations of the Hu–Wen administration, in particular with regard to the forthcoming housing policy reform. Under tremendous institutional constraints, social policy reform today seems to work on a crisis-response mechanism enforced by top political leadership rather than well-coordinated systemic efforts. This lack of systemic and prompt response entails a huge cost on the part of political authority.

Social policy as a whole might be compared with other public policy domains. Macroeconomic policy and public security and social stability are two good cases in point. The structure and distribution of voice for these two policy domains are not essentially different from social policy. However, unlike social welfare and social protection, there is little exit for the elite from macroeconomic disturbances or social instability. Indeed, the central and local political elite clearly enjoy higher stakes in economic growth and social stability due to the political benefits and costs based on achieving these two targets. Similarly, the economic elite are likely to lose more from the prospect of hyper-inflation and economic recession than ordinary citizens.

Local cadres could be mobilized as reliable and effective agents of economic growth and social stability, since these two tasks affect their political future and personal fortune. In consequence, there is commonly little lack of dynamics, policy input and usually remarkable achievements in these public

Table 8.1 Political dynamics of exit and voice in different social policy domains

	Social insurance	Social protection	Educational provision	Healthcare provision	Housing provision
Exit option	No exit from social risks for all classes	The elite and middle class	Limited exit for elite	Limited exit for elite	Substantial exit for the public sector elite
Major grievances	Level of coverage	Level of protection	Poor quality and inequity	Inequity, exclusion and high price	High price
Crowded-out social groups	Mostly rural and migrant workers	Mostly rural poor	Rural poor and migrant workers	Rural and urban poor, migrant workers	Urban middle class
Forms of "voice"/social resistance	Societal voice	Weak societal voice and violence	Strong societal voice, elite and middle class voice	Strong societal voice, middle-class voice	Strong societal voice, strong middle-class voice/protest
Institutional resistance to reform	No systemic resistance, fiscal constraints	No systemic resistance, fiscal constraints	Resistance from higher education sectors	Some resistance from healthcare sectors	Strong resistance from local government
State subsidy	Low	Low	High	High	High
Reform progress	Some progress/ clear blueprint	Some progress/ tentative blueprint	Some progress with no clear blueprint	Some progress with clear blueprint	Little progress with no clear blueprint

domains, as the recent stimulus package to promote GDP growth and maintain employment has vividly demonstrated. The potential costs and benefits to the reformers and their agents have largely dictated the reform agenda and conditioned the behavior of reformers. Social policy reform, as it involves redistribution of welfare benefits from the more privileged to the less privileged, is naturally much harder to find among competent and motivated agents as such. Table 8.1 summarizes the dynamics and progres in social policy reforms categorized into five policy areas as discussed above.

Policy implications

If examined from a historical perspective, most of these grievances have their origins in the social policy reform both in the narrow sense of welfare reform and in a broader sense as a restructuring of state–society relations. Much of the social injustice discussed above is rooted exactly in inequality and injustice in the distribution of social welfare. For example, the new burdens of expensive medication, education and housing are regarded as actual sources of grievances among various groups of the middle class in China today. High rates of crime, erosion of social cohesion and moral decay such as the spread of prostitution are likewise largely the result of basic educational inequity and the lack of social protection. Failure of the social policy reform to reduce the costs of essential welfare goods and provide protection for the majority is likely to result in further social instability.

Contrary to many skeptics, systematic social policy reform will not be unduly costly at least in the beginning. Part of the costs of welfare provisions, which will be shouldered by the state, is likely to prove to be economically efficient in the long run, as the input in education and healthcare effectively upgrades human capital accumulation in favor of continued growth in future, not to mention its contribution to social and political stability. In a similar vein, further investments in social insurance and social protection will also help to encourage consumption, relieve social tensions and remove some sources of social instability. State investment in social reform, while expensive at the outset, is likely to prove more effective than the stimulus packages that only serve to distort the economic structure further.

The Hu–Wen administration has made social policy an important and independent aspect of the public policy agenda. By expanding the coverage of social insurance, strengthening social protections for the poor and reforming market-oriented social provisions, the current social reform has achieved varying progress in all social policy domains. But the lack of reform dynamics is clearly a key obstacle. To a large extent reform is still limited in scope and falls short of the general public expectations. At a more profound level, further social policy reform will also require a broadened agenda to include readjustment in state–society relations. Such a necessary adjustment constitutes the political dimension of social reform.

Today, state–society relations are plagued by a myriad of special privileges for the political elite to access various welfare provisions. As discussions in earlier sections suggest, such widespread privileges provide exit options from the market for state employees, who otherwise will have to join the protest for better welfare provisions. The critical absence of voice from within the political elites generates a serious lack and delay in reform dynamics. In this sense, further reform will need to transform exclusive state-sponsored privileges and special interests into various forms of universally shared rights to social welfare, in addition to the existing bundle of rights to social insurance for all employees under the labor law, and means-tested social protection for eligible citizens across all social classes and professional boundaries.

In policy terms, special welfare rights of civil servants and former employees in monopoly SOEs must be adjusted and curtailed according to prevailing societal valuations. With the exit options withdrawn from the menu of choice for the political elite and a measure of universal citizen rights to state-sponsored social welfare, the voice for inexpensive and high quality welfare provisions will be significantly strengthened. The broadened social reform agenda thus will have to include, among others, creating rights of equal access to state-sponsored social provisions under a program of universal citizenship.

China's economic success is critically contingent on the mutual reinforcement between the dual dynamics of economic growth and social stability. But the current uneasy coupling of an economic growth model based on GDP-centered mobilization approach and a static form of social stability enforced by direct state control is replete with contradictions. A key source of contradictions, as discussed, is the lack of clearly envisioned and timely implemented social policies to compensate and protect social groups whose welfare positions are adversely affected by economic reform and current socio-economic institutions.

The absence of social policy reform will lead to increasing distrust between the state and society and disloyalty of the majority of the social groups, with profound political implications. In accordance with Samuel Huntington's classic study on comparative political development, mutual distrust and truncated loyalty effectively mean political disorganizations that in the long run will almost certainly undermine political instability, a scenario repeatedly enacted in the political upheavals in many Asian countries and most recently in Thailand (Huntington, 1968).[14]

As a recent study on institutional evolution suggests, modern state-building is critically dependent on open-access order in the political and economic domains for all potential social elites, otherwise the state will be unable to cope with the mounting violence by the excluded social forces against the existing exclusive political and social orders. The welfare regime is one of the most relevant domains in the context of China today in this connection. The exclusion of different social groups from the welfare regime is generating various degrees of violent and potential political reactions as indicated in the rising costs of maintaining public security. China is in urgent need of a shift from a privilege-based limited access to an open access order in its state-funded welfare system (North *et al.*, 2009).

With the widening of the income inequality gap and the dispossession of marginalized social groups, China may have entered a stage when economic growth is accompanied by potentially increasing social instability. Only sweeping reform in the social and economic structure will resolve the seething social conflicts and provide some institutional basis to social stability. The ongoing social policy reform will have to enshrine social injustice as the focus point and guiding principle (Zheng, 2009). Without a proper social policy reform among other major reforms to address the fundamental structural dilemmas, both social and economic development ahead will be unsustainable and liable to a vicious circle.

Notes

1 For a review of the history of politics of social policy in the West, refer to Manning (2008), Chapter 2.
2 "Zhongguo chengnuo wanshan shouruifenpei geju he longduan gaige" [China's Promise to reform monopoly sector and income distribution pattern] *People's Daily*, May 25, 2010.
3 The Internet has become an important institution of policy deliberation and public contention. See further discussions in Yang (2008) and Zheng (2007).

4 In most enterprises, although social insurances meet the legally required minimum, the level of protection remains relatively low and stagnant, especially enterprise pensions based on old-age insurance, which is only 20 percent of the prevailing wage level. The comparable figure in the government sector could be as high as 60–80 percent. Since the HPF involves no social risk sharing and incurs heavy funding, the fund is mostly concentrated in the government and monopoly SOEs.

5 As discussed earlier, urban MSLS originated from the need to cope with the social aftermath of the SOE reform in the mid-1990s, whereas later the rural MSLS, though adjusted many times to reflect true costs of living, lags behind the increase in general wage rate and essentially reflects the very basic subsistence line.

6 According to an independent comparative study by Liu Zhirong, China's minimum wage is only 25 percent of the average wage rate. This would rank China among the lowest of all countries with legalized minimum wage systems.

7 China's welfare spending only began to increase more rapidly than the whole budgetary spending since 2006, see Figure 8.4.

8 Despite the basic financial requirements, studying abroad is not strictly identity-based, at least less obviously so than the opportunity to access state-funded pension, healthcare and low price housing, which cater specifically for the politically and socially privileged civil servants.

9 "Declining proportions of rural undergraduate endangers social harmony," *China Youth Daily*, 24 January 2010.

10 China's education budget, like government financing for healthcare and public housing, share of education expenditure in government budget declined from 17.6 per cent in 1994 to 13.4 percent in 2006. But declines have been much more severe in the case of healthcare, social protection and public housing. Compared with developed welfare states, China's under-financing of healthcare and social protection is also more severe than that of education.

11 So far no systematic analysis of rent-seeking in local economic housing programs has been undertaken. Anecdotal stories are scattered around in various newspaper and magazine reports. The major cause is the scarce supply of economy housing available. China's economy housing only accounts for 6 percent of the total housing area.

12 The disappearing middle class," [Beixiaoshi de Zhongchanjieji], *China News Weekly*, Vol. 1, 2010.

13 Yan Jingjing, "How many elites are migrating abroad? What are they looking for?' [Duoshao jingying zai yimi, tamen za xunzhao shenme], *Southern Weekly*, 2 June 2010.

14 "Protests urge resignation of leaders in Thailand," *New York Times*, 14 March 2010.

References

Chan, K.C., Ngok, K.L. and Phillips, D. (2008) *Social Policy in China: Development and Well-being*, Bristol: The Policy Press.

Chan, L.H., Chen, L. and Xu, J. (2010) "China's engagement with global health diplomacy: was SARS a watershed?," *PLoS Med* 7(4): e1000266. doi:10.1371/journal.pmed.1000266.

Esping-Andersen, G. (1990) *The Three Worlds of Welfare Capitalism*, Princeton, NJ: Princeton University Press.

Gu, E. (2006) "From social insurance to social assistant: welfare policy change," in J. Wong and H. Lai (eds.) *China into the Hu–Wen Era: Policy Initiative and Challenges*, Singapore: World Scientific, pp. 405–36.

Hirschman, A. (1968) *Exit, Voice and Loyalty*, Cambridge, MA: Harvard University Press.

Hu, J. (2005) "Guanyu jianshe shehuizhuyi hexieshehui de jianghua" [On constructing a socialist harmonious society], Xinhua News Agency, 26 May 2005.

Huntington, S. (1968) *Political Order in Changing Society*, New Haven, CT: Yale University Press.

Li, C. (2006) "Deciphering Hu's leadership and defining new elites *politics*," in J. Wong and H. Lai (eds.) *China into the Hu–Wen Era: Policy Initiative and Challenges*, Singapore: World Scientific, pp. 68–73.

Liu,Z. (2005) "Institution and inequality: the hukou system in China," *Journal of Comparative Economics*, 33(1): 133–57.

Manning, N. (2008) "Politics of social policy," in J. Baldock (ed.) *Social Policy*, Oxford: Oxford University Press.

Naughton, B. (1995) *Growing Out of the Plan: Chinese Economic Reform, 1978–1993*, New York: Cambridge University Press.

North, D., Wallis, J. and Weingast, B. (2009) *Violence and Social Order*, Cambridge: Cambridge University Press.

Skcopol, T. (1992) *Protecting Soldiers and Mothers*, Cambridge, MA: Harvard University Press.

Tang, J. (2010) "Chengxiang dibao zhidu: lishi, xianzhuang yu qianzhan' [Urban and Rural MSLS: Past, Present and Future]. Beijing: the Institute of Sociology, Chinese Academy of Social Sciences.

Walder, A.G. (1986) *Communist Neo-Traditionalism, Work and Authority in Chinese Industry*, Berkeley, CA: University of California Press.

Yang, G. (2008) *The Power of the Internet: Citizen Activism Online*, New York: Columbia University Press.

Zhao, L. and Huang, Y. (2009) "China moves to reform its healthcare system," *EAI Background Brief No. 486*, East Asian Institute, National University of Singapore.

Zhao, Z. (2006) "Income inequality, unequal healthcare access, and mortality in China," *Population and Development Review*, 32(3): 461–83.

Zheng, Y. (2007) *Technological Empowerment: The Internet, State and Society in China*, Stanford, CA: Stanford University Press.

——(2009) "Economic reform, social policy and political transition," in L. Zhao and T. Lim (eds.) *China's New Social Policy: Initiative for a Harmonious Society*, Singapore: World Scientific, pp. 11–21.

9 Developmentalism, secularism, nationalism and essentialism

Current situation and challenges of the ethnic issue in China

Yongjia Liang

Introduction

In the spring of 2008 and summer of 2009, violence against and between civilians broke out in Lhasa and Urumqi, the capital cities of Tibet and Xinjiang, two of the largest ethnic autonomous regions in China, causing grave loss of lives and property. Different political powers engaged in complex interaction and struggles, heating up unprecedentedly the Chinese ethnic issue that has been marginalized by Chinese media and academics for decades. The violence reflects many problems in Chinese ethnic policies. In this chapter, I analyze the overall problem of the current ethnic issues in China, which, I argue, are faced with four challenges. First, developmentalism intended to alleviate ethnic conflicts is not sustainable. Second, secularism reveals the dilemma of the ideology of a "unified, multi-ethnic country," making it difficult for the state to encompass the ethnic minorities. Third, the current nationalist discourse is unable to accommodate the ethnic minorities. Fourth, the central problem of the Chinese ethnic issue is ethnic essentialism. I believe that the Chinese ethnic issue is an ideological one that goes beyond the question of social policy. It is an unsolved historical problem in the course of Chinese modernization as well as an urgent issue in the current social transformation.

Certainly, I am not the first to analyze the ethnic issues from the perspective of ideology. Such an approach already has been mooted (see, for example, Smith, 2001; Gellner, 2006), which Louis Dumont called the analysis of "fundamental ideas and values" (Dumont, 1983: 156), or "indigenous-idea-in-action" (Moffatt, 1986: xiv). In his paper "Nationalism and Communalism" (Dumont, [1966] 1998), Dumont argues that the partition of India and Pakistan was not so much a result of Britain's "malicious" policy, but a natural consequence of a century-long difference between Hinduism and Islam over the ideas of what makes a community. This conceptual difference seemingly resulted in two versions of nationalism, which was actually "communalism" that suffered from further demarcations when political parties resorted to Hindu and Islamic values to mobilize support. Therefore, though the Hindus and Muslims live side-by-side, they split easily when crisis arose.

If ideology plays such an important role in social life, ideology analysis is important to the study of ethnic issues.

There have been three judgments on the Chinese ethnic policy. First, the ethnic policy is believed to be an innovative system created by the Communist Party of China, hailed as a total victory: it needs some minor moderations but it has no fundamental defect (Mao, 2001; Jin, 2009). The judgment comes from those with a strong official background, some of whom are politicians themselves. Second, there are people who believe that the Chinese ethnic policy aims to assimilate the ethnic minorities with the cost of destroying the minority's social system and cultural heritage (Dreyer, 1977; Bulag, 2002; Mackerras, 2003). Again, these scholars are also largely premised by their political standpoint. Third, many from different backgrounds hold that there are structural flaws in the Chinese ethnic policy and without a comprehensive overhaul, it is potentially destructive and will be unable to deliver the desired ends (Ma, 2004; Gladney, 2004; Wang, 2008). I identify myself with the third group but with a new perspective: on the ethnic issues, what is at stake are not specific policies, but the ideology behind those policies.

Developmentalism and its sustainability

The logic of developmentalism is that the ethnic issue is part of the overall social problem. The ethnic difference is caused not only by class exploitation of the past, but also by he current situation of "economic and cultural backwardness." To promote economic development is the government's major responsibility because it provides the fundamental solution that is desired by the minority population themselves. It follows that once the economy is developed, the ethnic issues will be removed.

Developmentalism has been the official standpoint of the Chinese government since the 1980s. In an official document on the Tibetan issue released in April 1980, the Central Committee of the Chinese Communist Party (CCP) stated:

> Now that all Chinese ethnic nationalities have already undergone socialist transformation, the ethnic relations have become the relations of the labouring people. Therefore, the so-called "ethnic issue is by nature a class issue" is a wrong statement, which will severely distort the ethnic relations.
> (State Commission of Ethnic Affairs, *et al.* 1990: 34–5)

Two months later, in the famous Resolutions on Certain Questions in the History of Our Party Since the Founding of the People's Republic of China, the CCP admitted that

> in terms of the ethnic issue, in the past, especially during the Cultural Revolution, we had committed severe mistakes of over-enlarging class struggle, hurting many ethnic cadres and ethnic members. In our work,

we did not respect duly the rights of ethnic autonomy. We must always remember this lesson.

(ibid.: 109)

In one of his addresses, Deng Xiaoping (1993: 247) spelled out the shift from class struggle to developmentalism by stating that "we must develop the production and make the people rich. Only with these achievements can we strengthen the ethnic unity ... To evaluate an ethnic area, we should focus on whether that area has been developed and grow." In the 1980s, economic development was the key to Chinese ethnic policies, resulting in a huge flow of investment from the central government, along with the legislation of the Law of Ethnic Regional Autonomy. Top leaders also frequently visited the ethnic areas to seek quick and direct implementation of these policies.

The developmentalist policies gave way to the so-called "maintaining stability" (*weihu wending* or *weiwen*) policies in the 1990s, after the collapse of the Soviet Union and the rise of the third wave of nationalism. To a large extent, the areas under the jurisdiction of the Ethnic Regional Autonomy Law diverged institutionally: Though most of them, such as Guangxi, Yunnan, Guizhou, Sichuan, Inner Mongolia, joined the process of marketization, they were still left behind economically. On the other hand, Xinjiang Uyghur Autonomous Region and Tibet Autonomous Region remained in the redistribution system of the command economy, by which the government controlled most of the resources and imposed stricter surveillance on domains such as religion, propaganda and education. Anyone who lived in Xinjiang or Tibet for a fair period of time will feel the presence of the command economy. Compared with other parts of China, the basic national policies since the 1980s—birth control, opening-up, rule of law, marketization—have hardly been implemented in Xinjiang and Tibet. State purchase and sale of agricultural products still exist; the Xinjiang Production and Constructions Corps is itself a product of the command economy; the Population and Family Planning Commission's primary responsibility is marriage reform (for example, on Tibetan polygamy and polyandry) rather than birth control. There are also other policies such as "Two Less One Relax" in jurisdiction and "Three 60 percent" in terms of employment.[1] These policies are different from those for the eastern part of China where the Han population is overwhelmingly predominant, as well as from those for ethnic areas other than Xinjiang and Tibet. The national strategy of "Developing the West" since 2000 has drastically increased not only the GDP in Xinjiang and Tibet, but also the income disparity along ethnic lines because of a serious lack of relevant social policy, large inflow of other ethnicities (mainly Han) and the rapid growth of the indigenous ethnic population.

Take Xinjiang as an example. Although Xinjiang's GDP per capita has reached 20,000 RMB in China's largest autonomous region, the major contributing factor to this impressive growth is actually state-invested resource-dependent projects such as "west gas/petrol to east project" where most of the profits in the form of state revenue would be channeled back to the central government, leaving little for the local government. The profits to the derived businesses—transportation, tourism, the service industry—mainly go to the Chinese-speaking people, leaving little to the Uyghurs who also suffer from the rapid population growth. This is especially so in southern Xinjiang, where Uyghurs make up more than 90 percent of the population. In 2008, the total population of southern Xinjiang was 5.9 million, representing 31.8 percent of the entire autonomous region. Compared with that of the Han, the young Uyghurs are much less educated and non-Mandarin-proficient, making them underprivileged in job-hunting. The livelihood of people in southern Xinjiang is little more than oasis agriculture, utterly incapable of creating enough jobs to accommodate such an exploding population, so much so that out of 10 million Uyghurs, three million are unemployed (Jiateng, 2010).

CCP's Meeting on Xinjiang Work in May 2010 marked the decisive (re)turn to developmentalism to tackle the Xinjiang issue, especially the issue of "maintaining stability" through economic development. To display the central government's determination, the highest official in Xinjiang was replaced. The meeting laid down three new guidelines which are worthy of note. First, it changes the policy orientation from heavy-handed control to development, declaring that "[t]he social contradiction in Xinjiang, like that in the rest of the country, is still the material and cultural demand of the people and the backward social productivity."[2] Second, 19 provinces were assigned the task of aiding Xinjiang on a one-to-one basis. The decision is largely based on the logic of a command economy, which is different from that implemented in Tibet by the fact that it prioritizes projects that are intended to improve people's livelihood. Third, the city of Kashgar will be turned into a special economic zone and local resource revenue will be collected on the basis of price, instead of quantity. These policies are unlike those implemented previously, with the potential of delivering a novel mode of developing the ethnic areas, a mode that may exceed the policy-makers' intention.

Shortly after the Meeting on Xinjiang Work, the Party Committee of the Xinjiang Autonomous Region began to work out the goals laid out by China's top decision-makers. These goals included shanty hut renovation, power and gas supply, and income rise. Three policies which are meant to be achieved in 2012 are worth special attention: first, popularize two-year, pre-school bilingual (Chinese and ethnic language) education; second, provide employment guarantee to ethnic families without any wage-earner, and improve training on language and skill for ethnic college graduates; and third, establish the "New Rural Pension" system and basic healthcare system covering the entire region. The first is targeted at nurturing new generations of Chinese-speaking ethnic members. The second is to prevent extremist influence on the elites and the poor. The third is to increase the individual cost of antagonizing the system, on one hand, and expanding social security programs, on the other. These policies have unprecedented coverage with the purpose of greatly decreasing the rise and spread of various "unstable factors". As was claimed by Jiateng (2010), the commentator of *The Financial Times*, the new policy in Xinjiang "has good prospect."

Turning from heavy-handed control to developmentalism is certainly the right path to "maintain stability." It is generally believed that the extremism in central Asia is caused by the existence of a huge population of extremely poor people. Xinjiang was backed by the rapidly growing Chinese economy which is able to provide unparalleled assistance to improve the livelihood of its people. In his testimony in a Congress Hearing, Dru Gladney (2009: 24) defines the ethnic tension in Xinjiang as neither terrorism nor freedom-fighting, but "civil unrest." The Urumqi Incident in 2009 has nothing to do with Islam, but has a lot to do with the deep ethnic distrust caused by the social injustice in distribution and employment. The new policies in Xinjiang are intended to improve livelihoods through promoting development and enhance stability through promoting livelihoods. Certainly, the government is on the right track.

To improve livelihoods through economic development is the key to alleviating ethnic tensions, and it should be effective in the short run. However, development does not necessarily bring about "loyalty" for the following reasons. First, economic development itself does not guarantee social justice and equity. On the contrary, it may escalate social conflicts in the form of ethnic conflicts. Though the new policies in Xinjiang emphasize "livelihood," i.e. social justice and equity, the new immigrants from other parts of China may become the major beneficiaries, thereby further widening the income gap along ethnic lines. That the Lhasa Incident and the Urumqi Incident took the form of inter-ethnic conflict is largely due to the disadvantageous position of the two indigenous people in the economic system. In a study carried out in Tashqorgha, Yang Shengmin (2009) observes that in addition to the "three forces" (extremism, separatism and terrorism) and economic backwardness, the factors relevant to instability also include social insecurity and injustice, a situation he summarized as "inequality is more problematic than scarcity." How to balance the language disadvantage of the Turkic-speaking minorities will be a great challenge to the Xinjiang New Policy, not to mention the corruption issue that is now rampant in Xinjiang. Together with immigrant issues, corruption has the potential to undermine the new developmental approach to promoting development and improving livelihoods.

The second policy which aims to improve livelihoods and maintain stability may not work as expected either. The challenge lies in religion, a crucial element in the ethnic issue which economic development fails to address. Though improvements have been made in this area, the official attitude of the Chinese government towards religion is still shaped by two beliefs: first, religion should and must leave the public domain, i.e. the "state–church separation"; and second, religion will decline in the course of modernization. However, the religions of the world including China have never left the public domain, nor does the number of believers decline.[3] Most Chinese officials are atheists, lacking the basic knowledge of the social functions of religion.

Religious faith and practice are at best tolerated and taken as part of respecting and protecting the ethnic culture. However, most ethnic minorities in Xinjiang and Tibet are religious, upholding first and foremost the religious value they believe in. On one hand, the Han are often viewed as non-believers. On the other hand, the government often places religion under severe surveillance, on the pretext of state–church separation. Just as religion does not necessarily lead to separatism, atheist education does not necessarily brew loyalty. Faced with the vitality of various religions, the Chinese state policy of scientism and education and heavy-handed surveillance are not only insufficient to get rid of the problem, but are also damaging to the state's image by making itself look like a Han state.

If the state is unable to go beyond the Han's social values in ethics and morality and accommodate or even encompass the religious values of the ethnic minorities, and remains nothing but a tolerant inspector, then, any policy, including a developmentalist one, will be unable to convince the mass believers or secure their hearty support. Though recent unrest in Tibet and Xinjiang were non-religious ones and provoked by social and economic problems (Wang, 2008; Gladney, 2009), religion could sooner or later be the trigger because it is the ultimate value of ethnic societies in these regions. Various nationalist-separatist claims, including those in these regions, are easy to mobilize the support of the poor and of people who have suffered from injustice. However, these claims are in the final analysis a matter of ideology beyond the reach of developmentalism, and breed mainly among the better-off ethnic elites.[4] For an ethnic group where religious adherents predominate, if the state takes too long to establish its legitimacy in the ideological world of the ethnic people, or even neglects this issue by pretending that every ethnic member is an inborn patriot, the developmentalist policies—no matter how good they are—are but a waste of resources which may not only fail to obtain the desired respect from the ethnic groups, but also create opposition. Developmentalism, without addressing the issue of religion, is not sustainable.

Secularism: from empire to nation

A review of ethnic policies of the Qing Dynasty (1644–1911) is probably helpful for an understanding of the state's stand on religion. Comparatively speaking, the imperial ethnic policies under the Qing Dynasty were much more capable of accommodating differences (Wang, 2001). Its ideology was to encompass the ultimate value of different ethnic groups through the emperor's transcendence.[5] In particular, the Qing emperor encompassed different ethnicities with their different values. To the Manchurians, the Qing emperor was the head of the Eight Banners (*baqi*); to the Mongolians and Tibetans, he was the reincarnated Bodhisattva Mañjuśrī; to the Han, he was the Son of Heaven, the sage-ruler. In particular, the Qing emperor portrayed himself as a world ruler by submitting himself to the Manchu Shamanist lineage rule, Gelug Buddhism and Chinese Confucianism. He was a devoted Buddhist and a learned Confucian, two identities that made a great difference between the all-encompassing ethnic policies of the Qing court and the denial of Buddhist and Confucian values of the Nationalist and Communist governments. The ethnic policies of the Qing court should not be understood as something similar to the modern nation-state's governance (e.g. Hostetler, 2005; Perdue, 2005). Rather, its submission and assessment of the ultimate value of the "governed" people should be taken into consideration. Although its rule was fraught with violence, the Qing court did secure the support of the Han Confucian elites, the Eight Banners of the Manchurians and the aristocrats of Tibet and Mongolia, through its tolerance of the values of these people. Compared with plain, secularist nationalism that the nationalist and the contemporary communist governments impose on the ethnic areas, submission to the religious value of the subdued people has its unparalleled advantage.

Qing emperors took the ethnic issue seriously because they were from a minority who ruled a vast majority. Their ethnic policies for the northern ethnicities were intended to create allies to rule over the Han. The Qing court formed allies with Tibet and Mongolia through religion, while forbidding communication between these people and the Han, who were not allowed to migrate to these lands, or marry the people of Mongolia, Xinjiang or Tibet. Offices concerning the northern peoples—Generals of Yili, Heilongjiang, Jilin, and Shengjing, Envoy Ministers of Xinjiang, Mongolia and Tibet, Minister of the Court of Colonial Affairs—were exclusively available to the Manchurians. When the aristocrats, living Buddhas and Burkes of Mongolia, Xinijang and Tibet set out for regular meetings with the Emperor in Chengde, they were to avoid traveling through any Han area. After putting down the Dzungaria Revolt, the Qing court stationed Manchurian soldiers in southern Xinjiang. These institutions, though similar to what Qian Mu (2005) called "magic," was quite effective. Without successful ethnic policies, a mere one million Manchurians could not possibly rule more than 300 million of Chinese, Mongolians, Tibetans and other ethnic groups, for 270 years.

However, the Qing court's intention to ally with the Uyghur largely failed. From the Qing's conquest of the Uyghur in 1765 to the creation of Xinjiang Province in 1865, insurgences against the Qing control emerged one after another in southern Tengri Tagh (*Tianshan*). The "Holy War" of the House of Khwāja finally forced the Qing court to abandon the segregation policy, and adopt General Zuo Zongtang's strategy, turning Xinjiang into a province. It is generally believed that the Qing's failure in Xinjiang was caused by the corrupt Envoy Minister (*Zhuzai Dachen*) and the local chieftains (Burkes) (Wang, 2001: 184–5). It was not necessarily the case. In similar "corrupt" regions like Mongolia and Tibet, movements to break away from the Qing court became serious only at the end of the dynasty, though Xinjiang had seldom been stable after being turned into a directly ruled province. It can be said that the Qing failure in Xinjiang was not the segregation of the Muslims from the Han, but the inability of the Qing to encompass the Islamic faith of the Xinjiang people. A glance at the innumerable Muslim insurgences throughout the Qing dynasty suffices. On the other hand, the Qing court was able to establish its authority and secure the allegiance of the Tibetans, Mongolians and Han, through its submission to Tibetan Buddhism and Confucianism. The rebellions like the Jinchuan Insurgence and the Taiping Revolt that broke out among Tibetans and the Han were put down with success, precisely because of the loyal Tibetan aristocrats and the Han literati.

The Qing emperor's attitude towards Tibetan Buddhism and Han Confucianism was not simply an instrumental, involuntary political measure, but an embodied practice, a devoted pursuit of learning, and a voluntary belief. It is similar to the process of "superscription," what Prasenjit Duara (1988) described as an officialization process of the popular religions. The Qing emperors were successful in "superscribing" the religions of the Tibetans, Mongolians and the Han, but were never able to "superscribe" the Islamic faith in Xinjiang, and hence the allegiance of the believing mass and the religious leaders of the region. Shortly after conquering southern Tengri Tagh, the Qing court imposed a system similar to "state–church separation" system of today which was too radical to be accepted by the indigenous Islamic society. Therefore, it had no choice but to rely on the pricey, rootless Burkes, who were also unable to establish their authority in terms of religion.

An emperor is not merely a political figure, but a cosmocrator whose moral superiority is deeply embedded in the entire cosmology (Sahlins, 2008). That was part of the reason why the Qing emperor was able to gain legitimacy for himself among the Han, the Mongolian and the Tibetan, in addition to his military power. The Qing empire's failure in Xinjiang was not because of its military power, which in reality had been quite successful. Rather, it is a religious failure as the court could not establish its legitimacy in the Islamic world, or put it in another way, the court failed to "superscribe" Islam. The government of the Republic of China was so determined to build a modern nation-state that it voluntarily distanced itself from any religious involvement by creating national churches of different religions and then separated itself from them (Ji, 2008). The loss of the state's superscribing function left the state with nothing but secular power in Mongolia, Xinjiang, Tibet and Manchuria. The state became little more than a weak military power or a government with political plots. As a result, these areas were either under foreign control (i.e. Tibet under British aid or Xinjiang under the Soviet Union's indirect control), or separation (i.e. the independence of Outer Mongolia under the Soviet Union's patronage and Manchuria under Japanese control). The Republican government's rapid shift of ethnic policies, from expelling the Manchus to the Republic of Five Nations to Han-centric assimilation (Wang, 2001), reflected once again the nation-building dilemma in an era of Chinese transformation from empire to nation.

The first 30 years of the People's Republic of China witnessed the spread of the Mao cult all over the entire country. It seems that the Mao cult did wield superscribing power as in the ceremony of the "peaceful liberation of Tibet," the Dalai Lama bowed before Mao's image. Indeed, Mao's image and calligraphy served as powerful symbols of the "Democratic Reform" that incorporated ethnic minorities into a new system, to the extent that until today, "Chairman Mao" is still a venerated symbol to many older ethnic members. However, unlike imperial superscribing power, the cult of Mao was a replacing power that aimed to get rid of the ethnic religions. Mao Zedong himself was a non-believer unlike the Qing emperors who submitted themselves to religious faiths. The excessive desire to eradicate the old system in the ethnic areas was partly responsible for the armed insurgence that spread in Tibet, Xinjiang and other parts of west China during the Democratic Reform in the late 1950s. In other words, replacement was much more difficult than superscription. Since the 1980s, the Chinese government put even more emphasis on "state–church separation," promoting atheism and scientism as much as it can afford, further weakening its superscribing power over various religions.

On this, I must emphasize that I am not suggesting a restoration of imperial theocracy. I am simply arguing that a generally accepted ideology of a multi-ethnic China is still in the making. In the course of creating an ideology of a unified, multi-ethnic state, many issues have not been perfectly solved and remain questionable. Pure secularism, blatant scientism and unilateral patriotism are more wishful thinking than actual when ethnic religions, powerful in creating different versions of separatism, are in question. How to take a proper secularist standpoint in ethnic issues is not only a matter of power dynamics, but a matter of historical lessons marked by empire–nation shift. The promise of state secularism and the sacred nature of the state symbolism are actually in conflict, which has become all the more problematic since the overheated promotion of nationalism in the 1990s.

Nationalism: two concepts of China

Since the 1990s, state propaganda to promote Chinese nationalism has been extremely successful. Two or three young generations and many older ones have almost entirely accepted the nationalist ideology and are ready to believe whatever domestic media such as *Global Times* (*Huanqiu Shibao*)[6] have to say. This nationalist ideology is strongly charged with the protection of national sovereignty, the bitter memory of the wronged past and xenophobic sentiments that are hostile to foreign countries. It emphasizes the relation between overseas Chinese and their "motherland," especially those in Hong Kong, Macau, and Taiwan. However, Chinese nationalism has tremendous difficulty accommodating the ethnic minorities, a vast population of 100 million that inhabit 60 percent of the Chinese landmass, making it dangerous to slide into Han-centrism.

Xenophobic sentiments can be easily directed at domestic ethnic minorities, especially those who historically have ruled China. Because anti-Japanese sentiments in China are no longer limited to denouncing inhuman invasion and massacre, but extend to the hatred of the entire Japanese nation, it is easy for Chinese nationalists to apply the logic to those who conquered the Han, such as the Mongolians, Manchurians and the "five barbarians" (*wuhu*) of the remote past. Xenophobic sentiments infiltrate the recent wave with the re-evaluation of historical figures like Yue Fei, Wen Tianxiang, Yu Qian, Yuan Chonghuan, Wu Sangui, and Hong Chengchou,[7] a movement that promotes Han-centrism by equating China with the Han. Studies on racism in the Chinese past (Dikötter, 1992) and present (Chen, 2010) show that racism in China has deep historical roots and an extensive social seedbed. It is indeed the case. Racist opinions that would face criminal charges in many countries appear now and then on the Chinese Internet and other media. Because of a chronic lack of general education about ethnic unity and anti-racism, a mindset of hierarchy based on Han/non-Han demarcation is not uncommon in China. Ethnic assimilation and cultural diffusion are often viewed as a "backward" move. Word pairs such as *Putonghua* (Mandarin) and *Hanyu* (Han language), *Wushu* (Martial Arts) and *Guoshu* (National Arts), *Hanxue* (Sinology) and *Guoxue* (National Studies), *Zhongyi* (Chinese medicine) and *Guoyi* (National medicine) are pragmatically interchangeable words, without the slightest doubt. By the same logic, familiar words such as *Guohua* (national painting), *Guoyu* (national language), *Guoyi* (national craft) that fail to take ethnic minorities into due consideration have already penetrated the everyday life of the Chinese citizens. Slapping Yan Chongnian[8] and the boycotting of Christmas and Carrefour, together with the ignorant association of ethnic minorities, are all manifestations of Han-centrism in nationalist disguise.

One of the most conspicuous symptoms of Chinese nationalism is that many nationalist subscribers are ill informed when expressing their opinions. There is little awareness of the fact that their patriotic sentiment is the direct support of the love of the Han, especially of its writing system, and the equating of China with the Han heritage.

One problem with current Chinese nationalism is the discursive confusion with the terms *Zhonghua Minzu* (Chinese Nation), *Yanhuang Zisun* (Off-spring of the Yellow Emperor), *Huaxia Ernv* (Sinic Sons and Daughters), and *Longde Chuanren* (Descendants of the Dragon). It has already been the case that in pragmatics, all these terms could be used to describe the entire Chinese people. In most English dictionaries, all these words were translated to refer to the "Chinese people". However, a closer examination indicates that only the first justifies such a definition, while the other three can only be designated as the Han as most of the ethnic minorities do not share the legendary ancestors of the Yellow Emperor or the dragon. Nor were they a part of the Sinic people. Certainly, *Yanhuang Zisun*, *Huaxia Ernv* and *Longde Chuanren* are powerful symbols to unite the Chinese population in Hong Kong, Macau, Taiwan and other countries, whose ancestors came from southern China. As a result, many transnational ethnic minorities (Tibetans, Mongolians, Uyghur, Kazak, Khalkhas, Miao, Dai, Hani, and Korean) and several non-transnational minorities, when overseas, often associate with their own ethnic members rather than with the Han. Neither do they identify with

China as much as the Han. This is the case in not only neighboring countries such as Mongolia, the Middle Eastern countries, India and Burma, but also the developed countries of Europe, North America and Asia.

In 2002, the State Administration of Radio, Film and Television issued an official notice, highlighting the use of *Zhonghua Minzu* (Chinese Nation) rather than *Yanhuang Zisun* (Offspring of the Yellow Emperor) in the media in their report on the history of Chinese civilization. The need to put this clarification in writing shows the severity of the confusion of the two concepts. However, various propaganda authorities have to issue similar notices again and again since this notice indicates that the confusion is not easily eradicated.

Since 1980, in the tomb of the Yellow Emperor in Shaanxi Province, the annual public sacrifice (*Qingming Gongji Xuanyuan Huangdi Dianli*) to this legendary figure, whose footprint in the shrine indicated that he was an 18-meter-tall giant, has never failed to be performed on Ancestors Day. Monuments to commemorate the transfer of sovereignty of Hong Kong and Macau were also erected, demonstrating the major function of this quasi-religious site. In 2009, Mr. Lien Chan, honorary chairman of the Chinese Nationalist Party (KMT) in Taiwan attended the ceremony, while the Taiwan leader Ma Ying-jeou performed a "remote sacrifice" in Taipei. The short eulogy recited by the Shaanxi provincial governor elegantly eulogized the "Sinic Sons and daughters," "Hong Kong and Macau returned to the (Chinese) lineage," "across the (Taiwan) strait," and "blessed by our common ancestor." There was, however, not a single word of mention about the Chinese ethnic minorities, or "Chinese Nation" (*zhonghua minzu*). The cult of the Yellow Emperor is "ethnically narrow-minded" (Ma, 2010b) and historically invented by the nationalists of the late Qing dynasty to promote republican revolution (Sun, 2004). It is essentially a mindset of expelling the non-Han people.

In the past two decades, the Han have been synonymous with the Chinese nation and the Chinese nation with the Han because of the promotion of Chinese nationalism. Foreign countries represented as hostile people, such as the Japanese, the Americans, should be ideologically expelled from China and overseas Chinese, especially those who live in Taiwan, should be united under the banner of the Han ethnicity. Therefore, there have been two legitimate but incompatible concepts of China: a multi-ethnic China and a Yellow Emperor's China. Both concepts are officially legitimate but the latter seems to be more solidly founded in everyday life while the former is seldom substantiated. As a result, a constitutionally multi-ethnic China is ideologically recognized as a Han country and sliding into Han-centrism.

Ethnic essentialism: central problem of ethnic issue

In recent years, one of the most debated ideas on ethnic issue is the proposal by Professor Ma Rong (2007) to "de-politicize" and "culturalize" Chinese ethnicity. He believes that the culturalized concept of ethnicity was politicized in the era of the Chinese nation-state, especially after the ethnic classification project in 1950s, guided by Stalinism. Politicized ethnicity partly led to the collapse of the Soviet Union while culturalized ethnicity has proven successful in the United States. Therefore, China should learn from its own past and from the USA to "de-politicize" and "culturalize" ethnicity: replace *"minzu"* (nation) with *"zuqun"* (ethnic group), and make China a scheme of a politically unified, culturally diversified country with the preference for citizenship over ethnicity.

I agree with Ma Rong on the notion that the Chinese concept of ethnicity was politicized only after the collapse of the imperial system, but I also believe it is extremely difficult to "de-politicize" and "culturalize" ethnicity because of the following reasons. First, the semantics of a popular word such as *"minzu"* (nation) cannot be easily removed in a top-down manner. Second, "culture" and "politics" are not two separate domains. We are not strangers to "cultural nationalism" found all over the world. Third, separatism in Tibet and Xinjiang does not originate from ethnic classification. Instead, it appeared at the end of the Qing Empire when the ideology of "All under Heaven" disintegrated. In other words, before ethnic classification and ethnic regional autonomy, some ethnicities had already been "politicized."

In my opinion, the current problem of the ethnic issue is essentialism that penetrates the entire social, political and economic life. It is this stereotyped ideology that leads to a whole spectrum of problems, including separatism. Though there is an unlimited variety of viewpoints among different parties— the ethnic minorities, the Han, the Chinese government, overseas separatists, scholars—they surprisingly share the same views of an essentialized idea of ethnicity. We may call this idea "ethnic essentialism" that could be summarized as follows: an ethnicity must have an origin, an evolutionary history from the remote past all the way to the present, a common territory, economy, religion, art form, culture, language, writing, social organization, and so on and so forth. It should even have its particular scientific knowledge, physical appearance, personality, psychological makeup and patterns of behavior. All these features are shared by members of a given ethnicity and are different from those of other ethnicities. Since the introduction of *"minzu"* (nation, or ethnicity) in 1903, ethnic essentialism has been generally accepted. It met few challenges in the course of one of the most radical political and intellectual changes in world history (Pan, 2000), leading directly to the confusion in pragmatics of Chinese words for ethnicity (*minzu*), race (*zhongzu*), nation (*guozu*), state (*guojia*), and lineage (*zongzu*). The communist project of ethnic classification in 1950s further reified the ethnic essentialism with its Stalinist definition of ethnicity (the "four commons"). Caught by this idea, the government had no choice but to close the door to "identifying" new ethnicity in 1979, because there were too many new candidates to be "identified." However, new candidates began to surface again after the rise of "ethnic culture." The government and the public have to add thesuffix—*"Ren"* (people) instead of *"Zu"* (ethnicity)—to designate them, as in the case of "Mosuo Ren,"

"Zhan Ren," "Aini Ren," and "Akha Ren." Ethnic essentialism has this strong implication of evolutionism and social Darwinism. It even has the elements of racism. More problematic is that at present, ethnic essentialism is still seldom reflected in Chinese intellectual, political and public life.

Although ethnic essentialism is perfectly legitimate in the academic and historical sense, it hinders other possibilities of recognizing human groups. A case in point is the debate on whether the ancient kingdom of Nanzhao was established by the Chinese ethnicities of the Yi and the Bai, or by the Thais of Thailand (Liang, 2010). In the 1980s, Chinese scholars produced dozens of papers and books favoring the former. However, their evidence is intensely charged with a sense of racial history. While the Thai historians largely abandoned the racial historiography of "the Nanzhao as Thai" and even published a Chinese paper in a Chinese journal with the title explicitly saying "the Thai came from nowhere," the Chinese scholars never stop prodding the question of origin and produced a volume "Whence Came the Thai Race?". Cases like this show that as long as each ethnicity is compelled to find an origin by all means and to the extent of using DNA measures or dating an ethnicity back as long as possible, the ethnic essentialism will remain trapped by racial discourse.

One of the symptoms of ethnic essentialism is the sense of Han superiority which is articulated consciously or unconsciously and prevails in everyday life. This kind of superiority is officially called "Big Hanism" (*da hanzu zhuyi*), a development the government has always been against but without much effect, especially in the current nationalist heat. Though all ethnicities are constitutionally equal, the ethnic classification in the 1950s followed by the social-historical investigation was exactly intended to assess the "back-wardness" of each ethnicity. The result reveals that very few ethnicities are as "advanced" as the Han in the Marxist social ladder. Although the ethnic classification and the social-historical investigation were intended to bestow unprecedented political rights, all ethnic minorities have to remain backward as a condition for enjoying preferential policies. Even after ethnic relations were officially changed from class struggle to "new socialist ethnic relations" in the 1980s, and all ethnic groups were declared as having completed the socialist transformation, "economic and cultural backwardness" is still offi-cially declared as the most important difference, if not the only difference, between the ethnic minorities and the Han. As Harrell (1995) observed, the Chinese minorities are represented as ancestors (being primitive), children (being naïve), and/or women (being romantic). Most of the Chinese people still think of ethnic minorities as "backward" (*luohou*) and that some of them, such as the Jinuo and the Hezhe, are still in the near past and as backward as the Han were 5,000 years ago. The stereotyped images of being "good at singing and dancing," "romantic and sexually relaxed," and "mysterious and primitive" prevail in the Chinese society through the media. Though the government has always been cautious of ethnic discrimination, ethnic essen-tialism has already created an ethnic hierarchy so that discrimination often takes place unconsciously. The Chinese propaganda departments have to release notices from time to time, specifying the words which are pejorative or discriminatory, because the users have no knowledge of it. What is at stake here is the fact that in the twenty-first century, people from all walks of life in China, including most social scientists and civil service staff, know little more than what was known in the late nineteenth to early twentieth century on the issues of "what is ethnicity?" and "why are there ethnic differences?".

After the July 5 Urumqi Incident, the Ministry of Education decided to include "ethnic unity" in the curriculum of primary and secondary schools. Certainly it is good to end the near ignorance of ethnic structure in Chinese society. However, as Ma Rong (2009: 18) points out, "If the curriculum still follows the Stalinist version of ethnicity, the teaching may lead to the opposite result—strengthening the students 'ethnic consciousness'." The issue is still how to go beyond ethnic essentialism.

Ethnic essentialism also makes ethnic minorities engage in an unprecedented attempt at "self-orientalization." To develop the local economy, many autonomous ethnic governments went to the extent of "inventing traditions," which exceed the legal framework of excavating and protecting the ethnic cultural heritage. Most of the inventions follow the logic of ethnic essentialism, with some of them simply duplicating the Stalinist concept of ethnicity. Books on culture, custom, religion, philosophy, origin, migration and literature of a certain ethnicity are produced, while celebrations, rituals and ceremonies that never existed before are now extensively invented. All of them emphasize the "backwardness" of the given ethnic minority, constituting a process of "self-orientalization," a word rightly put forward by Louisa Schein (2000). Because of the mindset of ethnic essentialism, the invented traditions are more often than not about some "eccentric" customs, "mysterious" cults, or "primordial" art. For example, the capital city of the Diqing Tibet Autonomous Prefecture changed its name from Zhongdian to Shangeri-la. Lijiang promoted the indigenous "Naxi ancient music" (*naxi guyue*) which was actually a trans-ethnic art, and the Dongba characters claimed to be as early as a Neolithic invention. In the Dali Bai Autonomous Prefecture, the Gwer Sa La festival, one that tolerates temporary extra-marital relations, was a rather secret practice. However, the festival was recently openly acknowledged by the prefectural government in order to apply for national intangible cultural heritage, described as a custom that "not only implies the Bai's correction to the Confucian dogma, but also expresses the ultimate concerns of human nature." Recently, in order to apply for the status of UNESCO Intangible Cultural Heritage, numerous activities that never existed were invented.

Though these inventions of ethnic tradition may not be "harmful" for the time being, the ethnicization of many customs, festivals and art forms will leave each ethnicity in an awkward competition of exaggerating or even artificially creating its distinctiveness. As a result, the diffusion, borrowing, sharing, communication and merging naturally taking place in the past and present have to be deliberately understated or even denied. More importantly, the invention of tradition is one of the most important means of brewing nationalism (Hobsbawn and Ranger, 1983). Such versions of ethnic consciousness are part of the subaltern powers that are dislocating China (Gladney, 2004), a result of ethnic essentialism.

Conclusion

Challenges to the ethnic issues in China are not the so-called external forces, but the ideological difficulties as reflected in developmentalism, secularism and nationalism. The central problem is ethnic essentialism.

I am not suggesting a radical change to China's ethnic policies—the "New Policy" in Xinjiang may be exemplary, though not without challenge.[9] However, the ideological problem that current policies and legal framework frequently encounter must be solved anticipatorily. Economic development and preferential policies are not effective ways to build up a multi-ethnic country because the ethnic issue is not an economic issue, but an ideological one.

The first of such anticipatory measures is the interpretation of ethnic regional autonomy as "regional autonomy" instead of "ethnic autonomy" in multi-ethnic regions.[10] Regional autonomy is multi-ethnic autonomy, and that includes the Han. The preferential policies, or the "positive discrimination," should be based on regional difference, instead of ethnic differences. The advantages ethnic minorities enjoy should be intended to encourage their integration into the public life of the country such as language training, rather than encouraging ethnic segregation as some of current policies are doing. The preferential policies should not be based on the elusive "backwardness" of a given ethnicity.

The second anticipatory measure should be the elimination of ethnic identity in the public domain, such as household registration and ID card. The ethnic identity of a person should be gradually replaced by the identity of citizenship, and ultimately recorded for statistical purposes. Government budget should not be used to invent ethnic traditions. Meanwhile, the privatized ethnic identity could become flexible, such as allowing new ethnic identities and combined identities.

The third measure is the inclusion of ethnic unity as basic citizenship education, and the exclusion of the Stalinist concept of ethnicity. Measures should be taken to promote tolerance, understanding, respect and, most important of all, equality. Legislative and judicial measures should also be taken against discrimination and racism.

Current ethnic policies in China are suffering from ethnic essentialism as revealed in the current ideology of developmentalism, secularism and nationalism. The challenge of ethnic issues is first of all an ideological challenge. The state should stop filling in the knowledge gap with political power. The basic starting point is to substantiate the concepts of "unified, multi-ethnic country" and "Chinese nation" in a practical, holistic and accurate way, and in a way acceptable and understandable to the ordinary members of all ethnicities.

Notes

1 "Two Less One Relax" (*liangshao yikuan*) refers to the policy implemented since 1984, which requires the security/prosecution/judicial system, when enforcing law concerning ethnic minority members, to arrest less, criminalize less, and apply lighter punishment. "Three 60 per cent" is a policy that gives minimum quotas of ethnic minority employees in government departments and state-owned companies in the areas under Ethnic Regional Autonomy.
2 It is the official judgment of Chinese society based on the Chinese version of Marxism.
3 State–church separation and the decline of religion are two classic hypotheses of "secularization," largely abandoned by contemporary scholars. For example, Charles Taylor (2007) argues that secularism in the modern world should be understood as the situation where both believers and non-believers are aware of the existence of other paths of salvation. In China, there are many situations of mutual interference of religion and politics, a country modeled after the Christian world of "state–church separation." There are many unsolved issues concerning the religious status of Judaism, Eastern Orthodox, Hinduism, Baha'i faith and popular religion. The underground, family church, and the Vatican church are also such examples. Second, religious believers in China have been growing rapidly. Therefore, both state–church separation and religious decline in China should also be re-evaluated.
4 Ma Rong (2009) argues that the current danger of Chinese ethnic separatism is not the "Three Forces," but the nationalist consciousness among the ethnic elites within China. Though his argument is intended to address the Stalinist concept of ethnicity, the role that religion plays is certainly significant.
5 Here I apply the principle advanced by Louis Dumont (1998[1966]) through observation on traditional Indian and European societies. According to him, a given society has its ultimate value that penetrates every aspect of society, which often embodies religion. In non-Western societies, neither individualism nor egalitarianism is the ultimate value. The relation between the individual, subsystems, and society is usually that of hierarchy of encompassment.
6 The *Global Times* (*Huanqiu Shibao*) is a daily Chinese newspaper produced under the auspices of the official CCP newspaper. Its Chinese version, released in 1993, attracts a huge nationalist readership all over China. In 2009, over two million paper-based copies are produced daily, 89 percent of those go to those with a college degree. It has been accused of promoting Chinese nationalism.
7 They were either loyalists to the Han emperors against ethnic conquering forces, or traitors who helped the ethnic conquerors. In the official versions of Chinese history, they were neither considered as national heroes nor national traitors, because the conquests were interpreted as "internal conflicts of Chinese people." Recent waves of re-evaluation tend to go beyond this.
8 Yan Chongnian is a Manchurian scholar who is sympathetic to Qing imperial governance. In 2008, he was slapped in the face in Wuxi, by a young Han who claimed to be determined to revive the Han culture and protested at Yan's "denial" of the Manchus' massacre of the Han in the seventeenth century. In *The People's Website*, a public opinion investigation revealed that over 90 percent of subscribers thought Yan Chongnian deserved the slap.
9 Recent terrorist attacks in the city of Shihezi made Jia Qinglin, one of the top decision-makers of China, emphasize once again that "stability is the top priority in Xinjiang." The New Policy in Xinjiang is now faced with its first-round challenge.
10 For a detailed discussion, see Wang Hui (2008).

References

Bulag, U. (2002) *The Mongols at China's Edge: History and the Politics of National Unity*, Lanham, MD: Rowman & Littlefield.

Chen, K.H. (2010) *Asia as Method: Toward De-imperialisation*, Durham, NC: Duke University Press.

Deng, X. (1993) *Deng Xiaoping Wenxuan* [Selected Works of Deng Xiaoping], vol. 3, Beijing: Renmin Chubanshe.

Dikötter, F. (1992) *The Discourse of Race in Modern China*, London: C. Hurst & Co.

Dreyer, J. (1977) *China's Forty Millions: Minority Nationalities and National Integration in the People's Republic of China*. Cambridge, MA: Harvard University Press.

Duara, P. (1988) "Superscribing symbols: the myth of Guandi, Chinese God of war," *The Journal of Asian Studies*, 47: 778–95.

Dumont, L. ([1966] 1998) *Homo Hierarchicus*, New Delhi: Oxford University Press.

——(1983) "Stocktaking 1981: affinity as a value," in L. Dumont *Affinity as a Value*, Chicago: University of Chicago Press.

Gellner, E. (2006) *Nation and* Nationalism, 2nd edn, Malden, MA: Blackwell.

Gladney, D. (2004) *Dislocating China: Reflections on Muslims, Minorities and Other Subaltern Subjects*, London: C. Hurst & Co. Publishers.

——(2009) "Exploring the nature of Uighur nationalism: freedom fighters or terrorists?," Hearing Before the Committee on Foreign Affairs, House of Representatives, 101st Congress, First Session, 16 June 2009, serial no. 111–30.

Gu, X. ([1939] 2009) "Zhonghua minzu zhishi yige" [Here is only one Chinese nation], in R. Ma (ed.) *Minzu Shehuixue Yanjiu Tongxun* [Bulletin of Ethnic Sociology], 51: 2–7.

Harrell, S. (1995) "Introduction: the civilizing project and the reaction to them," in S. Harrell (ed.) *Cultural Encounter on China's Ethnic Frontiers*, Seattle: University of Washington Press.

Hobsbawn, E. and Ranger, T. (eds.) (1983) *The Invention of Tradition*, Cambridge: Cambridge University Press.

Hostetler, L. (2005) *Qing Colonial Enterprise: Ethnography and Cartography in Early Modern China*, Chicago: University of Chicago Press.

Ji, Z. (2008) "Secularization as religious restructuring: statist institution of Buddhism and its paradox," in M. Yang (ed.) *Chinese Religiosities*, Berkeley, CA: University of California Press.

Jiateng, Jiayi (Kato Yoshikazu) (2010) "Xinjiang xinzheng 'keqi'" ["The new policy" in Xinijang has good prospect], *Financial Times*. Available HTTP: www.ftchinese.com/story/001032895 (accessed 10 July 2010).

Jin, B. (2009) *Xin zhongguo minzu zhengce 60 nian* [60 Years of Ethnic Policies in New China], Beijing: Zhongyang Minzu Daxue Chubanshe.

Liang, Y. (2010) "Inalienable narration: Nanzhao history between Thailand and China," paper presented at international workshop on "Empire, Civilisation and the Anthropology of China", Singapore, 4–5 March 2010.

Ma, R. (2004) "A new perspective in guiding ethnic relations in the 21st century: 'de-politicization' of ethnicity in China," *Asian Ethnicity*, 8: 199–217.

——(2009) "Dangqian zhongguo minzu wenti de zhengjie yu chulu" [Central problems and solutions to the current ethnic issue in China], *Minzu Shehuixue Yanjiu Tongxun*, 51: 10–18.

——(2010a) "Zhongguo shehui de lingyilei 'eryuan jiegou'" (Another "dual structure" in Chinese society), *Minzu Shehuixue Yanjiu Tongxun*, 59: 1–11.

——(2010b) "Zhonghua minzu de gongtong wenhua yu 'huangdi chongbai' de zuqun xia'aixing" [The common culture and limits of "the Yellow Emperor cult"], *Minzu Shehuixue Yanjiu Tongxun*, 61: 7–11.

Mackerras, C. (2003) *China's Ethnic Minorities and Globalisation*, London: Routledge Curzon.

Mao, G. (2001) *Minzu wenti lunji* [Papers on Ethnic Issue], Beijing: Minzu Chebanshe.

Moffatt, M. (1986) "Editor's introduction to the English edition," in L. Dumont (ed.) *A South Indian Subcaste*, New Delhi: Oxford University Press, pp. xiii–xxi.

Pan, J. (2000) "Minzu de bolai ji xiangguan zhenglun" [The importing of "ethnicity" and its related debates], PhD Dissertation, Central University for Nationalities.

Perdue, P. (2005) *China Marches West: The Qing Conquest of Central Eurasia*, Cambridge, MA: Harvard University Press.

Qian, M. (2005) *Zhongguo lidai zhengzhi deshi* [Political Lessons of Chinese Dynasties], Beijing: Sanlian Shudian.

Sahlins, M. (2008) "The Stranger-king or, elementary forms of the politics of life," *Indonesia and the Malay World*, 36: 177–99.

Schein, L. (2000) *Minority Rules: The Miao and the Feminine in China's Cultural Politics*, Durham, NC: Duke University Press.

Schuck, P. (2010) "Minority preference policies in the United States," paper presented at the international workshop on Minority in China and U.S., American Academy of Arts and Sciences, Tufts University, Boston, June 27–28.

Shi, Z. (2010) "Baituo xizang yu xinjiang de shizuoyongzhe" [Getting rid of the creator of the Tibetan and Xinjiang issues], *Lianhe Zaobao*, May 24, 2010.

Smith, A. (2001) *Nationalism: Theory, Ideology, History*, Malden, MA : Polity Press.

State Commission of Ethnic Affairs, Documentary Studies of the Central Committee of the Chinese Communist Party (1990) *Xin Shiqi Minzu Gongzuo Wenxian Xuanbian* [Selected Documents of the Ethnic Work in New Era], Beijing: Zhonggong Zhongyang Wenxian Chubanshe.

Sun, L. (2004) *Lishi Xuejia de Jingxian*, Guilin: Guangxi Shifan Daxue Chubanshe.

Taylor, C. (2007) *A Secular Age*, Cambridge, MA: Harvard University Press.

Wang, H. (2008) "Dongfang zhuyi, minzu quyu zizhi yu zunyan zhengzhi" [Orientalism, ethnic regional autonomy and the politics of dignity], *Tianya*, 4.

Wang, K. (2001) *Minzu yu guojia: zhongguo duo minzu tongyi guojia de xixiang xipu* [Nation and State: A Genealogy of the Thought on Chinese Multiethnicism], Beijing: Shehui Kexue Chubanshe.

Xie, S. (1993) "Nanzhao, taiguo, yunnan guguo: dangdai zhongtai guozuzhuyi de jingzheng guocheng" [Nanzhao, Thailand, Yunnan's past: current nationalist contestation of Chinese and Thailand], *Kaogu Renleixue Xuekan*, 49: 50–69.

Yang, S. (2009) "Shehui wending hexie de jichu shi shenme?" [What is the foundation for social harmony and stability?], *Minzu Shehuixue Yanjiu Tongxun*, 49: 24–9.

Part III

China's social development in a comparative perspective

10 The evolving East Asian welfare regimes

The case of China

Chack Kie Wong

Introduction

The basic concept of the welfare state is the use of the state to provide welfare, from guaranteeing people a minimum income irrespective of their market value to offering all citizens without distinction of status and class the best standards available in relation to an agreed range of social services and benefits (Briggs, 1965). This is fundamentally different from the concept of the welfare society, primarily the family and voluntary associations that provide welfare (Rodger, 2000; Wong et al., 2002). Therefore, the welfare state is defined as using the state to provide welfare and benefits. In Western welfare theory, the welfare state is located at the interface of two sets of rights, or "rules of the game" (Gintis and Bowles, 1982, pp. 341–5)—citizen rights underlying the democratic institutions of society, and property rights underlying the capitalist market system. These two sets of rights are in constant and persistent contradiction with each other. According to neo-Marxist theorists, the contradictions underlying the welfare state are functional for the very existence of capitalism because they legitimize the accumulation function of capital (O'Connors, 1973; Gough, 1979; Offe, 1984).

When we study the welfare systems in East Asian societies where the underlying institutional arrangements are different from Western welfare states—the democratic institution and the capitalist economy were or are absent—we find that some systems may have different "rules of the game" or their institutional logic may take time to mature, such as the market economy in reform China and political democracy in Maoist and reform China, or rudimentary democracy in many East Asian societies. In other words, from the standard set by Western welfare capitalism, East Asian welfare systems can be described as "evolving" or immature (Tang, 2000; Kim, 2001).

Does it mean that we should look at East Asian welfare systems from the perspective of the welfare society and the welfare regime concepts, both de-emphasizing the state's role in welfare arrangements? The concept of the welfare society indicates an alternative and possible preference of the welfare system, predominated by families and voluntary organizations, over the welfare state (Burchell, 1995; Dean, 1995; Walters, 1997). What are the origins of the concept of the welfare regime? The welfare state regime was first used by

Esping-Andersen (1990) in his seminal work, Three Worlds of Welfare Capitalism. Later, he found the need to accommodate the contribution of different sectors in the distribution of benefits and costs in social settlements or welfare arrangements (Esping-Andersen, 1999), and he dropped the word "state" from "welfare state regime" (Gough, 1999).

The concept of regime in a welfare regime denotes the complex socio-political, legal and organizational features that are systematically interwoven in the relationship between the state and the economy as well as between the state and society (Esping-Andersen, 1990, p. 2; Walker and Wong, 2005, p. 6). That complex structure of relations between state, economy, and society is explained by Esping-Andersen's (1990) seminal work that found that class coalitions of power resources account for the regime types in the form of social settlements among capital, labor and state actors. In this light, the concept of the welfare regime looks more powerful and explains the outcome of social settlements, for example, welfare arrangements as major components between regime types.

On the basis of the above brief discussion, we should adopt a different approach to the study of East Asian welfare regimes. In fact, neither capital-ism nor democracy is necessary to constitute a welfare state or explain its development (Walker and Wong, 1996; 2004). Former Soviet bloc countries and Maoist China had many essential welfare services and provisions on a par with those in Western welfare capitalism. Also, the first batch of countries to initiate the core welfare state programmes, the social insurance schemes, were non-parliamentary regimes in Western Europe such as Austria, Denmark, Germany and Sweden (Flora and Heidenheimer, 1982, p. 70).

In other words, welfare development is driven not only by the institutional logics of capitalism and democracy; the driving force of welfare development in non-capitalist and non-democratic societies is often motivated by the need for political legitimacy of the authoritarian rule over society (Walker and Wong, 2005, p. 5). Therefore, it is necessary to look at the role of the state; in principle, it should be a state-led theory instead of a society-led theory such as a welfare regime. It is from this theoretical vantage point that we look at developmental state theory to explain the evolving Chinese welfare regime as a case of the East Asian welfare regime type.

On this basis, the organization of the chapter first introduces the tripartite framework, a framework larger than the institutional perspective above, and developed by Walker and Wong (2009) in their study of the relationship between economic policy and social policy. Analyses of the developmental state and their application in East Asian welfare regimes follow and finally, the chapter examines whether China is a developing welfare regime.

The tripartite framework

Walker and Wong (2009) use a tripartite framework to analyze the relationship between economic policy and social policy in a comparative analysis of social policy as a public burden in the West and China, despite direct or indirect social policy contributions to economic production and welfare creation.

First, it is institutional. The neo-Marxist analysis of the inherent contradiction of the accumulation and legitimization function in welfare capitalism (O'Conner, 1973; Gough, 1979; Offe, 1984) offers a starting point for the institutional perspective. However, this structural-functional analysis does not explain the acceptance of welfare state programmes across all social classes in advanced industrial societies (Ringen, 1987; Pierson, 1991; George and Wilding, 1993). The democratic institution of society provides the impetus or logic for welfare development in capitalist societies (Gintis and Bowles, 1982)—equality of political rights allows individuals, regardless of their status and means, access to a range of welfare benefits and provisions on an equal basis with their fellow citizens (Marshall,1950). In theory, the citizen rights underlying the democratic institution of society is a society-led explanation of the popular support of the welfare state and the driving force for welfare development.

However, China should have different institutional logic from that of Western welfare capitalism, especially in the Maoist era. This fact is vividly illustrated in the provision of comprehensive danwei (work unit) welfare to urban employees. Danwei welfare was like the "cradle to grave" Western welfare state, despite the fact that it was missing the two "rules of the game," citizen rights underlying the democratic institution of society and property rights underlying the capitalist market system (Walker and Wong, 1996). Now, China today is moving toward adopting a market mechanism and principles in its economy and even in the social sphere. The institutional logic of the capitalist market system should apply, but the democratic institution of society is still missing.

Second, it is ideology. China lacks a democratic society and is not a fully capitalist economy; nevertheless, it managed to provide sufficient social protection to its urban population through danwei welfare for decades. Since danwei are state-owned enterprises (SOEs) and government bureaus, including government-administered organizations such as universities and research institutes, they are part of the state apparatus through which the state decentralizes the tasks of national development to lower levels and organizations. In this institutional arrangement, danwei did not have to consider the cost of production in its welfare provisions to employees until economic reform was introduced in 1978 and in the early years of the reform period. So, the preclusion of the need for profit maximization should free individual danwei and the common people from constructing social policy or welfare as redundant or a waste of precious resources from economic production. However, this is not the case in China (Dixon, 1981; Leung and Nann, 1995). The legacy of traditional beliefs such as work ethics and family self-reliance reinforces the public perception of welfare as subordinate to economic production. Hence, those who receive social assistance were and still are regarded as secondary citizens. In other words, a lack of profit maximization or capital accumulation in the Chinese institutional arrangement of economic production did not prevent a dual perception of welfare distribution—danwei welfare was seen as legitimate and rightful while poverty relief was seen as dependent, with a social stigma (Walker and Wong, 2009). In this light, apart from the institutional logic, ideological factors should be included in the study of welfare development in the case of China as an evolving welfare regime.

Third, it is developmental. Economic development brings about an increase in wealth and some of the increased share can be allocated for redistribution (Wilensky, 1975; Pampel and Williamson, 1988); indeed, this is the modernization theory in explaining welfare development (Hill, 1996, pp. 20–1). Therefore, a "growth state" (Klein, 1980) can assign more growth dividend for welfare consumption. However, pre-reform China was not a "growth state," and this was Deng Xiaoping's rationale for initiating economic reform. However, the institutional arrangement of a command economy gave it the freedom to provide danwei welfare out of proportion to its national resources and fiscal capacity, a situation that happened not only in pre-reform China, but also in former socialist countries in Eastern and Central Europe (Kornai, 1997). However, for the larger population, it lacked the resources required for redistribution. In other words, the equalization of citizen rights in welfare, i.e., all citizens without distinction of status and class are offered the best standards available in welfare and benefits, is apparently an unlikely option for a developing economy like China.

Therefore, the developmental perspective is a logic underlying the often rudimentary nature of welfare regimes in East Asia. They do not command the required resources for redistribution through the welfare state, apart from the fact that the political elite in East Asia generally holds a negative view of the idea of the welfare state (Esping-Andersen, 1996; Wong and Wong, 2001; Chau and Yu, 2005).

In summary, the tripartite framework is seemingly more powerful than a single dimension of institutional analysis. Now, we come to a literature review on the developmental state and East Asian welfare regimes to see whether it has any new insights for the study of the case of China as an evolving welfare regime.

The developmental state and East Asian welfare regimes

The rationale of the developmental state is simple and straightforward. In order to catch up with advanced nations, developing countries need to use their state capacity to direct the economy and the society to accomplish national economic development (Leftwich, 1995, p. 401). The post-war Japanese economic success provides a good example of the developmental state theory in national development; the Japanese experience has been emulated by other Asian countries (Johnson, 1982; 1995).

According to Johnson (1982), a developmental state is a coalition consisting of government ministers and state bureaucrats that prioritizes economic growth over all else. In essence, it is a combination of political power and economic expertise that gives the developmental state much transformative power (Weiss, 2000). The transformative power or capacity of the developmental state comes from a number of components. They include a relatively autonomous and determined developmental elite, a powerful, competent and insulated economic bureaucracy, a weak and subordinated civil society, the effective management of non-state economic interest, and performance or ability to quell opposition and sustain legitimacy. In essence, a successful developmental state relies upon a weak society without autonomy that cannot challenge the developmental elite (Leftwich, 1995, p. 405).

Ironically, the success of the developmental state may pave the way for its own demise, because, as these countries achieve their economic growth, a clientelistic state evolves into a citizen-led state over time and the developmental elite has to make room for new autonomous institutions as well as popular interests (Barro, 1997; Lijphart, 1999). In this light, Pang (2000) talks about the end of the East Asian developmental states due to two major factors—democracy and financial globalization. Democracy implies the equalization of political power; this means that, with the success of the developmental state, economic affluence is likely to breed an assertive citizen state and the relatively autonomous developmental state will be difficult to maintain.

Financial globalization implies that domestic capitalists no longer require financial subsidies from the state to grow, because it provides them with low interest rates. Therefore, it is difficult to count domestic capitalists as strategic collaborators in national economic development. Then, a developmental state is forced to change into a regulatory state, in which the state intervenes less and is more concerned with the forms and procedures and the market forces and domestic capitalists are more assertive in economic decisions (Johnson, 1999; Walter, 2006; Pereira, 2008).

According to this analysis, the developmental states in East Asia, Taiwan, South Korea, and Japan ultimately lose their power over the economy and society. However, Singapore did not. Pereira (2008) finds two reasons for this divergence of Singapore from East Asia's tiger economies. First, Singapore effectively manages its non-state economic interests in its national development; Singapore's government does not collaborate with domestic capitalists, but transnational ones. Therefore, the domestic capitalist class has not developed into an autonomous and powerful social agent with the capacity to challenge the authority of the developmental elite. Second, because of a weak and subordinated civil society largely due to effective governance, Singapore's working class enjoys the fruit of the developmental state and its trade unions are tightly controlled by the state. For example, housing has never been an issue in Singapore, because more than 80 percent of Singapore's citizens buy their apartment from the government. The high ownership rate indicates, to a great extent, the effectiveness of an asset-based social policy (Sherraden et al., 1995; McCarthy et al., 2002). In other words, economic affluence does not come with an autonomous middle class and the state still has a firm grip on society.

Therefore, political democracy and a global economy explain the recent divergent national development of East Asian societies. Singapore's government, from the start of its developmental state, has effectively managed its non-state economic interests. It also sees welfare development as positive for its political legitimacy and sees it as a price to pay for maintaining a weak and subordinated civil society. Accordingly, Singapore is not a typical developmental state as social development is not at all subordinated to economic development (Lee, forthcoming).

The developmental state theory can also account for the welfare development in this region. Welfare developmentalism is the combination of welfare development and a developmental state; it suggests that the state subordinates welfare development to economic growth. We can also find similar idea in welfare productivism (Holliday, 2000). Welfare developmentalism in East Asia means that government intervention and policies are used extensively to promote industrialization by investing heavily in the education and health of the workforce to enhance the legitimacy of the government and to pacify labor (Tang, 2000; Kwon, 2002; Aspalter, 2006). Thus, welfare tends to target selective groups close to the developmental elite, consolidating its legitimacy and a premium is placed on those public and social policies that are growth-oriented. So, how could welfare developmentalism become inclusive welfare or universal welfare, such as the extension of the decommodified welfare programme? Political democracy seems to be the answer in view of the recent experiences in South Korea and Taiwan (Hort and Kuhnle, 2000; Kwon, 2002; Croissant, 2004; Ahn and Lee, 2005; Back, 2005; Hill and Hwang, 2005; Yasuhiro, 2005). However, it does not mean that population aging and other social factors are not important. This is an important explanation for the modernization theory in welfare development (Hill, 1996, pp. 18–24).

In the case of Korea's change to inclusive coverage, according to Kwon's account (2002, pp. 30–2), the development of universal health insurance was a long process fueled by democratization. In Korea, national health insurance first started in 1977 with typical exclusive developmental welfare features targeted at large-scale companies with more than 500 employees. It was extended to cover public sector workers and private school teachers in 1978. It was not until the 1988 presidential election that competitive campaigns under a democratic constitution forced all candidates to listen to the grievances of people left out of the national health insurance system. All candidates, including President-elect Roh Tae-woo, promised to extend health insurance coverage to all citizens. Even after health insurance became universal, the funds were managed separately in terms of collecting contributions and reimbursing their members' hospital treatment. In 2000, Kim Dae-jung's government decided to merge all funds (409 at the highest point) into a national health insurance fund (Kwon, 2002).

In the case of Taiwan's expansion of its decommodified welfare programme, both the Kuomintang and the Democratic Progressive Party applied a strategy of promising social welfare policies in highly competitive elections during the process of democratization (Aspalter, 2002, 2006; Ku, 2002; Wong, 2005). The expansion of the old age allowance, a non-developmental social expense programme, is an example. In the 1990s, local government chiefs of all parties began to address the issue of elderly poverty and pledged to establish a universal old-age allowance scheme in their cities or counties once they were elected. In 1997, even the popularly elected ruling Kuomintang President Lee Teng-Hui endorsed the idea of universal old-age allowance. In 2002, the universal old-age allowance was introduced by Taiwan's opposition party leader, Chen Shui-Bian of the Democratic Progressive Party, in his first presidential term (2000–2004).

On the basis of the analysis above, in the interplay of the developmental state with welfare development, there are two models demonstrated by the experiences of Korea, Taiwan and Singapore.

The first model, seen in Korea and Taiwan, is the shift from state-led welfare development to society-led after the democratic institution of society dominates. When civil society is weak, the developmental elite have more freedom to work on national development according to their judgment and expertise of what is good for the country. When the country has succeeded to some extent in its developmental goals and society is democratized, it shifts to a society-led model in welfare development.

In the second model, seen in Singapore, the developmental elite retain their power even in economic affluence. The development elite can devise deliberate policies (choice of economic collaborator and asset-based policy instead of redistribution) and exercise political control over trade unions that save them from subsuming to the degenerative logic of the developmental state, i.e., economic affluence breeds an assertive citizen state that eventually leads to a society-led model in welfare development.

The case of China as an evolving welfare regime

Now, we can incorporate the welfare development experiences of a few East Asian welfare regimes into the institutional dimension of our tripartite framework, fully aware that Western welfare theories—the society-led welfare regime theory and the neo-Marxist underlying contradictions of welfare capitalism—are inadequate in the study of East Asian welfare regimes.

Now, we look at the evidence in the study of the China's evolving welfare regime from a tripartite framework. Four types of statistical data are presented as empirical evidence for our tripartite analysis of China's evolving welfare regime; they are the share of social expenditure as a percentage of GDP, the share of SOE employment as a percentage of total urban employment, healthcare expenses, and the division of expenditure and revenue of central government and local governments.

The share of social expenditure as a percentage of GDP is an indicator of the commitment of the state to citizen rights. For example, inclusive welfare or decommodified welfare, especially social protection in healthcare and income maintenance programs of various kinds, are basically redistribution of the welfare state by cash transfer. Of course, East Asian welfare developmentalism is characterized by inadequate decommodification but is biased toward social investment. To compensate for this, public education expenses are included in the social expenditure figures. This type of statistical figure should indicate the extent of the universal coverage of welfare and benefits in a society.

The share of SOE employment to total urban employment indicates the extent of the need for redistribution by the welfare state in the Chinese welfare regime. China's dual welfare system is characterized by its bias toward SOEs and other danwei employers. In other words, the decline of SOE employment, one of the economic reform objectives, means that more employees are exposed to poor terms in remuneration, working conditions and benefits.

The statistical data on healthcare expenses provide an opportunity to look into a specific policy area of the need for social protection, as driven by the logic of capital accumulation. Therefore, we can see whether welfare development as depicted by macro-level data of social spending matches that of the micro-level specific policy area; perhaps a specific policy arrangement can remedy the inadequate finance in state welfare.

The statistical data of the division of the expenditure and revenue of central and local governments show whether China has commanded the required social resources for redistribution. In China, local governments are primarily responsible for the provision of public services, especially social welfare and benefits. The central government will reallocate part of its collected revenue to local governments in the second-round fiscal distribution for the sake of maintaining the financial balance between local governments and supporting specific policy objectives. For example, in the early 2000s, the matching-up of social assistance benefits from the central government enabled the urban Minimum Livelihood Security Line, the social assistance programme in China, to extend its coverage to those in need. Before this financial match-up, local governments had to choose between eligible applicants due to financial constraints (Tang, 2005). Of course, the reallocated revenue from the central government is not all for welfare and benefits; nevertheless, it indicates the extent of fiscal resources, i.e., the developmental dimension, available for redistribution to meet the need for political legitimization.

The institutional dimension

Table 10.1 reveals the social expenditure patterns of China during its economic reform and its different institutional arrangements of welfare. In the pre-reform period, China spent very little of its national wealth on social expenditure (a broader definition to include education and even cultural activities due to inseparable official statistics)—3.61 percent of GDP in 1978, when Deng Xiaoping started the reform process. That share increased to 9.48

Table 10.1 Social expenditure as percentage of gross domestic product (GDP) in China (selected years)

| Year | GDP (in 100 million yuan) | As % of GDP (in 100 million yuan) | | | Total social spending as % of GDP |
		Spending on culture, education, health care	Spending on pension and social welfare*	Subsidies to loss-making enterprises	
1978	3,645.2	3.09	0.52	N/A	3.61
1980	4,545.6	3.44	0.45	N/A	3.89
1985	9,016.0	3.51	0.35	5.62	9.48
1990	18,667.8	3.31	0.29	3.10	6.70
1995	60,793.7	2.41	0.19	0.54	3.14
2000	99,214.6	2.76	0.21	0.28	3.25
2001	109,655.5	3.07	0.24	0.27	3.58
2002	120,332.7	3.31	0.31	0.22	3.84
2003	135,822.8	3.32	0.37	0.17	3.86
2004	159,878.3	3.22	0.35	0.14	3.71
2005	183,084.8	3.33	0.39	0.11	3.83
2006	210,871.0	3.52	0.43	0.09	4.04
2007	249,529.9	4.01	2.18	N/A	6.19
2008	300,670.0	4.28	2.26	0.12	6.66

Note: * This refers to social relief and personal social services for the orphans, elderly and people with disability.
Source: Calculation based on *Statistical Yearbook of China 2006, 2008* and *2009,* the data of 2006 were retrieved August 6, 2008 from China data online; see the following websites and the 2008 and 2009 data are hard copies; price subsidies and subsidies to loss-making are not available on 2007 and 2008.
http://chinadataonline.org/member/yearbook/ybtableview.asp?ID=57575;
http://chinadataonline.org/member/yearbook/ybtableview.asp?ID=57433.

percent in 1985 because we include 5.62 percent of GDP as subsidies to loss-making enterprises in the social expenditure budget.

In this stage of economic reform, China needed to provide subsidies to loss-making SOE enterprises, not only because they were state-owned, but also because much of their loss was due to spending on labor insurance and welfare funds as part of the danwei welfare. For instance, in 1978, the SOEs spent an amount equivalent to 13.7 percent of their wage costs on workers' insurance. The amount rose to 24 percent in 1985, 28.2 percent in 1989, and 34 percent in 1993 (Walker and Wong, 1996, pp. 76–7). In Western welfare capitalism, a subsidy of this kind may be regarded as subsidies to social security.

That share of national wealth substantially decreased to an insignificant amount in 1995 and thereafter as a result of the gradual effect of the government's implementation of labor regulations on dismissal, recruitment, bankruptcy, and the establishment of the labor contract system since 1986 (Leung and Nann, 1995, p. 67). In other words, from the early stage of economic reform through the mid-1990s, the restructuring of SOEs was

Table 10.2 Employment of state-owned enterprises (SOEs) as percentage of total urban employment

Year	Total urban employment (in thousands)	Employment of SOEs (in thousands)	Employment of SOEs as % of total urban employment
1978	95,140	74,510	78.3
1980	105,250	80,190	76.2
1985	128,080	89,900	70.2
1990	170,410	103,460	60.7
1995	190,400	112,610	59.2
2000	231,510	81,020	35.0
2001	239,400	76,400	31.9
2002	247,800	71,630	28.9
2003	256,390	68,760	26.8
2004	264,760	67,099	25.3
2005	273,310	64,880	23.7
2006	283,100	64,300	22.7
2007	293,500	64,240	21.9
2008	302,100	64,470	21.3

Source: *Statistical Yearbook of China 2006, 2009.* The data of 2006 were retrieved August 6, 2008 from China data online; see the following website and the 2009 data are hard copies, http://chinadataonline.org/member/yearbook/ybtableview.asp?ID =57483.

necessary. This explains the drop in the subsidy from government to loss-making enterprises in mid-1990s. From 1995 on, the share of GDP as subsidies to loss-making enterprises was reduced to insignificance; for example, it was 0.54 percent in that year, not recorded in 2007, and was only 0.12 percent of GDP in 2008.

Table 10.2 shows the share of employment of SOEs as a percentage of total urban employment. In 1978, when Deng Xiaoping initiated economic reform, SOEs had 78.3 percent of total urban employment, but that figure declined to 35 percent in 2000, one year before China was admitted into the World Trade Organization. The share of SOE employment declined to 21.3 percent in 2008. This gradual decline of employment of SOEs as a percentage of total urban employment had an important implication for the welfare regime of China, a need for the state to intervene to alleviate the capital accumulation function, even though the SOE employment peaked in the mid-1990s in terms of the absolute number.

As mentioned above, the restructuring of SOEs that resulted in the rise of non-state sector employment implies that more employees are exposed to poor terms in remuneration, working conditions, and benefits. It is only in recent years that the central government in Beijing has realized the uneven primary distribution of market wages. For instance, recently a government minister in charge of human resources and social security suggested that since China had the right conditions such as GDP per capita exceeding US$4,000 and an annual growth rate of 8.6 percent in 30 years (1979–2008) (Renmin Zhengxie Bao, September 8, 2010), a 15 percent annual rise of wage was recommended in the upcoming 12th Five Year Plan.[1]

Therefore, it is clear that, despite the introduction of a capitalist market system, the protection of labor is at the mercy of the developmental elite because of inadequate citizen rights. If structural factors do not favor non-state sector employees, it is necessary to look at secondary distribution; that is, redistribution by the state in China's welfare regime. In this regard, we can look at evidence of redistribution in China's welfare regime.

As discussed above, social expenditure as a share of GDP does not make us excited about the redistribution of social resources in China. However, there were substantial increases recently—social expenditure as a share of GDP rose from 3.83 percent in 2005 to 4.04 percent in 2006, 6.19 percent in 2007, and 6.66 percent in 2008, substantial increases in a short time. In absolute terms, spending on culture, education and healthcare jumped from 610 billion yuan in 2005 to 1,286 billion yuan in 2008, an increase of 210 percent over four years. The corresponding rise in social expenditure on pension and social welfare was even more impressive, from 71.6 billion yuan in 2005 to 680.4 billion yuan in 2008, a jump of 950 percent in four years.

It can be concluded that redistribution in China is at a pretty low level but there have been impressive increases recently. We will explain this increase later. In the meantime, judging from the evidence available, the present level of social resource redistribution seems unlikely to legitimize the accumulation function of capital, using a comparative perspective. For example, in 2003, the average OECD country spent 12 percent of their GDP on cash benefits for redistribution, 5 percent as income support to the working age population and 7 percent as pensions for elderly and survivors (OECD, 2007).

Indirect empirical evidence supports this claim. For example, that inade-quate redistribution resulted in social miseries is paraphrased in terms of the "Three Mountains" facing people—education, healthcare and housing are not affordable. Sometimes, retirement is also added and termed the "Four Mountains" in public discourse. Social unrest is a great concern of the gov-ernment. In fact, a stability maintenance office was set up in 2006 in different tiers of the government to oversee social unrest and propose initiatives to maintain social stability. They are indicators of the insufficient political legit-imization function of the state.

Now we turn to a particular policy area, healthcare, to examine whether citizen rights to healthcare protection are prevalent in the urban reformed healthcare system. As mentioned above, China's danwei welfare was restruc-tured to facilitate the marketization of the economy. It is along these lines that unemployment, retirement, and healthcare protection are reformed. In other words, welfare reform in China is likely to work along the major tenet of welfare developmentalism—the subordination of social policy to economic and industrial policies.

Below, we will briefly outline the reform initiatives in the context of a dual system in healthcare protection and if healthcare engenders the right to affordable healthcare.

China has a dual healthcare system with urban and rural subsystems. Due to limited space, we confine our study to the urban healthcare system for employed persons. In the traditional urban system, labor and government insurance for healthcare was provided to employees of danwei, the former for SOE employees; the latter was provided to government civil servants and state-administered organization employees. The two traditional urban subsystems were not sustainable because they did not take cost into consideration and employees lacked the incentive to save for medical expenses. In the 1980s, initiatives such as cost sharing were launched to reform the traditional urban healthcare system. In 1993, the initiative to use a system of healthcare financing that combined a socially pooled fund with personal medical accounts was announced and piloted in Zhenjiang and Jiujiang, two medium-sized cities. In 1998, the new basic health insurance system was fully implemented to replace the traditional labor insurance and government insurance.

In terms of the source of financing of China's urban healthcare between 1998 and 2003, a span of five years after the new basic health insurance system was implemented, the share of the source of finance on the part of government insurance declined from 16 percent in 1998 to 4.0 percent in 2003, and 28.7 percent to 4.6 percent on the part of labor insurance in the corresponding years (Wong et al., 2006: Table 6.3). In other words, the reform in healthcare was successful because it reduced the financial burden over danwei, especially the productive SOEs. On closer scrutiny, the share of the source of finance was shifted to social insurance, i.e., basic health insurance, and its share rose from 4.7 percent in 1998 to 32.2 percent in 2003 (ibid.). Likewise, self-payment remained at a similar level, that is, 44.1 percent in 1998 and 44.8 percent in 2003 (ibid.).

From a neo-Marxist structural-functional perspective, the effect of this policy choice is clear. Healthcare reform is to enhance the capital accumulation function of the state in healthcare, albeit in China's case, it is to rescue the SOEs from loss-making. Therefore, it does not help in terms of political legitimization. Even though healthcare insurance coverage was extended to more private-sector employees, affordability remained a critical issue, for example, in 2003, 85.4 percent of respondents in survey of mid-China city residents agreed at different extents that "[t]he current medical and treatment expenses exceed what the general public can afford" (ibid., p. 101: Table 5.9). In other words, inclusive healthcare protection in terms of social insurance does not enhance any genuine citizen right in healthcare protection. Affordability of medical consultation is still one of the "Three Mountains" in public discourse about their hardship in daily life. The following two examples illustrate the tension due to the application of market mechanism into the operation of public hospitals in China. Reports suggested that public hospital doctors were called "white wolves" by patients[2] and some public hospitals had to ask police to be stationed in hospitals due to poor relations with patients.[3]

Relations between doctors and patients have not improved even after urban healthcare reform in 1998. The underlying problem is in the approach of the reform initiative—it aimed to control the demand for healthcare services without financial subsidy from the state to manage the political legitimization function in healthcare.

The underlying factor of the bad relationship between public hospital doctors and their patients can be traced back to the early 1980s when the central government began to freeze its subsidies to public hospitals (Zheng and Hillier, 1995). This forced hospitals to rely upon profits from two sources: charges on the use of high-end medical equipment and the sale of medicine. This started the decline of the subsidies from government as a share of the total income of public hospitals. For example, in 2008, the comprehensive public hospitals in China had an income of 500,655 million yuan, of which only 6.6 percent came from financial subsidies from the government and 0.79 percent from higher-tier government subsidies, with the remainder coming from income from fee charges, medical examinations, and medicine sales.[4]

The distribution of health expenses in China's comprehensive public hospitals indicates the inadequate financial subsidies from the government for healthcare provisions. In other words, this shows the very small role of the state in healthcare in terms of financing. Table 10.3 provides figures from a macro-level on the same vantage point of the distribution of China's healthcare expenses during reform, from 1980 to 2007.

In 1980, in the early years of Deng Xiaoping's economic reform, government healthcare expenses as a share of total healthcare expenses were 36.2 percent. They decreased to 25 percent in 1990 and then stabilized from 17 percent in 1995 to 15.6 percent in 1998 when the basic health insurance started. In the same vein, social health expenses (expenses of social insurance systems such as labor insurance and the basic health insurance) took a share of 42.6 percent in 1980, and then fell to 26.6 percent in 1998 when basic health insurance started; it increased to 34.5 percent in 2007, corresponding to the recent slight but continuous increases in government healthcare expenses.

Individual health expenses rose from 21.2 percent in 1980 to 57.8 percent in 1998, topped at 60.6 percent in 2000, and then decreased to 45.2 percent in 2007. Therefore, extending the coverage of basic health insurance, in practice, was not sufficient enough to mitigate the financial burden of individual patients. It was only recently that an increase in government healthcare expenses as a share of total healthcare expenses was correlated with the decline in individual healthcare expenses as a share of total healthcare expenses. For example, in 2007, the former reached 20.3 percent while the latter fell to 45.2 percent in the same year. Nevertheless, the share of individual healthcare expenses was still much larger than that in the early years of economic reform, e.g., 21.1 percent in 1980 compared to 45.2 percent in 2007.

Table 10.3 China's healthcare expenses and national wealth, selected years (at current price)

	1980	1990	1995	1997	1998	1999	2000	2001	2002	2003	2004	2005	2006	2007
Total health expenses (100 million yuan)	143.2	743.0	2257.8	3384.9	3776.5	4178.6	4764.0	5150.3[a]	5684.6	6584.1	7590.3	8659.9	9843.3	11,289.5
Government health expenses (%)	36.2	25.0	17.0	15.4	15.6	15.3	14.9	15.5	15.2	17.0	17.0	17.9	18.1	20.3
Social health expenses (%)	42.6	38.0	32.7	27.7	26.6	25.5	24.5	24.0	26.5	27.2	29.3	29.9	32.6	34.5
Individual health expenses (%)	21.2	37.0	50.3	56.9	57.8	59.2	60.6	60.5	58.3	55.9	53.6[+]	52.2	49.3	45.2
Per capita health expense (yuan)	14.51	65.0	190.6	273.8	302.6	331.9	376.4	403.6	442.6	509.5	583.9	662.3	748.8	854.4

Notes:
[a] Because of statistical adjustment, total health expenses in 2001 do not include health education at tertiary level, or residents' expenses on preventive medicines.
[+] It was revised to 5.16 in 2004.
Source: Ministry of Health (2004) Summary of China's Health Statistics, 2004, for 2003–2007, National Statistical Bureau of China (2009).

In general, the government has shied away from the financial role that opened the way for using market mechanism and principles in operating public hospitals, or maximizing profit through medical examination and the sale of medicine.

In summary, the inadequate financial role of the state transforms the structure of finance to the disadvantage of individual citizens. The institutionalization of healthcare provisions, because basic health insurance does not reflect any genuine citizen rights, has not affected the affordability of healthcare for average citizens in reform China. Apparently, the imbalance between capital accumulation and political legitimization, according to the neo-Marxist structural-functional perspective, is likely to create a context of change. Therefore, the Chinese welfare regime is not at its equilibrium—it is still an unfinished project and is evolving.

Ideological shift

When Deng Xiaoping launched economic reform in 1978, he followed the developmental state theory by using market forces to catch up with advanced countries in national development. In ideological terms, it is a shift from Mao Zedong's egalitarianism to market socialism, i.e., an ideology emphasizing "growth first" development and the subordination of social welfare and social development to economic development (Chau and Yu, 1999; Walker and Wong, 2009).

Nevertheless, Deng Xiaoping envisioned a stage-development in his "xiaokang" (small or moderate welfare) societal goal. When China reached the threshold of US$1,000 GNP per capital by the end of the twentieth century, it would have the resources necessary to tackle the rich–poor gap and regional disparity. In fact, the goal of building a "xiaokang" society was modified to the building of a "comprehensive xiaokang society" in 2002 by the Chinese Communist Party under the leadership of Jiang Zemin (2002); not only economic development was targeted, but also higher levels of democracy, culture, science and education, social harmony, and people's standard of living. However, Jiang's major ideological advancement was the "Three Represents," which includes the capitalist class as people, and not an ideological shift with direct implication on welfare development.

In late 2002, Hu Jintao became the Party Chief Secretary and the concept of social harmony was put forward. In his speech to the Party's high-level cadres on February 19, 2005, the six essential components of the concept of social harmony were presented; among them, the component of fairness and justice implied the reconciliation of the interests and relations of all parties concerned, under which people's internal and other social conflicts are properly settled and social equity and justice were implemented (Hu, 2005).

The discourse of social harmony by the new Chinese leadership indicates an ideological shift in developmental strategy from the growth-first development to a better coordination of economic and social development. This is also evident in the discourse of the "Five Co-ordinations" that Hu presented in 2003. They are the coordination of rural and urban development, regional development, economic and social development, humans and nature, and internal national development and the need to open China's door to the outside world in the 3rd Plenum of the 16th Central Committee of CCP (Central Committee of CCP, 2003).

Both constructing a harmonious society and the "Five Co-ordinations" indicate a shift from the trickle-down neo-liberal ideology of the market's unequal distribution—a few get rich first—to striking a proper balance between economic growth and social development and an emphasis on getting rich both in either the market's primary distribution or the welfare state's secondary distribution. It is evident in the recent ideological shift in the public discourse;.[5] in other words, the ideology of China's developmental elite is important in explaining the change as indicated in the empirical statistical data we presented above.

Developmental dimension

As we mentioned above, development means more resources available for redistribution. It is only when a developmental state has more social resources for redistribution that it can respond to society-led demands in terms of the increase in social expenditures. Of course, it is necessary but not sufficient to explain the shift in welfare development. It is necessary in the sense that insufficient social resources would limit the extent of the welfare coverage for all citizens in a developing country such as Maoist China, and will result in a dual welfare system.

In 2009, China's GDP was equivalent to US$4.985 trillion, making China the third largest economy in the world after the USA and Japan (Wall Street Journal, 2 July 2010). However, China is still a developing lower-medium income nation at best if its aggregate national wealth figure is divided by the vast population of 1.3 billion. Nevertheless, the sustained growth rate of up to 8–10 percent per year over a period of 30 years is phenomenal and has enabled the country to accumulate sufficient wealth for redistribution. This was especially the case after 1994 when the central government reformed the tax system and allowed the central government to have a greater share of tax money for redistribution. Table 10.4 illustrates this important turning point in terms of shares in tax money. The share of total fiscal income was 22.0 percent for central government and 78 percent for local governments in 1993. After the tax reform, it was reversed to 55.7 percent for central government and 44.3 percent for local governments. In other words, the central government had, from then on, a larger share of the revenue for redistribution for regional and social equitable purposes.

In this light, when Hu Jintao came to power, the ratio of central-local government in fiscal expenses declined from a 30.1/69.9 pattern in 2003 to a 21.3/78.7 pattern in 2008. This indicates that more social resources are

Table 10.4 Division of expenditure and revenue of central and local governments in China

Year	Revenue(100 million yuan)			Revenue (%)		Expenditure (100 million yuan)			Expenditure (%)	
	Total	Central	Local	Central	Local	Total	Central	Local	Central	Local
1978	1132.26	175.77	956.49	15.5	84.5	1122.09	532.12	589.97	47.4	52.6
1980	1159.93	284.45	875.48	24.5	75.5	1228.83	666.81	562.02	54.3	45.7
1985	2004.82	769.63	1235.19	38.4	61.6	2004.25	795.25	1209.00	39.7	60.3
1990	2937.10	992.42	1944.68	33.8	66.2	3083.59	1004.47	2079.12	32.6	67.4
1992	3483.37	979.51	2503.86	28.1	71.9	3742.20	1170.44	2571.76	31.3	68.7
1993	4348.95	957.51	3391.44	22.0	78.0	4642.30	1312.06	3330.24	28.3	71.7
1994	5218.10	2906.50	2311.60	55.7	44.3	5792.62	1754.43	4038.19	30.3	69.7
1995	6242.20	3256.62	2985.58	52.2	47.8	6823.72	1995.39	4828.33	29.2	70.8
1996	7407.99	3661.07	3746.92	49.4	50.6	7937.55	2151.27	5786.28	27.1	72.9
1997	8651.14	4226.92	4424.22	48.9	51.1	9233.56	2532.50	6701.06	27.4	72.6
1998	9875.95	4892.00	4983.95	49.5	50.5	10798.18	3125.60	7672.58	28.9	71.1
1999	11444.08	5849.21	5594.87	51.1	48.9	13187.67	4152.33	9035.34	31.5	68.5
2000	13395.23	6989.17	6406.06	52.2	47.8	15886.50	5519.85	10366.65	34.7	65.3
2001	16386.04	8582.74	7803.30	52.4	47.6	18902.58	5768.02	13134.56	30.5	69.5
2002	18903.64	10388.64	8515.00	55.0	45.0	22053.15	6771.70	15281.45	30.7	69.3
2003	21715.25	11865.27	9849.98	54.6	45.4	24649.95	7420.10	17229.85	30.1	69.9
2004	26396.47	14503.10	11893.37	54.9	45.1	28486.89	7894.08	20592.81	27.7	72.3
2005	31649.29	16548.53	15100.76	52.3	47.7	33930.28	8775.97	25154.31	25.9	74.1
2006	38760.20	20456.62	18303.58	52.8	47.2	40422.73	9991.40	30431.33	24.7	75.3
2007	51321.78	27749.16	23572.62	54.1	45.9	49781.35	11442.06	38339.29	23.0	77.0
2008	61330.35	32680.56	28649.79	53.3	46.7	62592.66	13344.17	49248.49	21.3	78.7

Source: Calculations based on *Statistical Yearbook of China 2009*. The 2009 data are hard copies.

available for the use of the local government. The substantial rise in social expenditure as a share of GDP and in absolute terms, as indicated in Table 10.1, suggests that the role of the state, as it was interpreted differently by China's developmental elite—between Jiang and Hu—is associated with the change in policy toward primary and secondary distribution in recent years. Of course, when we compare the share of social expenditure (excluding education) to GDP in mature Western welfare capitalism (e.g., OECD countries on average spent 20.5 percent of their GDP in 2005, and China's corresponding figure was 3.83 percent in 2005, and 6.66 percent in 2008),[6] in terms of social expenditure, China as a whole is still far from a mature welfare regime. Nevertheless, the enormous amount of wealth generated from China's growth state is impressive. The GDP in 2003 was 2,171.53 billion yuan. In 2008, it jumped to 6,133.04 billion yuan an enormous rise of 282 percent (Table 10.4). It is fair to say that China has the financial capacity to increase the extent of reallocation to local governments for equitable redistribution for welfare development for the political legitimization of the state.

Conclusion

China's welfare regime, the socio-political, legal, and organizational features in terms of the relations between state, economy and society, still favor the state and economy, and society needs the state for its protection. Prevalent Western welfare theories are inadequate in explaining the welfare development of China. China has a different institutional logic from that of the Western welfare capitalism because it is still a developmental state without political democracy; in other words, the society-led theory cannot explain welfare development and the Chinese welfare regime. Apparently, the developmental elite have the liberty to decide how welfare should be developed.

China's low social expenditure as a share of its national wealth is a clear indicator of its immaturity. But welfare reform is conducted to enhance capital accumulation and the cost of welfare is distributed unevenly to the disadvantaged groups. In this regard, the increasing share of non-SOE employment suggests that a larger share of urban employees receive second-class remuneration and welfare packages compared to their SOE counterparts. In principle, their poor conditions in primary distribution should be compensated by secondary distribution in welfare for the sake of the political legitimization of the state. On the contrary, welfare reform is found to shift the financial cost of state welfare to society as in the case of the basic health insurance for urban employment—the citizens included did not benefit from the reform initiative until the government increased its share in healthcare expenses.

Since the developmental elite is still in command, the shift of its ideology is significant to explain any shift in national and welfare development. The leadership of Hu Jintao, with the new discourse of constructing social harmony and the "Five Co-ordinations," indicates a departure from the "growth-first" developmental strategy and trickle-down neo-liberal ideology. This indicates that China has moved, at least ideologically, beyond welfare developmentalism, which is about the domination of social development by economic development. The ideological shift to a fine balance between economic development and social development coincided with a slow but continuous process of a rise in social expenditures in general and government healthcare expenses in particular. In relative terms, the social expenditure of the Chinese welfare regime is still small compared to Western welfare capitalism, but in absolute terms, the recent increases were substantial and a greater share of national revenue was channeled to local governments for redistribution after Hu Jintao took office in 2003. In other words, the developmental factor, i.e., resources, is also important. Of course, the size of social expenditure is not necessarily associated with citizen rights or affordability of healthcare protection, as demonstrated in the case of the United States (Lindert, 2004). But increase in social expenditure of a growth state is a necessary condition for welfare development—the basic tenet of the modernization theory (Hill, 1996).

Of course, we do not eliminate the possibility that the shift was due to structural factors as theorized by the need for political legitimization according to the neo-Marxist perspective. Accordingly, the ideological shift is reactive and a second-stage factor. Evidently, the public discourse of the "Three Mountains" and the establishment of the "stability maintenance offices" indicate the weak welfare state and insufficient political legitimization function of the state. Therefore, institutional and ideological are inter-related; this is the rationale that we use to study China's evolving welfare regime with a tripartite framework.

As a typical developmental state, welfare development in China and the well-being of its citizens depend very much on the ruling ideology and the transformative power of the developmental elite—the powerful political elite and the competent experts and bureaucrats in the design of a welfare regime and particular policy arrangement, on behalf of the society, with social settlements that are fair to the labor and common people. In this regard, abandoning the use of marketization in China's welfare reform is significant in enhancing the political legitimization function of the state. If China wants to lessen the social miseries resulting from capital accumulation and enhance its political legitimacy, the model of Singapore's non-typical developmental state seems a viable alternative, as social development is not at all subordinated to economic development.

Notes

1 See "China should be able to model after Japan on doubling its citizens' income." Available at: http://news.cts.com.tw/cnyes/money/201006/201006040488412.html (accessed July 16, 2010).
2 Doctors are "white wolves' or 'angels': the debate amongst members of the People's Political Consultative Conference." Available at: http://cppcc.people.com.cn/ GB/34952/4089344.html (accessed 9 July 2010).

3 Shanghai deploys police to station at hospital to cope with conflicts," published 23 January 2007. Available at: http://news.xinhuanet.com/legal/2007–01/23/content 5639758.htm (accessed 9 July 2010).
4 Source: Ministry of Health website, Table 4-3-1 Income and Expenses of all types of health institutes in 2008. www.moh.gov.cn (accessed 9 July 2010).
5 A recent news report suggests that readjusting income distribution was a topic raised frequently by the Chinese leaders in 2010. See "China's income distribution has entered into deepen readjusted stage." Available at: http://news.xinhuanet.com/politics/2010–03/02/content_1383133.htm (accessed 2 March 2010).
6 Social protection in OECD countries including pension, health care, unemployment, family, disability and housing, etc. Source: http://stats.oecd.org/wbos/Index.aspx?datasetcode=SOCX_AGG (accessed 15 July 2010).

References

Ahn, S.H. and Lee, S.C. (2005) "The development of the South Korea welfare regime," in A. Walker, and C.K. Wong (eds.) East Welfare Regimes in Transition: From Confucianism to Globalisation, Bristol: Policy Press.

Aspalter, C. (2002) Democratization and Welfare State Development in Taiwan, Aldershot: Ashgate.

——(2006) "The East Asian welfare model," International Journal of Social Welfare, 15: 290–301.

Back, S.W. (2005) "Does China follow the East Asian Development Model?," Journal of Contemporary Asia, 35: 485–98.

Barro, R. (1997) Getting it Right, Cambridge, MA: MIT Press.

Briggs, A. (1965) "The welfare state in historical perspective," in M.N. Zald (ed.) Social Welfare Institutions: A Sociological Reader, New York: Wiley.

Burchell, D. (1995) "The attributes of citizens: virtue, manners and the activity of citizenship," Economy and Society, 24: 540–58.

Central Committee (CCP) (2003) Communiqué of the Third Plenum of the 16th CPC Central Committee, on 14 October 2003 (in Chinese). Available HTTP: www.people.com.cn/GB/shizheng/1024/2133923.html (accessed 23 August 2006).

Chau, R.C.M. and Yu, W.K. (1999) "Social welfare and economic development in China and Hong Kong," Critical Social Policy, 19: 87–107.

——(2005) "Is welfare unAsian?," in A. Walker and C.K. Wong (eds.) East Welfare Regimes in Transition: From Confucianism to Globalisation, Bristol: Policy Press.

Croissant, A. (2004) "Changing welfare regimes in East and Southeast Asia: Crisis, change and challenge," Social Policy and Administration, 38: 504–34.

Dean, M. (1995) "Governing the unemployed self in an active society," Economy and Society, 24: 559–83.

Dixon, J. (1981) The Chinese Welfare System 1949–1979, New York: Praeger Publishers.

Esping-Andersen, G. (1990) The Three Worlds of Welfare Capitalism. Cambridge: Polity Press.

——(1996) Welfare State in Transition, London: Sage.

——(1999) Social Foundations of Post-industrial Economies, Oxford: Oxford University Press.

Faulks, K. (2000) Citizenship, London: Routledge.

Flora, P. and Heidenheimer. A.J. (eds.) (1982) The Development of the Welfare State in Europe and America. New Brunswick, NJ: Transaction.

George, V. and Wilding, P. (1993) Welfare and Ideology, Hemel Hempstead: Harvester Wheatsheaf.

Gintis, H. and Bowles, S. (1982) "The welfare state and long-term economic growth: Marxism, neoclassical, and Keynesian approaches," American Economic Review, 72: 341–5.

Gough, I. (1979) The Political Economy of the Welfare State, London: Macmillan.

——(1999) Welfare Regimes: On Adapting the Framework to Developing Countries, Bath: Global Social Policy Programme, Institute for International Policy Analysis, University of Bath.

Hill, M. (1996) Social Policy: A Comparative Analysis, London: Prentice Hall.

Hill, M. and Hwang, Y.S. (2005) "Taiwan: what kind of social policy regime?," in A. Walker and C.K. Wong (eds.) East Welfare Regimes in Transition: From Confucianism to Globalization, Bristol: Policy Press.

Holliday, I. (2000) "Productivist welfare capitalism: social policy in East Asia," Political Study, 48: 706–23.

Hort, S.E. and Kuhnle, S. (2000) "The coming of East and South-East welfare states," Journal of European Social Policy, 10: 162–84.

Hu, J. (2005) "Improve the ability of constructing a socialist harmonious society," a special seminar for provincial leaders to improve the ability of constructing a socialist harmonious society, 19 February 2005. Available at: http://news.enorth.com.cn/system//06/26/001054035.shtml (accessed 21 May 2006).

Jiang, Z. (2002) "Comprehensively building xiaokang society, spearheading the new era of Chinese socialist enterprise with special characteristic," Report at the 16th Party Congress of the Chinese Communist Party, 8 November 2002 (in Chinese).

Johnson, C. (1982) MITI and the Japanese Miracle: The Growth of Industrial Policy, 1925–1975, Stanford, CA: Stanford University Press.

——(1995) Japan: Who Governs? The Rise of the Developmental State, New York: W. W. Norton.

——(1999) "The developmental state: odyssey of a concept," in M. Woo-Cumings (ed.) The Developmental State, Ithaca, NY: Cornell University Press.

Kim, Y.M. (2001) "Welfare state or social safety nets? Development of the social welfare policy of the Kim Dae-Jung Administration," Korea Journal, 41: 169–201.

Klein, R. (1980) "The welfare state: a self-inflicted crisis," Political Quarterly, 51: 24–34.

Kornai, J. (1997) "Editorial: reforming the welfare state in post-socialist societies," World Development, 25: 1183–86.

Kwon, H.J. (2002) "Welfare reform and future challenges in the Republic of Korea: beyond the developmental welfare state?," International Social Security Review, 55: 23–38.

Ku, Y.W. (2002) "Towards a Taiwanese welfare state: demographic change, politics and social policy," in C. Aspalter (ed.) Discovering the Welfare State in East Asia, Westport, CT: Praeger.

Lee, K.C. (forthcoming) From Singapore's Housing and Social Security Case to Study the Relationship Between East Asian Developmentalism, Social Welfare and State Capacity, Hong Kong: Polytechnic University (in Chinese).

Leftwich, A. (1995) "Bringing politics back in: towards a model of the developmental state," The Journal of Developmental Studies, 31: 400–27.

Leung, J.C.B. and Nann, R.C. (1995) Authority and Benevolence: Social Welfare in China, Hong Kong: Chinese University Press.

Lindert, P.H. (2004) Growing Public: Social Spending and Economic Growth since the Eighteenth Century, Cambridge: Cambridge University Press.

Lijphart, A. (1999) Patterns of Democracy: Government Forms and Performance in Thirty-Six Countries, New Haven, CT: Yale University Press.

Marshall, T.H. (1950) Citizenship and Social Class and Other Essays, Cambridge: Cambridge University Press.

McCarthy, D., Mitchell, O.S. and Piggott, J. (2002) "Asset rich and cash poor: retirement provision and housing policy in Singapore," Journal of Pension, 1: 197–222.

National Statistical Bureau of China (2009) China Statistical Yearbook, 2009. Available at: www.stats.gov.cn/tjsj/ndsj/2009/image/shouyech.jpg (accessed 9 July 2010).

O'Connor, J. (1973) The Fiscal Crisis of the Welfare State, New York: St. James Press.

OECD (2007) The Social Expenditure Database: An Interpretive Guide, SOCX 1980–2003. Paris: OECD.

Offe, C. (1984) Contradictions of the Welfare State, London: Macmillan.

Pampel, F. and Williamson, J. (1988) "Welfare spending in advanced democracies, 1950–80," American Journal of Sociology, 93: 1424–56.

Pang, E.S. (2000) "The financial crisis of 1997–98 and the end of the Asian development state," Contemporary Southeast Asia, 22: 570–93.

Pereira, A. (2008) "Whither the developmental state? Explaining Singapore's continued developmentalism," Third World Quarterly, 29: 1189–203.

Pierson, C. (1991) Beyond the Welfare State? Cambridge: Polity Press.

Ringen, S. (1987) The Possibility of Politics, Oxford: Oxford University Press.

Rodger, J. J. (2000) From a Welfare State to a Welfare Society, Basingstoke: Macmillan.

Sherraden, M., Nair, S., Vasoo, S. and Ngiam, T.L. (1995) "Social policy based on assets: the impact of Singapore's Central Provident Fund," Asian Journal of Political Science, 3: 112–33.

Tang, J. (2005) The Urban and Rural Minimum Basic Livelihood Guarantee Systems: History, Present Conditions and Future Prospect, Beijing: Dajun Economic Research Centre.

Tang, K.L. (2000) Social Welfare Development in East Asia, Basingstoke: Palgrave.

Walker, A. and Wong, C. K. (1996) "Rethinking the western construction of the welfare state," International Journal of Health Services, 26: 67–92.

——(2004) "The ethnocentric construction of the welfare state," in P. Kennett (ed.) A Handbook of Comparative Social Policy, Cheltenham: Edward Elgar.

——(2005) East Welfare Regimes in Transition: From Confucianism to Globalization, Bristol: Policy Press.

——(2009) "The relationship between social policy and economic policy: constructing the public burden of welfare in China and the West," Development and Society, 38: 1–26.

Walter, A. (2006) "From developmental to regulatory state: Japan's new financial regulatory system," The Pacific Review, 19(4): 405–28.

Walters, W. (1997) "The active society: new designs for social policy," Policy and Politics 25: 221–34.

Weiss, L. (2000) "Developmental states in transition: adapting, dismantling, innovating, not normalizing," Pacific Review, 13: 21–55.

Wilensky, H. (1975) The Welfare State and Equality, Berkeley, CA: University of California Press.

Wong, C.K., Chau, K.L. and Wong, K.Y. (2002) "Neither welfare state nor welfare society," Social Policy and Society, 1: 293–301.

Wong, C.K., Lo, V.I. and Tang, K.L. (2006) China's Urban Healthcare Reform: Ffrom State Protection to Individual Responsibility, Lanham, MD: Lexington Books.

Wong, C.K. and Wong, K.Y. (2001) "Rhetoric and reality of East Asian welfare system-The case of Hong Kong," in Social Policy Research Centre, Repositioning of the State, Hong Kong: Hong Kong Polytechnic University, Joint Publishing (HK).

Wong, J. (2005) "Democracy, development and health in Taiwan," in H.J. Kwon (ed.) Transforming the Developmental Welfare State in East Asia, Basingstoke: Palgrave-Macmillan/UNEISD.

Yasuhiro, K. (2005) "Welfare states in East Asia: similar conditions, different past and divided future," 2nd East Asian Social Policy Conference, University of Kent, 30 June.

Zheng, X. and Hillier, S. (1995) "The reforms of the Chinese healthcare system: country level changes: the Jiangxi study," Social Science and Medicine, 41: 1057–64.

11 Singapore's social development experience

A relevant lesson for China?

Litao Zhao and John Wong

Introduction

In 1978, Deng Xiaoping made his first state visit to Singapore. He was very impressed by Singapore as a small city-state that had achieved successful economic and social development. In his *Nanxun* speech in early 1992, Deng specifically singled out Singapore as a country enjoying both high economic growth and good social development. China should learn from Singapore and do better than Singapore.

Ever since, the Chinese authorities have maintained a strong interest in Singapore's overall development experiences. More recently, Chinese leaders' attention has focused on Singapore's social development experiences. The government-to-government cooperation between China and Singapore thus expands from the economic to the social domain. After the China-Singapore Suzhou Industrial Park (which started in 1994), the China-Singapore Tianjin Eco-City is now under the construction, with greater attention paid to Singapore's experience in building an economically vibrant, environmentally friendly and socially harmonious city. Both sides of course realize that straightforward copying would not work. The question then is, what kind of lessons is relevant for China, given the difference between the two countries in terms of population and territory size, the stage of economic development, and the policy-making process?

Singapore's social development: strategies, features and performance

Globalization has facilitated the diffusion of dominant ideologies, policies and institutions across the globe, but the process of conversion and convergence is far from complete. Social policy to a large extent is still embedded in the historical-political-cultural complexity of the individual societies. From this perspective, any kind of learning from a foreign country has to be an eclectic one, and the learning process is conditioned by the degree of political, cultural, economic and social similarities between the two countries.

Social policy, whether broadly defined as government initiatives to enhance the social well-being of the population or narrowly defined as social protection of the poor and the vulnerable, involves a normative judgment about what is a good society and what is the best way to achieve it. Political philosophy, cultural traditions and the stages of economic development can all shape the thinking as well as the making of social policy. The distinction between socialism and capitalism, authoritarianism and democracy, individualism and familialism is central to our understanding of wide variations in social policy across the nations.

Different social policy regimes have different views about the role of the family, the market and the state in taking care of social needs. As Esping-Andersen (2001, p. 839) observes:

> Scandinavia responds [to a set of social risks] with social democracy and comprehensive welfare states, continental Europe and East Asia with familialism and corporatist social insurance, and the Anglo-Saxon world with targeted assistance and maximum markets.

Singapore's social policy has to be understood as based on its own history and development path as well. As we will show below, there is nothing much to say about Singapore's social policy if social policy is narrowly defined. From the perspective of state welfarism, one can question whether there is a social policy in Singapore. Singapore, however, clearly has its own social policy if social policy is to be broadly defined as state efforts to promote the general social well-being.

The ruling People's Action Party (PAP) had a strong social-democratic commitment in its early years. Nonetheless, the first generation leadership had known too well the problems of state welfarism. Its key members were educated in Britain at university there. Their personal experiences there fully convinced them that "state welfarism had the undesirable consequence of undermining the work ethic and contributed to a culture of dependency" (Tong and Lian, 2008, p. 1). To them, a welfare state should not be the future of Singapore. When they came back to Singapore, they faced the challenge of electoral politics. To win the election, they had to carefully deal with the tremendous pressure from the strong labor movement that called for a more radical set of socialist policies. Their triumph over the left wing of the PAP in the 1960s created the political condition to fend off such populist/socialist pressure. As they consolidated the PAP rule, they were able to steer Singapore away from both socialist and capitalist systems.

As a counter-discourse to Western liberalism and state welfarism, the PAP leadership turned to "Asian values" as an alternative model for social policy. The first generation leadership repeatedly stressed the role of family and self-responsibility in social development in general, and in social security provision in particular. The core "Asian values" included self-help, thrift, discipline and filial piety. The PAP leadership saw these values not only as an important contribution to Singapore's economic success, but also treated them as a cure to cope with the undesirable consequences of its economic success, namely excessive Westernization, in the form of delinquency, abortion, divorce and drug use (Lian, 2008).

The PAP leadership did not treat social development as an independent domain to be separated from economic development. Social development was not even seen as an end in itself, but instead as an instrument to promote and support economic development, and as part of the political project to create a common identity in a society without much shared historical experience. In terms of the relationship between economic development and social development, the practical PAP leadership believed that they were interrelated, but there was a sequence: economic development first, social development second. Economic development creates social friction, but also generates material resources to cope with them (Wong, 1995).

In the view of the PAP leadership, the best way to promote general social well-being was through economic growth rather than redistribution. To promote economic growth, the right incentive for individuals to work hard is as important as the state interventionist policies. Letting individuals and families take care of their basic needs is both a cultural practice that can help hold the society together, and an essential part of the right incentive needed for economic growth. Thus workfare is preferred and welfare is rejected. The state should create a favorable environment to develop individuals to their fullest potential, and use meritocracy to select and reward talents. In addition, priority should be given to "productive" social investment instead of "redistributive" social welfare consumption.

In the early stages of its economic development, Singapore focused on public housing and basic education as "social investment" in order to spur industrialization. Subsequently, education was focused on skill training and high level manpower development to facilitate Singapore's industrial upgrading. More recently, education has targeted the "knowledge economy", with a special focus on higher education and R&D. However, there is no minimum wage provision and no unemployment insurance. As a last resort of social protection, public assistance to the needy is by no means generous.

Economically, Singapore has transformed from a "Third World" to a "First World" country in about three decades. One suspects that Singapore's economic development may have come at the cost of social development, given that its social policy is geared toward economic development. Table 11.1 presents some key social indicators for Singapore over time. Clearly Singapore has been making good progress in terms of social development. Its basic education has been expanding, and the adult literacy rate constantly improving. There was near full employment after 1970. Healthcare has become more accessible, with the number of doctors increasing considerably faster than that of the population. The infant mortality rate has been declining to one of the lowest in the world. The share of the population living in public housing is extremely high, always above 80 percent since the mid-1980s. Singapore has been a very safe city-state by international standards, but it was still able to substantially reduce the crime rate over time.

From a comparative perspective, Singapore's progress in social development is commensurate with its progress in economic development. An often used indicator for the international comparison of social development is the Human Development Index (HDI), which combines life expectancy, educational attainment and income indicators to give a composite measure of human

Table 11.1 Singapore's major social indicators, 1970–2008

	1970	1980	1990	2000	2008
Population (million)	2.1	2.4	3.0	4.0	4.8
Infant mortality rate (per 1,000 live births)	20.5	8	6.6	2.5	2.1
Total fertility rate	3.1	1.8	1.8	1.6	1.3
Gross enrollment ratio in primary education (%)	–	78.6	93.6	87.8	96.6
Adult literacy rate (% aged 15 and above)	–	84	87.6	92.5	96
Unemployment rate (% aged 15 and above)	6	3.5	1.8	3.6	2.3
Health (persons per doctor)	–	909	769	667	625
Population living in HDB flats (%)	–	73	88	85	82
Total offenses (per 10,000 population)	–	123	198	90	67

Source: Department of Statistics, *Yearbook of Statistics*, Singapore, various years.

development. Table 11.2 presents HDI and individual items for Singapore and selected East Asian economies. In 2009, it had the second highest HDI in Asia after Japan. Overall, it ranked 23 out of 182 countries/regions, as one of the group with very high human development, along with Japan and other Newly Industrialized Economies (NIEs) such as Hong Kong and South Korea.[1] In comparison, Malaysia was the only country in Southeast Asia to make the list of high human development. China so far is a country with medium human development, alongside with Thailand, the Philippines and Indonesia.

Based on social indicators measuring education, health, income and safety, Singapore is a developed country in terms of social development, although many people believe Singapore still has a room to improve in the aspect of "social grace." What is remarkable about Singapore's development experience is two-fold. On the one hand, it has achieved high economic growth with relatively low social cost. Industrial relations have been stable, so are the ethnic relationships. Its physical environment is clean and green, pollution is low, and city traffic still manageable. Above all, its streets are safe, with the crime rate low by the standard of any metropolitan city. Although income inequality has been increasing and is at a high level, its negative consequences on social stability and distributive justice are partially offset by near full employment and high homeownership rate.

On the other hand, Singapore has achieved a high level of social development without vast amounts of government spending. The growth of government expenditures is deliberately kept lower than GDP growth; government spending on education as a percentage of GDP is low by international standards; even more remarkably, government spending on healthcare is extremely low by international standards.

Table 11.3 shows how the Singapore government spends its revenue. As a general trend, the total government expenditure has been increasing, but at a

Table 11.2 Socio-economic development in selected East Asian economies

	GDP per capita (US$)	Total Fertility Rate	Life expectancy at birth		Infant mortality rate (per 1,000 live births)	Gross enrollment ratio into education					Human Development Index	
						Secondary		Tertiary				
			Female	Male		Female	Male	Female	Male	Year	Value	Rank
	2009	2009	2009	2009	2009						2009	2009
China	3,556	1.4	72	76	20	78	77	23	23	2007	0.772	92
Japan	32,600	1.2	82	85	2.8	101	101	54	62	2007	0.960	10
NIEs												
S. Korea	16,491	1.2	76	82	4.3	94	98	69	65	2007	0.937	26
Taiwan	15,552	1.2	75	81	5.4	99	98	85	79	2007	–	–
Hong Kong	24,626	1.0	79	85	2.6	86	86	34	33	2007	0.944	24
Singapore	35,022	1.1	77	81	2.3	73	75	40	47	2007	0.944	23
ASEAN-4												
Indonesia	2,142	2.3	68	73	30	74	73	32	19	2007	0.734	111
Malaysia	8,065	3.0	71	76	16	72	70	33	27	2006	0.829	66
the Philippines	1,639	3.3	68	74	21	87	79	32	25	2006	0.751	105
Thailand	4,036	1.7	71	76	18	88	79	45	38	2006	0.783	87
India	946	2.7	65	67	51	49	53	10	14	2006	0.612	134

Note: Human Development Index combines life expectancy, educational attainment and income indicators to give a composite measure of human development.
Source: Compiled from the CIA, *World Fact Book*, https://www.cia.gov/library/publications/the-world-factbook/, the United Nations Database, and the Asian Development Bank.

Table 11.3 Singapore's government expenditures (million, S$), 1998–2009

	1998			2003			2008			2009		
	Government expenditure	% of total government expenditure	% of GDP	Government expenditure	% of total government expenditure	% of GDP	Government expenditure	% of total government expenditure	% of GDP	Government expenditure	% of total government expenditure	% of GDP
Security*	8,665	34.9	6.3	10,328	38.0	6.4	14,450	38.6	5.6	14,402	35.6	5.4
Social development	10,025	40.4	7.3	12,392	45.6	7.6	15,453	41.2	6.0	16,554	40.9	6.2
Education	4,824	19.5	3.5	6,200	22.8	3.8	8,154	21.8	3.2	8,180	20.2	3.1
Healthcare	1,197	4.8	0.9	1,758	6.5	1.1	2,541	6.8	1.0	3,339	8.2	1.3
Economic development	4,705	19.0	3.4	3,188	11.7	2.0	6,335	16.9	2.5	8,261	20.4	3.1
Government administration	1,399	5.6	1.0	1,282	4.7	0.8	1,231	3.3	0.5	1,266	3.1	0.5
Total	24,795	–	18.0	27,189	–	16.7	37,469	–	14.6	40,483	–	15.3

Note: * Includes government expenditures on security and external relations.
Source: Department of Statistics, *Yearbook of Statistics*, Singapore, various years.

rate lower than GDP growth, so that as a percentage of GDP it was declining between 1998 and 2009. It reflects Singapore government's decision not to let government expenditure run ahead of economic growth. As is always the case with Singapore, security and external relations account for a large chunk of government spending. On social development, Singapore government consistently spends over 40 percent of total government expenditure. Of the two major items of social development, education accounts for over 20 percent of total government expenditures, much higher than government spending on healthcare. Measured against GDP, government spending on education is low by international standards, consistently below 4 percent of GDP. In fact, it has been declining from 3.8 percent of GDP in 2003 to 3.1 percent in 2009.

Singapore's government spending on health is even more remarkably low, at around 1 percent of GDP between 1998 and 2008. There was a substantial increase in 2009, but still as low as 1.3 percent of GDP. Private expenditure on health is not particularly high either. According to World Health Statistics (World Health Organization, 2009, pp. 108–15), in 2006, Singapore's government spending made up about one-third of total expenditure on health, about 1.1 percent of GDP, and private expenditure made up the other two-thirds, about 2.2 percent of GDP. Measured against GDP, private expenditure is much lower in Singapore than in the United States (8.3 percent in 2006), and not considerably higher than in the welfare states (for instance, 1.8 percent in Sweden and 1.0 percent in the UK). As a result of the extremely low government expenditure and the comparatively low private expenditure, total expenditure on healthcare was only 3.3 percent of GDP for Singapore, compared to 8.2 percent for the UK, 9.2 percent for Sweden and an astonishing 15.3 percent for the USA. Despite lower spending on healthcare, Singapore's health indicators are as good as those of the developed countries, including the welfare states.

Clearly, Singapore's social policy has worked well. From a comparative perspective, it has an additional advantage of delivering good results with much less spending, particularly government spending. This advantage becomes an attractive feature of Singapore's development experience, particularly in the aftermath of the 2008 global financial crisis, when government deficit has become a headache for many welfare states. If anything, Singapore's experience shows that self-help, individual responsibility and filial piety, supported by an enabling environment that stresses meritocracy and provides good education and skills training, can form the basis of an alternative model of social policy and social development.

Singapore's social policies

The Central Provident Fund (CPF)

Singapore's primary form of social security is the Central Provident Fund (CPF). It has a longer history than Singapore as an independent state. Many

British colonial territories established provident funds in the 1950s as a savings scheme for retirement. This was the period of decolonization in Singapore. There was substantial pressure on political parties in Singapore to improve the livelihoods of the impoverished masses quickly, either by establishing a universal and comprehensive social insurance scheme as advocated by the British Labour Government's *Beveridge Report*, or through radical redistribution as practiced by the newly-formed governments of China, India, and Indonesia. The PAP leadership had known too well of the problems of either state welfarism or socialist experiments. Once they consolidated their power within the party and against other opposition parties, they were able to carry out policies that best fit with their vision for Singapore (Lian, 2008).

The PAP inherited the CPF for at least two reasons. First, CPF fits well with the PAP ideology of self-help, diligence, discipline and family support. One defining feature of CPF is that contributions are not pooled. Instead, it is a fully funded program, with regular payroll contributions from employees and employers into a personal savings account. Accumulations in the personal account can be withdrawn for a specified contingency. In this way, CPF is save-as-you-earn instead of pay-as-you-go which characterizes many social insurance programs. There is no cross-subsidization across CPF members. As such, there is no redistribution from the rich to the poor, from the young to the old beyond the family.

Second, CPF as a publicly managed fund can be used for economic development. Back in the 1950s and 1960s, with a sizable portion of the population living in poverty and the majority living in badly overcrowded conditions, it was difficult to launch the development process in Singapore. Without either an agricultural or industrial base to support economic takeoff, CPF was seen by Goh Keng Swee, the economic architect of Singapore, as a useful means of capital formation (Barr, 2000, pp. 116–17). In fact, the Singaporean provident fund is the best known among all the provident funds, largely because of "the effective use of accumulations by the government for housing construction and economic development projects" (Tang and Midgley, 2008).

CPF started off as a pension program, with a 5 percent payroll contribution from the employee and another 5 percent from the employer. Its functions, however, gradually expanded to meet the changing needs of an increasingly affluent population. It evolved in the next five decades to become the most elaborate and complex scheme of its kind in the world. The first major change took place in 1968, when Singaporeans were allowed to use their CPF savings to buy flats built by the government. The tie-up between CPF and public housing is widely seen by many as a milestone in the construction of Singapore society (Chua, 1997; Hill and Lian, 1995; Lian, 2008). From 1964, the government began to promote homeownership as an essential part of nation-building. The initial take-up rate of public housing was low until the liberalization of CPF in 1968, which made public housing affordable to the majority of working-class families.

Another landmark development came in 1984 with the introduction of the Medisave Scheme, a self-funded healthcare program. From that time on, CPF was also closely linked to Singapore's healthcare system. CPF continued to evolve as a framework for other social policies. For instance, from 1989, CPF savings could be used to finance higher education in local universities. Moreover, the CPF system was flexible enough to be linked to and supplemented by insurance programs. For example, the Medishield Program, set up in 1990, is a medical insurance scheme with risk-pooling and co-payment features. It is designed to pay part of the expenses arising from prolonged hospitalization and certain outpatient treatment for serious illness.

To increase the return rate and add flexibility to the management of account balances, CPF members can invest their savings under certain conditions. Put it simply, while CPF retains its core feature as a savings scheme, it has evolved to become the most elaborate and complex scheme of its kind in the world, taking on functions as diverse as pensions, homeownership, healthcare, insurance, education and investment (see Table 11.4 for the development of Singapore's CPF system).

Table 11.4 The evolution of the CPF system

Year	Scheme	Function
1955	Central Provident Fund (CPF)	Pension
1968	Approved Housing Scheme	Home-ownership
1978	Singapore Bus Services (1978) Ltd. Share Scheme	Investment
1981	Approved Residential Property Scheme	Home-ownership
1982	Home Protection Insurance Scheme	Insurance
1984	Medisave Scheme	Healthcare
1986	Approved Non-Residential Properties Scheme[a]	Investment
1986	Approved Investment Scheme[b]	Investment
1987	Minimum Sum Scheme	Pension
1989	Dependents' Protection Insurance Scheme	Insurance
1989	Financing of Tertiary Education in Singapore	Education
1990	Medishield Scheme	Healthcare/insurance
1992	Edusave Scheme	Education
1993	Shared Ownership Top-Up Scheme	Other
1995	CPF Top-Up Scheme	Other
1997	CPF Investment Scheme	Investment
2001	Supplementary Retirement Scheme	Pension
2002	Eldershield Scheme	Insurance
2007	Eldershield Supplements Scheme	Insurance
2009	CPF Life	Pension payout

Notes:

a This scheme was phased out in 2006. Instead, CPF members can use the CPF Investment Scheme to purchase non-residential properties.

b Since October 2003, this scheme has been divided into the Basic and Enhanced investment schemes; since January 1, 1997, the Approved Investment Scheme has been replaced by the CPF Investment Scheme.

Under the current system, each CPF member holds three accounts with the CPF Board: the ordinary, the special and the medisave accounts. The ordinary account is set up to finance the purchase of a home, approved investments, CPF insurance and education, under certain conditions. It can be withdrawn at age 55, subject to the retention of the minimum sum. The remaining balances will be held in the retirement account established for CPF members at age 55. Since 1986, the interest is a weighted average of the 12-month deposit and month-end savings rate, subject to a minimum rate of 2.5 percent according to the CPF Act. Currently the interest is paid at 2.5 percent. CPF savings are not protected against inflation, however. For those below 55 years, between 66.7 percent and 45.6 percent of the contributions is channeled into this account, with the rate higher for younger cohorts.

The special account is for old-age provisions. Funds in this account cannot be touched until age 62, except for certain low-risk investments through the CPF Investment Scheme (CPFIS). CPFIS was introduced in 1997 to replace an earlier model dating from 1986. It allows CPF members to invest part of ordinary and special account balances in Singapore government bonds, bonds of statutory boards, gold, investment-linked insurance policies, unit trusts, corporate bonds, shares, and so on. A minimum sum must be retained before the ordinary and special account balances can be withdrawn. By 2013, the minimum sum will be S$120,000 in 2003 dollars (Reisman 2007). Currently savings in this account enjoys a higher interest rate of 4 percent, subject to a specified ceiling. For those below 55 years, between 14.5 percent and 24.6 percent of the contributions is channeled into this account, with the proportion increasing with age.

The medisave account can be used for hospital care, outpatient treatment, and approved medical insurance. Unlike the other two accounts, the self-employed are required to contribute to this account. For those below 55 years, between 18.8 percent and 29.8 percent of the contributions is channeled into the medisave account. Savings in this account enjoy the interest rate of 4 percent.

The CPF contribution rate increased over time as its functions expanded. Initially at 10 percent of payroll between 1955 and 1968 when CPF was only for old-age provision, the contribution rate increased all the way to the peak of 50 percent in 1984. From the mid-1980s, the CPF contribution rate has been adjusted downward based on economic considerations. The rate is reduced when the economy falls into recession, both for employee contribution and employer contribution. For employers, the main purpose is to encourage retention of workers by reducing the cost of hiring; for employees, a lower contribution rate means more cash available for immediate consumption. Together lower rates help to stabilize the labor market and boost the domestic consumption. By allowing the CPF contribution rate to fluctuate within a certain range, CPF also becomes an instrument for economic adjustment. The long-term contribution rate would be 10–16 percent for employees, and 20 percent for employers (see Table 11.5 for the historical changes in the CPF contribution rate).

Table 11.5 CPF contribution rates (for workers aged 50 and below) since 1955 (%)

Year	Employer	Employee	Total
1955	5	5	10
1968	6.5	6.5	13
1974	15	15	30
1984	25	25	50
1986	10	25	35
1988	12	24	36
1989	15	23	38
1990	18	22	40
1993	18.5	21.5	40
1994	20	20	40
1999	10	20	30
2000	12	20	32
2001	16	20	36
2003	13	20	33
2007	14.5	20	34.5
2010	15	20	35
2011	15.5	20	35.5
Long term	10–16	20	30–36

Source: Low (2004); CPF publications.

The CPF system so far has worked well for Singapore. As a social security system, it has the advantage of delivering good performance in social indicators without large amounts of government spending. Even the private expenditure is not particularly large compared with the welfare states where the government is primarily responsible for welfare provision. As a policy tool for facilitating economic growth, CPF frees employers from the burden of providing supplemental pensions and medical benefits and becomes one of the selling points to attract multinational companies to Singapore. Moreover, CPF has the advantage of building up substantial reserves for massive investment in government-led projects (Lee and Vasoo, 2008). CPF continues to accumulate with contributions exceeding withdrawals, up to 63 percent of GDP by the end of 2009 (see Table 11.6).

Provident funds as compared to social insurance-based social security system have been criticized for failing to provide universal coverage, and for inadequate protection to low-income earners and workers without long employment before retirement (International Social Security Association, 1975). Singapore has worked out a way to minimize such disadvantages through full employment. As different social security systems face the same challenge of fertility declining and population ageing, CPF has the great advantage as a fully-funded program, which does not add much burden to public finance. CPF has shown some degree of flexibility in coping with population ageing. By reducing employer contribution rates, Singapore encourages employers to retain or recruit senior workers above 55 years by lowering the cost of hiring.

Table 11.6 Selected indicators of Singapore's Central Provident Fund (CPF)

	2009
Members (million)[a]	3.29
Active members (million)	1.64
Members' balance (S$ million)[a]	166,804
– Ordinary Account (%)	42.3
– Special Account (%)	21.2
– Medisave Account (%)	27.7
– Retirement Account and others (%)	8.7
Members' balance as % of GDP[a]	62.9
Contributions (S$ million)[b]	4,764.3
Withdrawals[b]	
– total (S$ million)	3,093.0
– retirement (%)	22.7
– housing (%)	54.0
– healthcare (%)	15.8
– investment (%)	6.6
– other[c] (%)	0.8

Notes:
a As at 31 December 2009.
b Period from October to December 2009.
c Other Schemes include Home Protection Scheme, Dependents' Protection Scheme, Education Scheme, Special Discounted Shares Scheme, and so on.
Source: http://mycpf.cpf.gov.sg/CPF/About-Us/CPF-Stats/CPF_Stats2009q4.htm.

The Housing Development Board (HDB)

Public housing has been regarded by many as an area in which Singapore truly stands out, unsurpassed by any city in the world in terms of providing low-cost accommodation to the majority of the population, and integrating public housing with community development. When the PAP government came to power in 1959, Singapore had one of the largest urban slums in South-East Asia. Now Singapore has changed into a clean, green garden city, or a city in the garden, with Singaporeans enjoying considerably larger living space than their counterparts in other metropolitan cities.

The change began with the establishment of the Housing Development Board (HDB) in 1960, the public housing authority in Singapore. Initially, public housing was for rental only. In 1964, the PAP government introduced the concept of homeownership on the political ground that a home-owning society is more stable and responsible. The best explanation is offered by Lee Kuan Yew, Prime Minister of Singapore between 1959 and 1990:

> My primary preoccupation was to give every citizen a stake in the country and its future. I wanted a home-owning society. I had seen the contrast between the low-cost rental flats, badly misused and poorly

maintained, and those of house-proud owners, and was convinced that if every family owned its home, the country would be more stable … I believed this sense of ownership was vital for our new society which had no deep roots in a common historical experience.

(Lee, 2000, pp. 116–17)

The real breakthrough came in 1968 when CPF balances could be used to purchase HDB flats. Under the Approved Housing Scheme, CPF members can use CPF savings to pay the monthly installments over a maximum period of 25 years after they have paid a down payment of 5 to 10 percent of the purchase price. By 1970, HDB had built 100,000 units, housing 30 percent of the population (Reisman, 2007, p. 161). With the growth of middle-class families and the growing need for better living environment of HDB estates, the HDB has adjusted its priority from building smaller flats (1-room, 2-room or 3-room) to building larger flats and upgrading the existing estates (see Table 11.7). For more than two decades since the 1980s, more than 80 percent of Singaporeans have lived in HDB flats.

What is significant about the Singapore experience of public housing is that public housing is not planned as a welfare provision to the low-income population. It is first and foremost a political project, meant to make every Singaporean a stakeholder in the survival and growth of a young country without a long history and facing a lot of uncertainties. For this purpose, public housing also becomes an instrument for social engineering. In 1989, the government made explicit the rule that the HDB estates must have an ethnic mix roughly in proportion to that of Singapore as a whole. Such a *de facto* quota system is designed to promote racial harmony.

Integration also extends to class. Each HDB block has small rental flats as well as flats of different sizes to be sold to families with different income levels. The less well-off often live in 3-room or 2-room flats and the better off choose 4-room or 5-room flats, but they live side-by-side to avoid the problem of class-based segregation or isolation (Reisman, 2007). Such a residential pattern in turn affects integration in schools, shops, community clubs, food courts and other local amenities, further fostering shared experiences and promoting racial harmony and social stability.

The amazing fact that more than 80 percent of Singaporeans live in the HDB flats sets Singapore apart from most other countries in the area of public housing. In countries where public housing is provided as a form of social welfare to low-income families, public housing estates often quickly degenerate into slums or become hotbeds of crime. In Singapore, the majority of the population live in public housing owned by their families. Whether less well-off or better-off, and regardless of their ethnicity, they have formed a common identity as "the HDB heartlanders."

Another remarkable feature of Singapore's public housing program is that the housing policy is closely integrated with the economic policy. From the outset, in addition to political considerations, public housing was also

Table 11.7 Resident households by type of dwelling in Singapore

Year	Total (1,000)	HDB (% of total resident households)					Condominiums (% of total resident households)	Landed property (% of total resident households)	Other (% of total resident households)
		Total HDB	1-2 room	3-room	4-room	5-room & larger flats			
1980	472.7	68.5	21.9	32.2	9.8	3.5	2.3	8.5	20.6
1990	661.7	84.6	8.1	35.3	27.4	13.0	4.1	7.0	4.3
2000	915.1	87.7	5.0	25.8	33.1	23.5	6.3	5.1	1.0
2005	1,024.5	84.4	4.3	20.7	32.5	26.6	9.7	5.4	0.5
2009	1,119.6	83.5	4.4	20.2	32.0	26.6	10.4	5.5	0.6

Source: Adapted from Department of Statistics (2010).

considered a productive social investment. Cheap public housing means that labour can live on relatively lower wages, which is attractive to foreign investment and conducive to the development of labor-intensive industries.

Singapore's public housing program also benefits from this type of integration. As discussed earlier, CPF is an important source of credit to the government in the form of government bonds. The government in turn provides development loans and grants to HDB for building, upgrading and maintaining the HDB estates. HDB then offers a very low mortgage rate at 0.1 percent above the CPF interest rate, about 2 percent below the market rate. The circuit of capital is completed when CPF services the monthly installments to HDB on behalf of public housing buyers. Such a tie-up of CPF and HDB is central to the success of Singapore's public housing program (Lee and Vasoo, 2008, p. 279).

Education

Education is an integral part of Singapore's social policy. In the view of the Singapore leadership, without any natural resources, human resources have to be the most important source of economic growth for Singapore. The small population size makes nurturing talent even more important. Investment in education also fits well with the PAP ideology of self-help and meritocracy.

Other countries have also recognized the importance of education for economic and social development. Nonetheless, Singapore has developed its education system into one of the best in the world in just a few decades while most developing countries fail to catch up. To a large extent, Singapore's success in education lies in the fact that education is not seen as a separate domain to be isolated from the larger agendas. Instead, education is part of human resource development that is closely linked to Singapore's overall development strategies.

A lesson from Singapore is that educational development should be in line with economic development. In the 1960s and 1970s, Singapore focused on basic education, to provide workers with basic literacy and numeracy skills for labor-intensive industries. At that time there was relatively small demand for skilled labor. Since the late 1970s when the economy began to enter the next phase of more intensive industrialization based on higher value-added activities, the focus shifted to rapidly expanding education and training facilities at all levels. Into the 1990s, with the concept of the knowledge economy increasingly gaining popularity, there was unprecedented emphasis on higher education and R&D (see Table 11.8 for changes in the allocation of government spending on various levels of education).

Singapore adopts a manpower approach to educational development. Despite stressing the importance of education, the government does not want higher education to expand too quickly, to the point that the labor market cannot absorb the results. The government also wants the education sector to provide employable skills to the students. The government has been mindful

Table 11.8 Singapore government expenditure on education (million, S$)

	1980		1985		1990		1995		2000		2005		2008	
	Amount	Share (%)	Amount	Share (%)	Amount	Share (%)	Amount	Share (%)	Amount	Share (%)	Amount	Share (%)	Amount	Share (%)
Total	688	100	1,776		2,108		3,633		5,868		6,082		8,246	
Growth (1980 as 100)	100		258		306		528		853		884		1,198	
Recurrent expenditure	589	100	1,388	100	1,808	100	2,760	100	4,277	100	5,215	100	7,486	100
Primary schools	210	35.7	423	30.5	540	29.9	695	25.2	995	23.3	1,126	21.6	1,561	20.9
Secondary schools and junior colleges	212	36.0	432	31.1	582	32.2	845	30.6	1,167	27.3	1,566	30.0	2,214	29.6
Vocational schools	30	5.1	80	5.8	86	4.8	110	4.0	148	3.5	204	3.9	275	3.7
Polytechnics	24	4.1	110	7.9	153	8.5	351	12.7	524	12.3	624	12.0	932	12.4
Universities	75	12.7	254	18.3	339	18.8	568	20.6	899	21.0	1,058	20.3	1,811	24.2
Others	39	6.6	89	6.4	108	6.0	191	6.9	544	12.7	637	12.2	693	9.3
Development expenditure	99		387		300		873		1,591		867		760	

Note: % in parentheses is the share of each level of education in total recurrent expenditure for all levels of education.
Source: Ministry of Education, Singapore.

of the problems of overexpansion of higher education, including educated unemployment and enormous wastages in producing graduates without employable skills. Although Singapore lags behind Taiwan and South Korea in terms of higher education attainment (see Table 11.2), but this is not necessarily viewed as a problem by the Singapore leadership.

Keeping education development in line with economic development is part of the reason why Singapore can develop a world-class education system without huge government spending. To be sure, teachers in Singapore are well paid, classrooms are well equipped, and research labs are furnished with cutting edge facilities. Still, government expenditure on education is lower than 4 percent of GDP, not high by international standards. Remarkably, it has been declining to 3.1 percent as of 2009. The unparalleled efficiency displayed in the Singapore education system has a great deal to do with the manpower approach that restricts education from growing faster than the economy and the labor market.

Healthcare

Healthcare is another area in which Singapore has shown impressive performance. Its healthcare system is a very effective one so that Singaporeans are as healthy as people in other developed countries. Life expectancy at birth has increased from 70 in 1965 to 81 in 2008. Infant mortality rate has declined from 26.3 per 1000 live births in 1965 to 2.1 per 1000 live births in 2008, among the lowest in the world. Behind this progress is improved access to healthcare over time. In 1965, on average a doctor had to take care of 2,053 persons. The number dropped to 909 in 1980, 769 in 1990, 667 in 2000, and further down to 625 in 2008.

Another feature of Singapore healthcare system is its unparalleled efficiency in terms of achieving good health indicators without heavy investment. Singapore has constantly kept the national healthcare expenditure below 4 percent of GDP, extremely low by the standard of developed countries. In particular, government expenditure on healthcare has been hovering around 1 percent of GDP for a long time, before it increased significantly to 1.3 percent in 2009. In arguing that the Singapore model may offer the solution to America's healthcare woes, Callick (2008) forcefully points out that Singaporeans are healthier than Americans, yet pay only one-fifth of what Americans pay for their healthcare. Also in per capita terms, Singapore government spends one-seventh of what the US government spends on health.

The Singapore healthcare system features multiple layers of protection. As the first tier of protection, the government provides up to 80 percent of the total bill in public hospital wards. The second tier of protection is provided by Medisave, introduced in 1984 as a compulsory medical savings scheme under CPF. Contributions from working Singaporeans and their employers are saved in the Medisave accounts for future medical needs. As a feature of CPF, there is no cross-subsidization between CPF members. This makes

Singaporeans keenly aware of their responsibility for their own health. It also helps to avoid the problems stemming from demand-side moral hazard. The third tier of protection is provided by Medishield, a catastrophic illness insurance scheme introduced in 1990 to help members meet the medical expenses of major and prolonged illnesses. Medisave often proves insufficient to cover such expenses, making a risk-pooling scheme like Medishield necessary as part of the healthcare system. Medishield has co-payment and deductible features to minimize the problems of insurance-induced moral hazard. Finally, for those who cannot pay the subsidized bills despite Medisave and Medishield coverage, Medifund acts as the last line of defense. It is an endowment fund set up by the government in 1993 to help the needy Singaporeans pay their medical bills.

Singapore operates a mixed delivery model, with public providers delivering 80 percent of services in acute care sectors, private providers delivering 80 percent of services in the primary care sector, and voluntary welfare organizations mainly providing services in the step-down care sector (nursing homes, community hospitals and hospices). This mixed delivery model works well in Singapore to give the government an instrument to intervene in the healthcare sector (through public hospitals), on one hand, and to increase competition between different healthcare providers for greater efficiency and higher quality, on the other.

Singapore has used various ways to contain healthcare costs. In recognition of prevention better than cure, the government has been promoting a healthy lifestyle. Medisave is a key mechanism in containing the rising healthcare costs. By stressing the crucial role of the individual in promoting and maintaining his/her own health, the government uses Medisave to reward the healthy and shift the onus of healthcare to the individual. Co-payment and deductibles are used to curb problems of moral hazard, and competition and transparency among healthcare providers are emphasized to increase efficiency and help consumers make better choices.

Public assistance

As Singapore focuses on "productive" social investment, such as public housing, education and healthcare, programs that are "redistributive" in nature and are considered social consumption are discouraged. The first generation PAP leadership is well known to be averse to social welfare handouts. To promote the work ethic, there is no minimum wage and no unemployment insurance in Singapore. During the economic crisis when income maintenance becomes a challenge, the government reacts with support programs that subsidize employers for hiring, and subsidize employees for skills upgrading. This alternative approach is in stark contrast to the welfarist approach that directly provides unemployment benefits to laid-off workers.

As Singapore leaders see it, the state should not replace the traditional function of the family in caring for their family members. In this context, public assistance operates as the last line of defense. It is provided to the "needy" who lack the ability to support themselves and whose family does not have that ability. The government categorizes the needy into three groups: The first group consists of those unable to work and with no family support; the second group includes those who can support themselves in good times, but lose their jobs or have their wages cut during the economic downturn; the third group is composed of dysfunctional families plagued by a variety of financial and non-financial problems (Balakrishnan, 2009).

To help the needy (the bottom 20 percent of the society), the government set up the ComCare Fund in June 2005, standing at S$800 million by 2009. Assistance to the needy is delivered through the Community Development Councils (CDCs). To the first group of the needy, the CDCs provide public assistance through ComCare Enable, a scheme for long-term support. The CDCs also work with hospitals and HDB to apply for Medifund and rental flats respectively for the needy. To the second group, targeted, conditional and interim assistance is provided through ComCare SelfReliance. For the third group, the focus is on the developmental needs of children from needy families. The CDCs administer childcare, kindergarten and student care subsidies and bursaries through ComCare Grow, which is designed to help children from needy families do well in schools and lift them out of poverty trap.

The government adopts the approach of "Many Helping Hands" to involve citizens, grassroots organizations and voluntary welfare organizations in delivering social assistance. From a comparative perspective, public assistance is not a large program. In 2009, the government provided subsidies up to S$100 million directly to the needy families, and another S$140 million to voluntary welfare organizations. The sum is small compared to the government budget of S$29 billion. This is not surprising given Singapore's emphasis on workfare over welfare.

What relevant lessons for China?

To start with, Singapore is a small and efficient city-state, while China is huge and diverse. The two countries differ in the size of population and territory, the level of economic development, the number of layers of government, and the process of policy-making and implementation. These differences should have important implications for China's policy priority. For example, Singapore has long passed the stage in which poverty is a preoccupation. In contrast, poverty remains a serious challenge for China and should receive substantial policy attention. Singapore as a city-state does not have the problem of the rural–urban gap and regional disparity. China, by comparison, has to cope with the large inequalities along the rural/urban and regional dimensions. More importantly, China is not developing its social policy from scratch. It has its own policy framework that will shape the ongoing policy reform. It is therefore unrealistic and problematic to expect that China will replicate the Singapore experience in its socio-economic development.

Despite the profound differences between China and Singapore, the two countries also have similarities in many aspects, making the Singapore experience a relevant and valuable reference for China. In fact, China's social security system is a mixed one. Its pension program has both a social pooling account and a personal savings account. As is the case with China's practical approach to the economic reform, China's social policy framework also exhibits some degree of flexibility to allow for selective learning of foreign experience.

What lessons can Singapore offer to China in terms of social development?

1   GDP growth is a top priority in both countries. As we have shown, Singapore is able to balance economic and social development. As a result, it has achieved a high level of economic development with relatively low social costs, and it has become a developed country in both economic and social development. China's trajectory is different. While its economic growth is as rapid as Japan and the four "little dragons" of South Korea, Taiwan, Hong Kong and Singapore in the earlier stage of economic take-off, China's social development is lagging behind. China's unbalanced development strategy has created enormous stresses and strains. The very first lesson that the Singapore experience offers is that economic development does not have to come at the cost of social development, at the price of rising social challenges and growing social instability.

2   Both countries emphasize the family as the foundation of the society. This has become part of the national ideology in Singapore. Singapore reinforces this ideology through institutions and policies that emphasize family support, encourage filial piety and engage dysfunctional families. CPF is such an institution. CPF members can top up the account balances, and use their account balances to pay for the medical costs of their family members. Housing policy is designed to give incentives for married children to live within 2 kilometres of their parents, or for elderly parents to relocate for the same sake. It also encourages the extended family of three generations to occupy a single flat. In China, the rhetoric of family as the building block of the society is not matched by any specific policy. To make it worse, the functions of family have been seriously weakened by migration and poverty. In particular, the household registration or *hukou* system that allows farmers to work in the cities but denies them access to social services such as social security, public housing and education has restricted full-family migration, leaving the spouse or children back in the countryside.

3   Singapore has put a great deal of emphasis on self-help. It has become the ideological core of Singapore's social policy. CPF is an institution that best reflects this ideology. Self-help does not mean government inaction. The Singapore experience shows that the government has to create an enabling environment to help individuals succeed. In Singapore, self-help as a value and ideology is supported by a good education system, programs of skills upgrading and the practice of meritocracy in social mobility. In China,

self-help is the reality. However, this is less the result of the state ideology than the result of marketization of healthcare and to some extent education, which has substantially increased the financial burden on households. Even if self-help is a cherished value as in the historical past, it lacks strong state support in personal capacity building, and is problematized by poverty, inequality and corruption.

4   Conceptually and operationally, Singapore's social policy is integrated with its economic policy and the overall agenda. As discussed earlier, public housing is an instrument for nation-building, social engineering and economic competitiveness. CPF is another instrument for economic development and economic competitiveness. And public housing and CPF are closely integrated to the extent that they are seen as two sides of the same coin. The Singapore experience holds a positive lesson for the international debate whether social security is compatible with economic growth. It shows that coherent economic and social policy can benefit both economic and social development. This can be an important lesson for China. China's economic and social policies are often characterized as uncoordinated and unbalanced. The uncoordinated policies are further complicated in implementation by the central–local relationship, leading to a variety of problems in the form of inequalities, pollution, social instability and social anomie.

5   Singapore has seen growing government spending on social development, in the areas of education, public housing and healthcare. Nonetheless, Singapore has always planned for the long term. The government is very careful not to overspend in good times, so that government expenditures on social development and other areas are not allowed to grow faster than GDP growth. As a result, the government is in a better position to tackle short-term problems such as economic downturn and long-term problems such as population ageing. China has also seen rapid growth of government spending on social development, with certain expenditure (e.g. education) increasing faster than GDP and government revenue growth. The central government is also in a good fiscal position. However, there is tremendous inefficiency and wastage within the system. In 2008, China's government spending on education reached 3.5 percent of GDP, higher than the 3.2 percent for Singapore. According to the most recent data from the World Health Organization, government expenditure on health was 1.87 percent of GDP in 2006, and private expenditure was 2.73 percent, compared to 1.1 percent and 2.2 percent respectively. In light of the Singapore experience, the issue for China is not just how much money, but also how money is spent on social development.

6   Singapore has kept social development in line with economic development, using social policy to support economic development on one hand, and using industrial upgrading to improve people's working environment and living standards on the other hand. During the bad times of economic crisis, Singapore has a tripartite system—the government, employers and employees—in place to reach compromise on issues such as job retention,

wage cut and skills upgrading. In China, economic competiveness is less based on skills upgrading than on the extended period of low wages and sub-standard employment. The industrial relations are seriously biased in favor of the employers. There is rising labor unrest with the demographic shift to the second generation migrant workers who are less tolerant of low wages, bad working conditions, and long working hours.
7 Singapore has sought to integrate social policy with community develop- ment to create a stable yet vibrant society, empowering grassroots organi- zations to engage people of different races and classes and encouraging non-governmental organizations to play a salient role in welfare delivery. By comparison, the Chinese Communist Party has yet to find a way to work with non-governmental organizations more effectively in delivering public goods and ensuring social stability amidst rapid industrialization and urbanization.

To conclude, Singapore has established a model in social policy in general, and social security in particular. This model of course faces the challenge of globalization and population ageing, but the past experience has confirmed its adaptability and flexibility. What it needs is to fine-tune itself in the changing circumstances. China is in search of a model with Chinese characteristics. So far a distinct yet scalable Chinese model in social security or social policy is lacking. The pressing need for China is not to fine-tune, but to "reform" or "create" through selective learning and innovative policy-making. Singapore's experience in social development can offer valuable lessons in this.

Note

1 As Taiwan is not a member of the United Nations, the HDI report does not include data for Taiwan. Taiwan would rank 25 if it were to be included, as cal- culated by its government. Other Asian countries that made the list of very high human development were a few Middle Eastern countries.

References

Balakrishnan, V. (2009) "Speech as Minister of Community Development, Youth and Sport at the FY 2009 Committee for Supply Debate," 11 February. Available at: www. parliament.gov.sg/mp/vivian-balakrishnan.
Barr, M. D. (2000) "Lee Kuan Yew's Fabian phase," *Australian Journal of Politics and History*, 46: 110–25.
Callick, R. (2008) "The Singapore model," *The American*. Available at: www.american.com/archive/2008/may-june-magazine-contents/the-Singapore-model (accessed June 28, 2010).
Chua, B. H. (1997) *Political Legitimacy and Housing: Stakeholding in Singapore*, London: Routledge.
Department of Statistics (2010) *Yearbook of Statistics 2010*, Singapore: Government Printer.

Esping-Andersen, G. (2001) "Social foundations of postindustrial economies," in D. Grusky (ed.) *Social Stratification*, Boulder, CO: Westview Press.

Hill, M. and Lian K. F. (1995) *The Politics of Nation Building and Citizenship in Singapore*, London: Routledge.

International Social Security Association (1975) "Transformation of provident funds into pension schemes," *International Social Security Review* 28: 276–89.

Lee, J. and Vasoo, S. (2008) "Singapore: social investment, the state and social security," in J. Midgley and K. L. Tang (eds) *Social Security, the Economy and Development*, New York: Palgrave Macmillan.

Lee, K. Y. (2000) *From Third World to First: The Singapore Story: 1965–2000*, New York: HarperCollins.

Lian, K. F. (2008) "Is there a social policy in Singapore?," in K. F. Lian and C. K. Tong (eds) *Social Policy in Post-Industrial Singapore*, Boston: Brill.

Low, L. (2004) "How Singapore's Central Provident Fund fares in social security and social policy," *Social Policy and Society*, 3: 301–10.

Reisman, D. (2007) "Housing and superannuation: social security in Singapore," *International Journal of Social Economics*, 34: 159–87.

Tang, K.L. and Midgley, J. (2008) "The origins and features of social security," in J. Midgley and K. L. Tang (eds) *Social Security, the Economy and Development*, New York: Palgrave Macmillan.

Tong, C.K. and Lian K F. (2008) "Social policy issues in a post-industrial society," in K. F. Lian and C. K. Tong (eds) *Social Policy in Post-Industrial Singapore*, Boston: Brill.

Wong, J. (1995) "The social dimensions of Singapore's economic restructuring," in UNESCAP (ed.) *Social Costs of Economic Restructuring in Asia and the Pacific*, Bangkok: United Nations Publication.

World Health Organization (2009) *World Health Statistics 2009*. Available at: www.who.int/whosis/whosat/EN_WHS09_Full.pdf (accessed June 28, 2010).

Index

All-China Federation of Trade Unions 34–35
All-China Women's Federation 34
Anju project 129–37
Asian Values 231

Basic Health Insurance Scheme (BHI) 104
Beijing 74, 110, 116, 119–25, 216
Beijing Consensus 40
Buddhism: Gelug 191; Tibetan 193

central-local relationship 3, 250
Central Provident Fund (CPF) 15, 154, 236–41
China Center for Population and Development 147
China-Singapore Suzhou Industrial Park 15, 230
China-Singapore Tianjin Eco-City 15, 230
Chinese Communist Party (CCP) 19–21, 58, 106, 187, 221, 257
Chinese Nationalist Party (KMT) 196
Chinese People's Political Consultative Conference (CPPCC) 35, 171
civil society 5, 14, 47, 211–13
commercialization 3
Communist Youth League 34
Confucianism 191–93
Consumption 57–59, 61, 117, 182, 239: domestic 239; government 57; household 57, 61; propensity 77; smoothing 61; social 247; stimulation 61; welfare 210, 232
Cooperative Medical System (CMS) 84, 87, 90, 101, 105
Cultural Revolution 19, 24, 144–45, 187

Decentralization 3–5, 24–25, 111, 176
Democratic Progressive Party 212–13
demographic dividends 141, 153, 172
demographic transition 12–13, 141–48
Deng Xiaoping 5–6, 19, 24, 31, 45, 188, 210, 214–21, 230
dependency ratio 12, 41, 46, 141–54: child 142–43, 149, 153; elderly 46, 142–43, 149–52, 157; old 13; overall 141; total 143
Development Research Center of the State Council 105
developmental states 2, 5, 14–15, 211
diagnosis-related groups (DRG) 109
Dumont, Louis 186, 201
Dzungaria Revolt 192

Eight Banners 191–92
ethnic essentialism 14, 186, 196–200
ethnicity 28, 34, 196–201: culturized 197; politicized 197

federalism 24, 110
fee-for-service (FFS) 109
fertility rate 12, 141–54, 233
financial target responsibility system 104
fiscal expenditure 10, 83–97
Fujian 25, 110

Gansu 29
Gini coefficient 5, 27, 43, 51–52, 79
global financial crisis 7–9, 40–41, 52–53, 61, 71, 75, 85, 236
Great Leap Forward 24
Guangdong 25, 66, 72
Guangxi 29, 188
Guizhou 29, 188

Hainan 25
healthcare 112, 161–69, 174–84, 213,
  217–19, 232–38, 246, 250: costs 247;
  coverage 112; expenses 213–14, 219,
  224–25, 246; providers 247; public
  142; reform 112, 162; system 112, 189,
  217–18, 238
Hirschman, Albert 13, 162, 169
Household Responsibility System (HRS)
  163
Housing 5–7, 11–15, 34, 44–46, 53, 61,
  73–75, 85–86, 91–96, 115–36, 161–67,
  174–80, 211, 217, 237–50: commercial
  6, 74; market 6, 73, 124–25, 135, 179;
  needs 6, 74; poverty 123, 135; prices
  73–74, 78, 85, 95, 135–36, 168, 180;
  private 12, 125, 130; privatization 73,
  125–26, 133; public 5–8, 73–78, 115–
  26, 136, 162–80, 232, 237–44; reforms
  6, 15, 73, 125–31, 136; rental 12, 85,
  95; security 6, 10, 73, 95, 97;
  subsidized 12, 74–75, 132, 179; supply
  117–24, 127, 131–33; welfare 126
Housing Development Board (HDB)
  241
Housing Provident Fund (HPF) 90, 95,
  126, 128, 172
Hu Jintao 5–6, 10, 32–34, 110, 161–65,
  221–25
Human Development Index (HDI) 232

Inequality 2, 28, 106, 123–24, 167,
  173–81, 190, 233, 250: housing 132;
  income 5–8, 43, 51–53, 60–61; 77–79;
  93–97; 183; welfare 165
Inner Mongolia 29, 188

Jiang Zemin 6, 30, 165, 221
Jingji Shiyong Fang 73, 131, 134–37

Labor Insurance Scheme (LIS) 101
labor mobility 55, 77
Lhasa 14, 186, 190
life expectancy 1, 99, 142, 158, 232–34,
  246

Manchuria 191–95
Mao Zedong 19, 31, 165, 194, 221
marketization 3–6, 111, 127–31, 161–78,
  188, 217, 225, 250
mass consumption 8–9, 44–45
mass incidents 1, 30, 171
mass organizations 34
McKinsey 107

Medical Savings Account (MSA) 104
migrant workers 2, 7, 10, 32–35, 46,
  51–78, 96–98, 105, 117, 121–32,
  165–81, 251
Minimum Living Standard Guarantee
  (MLSG) 60–62
Minimum Standard of Living Scheme
  (MSLS) 173
Ministry of Civil Affairs 33, 62
Ministry of Health 109

National Council for the Social Security
  Fund (NCSSF) 90
Nationalism 14, 186–94, 200: Chinese
  194–96; cultural 197; Han 14
New Cooperative Medical System
  (NCMS) 105
New Rural Cooperative Medical
  Insurance (NRCMI) 64
Ningxia 29
non-governmental organizations
  (NGOs) 33–34, 47, 171

Olson, Mancur 8, 20–24
One Child Policy 117–19
open-door policy 2, 19–23

Peking University 107, 156–57
People's Action Party 15, 231
People's Congress 35, 115, 156, 171
People's Liberation Army 30
people's organizations 34
Polanyi, Karl 20–23, 30, 33
policy gridlock 110
private non-enterprise organizations
  (PNEOs) 33
professional management unit 33–34
property owners' committees 34
Property Rights Bill 32
poverty 1, 10, 24, 27, 51–53, 60–63, 101,
  173, 237, 249–50: absolute 91–93;
  alleviation 83; elderly 213; line 52–55,
  63–64, 77, 115; reduction 1, 10, 27,
  34, 51, 60–63, 96, 105, 154; relief
  58–60, 77, 210; trap 60, 132, 248
privatization 4, 24, 73, 112–13, 125–34
public assistance 7, 10, 232, 247–48
public service 3–8, 44, 53–62, 77, 85, 214

Qing 191–201
Qinghai 29

regional disparity 4–6, 98, 221, 248
rural-urban gap 4, 28, 248

sannong issues 29
secularism 14, 186–201
Shaanxi 196
Shanghai 92, 115–19, 124–25, 137, 163, 173, 226
Shenzhen 65, 74, 109, 118–19
Sichuan 188
Singapore 2, 5, 14–15, 26, 40, 104, 129, 154, 211–13, 225, 230–51
social insurance 10–13, 23, 59–60, 83–94, 104, 128–29, 155–59, 162–73, 181–84, 208, 218–19, 231–40
social justice 6, 37, 165, 190
social security 8–15, 29, 44–47, 51–62, 77, 83–98, 104, 134, 164, 215–16, 231, 236, 250–51; accounts 7–12; expenditure 83–86, 96–97; fund 90, 155; programs 7, 10, 62, 93, 189; reform 10–11; schemes 129; system 9, 44–46, 51–62, 77, 83–97, 141, 153–57, 178, 240, 249; subsidy 89
Special Economic Zones (SEZs) 25
superscription 193–94
sustainable development 9, 20–21, 40–41

Three Mountains 217–18, 225
Three Represents 30, 221

Tianjin 115–21
Tibet 29, 186–99
township and village enterprises (TVEs) 161, 163

unemployment 52, 57–61, 75, 158, 172–73, 217, 226, 246: insurance 55, 59–61, 75–78, 83–93, 172, 232, 247; pressure 41, 55, 75–77; rate 55–56, 75, 135, 233
United Nations Development Programmes 1
Urban Residents Basic Medical Insurance (URBMI) 64
urbanization 3–7, 45–46, 56, 85, 122, 251
Urumqi 14, 186, 190, 199

welfare capitalism 207–15, 224–25
welfare regime 14–15, 164, 175, 183, 207–25: Chinese 208, 214–25; East Asian 207–13; western 14
Wen Jiabao 5, 10, 15, 36, 70, 79, 84, 107, 110, 161, 164
work unit 3, 6, 89, 155, 163, 172, 178, 209
Worker Basic Medical Insurance (WBMI) 64

For Product Safety Concerns and Information please contact our EU
representative GPSR@taylorandfrancis.com
Taylor & Francis Verlag GmbH, Kaufingerstraße 24, 80331 München, Germany

www.ingramcontent.com/pod-product-compliance
Lightning Source LLC
Chambersburg PA
CBHW061720270326
41928CB00011B/2055